PETER NORTON'S

Essential Concepts

Sixth Edition

McGraw Hill **Technology Education**

Boston   Burr Ridge, IL   Dubuque, IA   Madison, WI   New York   San Francisco   St. Louis
Bangkok   Bogotá   Caracas   Kuala Lumpur   Lisbon   London   Madrid   Mexico City
Milan   Montreal   New Delhi   Santiago   Seoul   Singapore   Sydney   Taipei   Toronto

The *McGraw-Hill* Companies

Technology Education

PETER NORTON'S® ESSENTIAL CONCEPTS
Published by McGraw-Hill Technology Education, a business unit of The McGraw-Hill Companies, Inc.,
1221 Avenue of the Americas, New York, NY, 10020. Copyright © 2006 by The McGraw-Hill Companies, Inc.
All rights reserved. No part of this publication may be reproduced or distributed in any form or by any means,
or stored in a database or retrieval system, without the prior written consent of The McGraw-Hill Companies, Inc.,
including, but not limited to, in any network or other electronic storage or transmission, or broadcast for distance learning.

Some ancillaries, including electronic and print components, may not be available to customers outside the United States.

This book is printed on acid-free paper.

1 2 3 4 5 6 7 8 9 0 QPD/QPD 0 9 8 7 6 5

ISBN 0-07-297849-X

Editor in chief: *Bob Woodbury*
Senior sponsoring editor: *Christopher Johnson*
Developmental editor: *Pamela Woolf*
Marketing manager: *Sankha Basu*
Director, Sales and Marketing: *Paul Murphy*
Lead producer, Media technology: *Ed Przyzycki*
Senior project manager: *Lori Koetters*
Lead production supervisor: *Michael R. McCormick*
Senior designer: *Mary E. Kazak*
Senior photo research coordinator: *Jeremy Cheshareck*
Photo researcher: *Teri Stratford*
Supplement producer: *Lynn M. Bluhm*
Senior digital content specialist: *Brian Nacik*
Cover design: *Melissa Welch/Studio Montage*
Cover images: *© Corbis; © Getty*
Peter Norton photos: *Kelly Barrie*
Interior design: *Amanda Kavanagh/Ark Design Studio*
Typeface: *10/12 Sabon*
Compositor: *Cenveo*
Printer: *Quebecor World Dubuque Inc.*

Library of Congress Cataloging-in-Publication Data

Norton, Peter.
    Peter Norton's essential concepts.—6th ed.
        p. cm.
    ISBN 0-07-297849-X (alk. paper)
    1. Computers. 2. Computer software. I. Title: Essential concepts. II. Title.
QA76.5.N674 2006
004—dc22

                                        2004061018

www.mhhe.com

About Peter Norton

Acclaimed computer software entrepreneur Peter Norton is active in civic and philanthropic affairs. He serves on the boards of several scholastic and cultural institutions and currently devotes much of his time to philanthropy.

Raised in Seattle, Washington, Mr. Norton made his mark in the computer industry as a programmer and businessman. *Norton Utilities*™, *Norton AntiVirus*™, and other utility programs are installed on millions of computers worldwide. He is also the best-selling author of computer books.

Mr. Norton sold his PC-software business to Symantec Corporation in 1990 but continues to write and speak about computers, helping millions of people better understand information technology. He and his family currently reside in Santa Monica, California.

Editorial Consultant

Tim Huddleston

Academic Reviewers

Michael Anderson
ECPI College of Technology, VA

Lee Cottrell
Bradford School, PA

Lynn Dee Eason
Sault College of Applied Arts & Technology, Ontario

Terry Ann Felke
William Rainey Harper College, IL

Timothy Gottleber
North Lake College, TX

Captain Jim Jackson
West Point Academy, NY

Yvonne Ng Ling
Temasek Polytechnic, Singapore

Keith Samsell
Florida Metropolitan University

Cherie Ann Sherman
Ramapo College, NJ

Erik Sorensen
College of Redwoods, CA

Karen Stanton
Los Medanos College, CA

Umesh Varma
Campbell University, NC

ACKNOWLEDGEMENTS

Special thanks go to others who contributed to the content and development of this project: Kenny Atkins, Brian Carroll, Scott Clark, Lee Cottrell, Timothy Gottleber, Jane and Chuck Holcombe, Richard Mansfield, Bridget McCrea, Dan Shoemaker, Corey Schou, Natalie Walker Whitlock, and Teri Stratford.

Why Study Computer Technology?

The computer is a truly amazing machine. Few tools can help you perform so many different tasks. Whether you want to track an investment, publish a newsletter, design a building, or practice landing an F14 on the deck of an aircraft carrier, you can use a computer to do it. Equally amazing is the fact that the computer has taken on a role in nearly every aspect of our lives. Consider the following examples:

>> Tiny embedded computers control our alarm clocks, entertainment centers, and home appliances.

>> Today's automobiles could not even start—let alone run efficiently—without embedded computer systems.

>> In the United States, more than half of all homes now have at least one personal computer, and the majority of those computers are connected to the Internet.

>> An estimated 10 million people now work from home instead of commuting to a traditional workplace, thanks to PCs and networking technologies.

>> People use e-mail for personal communications nearly 10 times as often as ordinary mail, and nearly five times more often than the telephone.

>> Routine, daily tasks such as banking, using the telephone, and buying groceries are affected by computer technologies.

Here are just a few personal benefits you can enjoy by developing a mastery of computer technology:

>> **Improved Employment Prospects.** Computer-related skills are essential in many careers. Whether you plan a career in automotive mechanics, nursing, journalism, or archaeology, having computer skills will make you more marketable to prospective employers.

>> **Skills That Span Different Aspects of Life.** Many people find their computer skills valuable regardless of the setting—at home, work, school, or play. Your knowledge of computers will be useful in many places other than your work.

>> **Greater Self-Sufficiency.** Those people who truly understand computers know that computers are tools—nothing more or less. We do not give up control of our lives to computer systems; rather, we use computer systems to suit our needs. By knowing how to use computers, you can actually be more self-sufficient, whether you use computers for research, communications, or time-management.

>> **A Foundation of Knowledge for a Lifetime of Learning.** Basic computing principles have not changed over the past few years, and they will be valid well into the future. By mastering fundamental concepts and terminology, you will develop a strong base that will support your learning for years to come.

Regardless of your reasons for taking this course, you have made a wise decision. The knowledge and skills you gain should pay dividends in the future, as computers become even more common at home and at work.

CONTENTS AT A GLANCE

Chapter 1: Introducing Computer Systems   2

Lesson 1A: Exploring Computers and Their Uses   3
Lesson 1B: Interacting with Your Computer   24

Chapter 2: Presenting the Internet   48

Lesson 2A: The Internet and the World Wide Web   49
Lesson 2B: E-Mail and Other Internet Services   76

Computing Keynotes: Creating Your Own Web Page   94

Chapter 3: Computing Alone and in Groups   102

Lesson 3A: Transforming Data into Information   103
Lesson 3B: Networking Basics   136

Chapter 4: Introduction to Software   158

Lesson 4A: Operating System Basics   159
Lesson 4B: Productivity Software   182

Computing Keynotes: Computer Viruses   202

Chapter 5: Living in the Online World   208

Lesson 5A: Doing Business in the Online World   209
Lesson 5B: Staying Safe in the Online World   224

Appendix A: History of Microcomputers   248
Appendix B: Self-Check Answers   268

FEATURE ARTICLES

At Issue

Computerized Disease Management   18
Stomping Out Spam   80
Cyborgs among Us: Wearable Technology   128
Who Really Owns the Software on Your PC?   176
On the Beat with Techno-Cops   218

Norton Notebook

Speech Recognition   32
Internet Time Travel: The Wayback Machine   58
What *Is* a Computer Chip?   116
Why Own When You Can Rent?   188
Business, the Internet, and Everything   214

Productivity Tip

Choosing the Right Tool for the Job   8
Evaluating the Reliability of Search Results
and Web Sites   68
The Telecommuter's Checklist   142
Do-It-Yourself Tech Support   168
Keeping Your PC Up to Date   236

Computers In Your Career

Using Computers Outside of the IT Industry   40
Documentation and Online Help System Designer   86
Careers in Networking   150
Help Desk and Technical Support Specialists   194
Career Opportunities and the Internet   238

Computing Keynotes

Creating Your Own Web Page   94
Computer Viruses   202

CONTENTS

CHAPTER 1::
Introducing Computer Systems   2
Chapter Contents   2

Lesson 1A:
Exploring Computers and Their Uses   **3**

Overview: Computers in Our World   3
The Computer Defined   4
Computers for Individual Users   4
   Desktop Computers   4
   Workstations   5
   Notebook Computers   5
   Tablet PCs   5
   Handheld PCs   6
   Smart Phones   6
Computers for Organizations   6
   Network Servers   6
   Mainframe Computers   6
   Minicomputers   7
   Supercomputers   8
Productivity Tip: Choosing the Right Tool for the Job   **8**
The Parts of a Computer System   9
Essential Computer Hardware   10
Software Brings the Machine to Life   13
   System Software   14
   Application Software   14
Computer Data   16
At Issue: Computerized Disease Management   **18**
Lesson 1A Review   **20**

Lesson 1B:
Interacting with Your Computer   **24**

Overview: Input and Output   24
Common Input Devices   25
   The Keyboard   25
      Alphanumeric Keys   *25*
      Modifier Keys   *25*
      Numeric Keypad   *25*
      Function Keys   *26*
      Cursor-Movement Keys   *26*
   The Mouse and Its Variants   26

   Types of Mice   *26*
   Mouse Variants   *27*
Other Input Devices   28
   Digital Pens   *28*
   Touch Screens   *29*
   Game Controllers   *29*
   Bar Code Readers   *29*
   Image Scanners   *29*
   Microphones   *30*
   Video Cameras   *30*
   Digital Cameras   *31*
Common Output Devices   31
   Monitors   31
      CRT Monitors   *31*
Norton Notebook: Speech Recognition   **32**
      Flat-Panel Monitors   *34*
      Comparing Monitors   *34*
      Video Cards   *36*
   Sound Systems   37
   Printers   37
      Dot Matrix Printers   *37*
      Ink Jet Printers   *38*
      Laser Printers   *38*
      Comparing Printers   *38*
**Computers In Your Career: Using Computers
Outside of the IT Industry**   **40**
Lesson 1B Review   **42**
Chapter Skills Review   **46**
   Chapter Labs   46
   Discussion Questions   47
   Research and Report   47
   Ethical Issues   47

CHAPTER 2::
Presenting the Internet   48
Chapter Contents   48

Lesson 2A:
The Internet and the World Wide Web   **49**

Overview: What Is the Internet?   49
The Internet's History   50

The Beginning: A "Network of Networks"   50
Today: Still Growing   51
The Internet's Major Services   52
Understanding the World Wide Web   52
  How the Web Works   53
  Web Browsers and HTML Tags   54
  URLs   55
  Helper Applications and Multimedia Content   56
Norton Notebook: Internet Time Travel:
The Wayback Machine   **58**
Using Your Browser and the World Wide Web   59
  Launching Your Browser   60
  Navigating the Web   60
   Using URLs   *60*
   Using Hyperlinks   *61*
   Using the Browser's Navigation Tools   *62*
  Closing Your Browser   62
  Getting Help with Your Browser   63
Searching the Web   63
  Using a Directory   65
  Using a Search Engine   65
   Using Boolean Operators in Your Searches   *66*
   Using Advanced Search Options   *67*
Productivity Tip: Evaluating the Reliability of
Search Results and Web Sites   **68**
  Using a Metasearch Engine   70
  Sponsored versus Nonsponsored Links 70
  Using Site-Specific Search Tools   71
Lesson 2A Review   **72**

Lesson 2B:
E-Mail and Other Internet Services   **76**
Overview: Communicating through the Internet   76
Using E-Mail   77
  Understanding E-Mail   77
   E-Mail Addresses   *77*
   Listserv Systems   *78*
  Using an E-Mail Program   78
   Creating a Message   *78*
   Receiving and Reading a Message   *79*
At Issue: Stomping Out Spam   **80**

Using Web-Based E-Mail Services   81
More Features of the Internet   81
  News   81
  FTP   83
  Internet Relay Chat (IRC) and Web-Based Chat   84
  Instant Messaging   85
  Online Services   85
Computers In Your Career: Documentation and
Online Help System Designer   **86**
  Peer-to-Peer Services   86
Lesson 2B Review   **88**
Chapter Skills Review   **92**
  Chapter Labs   92
  Discussion Questions   93
  Research and Report   93
  Ethical Issues   93

**Computing Keynotes: Creating Your
Own Web Page**   **94**

CHAPTER 3::
Computing Alone and in Groups   **102**
Chapter Contents   102

Lesson 3A:
Transforming Data into Information   **103**
Overview: The Process of Processing Data   103
How Computers Represent Data   104
  Number Systems   104
  Bits and Bytes   104
  Text Codes   105
   EBCDIC   *105*
   ASCII   *105*
   Extended ASCII   *105*
   Unicode   *105*
How Computers Process Data   107
  The CPU   107
  Memory   108
   Nonvolatile Memory   *108*

Flash Memory   108
Volatile Memory   108
Factors affecting Processing Speed   109
Registers   109
Memory and Computing Power   110
The Computer's Internal Clock   111
The Bus   111
Cache Memory   112
A Look inside the Processor   113
Microcomputer Processors   114
Intel Processors   115
Advanced Micro Devices (AMD) Processors   115
Freescale Processors   115
Norton Notebook: What *Is* a Computer Chip?   **116**
IBM Processors   117
Comparing Processors   117
Extending the Processor's Power to Other Devices 118
Standard Computer Ports   118
Mouse and Keyboard Ports   118
Two Universal Serial Bus (USB) Ports   118
Serial Port   118
Parallel Ports   118
Audio Ports   118
Network Port   118
Modem Port   118
Monitor Port   118
Serial and Parallel Ports   119
Specialized Expansion Ports   119
SCSI   119
USB   119
IEEE 1394 (FireWire)   120
Musical Instrument Digital Interface (MIDI)   120
Expansion Slots and Boards   120
PC Cards   120
Storage Devices   121
Magnetic Storage Devices   121
How Data Is Stored on a Disk   121
How Data Is Organized on a Magnetic Disk   122
How the Operating System Finds Data on a Disk   124
Diskettes (Floppy Disks)   125
Hard Disks   126

Removable High-Capacity Magnetic Disks   126
Tape Drives   127
Optical Storage Devices   127
CD-ROM   127
At Issue: Cyborgs among Us: Wearable Technology **128**
DVD-ROM   129
Recordable Optical Technologies   129
Lesson 3A Review   **131**

Lesson 3B:
Networking Basics   **136**
Overview: Sharing Data Anywhere, Anytime   136
The Uses of a Network   137
Simultaneous Access   137
Site Licenses   138
Network Versions   138
Shared Peripheral Devices   138
Personal Communications   139
Easier Data Backup   139
Common Types of Networks   140
Local Area Networks (LANs)   140
Wide Area Networks (WANs)   140
Hybrid Networks   140
Campus Area Networks (CANs)   141
Metropolitan Area Networks (MANs)   141
Home Area Networks (HANs)   141
How Networks Are Structured   141
Server-Based Networks   141
Productivity Tip: The Telecommuter's Checklist **142**
Client/Server Networks   143
Peer-to-Peer Networks   144
Network Topologies and Protocols   145
Network Media   146
Wire-Based Media   146
Wireless Media   146
Network Hardware   146
Network Interface Cards (NICs)   147
Network Linking Devices and Technologies   147
Protocols   149
Computers In Your Career: Careers in Networking **150**
Lesson 3B Review   **152**

Chapter Skills Review	**156**
Chapter Labs	156
Discussion Questions	157
Research and Report	157
Ethical Issues	157

CHAPTER 4::
Introduction to Software

Introduction to Software	158
Chapter Contents	158

Lesson 4A:
Operating System Basics   159

Overview: The Purpose of Operating Systems	159
Types of Operating Systems	160
Providing a User Interface	161
Graphical User Interfaces	161
Command-Line Interfaces	164
Running Programs	164
Sharing Information	165
Managing Hardware	166
PC Operating Systems	167
DOS	167
Productivity Tip: Do-It-Yourself Tech Support	**168**
Windows NT Workstation	168
Windows 9x	170
Windows 2000 Professional	171
Windows XP	171
The Macintosh Operating System	172
UNIX for the Desktop	173
Linux for the Desktop	173
Network Operating Systems	173
Embedded Operating Systems	175
At Issue: Who Really Owns the Software on Your PC?	**176**
Lesson 4A Review	**178**

Lesson 4B:
Productivity Software   182

Overview: Software to Accomplish the Work of Life	182
Word Processing Programs	183
The Word Processor's Interface	183
Entering and Editing Text	184
Formatting Text	185
Spreadsheet Programs	186
The Spreadsheet's Interface	186
Entering Data in a Worksheet	186
Labels	187
Values	187
Dates	187
Norton Notebook: Why Own When You Can Rent?	**188**
Presentation Programs	190
The Presentation Program's Interface	190
Creating a Presentation	191
Presenting Slide Shows	192
On a Large-Format Monitor	193
On a Television Screen	193
From a Data Projector	193
Personal Information Managers	193
Computers In Your Career: Help Desk and Technical Support Specialists	**194**
Lesson 4B Review	**197**
Chapter Skills Review	**200**
Chapter Labs	200
Discussion Questions	201
Research and Report	201
Ethical Issues	201

Computing Keynotes: Computer Viruses   202

CHAPTER 5::
Living in the Online World   208

Chapter Contents	208

Lesson 5A:
Doing Business in the Online World   209

Overview: Commerce on the World Wide Web	209
E-Commerce at the Consumer Level	210
Online Shopping	210
Online Stores versus Physical Locations	211
Using Online Catalogs	211

Paying for Purchases 212
Getting Customer Service 212
Online Banking and Finance 213
Online Banking 213
Norton Notebook: Business, the Internet, and Everything 214
Online Finance 215
E-Commerce at the Business Level 216
Business-to-Business (B2B) Transactions 216
Intranets and Extranets 217
Telecommuters 217
At Issue: On the Beat with Techno-Cops 218
Security 218
Lesson 5A Review 220

Lesson 5B:
Staying Safe in the Online World 224

Overview: Keeping Your System Safe 224
Protecting Yourself 225
Avoiding Identity Theft 225
Managing Your Papers 226
Guarding Personal Information 226
Looking at the Big Picture 227
Protecting Your Privacy 227
Keeping Marketers at Bay 228
Knowing Your Rights 228
Managing Cookies, Spyware, and Other "Bugs" 229
Dealing with Cookies 230
Removing Web Bugs and Spyware 231
Evading Spam 231

Keeping Your Data Secure 233
Restricting Access to Your System 234
Limiting Physical Access 234
Using a Firewall 234
Backing Up Data 235
Safeguarding Your Hardware 235
Productivity Tip: Keeping Your PC Up to Date 236
Using Automated Warnings 236
Computers in Your Career: Career Opportunities and the Internet 238
Handling Storage Media 238
Storing Computer Equipment 239
Keeping Your Computer Clean 240
Lesson 5B Review 241
Chapter Skills Review 245
Chapter Labs 245
Discussion Questions 245
Research and Report 246
Ethical Issues 246

Appendix A:
History of Microcomputers 248
Appendix B:
Self-Check Answers 268
Glossary 269
Credits 287
Index 288

STUDENT AND INSTRUCTOR RESOURCES

This textbook is supplemented by a variety of resources for students and teachers.

SimNet™ XPert

SimNet XPert is a complete learning and assessment program of Microsoft Office applications and computer concepts.

The **Learning Component** is a computer-based program that teaches skills and tasks using a variety of methods.

>> **Teach Me** mode introduces the skill using text, graphics, and interactivity.

>> **Show Me** mode employs narration and animation to illustrate how the skill is used.

>> **Let Me Try** mode enables you to practice and improve your proficiency in SimNet XPert's non-threatening simulated environment.

The **Assessment Component** allows you to take practice exams and assessment tests assigned by your instructor in SimNet XPert's robust simulated environment. This means your proficiency in any of these applications can finally be tested as you perform a task, rather than based on how well you can answer true/false and multiple choice questions.

Peter Norton Web Site (www.mhhe.com/peternorton)

The Peter Norton Web site includes a variety of resources for students and teachers. For students, the Web site offers a variety of learning resources, including:

>> Web link database

>> Internet labs and activities

>> Course outlines and slides

>> Online quizzes

>> Ezine articles that offer news about technology trends

>> Information about IT careers

For instructors, the Web site provides additional materials that help teach the course using the textbook:

>> Course outlines

>> Classroom presentations

>> Teaching tips and discussion topics

>> Extra projects

Instructor Resource Kit

In addition to the Web site, an instructor's resource kit is available on CD-ROM. The CD-ROM includes:

>> An Instructor's Manual and Answer Key

>> ExamView Pro test bank software with hundreds of questions

>> Instructor Classroom Presentations

>> SCANs Correlations

>> PageOut™, an online instructor tool

>> WebCT and Blackboard Distance Learning Platforms

PREREQUISITES

What You Should Know Before Using This Book

This book assumes that you have never used a computer before or that your computer experience has been very brief. If so, you may need to learn some basic computer skills before proceeding with this course. This Prerequisites section introduces basic skills, using illustrations to help you recognize and remember the hardware or software involved in each skill. Some of these skills are covered in greater detail in other units of this book. In such cases, you will find references that point you to more information.

Equipment Required for This Book's Exercises

>> IBM-compatible personal computer
>> Keyboard
>> Two-button mouse
>> Windows 98 or higher
>> Internet connection
>> Web browser

Turning the Computer On and Off

Turning the Computer On

As simple as it may sound, there is a right way to turn a computer's power on and off. If you perform either of these tasks incorrectly, you may damage the computer's components or cause problems for the operating system, programs, or data files.

1. Before turning on your computer, make sure that all the necessary cables (such as the mouse, keyboard, printer, modem, etc.) are connected to the system unit. Also make sure that the system's power cords are connected to an appropriate power source.

2. Make sure that there are no diskettes in the computer's diskette drive, unless you must boot the system from a diskette. (The term *booting* means starting the computer.) If you must boot the system from a diskette, ask your instructor for specific directions.

3. Find the On/Off switch on each attached device (the monitor, printer, etc.) and place it in the ON position. A device's power switch may not be on the front panel. Check the sides and back to find the On/Off switch if the switch is not located on the front panel.

4. Find the On/Off switch on the computer's system unit—its main box into which all other components are plugged—and place it in the ON position.

Most computers take a minute or two to start. Your computer may display messages during the start-up process. If one of these messages prompts you to perform an action (such as providing a network user ID and password), ask your instructor for directions. After the computer has started, the Windows desktop will appear on your screen.

Turning the Computer Off

In Windows-based systems, it is critical that you shut down properly, as described here. Windows creates many temporary files on your computer's hard disk when running. By shutting down properly, you give Windows the chance to erase those temporary files and do other "housekeeping" tasks. If you simply turn off your computer while Windows or other programs are running, you can cause harm to your system.

Note: The illustration shows the shut-down process in Windows 98. The process, menus, and dialog boxes are the same in all versions of Windows except Windows XP, as noted in the following instructions.

1. Remove any disks from the diskette and CD-ROM drives and make sure that all data is saved and all running programs are closed. (For help with saving data and closing programs, ask your instructor.)

2. Using your mouse pointer, click the Start button, which is located on the taskbar. The Start menu will appear. On the Start menu, click Shut Down. (If you use Windows XP, click the Turn Off Computer option.) The Shut Down Windows dialog box will appear. (In Windows XP, the Turn Off Computer dialog box will appear.)

For more information on Windows and other operating systems, see Chapter 7, "Using Operating Systems."

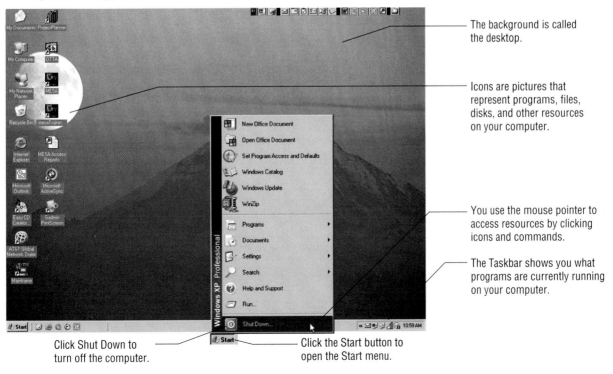

The background is called the desktop.

Icons are pictures that represent programs, files, disks, and other resources on your computer.

You use the mouse pointer to access resources by clicking icons and commands.

The Taskbar shows you what programs are currently running on your computer.

Click Shut Down to turn off the computer.

Click the Start button to open the Start menu.

Windows will begin the shut-down process. Windows may display a message telling you that it is shutting down. Then it may display the message "It is now safe to turn off your computer." When this message appears, turn off the power to your system unit, monitor, and printer.

In some newer computers, the system unit will power down automatically after Windows shuts down. If your computer provides this feature, you need to turn off only your monitor and other devices.

Using the Keyboard

If you know how to type, then you can easily use a computer keyboard. The keyboard contains all the alphanumeric keys found on a typewriter, plus some keys that perform special functions.

:: *The keyboard is covered in detail in Lesson 3A, "Using the Keyboard and Mouse."*

1.

2.

3.

4.

1. In Windows, the ENTER key performs two primary functions. First, it lets you create paragraph ("hard") returns in application programs such as word processors. Second, when a dialog box is open, pressing ENTER is like clicking the OK button. This accepts your input and closes the dialog box.

2. The SHIFT, CTRL (control), and ALT (alternate) keys are called modifier keys. You use them in combination with other keys to issue commands. In many programs, for example, pressing CTRL+S (hold the CTRL key down while pressing the S key) saves the open document to disk. Used with all the alphanumeric and function keys, the modifier keys let you issue hundreds of commands.

3. In Windows programs, the ESC (escape) key performs one universal function. That is, you can use it to cancel a command before it executes. When a dialog box is open, pressing ESC is like clicking the CANCEL button. This action closes the dialog box and ignores any changes you made in the dialog box.

4. Depending on the program you are using, the function keys may serve a variety of purposes or none at all. Function keys generally provide shortcuts to program features or commands. In many Windows programs, for example, you can press F1 to launch the online help system.

5. In any Windows application, a blinking bar—called the cursor or the insertion point—shows you where the next character will appear as you type. You can use the cursor-movement keys to move the cursor to different positions. As

their arrows indicate, these keys let you move the cursor up, down, left, and right.

6. The DELETE key erases characters to the right of the cursor. The BACKSPACE key erases characters to the left of the cursor. In many applications, the HOME and END keys let you move the cursor to the beginning or end of a line, or farther when used with a modifier key. PAGE UP and PAGE DOWN let you scroll quickly through a document, moving back or ahead one screen at a time.

5. I am what I am. | ⸻ Cursor (or insertion point)

⸻ Cursor-movement keys

6.

Backspace key

Using the Mouse

The mouse makes your computer easy to use. In fact, Windows and Windows-based programs are mouse-oriented, meaning their features and commands are designed for use with a mouse.

1. This book assumes that you are using a standard two-button mouse. Usually, the mouse's left button is the primary button. You click it to select commands and perform other tasks. The right button opens special "shortcut menus," whose contents vary according to the program you are using.

2. You use the mouse to move a graphical pointer around on the screen. This process is called pointing.

3. The pointer is controlled by the mouse's motions across your desktop's surface. When you push the mouse forward (away from you), the pointer moves up on the screen. When you pull the mouse backward (toward you), the pointer moves down. When you move the mouse to the left or right, or diagonally, the pointer moves to the left, right, or diagonally on the screen.

1.

▪▪ *The mouse is covered in greater detail in Lesson 3A, "Using the Keyboard and Mouse."*

2.

3.

❶ When the mouse moves...

❷ ...the rolling mouse ball spins the rollers.

❸ The information from the spinning rollers is sent to the system software, which controls the pointer.

"click"

4.

"click click"

5.

"click"

6.

7.

4. To click an object, such as an icon, point to it on the screen, then quickly press and release the left mouse button one time. Generally, clicking an object selects it, or tells Windows that you want to do something with the object.

5. To double-click an object, point to it on the screen, then quickly press and release the left mouse button twice. Generally, double-clicking an object selects and activates the object. For example, when you double-click a program's icon on the desktop, the program launches so you can use it.

6. To right-click an object, point to it on the screen, then quickly press and release the right mouse button one time. Generally, right-clicking an object opens a shortcut menu that provides options for working with the object.

7. You can use the mouse to move objects around on the screen. For example, you can move an icon to a different location on the Windows desktop. This procedure is often called drag-and-drop editing. To drag an object, point to it, press and hold down the left mouse button, drag the object to the desired location, then release the mouse button.

ABOUT THIS BOOK

Effective Learning Tools

This pedagogically rich book is designed to make learning easy and enjoyable. It will help you develop the skills and critical thinking abilities that will enable you to understand computers and computer technology, troubleshoot problems, and possibly lead you into an IT career.

Self-check quizzes keep the students engaged and test their understanding of the lesson topics.

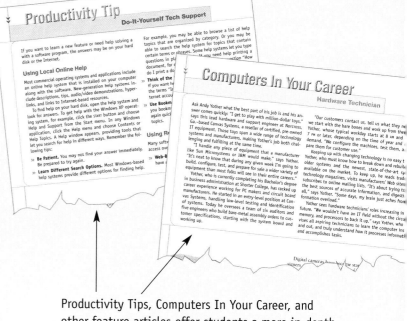

Each chapter includes . . .

>> **Learning objectives** that set measurable goals for lesson-by-lesson progress

>> **Four-color illustrations** that give you a clear picture of the technologies

>> **More review materials at the end of each chapter *and* lesson:** Key terms quiz, multiple choice questions, short answer review questions, lab activities, discussion questions, research and report assignments, and ethical issue discussions

Productivity Tips, Computers In Your Career, and other feature articles offer students a more in-depth discussion of today's technology and how it affects their everyday lives.

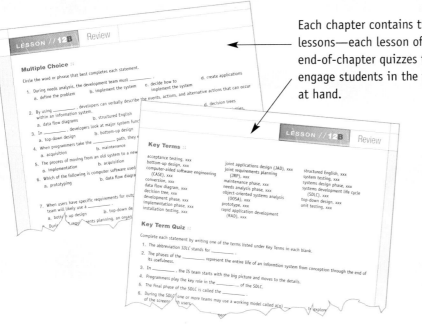

Each chapter contains two lessons—each lesson offers end-of-chapter quizzes that engage students in the topics at hand.

This book is full of detailed IT concepts and current photographs of the latest technologies. Norton Online sidebars point students to the new Norton web site accompanying this textbook where students can find more information on IT-specific topics.

>> **Self-check quizzes** in each lesson (two per chapter) help students apply their knowledge as they work through the lesson

Feature articles

>> **Norton Notebooks** offer insightful thoughts about emerging technologies and computers in our society.

>> **At Issue** articles spotlight trends in information technology and offer a compelling look at how technology is used to help people enhance their lives.

>> **Computers In Your Career** offer students a "human face" into IT professions by providing IT interviews and ideas for where an IT career might take today's students.

>> **Productivity Tips** cover topics such as adding RAM, printer maintenance, and sharing Internet connections.

Important Technology Concepts

Information technology (IT) offers many career paths leading to occupations in such fields as PC repair, network administration, telecommunications, Web development, graphic design, and desktop support. To become competent in any IT field you need certain basic computer skills. *Peter Norton's Introduction to Computers*, 6e, builds a foundation for success in the IT field by introducing you to fundamental technology concepts and giving you essential computer skills.

Your IT career starts here!

PETER NORTON'S

Essential
Concepts

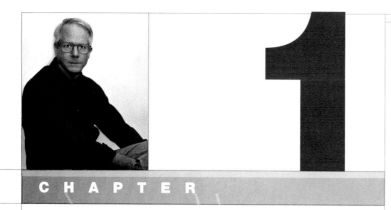

CHAPTER

1

Introducing Computer Systems

01 02 03 04 05 06 07 08 09 10 11 12 13 14

CHAPTER CONTENTS ::

This unit contains the following lessons:

Lesson **1A:**
Exploring Computers and Their Uses

>> The Computer Defined
>> Computers for Individual Users
>> Computers for Organizations
>> The Parts of a Computer System
>> Essential Computer Hardware
>> Software Brings the Machine to Life
>> Computer Data

Lesson **1B:**
Interacting with Your Computer

>> Common Input Devices
>> Common Output Devices

Exploring Computers and Their Uses

Overview: Computers in Our World

Consider this sentence: "Computers are everywhere." Does it sound like an overstatement? An understatement? A cliché? No matter how you perceive the impact of computers on our world, the statement is true. Computers *are* everywhere. In fact, you can find them in some pretty unlikely places, including your family car, your home appliances, and even your alarm clock!

In the past two decades, computers have reshaped our lives at home, work, and school. The vast majority of businesses now use computerized equipment in some way, and most companies are networked both internally and externally. More than half of all homes in the United States have at least one computer, and most of them are connected to the Internet. Workers who once had little use for technology—such as cashiers, secretaries, and delivery persons—now interact with computers every day.

As a first step toward understanding computer technology, this lesson examines the many types of computers that are in common use today. Although this class will focus on personal computers (the ones that seem to sit on every desktop), you will first learn about the wide variety of computers that people use, and the reasons they use them. As your knowledge of computers grows, you will understand that all computers—regardless of their size or purpose—are basically similar. That is,

OBJECTIVES ::

>> In basic terms, define the word *computer*.

>> Differentiate between computers designed for individual users and those designed for use by organizations.

>> Identify four categories of computer hardware.

>> List four units of measure for computer memory and storage.

>> Name and differentiate the two main categories of computer software.

>> Explain the difference between data, information, and programs.

they all operate on the same fundamental principles, are made from the same basic components, and need instructions to make them run.

The Computer Defined

In basic terms, a computer is an electronic device that processes data, converting it into information that is useful to people. Any computer—regardless of its type—is controlled by programmed instructions, which tell the machine what to do.

The computers discussed in this book—and which are everywhere around you—are digital computers. Digital computers are so called because they break all types of information into tiny units, and use numbers to represent those pieces of information. Digital computers also work in very strict sequences of steps, processing each unit of information individually, according to the highly organized instructions they must follow.

Computers for Individual Users

Most computers are meant to be used by only one person at a time. Such computers are often shared by several people (such as those in your school's computer lab), but only one user can work with the machine at any given moment.

These systems are all examples of personal computers (PCs)—a term that refers to any computer system that is designed for use by a single person. Personal computers are also called microcomputers, because they are among the smallest computers created for people to use. Note, however, that the term *personal computer* or *PC* is most often used to describe desktop computers. There are six basic types of personal computer:

>> **Desktop Computers**   The most common type of personal computer is the desktop computer—a PC that is designed to sit on (or under) a desk or table. As its name implies, a desktop computer is a full-size computer that is too big to be carried around. The main component of a desktop PC is the system unit, which is the case that houses the computer's critical parts, such as its processing and storage devices. There are two common designs for desktop computers (see Figure 1A.1). The more traditional desktop model features a

FIGURE 1A.1

A traditional desktop PC and a "tower" model.

horizontally oriented system unit, which usually lies flat on the top of the user's desk. Many users place their monitor on top of the system unit. Vertically oriented tower models have become the more popular style of desktop system. This design allows the user to place the system unit next to or under the desk, if desired.

» **Workstations** A workstation is a specialized, single-user computer that typically has more power and features than a standard desktop PC (see Figure 1A.2). These machines are popular among scientists, engineers, and animators who need a system with greater-than-average speed and the power to perform sophisticated tasks. Workstations often have large, high-resolution monitors and accelerated graphics–handling capabilities, making them suitable for advanced architectural or engineering design, animation, and video editing.

» **Notebook Computers** Notebook computers, as their name implies, approximate the shape of an 8.5- by 11-inch notebook and easily fit inside a briefcase. Because people frequently set these devices on their lap, they are also called laptop computers. Notebook computers can operate on alternating current or special batteries. These amazing devices generally weigh less than eight pounds, and some even weigh less than three pounds! During use, the computer's lid is raised to reveal a thin monitor and a keyboard. When not in use, the device folds up for easy storage. Notebooks are fully functional microcomputers; the people who use them need the power of a full-size desktop computer wherever they go (see Figure 1A.3). Because of their portability, notebook PCs fall into a category of devices called mobile computers—systems small enough to be carried by their user.

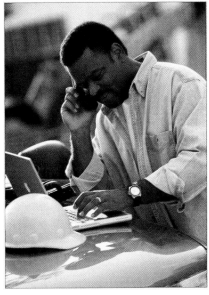

FIGURE 1A.3

Notebook computers have the power of desktop PCs but are light and portable.

» **Tablet PCs** The tablet PC is the newest development in portable, full-featured computers (see Figure 1A.4). Tablet PCs offer all the functionality of a notebook PC, but they are lighter and can accept input from a special pen—called a stylus or a digital pen—that is used to tap or write directly on the screen. Many tablet PCs also have a built-in microphone and special software that accepts input from the user's voice. A few models even have a foldout keyboard, so they can be transformed into a standard notebook PC. Tablet PCs run specialized versions of standard programs and can be connected to a network. Some can be connected to a keyboard and a full-size monitor.

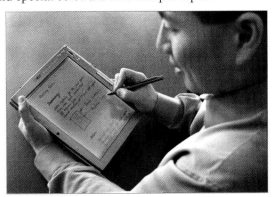

FIGURE 1A.4

Tablet PCs are popular among users who take notes or use hand-drawn documents.

PDAs put a computer in your pocket and can be used in many different ways.

>> **Handheld PCs**   Handheld personal computers are computing devices small enough to fit in your hand (see Figure 1A.5). A popular type of handheld computer is the personal digital assistant (PDA). A PDA is no larger than a small appointment book and is normally used for special applications, such as taking notes, displaying telephone numbers and addresses, and keeping track of dates or agendas. Many PDAs can be connected to larger computers to exchange data. Most PDAs come with a stylus that lets the user write on the screen. Some handheld computers feature tiny built-in keyboards or microphones that allow voice input.

>> **Smart Phones**   Some cellular phones double as miniature PCs (see Figure 1A.6). Because these phones offer advanced features not typically found in cellular phones, they are sometimes called smart phones. These features can include Web and e-mail access, special software such as personal organizers, or special hardware such as digital cameras or music players. Some models even break in half to reveal a miniature keyboard.

FIGURE 1A.6

New cellular phones, like the Nokia 9500 Communicator, double as tiny computers, offering many of the features of PDAs.

Computers for Organizations

Some computers handle the needs of many users at the same time. These powerful systems are most often used by organizations, such as businesses or schools, and are commonly found at the heart of the organization's network:

>> **Network Servers**   Today, most organizations' networks are based on personal computers. Individual users have their own desktop computers, which are connected to one or more centralized computers, called network servers. A network server is usually a powerful personal computer with special software and equipment that enable it to function as the primary computer in the network.

PC-based networks and servers offer companies a great deal of flexibility. For example, large organizations may have dozens or hundreds of individual servers working together at the heart of their network (see Figure 1A.7). When set up in such groups—sometimes called *clusters* or *server farms*—network servers may not even resemble standard PCs. In these large networks, different groups of servers may have different purposes, such as supporting a certain set of users, handling printing tasks, enabling Internet communications, and so on.

simnet™

Norton
ONLINE

For more information on computers for organizations, visit **http://www.mhhe.com/ peternorton**.

Large corporate networks can use hundreds of servers.

>> **Mainframe Computers**   Mainframe computers are used in large organizations such as insurance companies and banks, where many people frequently need to use the same data. Mainframes are large, powerful systems (see Figure 1A.8). The largest mainframes can handle the processing needs of thousands of users at

any given moment. But what these systems offer in power, they lack in flexibility. Most mainframe systems are designed to handle only a specific set of tasks. In your state's Department of Motor Vehicles, for example, a mainframe system is probably devoted to storing information about drivers, vehicles, and driver's licenses, but little or nothing else. By limiting the number of tasks the system must perform, administrators preserve power for required operations.

In a traditional mainframe environment, each user accesses the mainframe's resources through a device called a terminal (see Figure 1A.9). There are two kinds of terminals. A *dumb terminal* does not process or store data; it is simply an input/output (I/O) device that functions as a window into a computer located somewhere else. An *intelligent terminal* can perform some processing operations, but it usually does not have any storage. In some mainframe environments, however, workers can use a standard personal computer to access the mainframe.

» **Minicomputers** First released in the 1960s, minicomputers got their name because of their small size compared to other computers of the day. Because the minicomputer's capabilities are somewhere between those of mainframes and personal computers, they are often called midrange computers.

FIGURE 1A.8

Mainframe computers are often housed alone, away from their users.

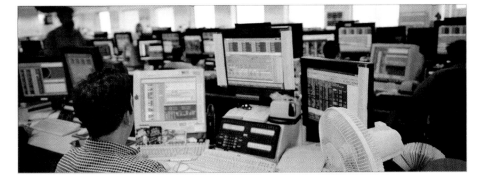

FIGURE 1A.9

Hundreds or thousands of mainframe users can access the central computer.

Buying a computer is a lot like buying a car because there are so many models and options from which to choose! Before deciding which model is best for you, identify the type of work for which you want to use the computer.

Depending on your job, you may need to use a computer on a limited basis. A handheld system is great if you want to

>> **Manage Your Schedule on a Daily or Hourly Basis** Handheld computers are popular for their calendar and schedule-management capabilities, which enable you to set appointments, track projects, and record special events.

>> **Manage a List of Contacts** If you need to stay in touch with many people and travel frequently, personal digital assistants provide contact-management features.

>> **Make Notes on the Fly** Some PDAs feature small keyboards, which are handy for tapping out quick notes. Others feature pens, which enable the user to "write" directly on the display screen. Many newer handheld systems also provide a built-in microphone, so you can record notes digitally.

>> **Send Faxes and E-Mail** Most popular handheld PCs have fax and e-mail capabilities and a port that lets them exchange data with a PC.

If your job requires you to travel, but you still need a full-featured computer, you may consider using a laptop or notebook computer. This option is the best choice if you want to

>> **Carry Your Data with You** If you need to make presentations on the road or keep up with daily work while traveling, portable PCs are ideal. Laptop systems offer as much RAM and storage capacity as desktop models. Many portables have built-in CD-ROM or DVD drives; others accept plug-in CD-ROM, DVD, and hard drives, which can greatly increase their capacity.

>> **Be Able to Work Anywhere** Portable PCs run on either rechargeable batteries or standard current.

>> **Communicate and Share Data from Any Location** Most portable computers have built-in modems or slots for plugging in a modem.

>> **Supercomputers** Supercomputers are the most powerful computers made, and physically they are some of the largest (see Figure 1A.10). These systems can process huge amounts of data, and the fastest supercomputers can perform more than one trillion calculations per second. Some supercomputers can house thousands of processors. Supercomputers are ideal for handling large and highly complex problems that require extreme calculating power. For example, supercomputers have long been used in the mapping of the human genome, forecasting weather, and modeling complex processes.

FIGURE 1A.10

Supercomputers are most common in university and research settings, but a few government agencies and very large businesses use them as well.

SELF-CHECK ::

Circle the correct answer for each question.

1. Any computer is controlled by _____ .
    a. hardware   **b.** information   **c.** instructions

2. Which of these is a powerful type of personal computer, favored by professionals such as engineers?
    a. workstation   **b.** notebook   **c.** mainframe

3. Which type of computer will you most likely encounter at the Department of Motor Vehicles?
    a. smart phone   **b.** mainframe   **c.** supercomputer

If you work in one place and need to perform various tasks, a desktop computer is the best choice. Choose a desktop computer if you want to

>> **Work with Graphics-Intensive or Desktop Publishing Applications** Complex graphics and page-layout programs require a great deal of system resources, and a desktop system's large monitor reduces eye fatigue.

>> **Design or Use Multimedia Products** Even though many portable computers have multimedia features, you can get the most for your money with a desktop system. Large screens make multimedia programs easier to see, and stereo-style speakers optimize sound quality.

>> **Set Up Complex Hardware Configurations** A desktop computer can support multiple peripherals—including printers, sound and video sources, and various external devices—at the same time. If you want to swap video or audio cards easily, increase RAM, or perform other configuration tasks, a desktop system will provide many options.

Portable computers enable you to work almost anywhere.

The Parts of a Computer System

No matter how big it is or how it is used, every computer is part of a system. A complete computer system consists of four parts, as shown in Figure 1A.11.

The mechanical devices that make up the computer are called hardware. Hardware is any part of the computer you can touch. A computer's hardware consists of

simnet™

DATA (information)

HARDWARE (the computer)

SOFTWARE (programs)

PageMaker · Excel · PowerPoint · Illustrator · Windows

Memo

Software installed on the computer

PEOPLE (users)

Converting pieces of data into useful information is a key task of computers.

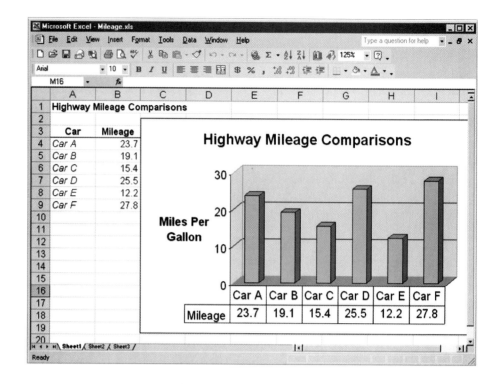

interconnected electronic devices that you can use to control the computer's operation, input, and output. (The generic term device refers to any piece of hardware.)

Software is a set of instructions that makes the computer perform tasks. In other words, software tells the computer what to do. (The term program refers to any piece of software.) Some programs exist primarily for the computer's use to help it perform tasks and manage its own resources. Other types of programs exist for the user, enabling him or her to perform tasks such as creating documents.

Data consists of individual facts or pieces of information that by themselves may not make much sense to a person. A computer's primary job is to process these tiny pieces of data in various ways, converting them into useful information. For example, if you saw the average highway mileages of six different cars, all the different pieces of data might not mean much to you. However, if someone created a chart from the data that visually compared and ranked the vehicles' mileages, you could probably make sense of it at a glance (see Figure 1A.12). This is one example of data being processed into useful information.

People are the computer operators, also known as users. It can be argued that some computer systems are complete without a person's involvement; however, no computer is totally autonomous. Even if a computer can do its job without a person sitting in front of it, people still design, build, program, and repair computer systems. This lack of autonomy is especially true of personal computer systems, which are the focus of this book and are designed specifically for use by people.

Essential Computer Hardware

For more information on computer hardware, visit **http://www.mhhe.com/ peternorton**.

A computer's hardware devices fall into one of four categories (see Figure 1A.13): the processor, memory, input and output, and storage.

The procedure that transforms raw data into useful information is called processing. To perform this transformation, the computer uses two components: the processor and memory.

The processor is like the brain of the computer; it organizes and carries out instructions that come from either the user or the software. In a personal computer, the processor usually consists of one or more specialized chips, called microprocessors, which are slivers of silicon or other material etched with many tiny electronic circuits. To process data or complete an instruction from a user or a program, the computer passes electricity through the circuits.

As shown in Figure 1A.14, the microprocessor is plugged into the computer's motherboard. The motherboard is a rigid rectangular card containing the circuitry that connects the processor to the other hardware. The motherboard is an example of a circuit board. In most personal computers, many internal devices—such as video cards, sound cards, disk controllers, and other devices—are housed on their own smaller circuit boards, which attach to the motherboard. In many newer computers, these devices are built directly into the motherboard. Some newer microprocessors are large and complex enough to require their own dedicated circuit boards, which plug into a special slot in the motherboard. You can think of the motherboard as the master circuit board in a computer.

A personal computer's processor is usually a single chip or a set of chips contained on a circuit board. In some powerful computers, the processor consists of many chips and the circuit boards on which they are mounted. In either case, the term central processing unit (CPU) refers to a computer's processor. People often refer to computer systems by the type of CPU they contain. A "Pentium 4" system, for example, uses a Pentium 4 microprocessor as its CPU.

In a computer, memory is one or more sets of chips that store data and/or program instructions, either temporarily or permanently. Memory is a critical processing component in any computer. Personal computers use several different types of memory, but the two most important are called random access memory (RAM) and read-only memory (ROM). These two types of memory work in very different ways and perform distinct functions.

The most common type of memory is called random access memory (RAM). As a result, the term *memory* is typically used to mean RAM. RAM is like an electronic scratch pad inside the computer. RAM holds data and program instructions while the CPU works with them. When a program is launched, it is loaded

Motherboard

Circuit board

The microprocessor is inside this case.

FIGURE 1A.14

Processing devices.

Random access memory (RAM).

into and run from RAM. As the program needs data, it is loaded into RAM for fast access. As new data is entered into the computer, it also is stored in RAM—but only temporarily. Data is both written to and read from this memory. (Because of this, RAM is also sometimes called *read/write memory*.)

Like many computer components, RAM is made up of a set of chips mounted on a small circuit board (see Figure 1A.15).

RAM is volatile, meaning that it loses its contents when the computer is shut off or if there is a power failure. Therefore, RAM needs a constant supply of power to hold its data. For this reason, you should save your data files to a storage device frequently, to avoid losing them in a power failure. (You will learn more about storage later in this chapter.)

RAM has a tremendous impact on the speed and power of a computer. Generally, the more RAM a computer has, the more it can do and the faster it can perform certain tasks. The most common measurement unit for describing a computer's memory is the byte—the amount of memory it takes to store a single character, such as a letter of the alphabet or a numeral. When referring to a computer's memory, the numbers are often so large that it is helpful to use terms such as kilobyte (KB), megabyte (MB), gigabyte (GB), and terabyte (TB) to describe the values (see Table 1A.1).

TABLE 1A.1

Units of Measure for Computer Memory and Storage

Unit	Abbreviation	Pronounced	Approximate Value (bytes)	Actual Value (bytes)
Kilobyte	KB	KILL-uh-bite	1,000	1,024
Megabyte	MB	MEHG-uh-bite	1,000,000 (1 million)	1,048,576
Gigabyte	GB	GIG-uh-bite	1,000,000,000 (1 billion)	1,073,741,824
Terabyte	TB	TERR-uh-bite	1,000,000,000,000 (1 trillion)	1,099,511,627,776

Today's personal computers generally have at least 256 million bytes (256 MB) of random access memory. Many newer systems feature 512 MB or more.

Unlike RAM, read-only memory (ROM) permanently stores its data, even when the computer is shut off. ROM is called non-volatile memory because it never loses its contents. ROM holds instructions that the computer needs to operate. Whenever the computer's power is turned on, it checks ROM for directions that help it start up, and for information about its hardware devices.

A personal computer would be useless if you could not interact with it because the machine could not receive instructions or deliver the results of its work. Input devices accept data and instructions from the user or from another computer system. Output devices return processed data to the user or to another computer system. (You will learn more about input and output devices in the next lesson.)

A computer can function with only processing, memory, input, and output devices. To be really useful, however, a computer also needs a place to keep program files and related data when they are not in use. The purpose of storage is to hold data permanently, even when the computer is turned off.

You may think of storage as an electronic file cabinet and RAM as an electronic worktable. When you need to work with a program or a set of data, the computer locates it in the file cabinet and puts a copy on the table. After you have finished working with the program or data, you put it back into the file cabinet. The changes you make to data while working on it replace the original data in the file cabinet (unless you store it in a different place).

There are many types of computer storage, but the most common is the magnetic disk. A disk is a round, flat object that spins around its center. (Magnetic disks are almost always housed inside a case of some kind, so you can't see the disk itself unless you open the case.) Read/write heads, which work in much the same way as the heads of a tape recorder or VCR, are used to read data from the disk or write data onto the disk.

The hard disk is built into the computer's case.

Diskettes can be inserted into and removed from the diskette drive.

The device that holds a disk is called a disk drive. Some disks are built into the drive and are not meant to be removed; other kinds of drives enable you to remove and replace disks (see Figure 1A.16). Most personal computers have at least one nonremovable hard disk (or hard drive). In addition, there is also a diskette drive, which allows you to use removable diskettes (or floppy disks). The hard disk serves as the computer's primary filing cabinet because it can store far more data than a diskette can contain. Diskettes are used to load data onto the hard disk, to trade data with other users, and to make backup copies of the data on the hard disk.

In addition to magnetic storage, nearly every computer sold today includes at least one form of optical storage—devices that use lasers to read data from or write data to the reflective surface of an optical disc.

The CD-ROM drive is the most common type of optical storage device. Compact discs (CDs) are a type of optical storage, identical to audio CDs (see Figure 1A.17). Until recently, a standard CD could store about 74 minutes of audio or 650 MB of data. A newer breed of CD can hold 80 minutes of audio or 700 MB of data. The type used in computers is called Compact Disc Read-Only Memory (CD-ROM). As the name implies, you cannot change the information on the disc, just as you cannot record over an audio CD.

If you purchase a CD-Recordable (CD-R) drive, you have the option of creating your own CDs. A CD-R drive can write data to and read data from a compact disc. To use a CD-R drive, you must use a special CD-R disc, which can be written on only once, or a CD-ReWritable (CD-RW) disc, which can be written to multiple times.

An increasingly popular data storage technology is the Digital Video Disc (DVD), which is revolutionizing home entertainment. Using sophisticated compression technologies, a single DVD (which is the same size as a standard compact disc) can store an entire full-length movie. DVDs can hold a minimum of 4.7 GB of data and as much as 17 GB. Future DVD technologies promise much higher storage capacities on a single disc. DVD drives also can locate data on a disc faster than standard CD-ROM drives.

FIGURE 1A.16

Standard PCs have a built-in hard disk and a diskette drive.

FIGURE 1A.17

Software makers commonly sell their products on CD because of the disc's high storage capacity.

Software Brings the Machine to Life

The ingredient that enables a computer to perform a specific task is software, which consists of instructions. A set of instructions that drive a computer to perform specific tasks is called a program. These instructions tell the machine's physical components what to do; without the instructions, a computer could not do anything at all. When a computer uses a program, it is said to be running or executing that program.

simnet™

Although the array of available programs is vast and varied, most software falls into two major categories: system software and application software.

System Software

System software is any program that controls the computer's hardware or that can be used to maintain the computer in some way so that it runs more efficiently. There are three basic types of system software:

>> An operating system tells the computer how to use its own components. Examples of operating systems include Windows, the Macintosh Operating System, and Linux (see Figure 1A.18). An operating system is essential for any computer, because it acts as an interpreter between the hardware, application programs, and the user. When a program wants the hardware to do something, it communicates through the operating system. Similarly, when you want the hardware to do something (such as copying or printing a file), your request is handled by the operating system.

>> A network operating system allows computers to communicate and share data across a network while controlling network operations and overseeing security.

>> A utility is a program that makes the computer system easier to use or performs highly specialized functions. Utilities are used to manage disks, troubleshoot hardware problems, and perform other tasks that the operating system itself may not be able to do.

Application Software

Application software tells the computer how to accomplish specific tasks, such as word processing or drawing, for the user. Thousands of applications are available for many purposes and for people of all ages. The major categories of these applications include

>> Word processing software for creating text-based documents such as newsletters or brochures (see Figure 1A.19).

>> Spreadsheets for creating numeric-based documents such as budgets or balance sheets.

FIGURE 1A.18

Windows is the most popular of all PC operating systems, running on about 90 percent of all personal computers.

>> Database management software for building and manipulating large sets of data, such as the names, addresses, and phone numbers in a telephone directory.

>> Presentation programs for creating electronic slide shows (see Figure 1A.20).

>> Graphics programs for designing illustrations or manipulating photographs, movies, or animation.

>> Multimedia authoring applications for building digital movies that incorporate sound, video, animation, and interactive features.

>> Entertainment and education software, many of which are interactive multimedia events.

>> Web design tools and Web browsers, and other Internet applications such as newsreaders and e-mail programs.

>> Games, some of which are for a single player and many of which can be played by several people over a network or the Internet.

FIGURE 1A.19

Word processing software is designed for creating documents that consist primarily of text, but also lets you add graphics and sounds to your documents. It also provides layout features that let you create brochures, newsletters, Web pages, and more.

FIGURE 1A.20

Presentation software is most often used for creating sales presentations, although it can be effective for any type of electronic slide show.

Computer Data

You have already seen that, to a computer, data is any piece of information or fact that, taken by itself, may not have much or any meaning to a person. For example, you might think of the letters of the alphabet as data. Taken individually, they do not mean a lot. But when grouped into words and sentences, they make sense; that is, they become information (see Figure 1A.21). Similarly, basic geometric shapes may not have much meaning by themselves, but when they are grouped into a blueprint or a chart, they become useful information.

The computer reads and stores data of all kinds—whether words, numbers, images, or sounds—in the form of numbers. Consequently, computerized data is digital, meaning that it has been reduced to digits, or numbers. This is because the computer can work only with strings of numbers. Just as people represent their own language by using strings of letters to make up words and sentences, computers use strings of numbers to represent every type of data they must handle. Following instructions from the software and the user, the computer manipulates data by performing calculations, doing comparisons, or arranging the bits of information so they make sense to the user.

FIGURE 1A.21

A piece of data, like a letter of the alphabet, has little meaning by itself. When pieces of data are combined and placed in some sort of context, such as a resume, they become meaningful information.

A	B	C	D
E	F	G	H
I	J	K	L
M	N	O	P
Q	R	S	T
U	V	W	X
Y	Z		

Data = Piece of information without context

RESUME

Johnathon Smith
1512 N. Main Street
Troy, NC 28265

704-555-5555
smith@try.net
www.jon.com

Objective
A career as a sales associate with a leading grocery chain

Education
- Ph.D, Nuclear Phsyics, *Massachussetts Institute of Technology*, 1998.
- M.S., Physics, *Duke University*, 1996
- B.S., Chemistry/Physics, *Center College*, 1994

Maintained average GPA of 3.8 during collegiate career.

Experience
2000 – Present. Head Bag Boy, *Tom's QuickShop*, Cambriage City, IN
1999 – 2000. Bag Boy, *The Vilage Pantry*, Nitro, W.V.
1998 – 1999. Assistant Janitor, *McCreary County Jail*, Whitley City, KY

Special Skills
- Expert in the programming of differential analysers
- Proficient at operation of particle accelerators
- Developed method for creating anti-matter in standard household bathroom

References
Available on request.

Information = Data placed in context

Just as computer data is different from information, it also differs from programs. Recall that a software program is a set of instructions that tells the computer how to perform tasks. Like data, these instructions exist as strings of numbers so the computer can use them. But the resemblance ends there. You can think of the difference between data and programs this way: data is for people to use, but programs are for computers to use.

Within the computer, data is organized into files. A file is simply a set of data that has been given a name. A file that the user can open and use is often called a document. Although many people think of documents simply as text, a computer document can include many kinds of data (see Figure 1A.22). For example, a computer document can be a text file (such as a letter), a group of numbers (such as a budget), a video clip (which includes images and sounds), or any combination of these items. Programs are organized into files as well; these files contain the instructions and data that a program needs in order to run and perform tasks.

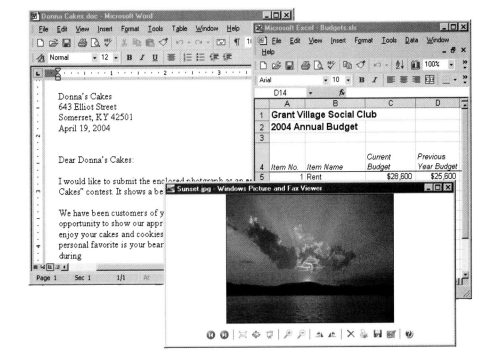

FIGURE 1A.22

A letter, a budget, a picture—each one is an example of a document that a person can use.

At Issue

Computerized Disease Management

Despite the abundance of widely recognized, evidence-based standards, health care is notoriously inconsistent from one doctor to the next, one hospital to the next, and one region to the next. So much so, that the experts at the National Academies Institute of Medicine have proclaimed it to be a health system quality chasm.

Through the use of global information technology, new technology-driven disease management systems are offering the health care industry a solution to the high variability of practice. Interactive computerized disease management programs promise to close this "quality chasm."

The goal of interactive computerized disease management (DM) programs is to monitor patients with chronic diseases such as heart disease or diabetes, track their progress, and encourage compliance with medical best practices. Through wireless telephony or Web interfaces, patients report vital signs, symptoms, and other medical information to their caregivers. In some cases, patients are hooked up to remote monitoring devices that automatically transmit information to a physician or medical database. Case managers then monitor patient data, looking for early problems and intervening before costly emergencies arise.

Computerized DM systems have been shown to facilitate communication between patients and health care providers, cut health care costs, and improve quality of care.

One leading provider of these systems is LifeMasters Supported SelfCare, Inc. LifeMasters offers high-tech DM programs that create cooperative health partnerships among patients, physicians, and payors.

With the LifeMasters program, computers monitor disease across large patient groups; report patient status to doctors and their clinical teams; send reminders when patients are due for testing, evaluation, and treatment; and track the outcomes to support improvement and continuity of care. LifeMasters claims their computerized information technology system improves quality of life for individuals with chronic illnesses, supports physicians with improved DM tools, and reduces chronic-disease costs for payors.

Headquartered in Irvine, California, LifeMasters currently provides DM services for more than 275,000 patients with diabetes, congestive heart failure, coronary artery disease, chronic obstructive pulmonary disease, hypertension, and asthma in all 50 states, the District of Columbia, and Puerto Rico.

Taking the computerized DM model one step further, LifeMasters also maintains the LifeMasters Online Web site, the first fully interactive health monitoring and management service for individual use.

LifeMasters Online offers health management tools and content similar to those offered through LifeMasters' caregiver-supervised model, but it is available free to the general public. Here, users enter their own vital-sign and symptom information via the Web site or through a Touch-Tone phone. The information goes into a database and, when the data indicates that medical intervention is required, the patient's physician is notified.

Patients have access to support groups and medical information on a 24 × 7 basis. LifeMasters Online also provides self-directed health education and behavior modification modules addressing health concerns such as diet, exercise, and smoking cessation.

"We built this for the future," says Christobel Selecky, LifeMasters CEO. "As the Baby Boom generation ages and develops chronic diseases, we're going to need to use technology tools to help physicians and their patients manage their health care more effectively and efficiently than in traditional ways."

Summary ::

>> A computer is an electronic device that processes data, converting it into information.

>> Computers designed for use by a single person include desktop computers, workstations, notebook computers, tablet computers, handheld computers, and smart phones.

>> The desktop computer is the most common type of personal computer. This computer is designed to sit on top of a desk or table and comes in two basic styles.

>> A workstation is a specialized, single-user computer that typically has more power and features than a standard desktop PC.

>> Notebook computers (or laptop computers) are full-featured PCs that can easily be carried around.

>> A tablet PC is another type of portable PC, but it can accept handwritten input when the user touches the screen with a special pen.

>> Handheld personal computers are computing devices that are small enough to fit in your hand; the personal digital assistant (PDA) is an example of a handheld computer.

>> Smart phones are digital cellular phones that have features found in personal computers, such as Web browsers, e-mail capability, and more.

>> Some types of computers—such as network servers, mainframes, minicomputers, and supercomputers—are commonly used by organizations and support the computing needs of many users.

>> A network server is a powerful personal computer that is used as the central computer in an organization's network.

>> Mainframes are powerful, special-purpose computers that can support the needs of hundreds or thousands of users.

>> Minicomputers are like small mainframe systems and often support dozens or hundreds of users at one time.

>> Supercomputers are the largest and most powerful computers made and are used for sophisticated tasks such as genome mapping and weather forecasting.

>> A complete computer system includes hardware, software, data, and users.

>> Hardware consists of electronic devices, the parts you can touch.

>> Software, also known as programs, consists of instructions that control the computer.

>> Data consists of text, numbers, sounds, and images that the computer can manipulate.

>> People who operate computers are called users.

>> A computer's hardware devices fall into four categories: processor, memory, input and output (I/O), and storage.

>> The operating system tells the computer how to interact with the user and how to use the hardware devices attached to the computer.

>> Application software tells the computer how to accomplish tasks the user requires.

>> In a computer, data consists of small pieces of information that, by themselves, may not make sense to a person. The computer manipulates data into useful information.

Key Terms ::

application software, 14
byte, 12
CD-Recordable (CD-R), 13
CD-ReWritable (CD-RW), 13
CD-ROM drive, 13
central processing unit (CPU), 11
circuit board, 11
compact disc (CD), 13
Compact Disc Read-Only Memory
   (CD-ROM), 13
computer, 4
computer system, 9
data, 10
desktop computer, 4
device, 10
digital, 16
digital pen, 5
Digital Video Disc (DVD), 13
disk drive, 13
diskette, 13
diskette drive, 13
document, 17
execute, 13
file, 17
floppy disk, 13

gigabyte (GB), 12
handheld personal computer, 6
hard disk, 13
hard drive, 13
hardware, 9
input device, 12
input/output (I/O) device, 7
kilobyte (KB), 12
laptop computer, 5
magnetic disk, 13
mainframe, 6
megabyte (MB), 12
memory, 11
microcomputer, 4
microprocessor, 11
midrange computer, 7
minicomputer, 7
mobile computer, 5
motherboard, 11
network operating system, 14
network server, 6
nonvolatile, 12
notebook computer, 5
operating system, 14
optical storage, 13

output device, 12
personal computer (PC), 4
personal digital assistant (PDA), 6
processing, 10
processor, 10
program, 10
random access memory (RAM), 11
read-only memory (ROM), 12
read/write head, 13
run, 13
smart phone, 6
software, 10
storage, 12
stylus, 5
supercomputer, 8
system software, 14
system unit, 4
tablet PC, 5
terabyte (TB), 12
terminal, 7
user, 10
utility, 14
volatile, 12
workstation, 5

Key Term Quiz ::

Complete each statement by writing one of the terms listed under Key Terms in each blank.

1. The _____ is the case that holds the computer's critical components.

2. A(n) _____ is a specialized, single-user computer that typically has more power than a standard PC.

3. A(n) _____ is usually a powerful personal computer that functions as the primary computer in a network.

4. A complete _____ is a combination of hardware, software, data, and a user.

5. A(n) _____ is a set of data or program instructions that has been given a name.

6. A(n) _____ is a device that holds a disk.

7. Electronic instructions that tell the computer's hardware what to do are known as _____ .

8. The generic term _____ refers to a piece of hardware.

9. Data and program instructions are temporarily held in _____ while the processor is using them.

10. One _____ is roughly equivalent to one million bytes of data.

LESSON // 1A   Review

Multiple Choice ::

Circle the word or phrase that best completes each statement.

1. A computer converts data into this.
   - a. information
   - b. charts
   - c. software
   - d. input/output

2. Personal computers are also called _____ .
   - a. minicomputers
   - b. microcomputers
   - c. maxicomputers
   - d. supercomputers

3. Many scientists, engineers, and animators use specialized computers, called _____ .
   - a. personal digital assistants
   - b. minicomputers
   - c. workstations
   - d. networks

4. Notebook PCs fall into a category of devices called _____ .
   - a. mobile computers
   - b. small computers
   - c. handheld computers
   - d. minicomputers

5. Network servers are sometimes set up in groups that may be called _____ or server farms.
   - a. units
   - b. workgroups
   - c. clusters
   - d. racks

6. Which of the following devices stores instructions that help the computer start up?
   - a. joystick
   - b. RAM
   - c. ROM
   - d. monitor

7. Which of the following is *not* an essential part of a complete personal computer system?
   - a. hardware
   - b. software
   - c. user
   - d. terminal

8. Which of the following units represents the largest amount of data?
   - a. kilobyte
   - b. terabyte
   - c. gigabyte
   - d. megabyte

9. A file that the user can open and use is called a(n) _____ .
   - a. application
   - b. program
   - c. document
   - d. data

10. Because computer data has been reduced to numbers, it is described as being _____ .
    - a. digital
    - b. numeral
    - c. digitic
    - d. numeric

22   Chapter 1

Review Questions ::

In your own words, briefly answer the following questions.

1. What is a computer?
2. List six types of computers that are designed for use by a single person.
3. List four types of computers that are designed for use by organizations and are commonly used by multiple people at the same time.
4. List the four parts of a complete computer system.
5. Identify four categories of computer hardware.
6. List four units of measure for computer memory and storage, not including the byte.
7. Name the two main categories of storage devices.
8. Name the two main categories of computer software.
9. What is the difference between data and information?
10. What is a fundamental difference between data and programs?

Lesson Labs ::

Complete the following exercises as directed by your instructor.

1. During the course of a normal day, keep a list of your encounters with computers of various kinds. Your list should show the place and time of the encounter, the type of interaction you had with the technology, and the results of that interaction. (Remember, computers can take many sizes and forms, so be alert to more than just PCs.) Share your list with the class.
2. What type of computer system do you use in class or in the lab? How much can you tell about the system by looking at it? List as much information as you can about the computer. Is it a desktop or tower model? What brand is it? What type of processor does it have? What are the model and serial numbers? What external devices does it have? Is it connected to a network or printer?

Interacting with Your Computer

Overview: Input and Output

From the user's point of view, input and output devices are just as important as the CPU, perhaps even more important. After you buy and set up the computer, you may take the CPU for granted because you interact directly with input and output devices and only indirectly with the CPU.

An input device does exactly what its name suggests: it enables you to enter information and commands into the computer. The most commonly used input devices are the keyboard and the mouse. If you buy a new personal computer today, it will include a keyboard and mouse unless you specify otherwise. Other types of input devices are available as well, such as variations of the mouse and specialized input devices such as microphones and scanners.

An output device enables the computer to present processed information back to you, whether as text, pictures, sounds, numbers, or music. The most common output devices are monitors and printers.

This lesson introduces you to input and output devices. You will learn the importance of these devices and the many tasks they enable you to perform on your PC.

OBJECTIVES ::

>> Identify the five key groups on a standard computer keyboard.

>> Describe the purpose of the pointing device and the role it plays in computing.

>> List the two most commonly used types of computer monitors.

>> List the three most commonly used types of printers.

>> List the four criteria you should consider when evaluating monitors or printers.

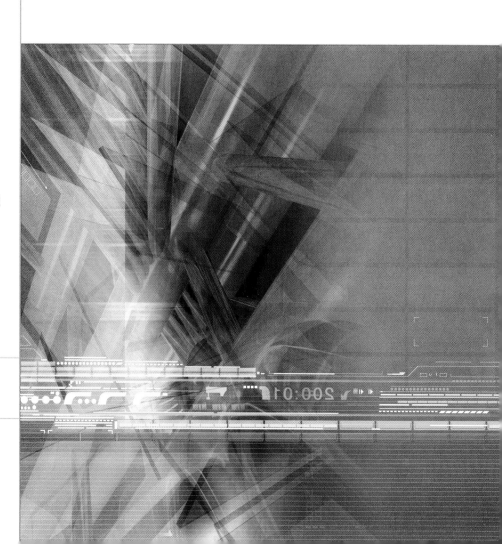

Common Input Devices

Input devices are the tools you use for issuing commands to the computer. Input devices also enable you to provide data for the computer to process, such as text, numbers, pictures, or sounds. There are many kinds of input devices; some serve a wide range of purposes, while others have a very specific use. As you work with computers, you will probably use many different kinds of input devices.

The Keyboard

The keyboard was one of the first peripherals to be used with computers, and it is still the primary input device for entering text and numbers. Keyboards come in many styles. The various models differ in size, shape, and feel; except for a few special-purpose keys, most keyboards are laid out almost identically. Among personal computers, the most common keyboard layout is the IBM Enhanced Keyboard. It has about 100 keys, as shown in Figure 1B.1.

A standard keyboard's keys are arranged in five groups:

>> **Alphanumeric Keys** The alphanumeric keys—the area of the keyboard that looks like a typewriter's keys—are arranged the same way on almost every keyboard. Sometimes this common arrangement is called the QWERTY (pronounced KWER-tee) layout because the first six keys on the top row of letters are Q, W, E, R, T, and Y. Along with the keys that produce letters and numbers, the alphanumeric key group includes four keys—TAB, CAPS LOCK, BACKSPACE, and ENTER—that have specific functions.

>> **Modifier Keys** The SHIFT, ALT (Alternate), and CTRL (Control) keys are called modifier keys because they modify the input of other keys. In other words, if you hold down a modifier key while pressing another key, then you are changing the second key's input in some way. For example, if you press the J key, you input a small letter *j*. But if you hold down the SHIFT key while pressing the J key, you input a capital *J*. Modifier keys are extremely useful because they give all other keys multiple capabilities.

>> **Numeric Keypad** The numeric keypad is usually located on the right side of the keyboard, as shown in Figure 1B.1. The numeric keypad looks like a calculator's keypad, with its 10 digits and mathematical operators (+, -, *, and /). The numeric keypad also features a NUM LOCK key, which forces the

Norton
ONLINE

For more information on keyboards, visit
http://www.mhhe.com/ peternorton.

FIGURE 1B.1

Most IBM-compatible PCs use a keyboard like this one.

Alphanumeric keys

The cursor, or insertion point, shows where the next letter typed will appear.

Now is the time for all good men to |

The cursor, or insertion
point, in a document

numeric keys to input numbers. When NUM LOCK is deactivated, the keys perform cursor-movement control and other functions.

» **Function Keys** The function keys, which are labeled F1, F2, and so on, are usually arranged in a row along the top of the keyboard. They allow you to input commands without typing long strings of characters or navigating menus or dialog boxes. Each function key's purpose depends on the program you are using. For example, in most programs, F1 is the help key. When you press it, a special window appears to display information about the program you are using. Most keyboards have 12 function keys. Many programs use modifier keys to give the function keys more capabilities.

» **Cursor-Movement Keys** Most standard keyboards also include a set of cursor-movement keys, which let you move around the screen without using a mouse. In many programs and operating systems, a mark on the screen indicates where the characters you type will be entered. This mark, called the cursor or insertion point, appears on the screen as a blinking vertical line, a small box, or some other symbol to show your place in a document or command line. Figure 1B.2 shows an insertion point in a document window.

The Mouse and Its Variants

Today, every new PC includes a pointing device as standard equipment, as shown in Figure 1B.3. Full-size PCs usually include a mouse as the pointing device. A mouse is an input device that you can move around on a flat surface (usually on a desk or keyboard tray) and controls the pointer. The pointer (also called the *mouse pointer*) is an on-screen object, usually an arrow, that is used to select text; access menus; and interact with programs, files, or data that appears on the screen. Figure 1B.4 shows an example of a pointer in a program window.

Types of Mice

The mechanical mouse is the most common type of pointing device. A mechanical mouse contains a small rubber ball that protrudes through a hole in the bottom of

FIGURE 1B.3

Most modern personal computers are equipped with a mouse.

FIGURE 1B.4

An example of a pointer as it might appear on a computer screen.

Norton
ONLINE

For more information on mice, visit **http://www.mhhe.com/ peternorton**.

FIGURE 1B.5

The parts of a mechanical mouse, seen from the bottom.

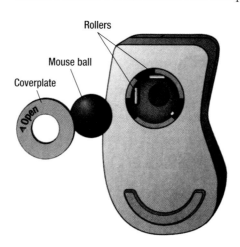

Rollers

Mouse ball

Coverplate

the mouse's case (see Figure 1B.5). The ball rolls inside the case when you move the mouse around on a flat surface. Inside the mouse, rollers and sensors send signals to the computer, telling it the distance, direction, and speed of the ball's motions (see Figure 1B.6). The computer uses this data to position the mouse pointer on the screen.

Another popular type of mouse, the optical mouse, is nonmechanical. This type of mouse emits a beam of light from its underside; it uses the light's reflection to judge the distance, direction, and speed of its travel (see Figure 1B.7).

1 When the mouse moves...

2 ...the rolling mouse ball spins the rollers.

3 The information from the spinning rollers is sent to the system software, which controls the pointer.

FIGURE 1B.6

How the mouse controls the pointer.

FIGURE 1B.7

The underside of an optical mouse.

The mouse offers two main benefits. First, the mouse lets you position the cursor anywhere on the screen quickly without using the cursor-movement keys. You simply move the pointer to the on-screen position you want and press the mouse button; the cursor appears at that location. Second, instead of forcing you to type or issue commands from the keyboard, the mouse and mouse-based operating systems let you choose commands from easy-to-use menus and dialog boxes (see Figure 1B.8).

Mouse Variants

There are three common variations on the mouse, all of which are very popular:

>> **Trackballs** A trackball (see Figure 1B.9) is a pointing device that works like an upside-down mouse. You rest your index finger or thumb on an exposed ball, then place your other fingers on the buttons. To move the pointer around the screen, you roll the ball with your index finger or thumb. Because you do not move the whole device, a trackball requires less space than a mouse. Trackballs gained popularity with the advent of laptop computers, which typically are used on small work surfaces that have no room for a mouse.

>> **Trackpads** The trackpad (also called a touchpad) is a stationary pointing device that many people find less tiring to use than a mouse or trackball. The movement of a finger across a small touch-sensitive surface is translated into pointer movement on the

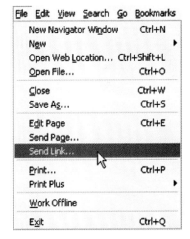

FIGURE 1B.8

Using the mouse to choose a command from a menu.

FIGURE 1B.9

Trackballs come in many shapes and sizes.

Some notebook computers and desktop keyboards feature a built-in trackpad.

Norton
ONLINE

For more information on mouse variants, visit **http://www.mhhe.com/ peternorton**.

Trackpad

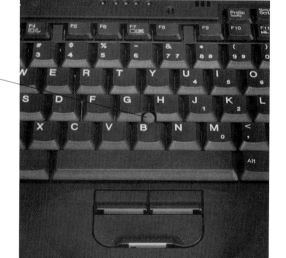

TrackPoint

FIGURE 1B.11

IBM's ThinkPad computers feature the TrackPoint pointing device; similar devices are found in many other portable PCs.

FIGURE 1B.12

To interact with a pen-based computer, you can use the pen to point, tap, drag, draw, and even write on the device's screen.

computer screen. The touch-sensitive surface may be only 1.5 or 2 inches square, so the finger never has to move far. The trackpad's size also makes it suitable for a notebook computer. Some notebook models feature a built-in trackpad rather than a mouse or trackball (see Figure 1B.10).

>> **Integrated Pointing Devices** Many portable computers feature a small joystick positioned near the middle of the keyboard, typically between the G and H keys. The joystick is controlled with either forefinger, and it controls the movement of the pointer on screen. Because users do not have to take their hands off the keyboard to use this device, they can save a great deal of time and effort. Two buttons that perform the same function as mouse buttons are just beneath the spacebar and are pressed with the thumb. Several generic terms have emerged for this device; many manufacturers refer to it as an integrated pointing device, while others call it a 3-D point stick. On IBM's ThinkPad notebook computers, this pointing device is called the TrackPoint (see Figure 1B.11).

Other Input Devices

Although the keyboard and the mouse are the input devices that people use most often, there are many other ways to input data into a computer:

>> **Digital Pens** Pen-based systems—including many tablet PCs, personal digital assistants, and other types of handheld computers—use a digital pen for data input (see Figure 1B.12). This device is sometimes called a stylus. You hold

the pen in your hand and write on a special pad or directly on the screen. You also can use the pen as a pointing device, like a mouse, to select commands by tapping the screen. Pen-based computers are often used for taking notes, not for entering large amounts of text.

» **Touch Screens** Touch screens accept input by allowing the user to place a fingertip directly on the computer screen, usually to make a selection from a menu of choices. Most touch-screen computers use sensors on the screen's surface to detect the touch of a finger, but other touch-screen technologies are in use as well. They are well-suited for simple applications, such as automated teller machines or public information kiosks (see Figure 1B.13).

» **Game Controllers** A game controller can be considered an input device because a computer game is a program, much like a word processor. Game controllers generally fall into two broad categories: game pads and joysticks (see Figure 1B.14). Joysticks enable the user to "fly" or "drive" through a game, directing a vehicle or character. A game pad is a small, flat device that usually provides two sets of controls—one for each hand. These devices are extremely flexible and are used to control many kinds of games.

» **Bar Code Readers** Bar code readers are one of the most widely used input devices. The most common type of bar code reader is the flatbed model, which is commonly found in supermarkets and department stores (see Figure 1B.15). Workers for delivery services, such as FedEx, also use handheld bar code readers in the field to identify packages. These devices read bar codes, which are patterns of printed bars that appear on product packages. The bar codes identify the product. The bar code reader emits a beam of light—frequently a laser beam—that is reflected by the bar code image. A light-sensitive detector identifies the bar code image.

» **Image Scanners** The bar code reader is a special type of image scanner. Image scanners (also called *scanners*) convert any printed image into electronic form by shining light onto the image and sensing the intensity of the light's reflection at every point. Figure 1B.16 illustrates the scanning process. The image scanner is useful because it translates printed images into an electronic format that can be stored in a computer's memory. Then you can use software to organize or manipulate the electronic image. For example, if you scan a photo, you can use a graphics program such as Adobe Photoshop to increase the contrast or adjust the colors. If you scan a text document,

FIGURE 1B.13

This student is using a touch-screen system to get information at a public-information kiosk.

FIGURE 1B.14

Some game controllers even provide tactile feedback, such as vibrations or pulses, to help players "feel" the action in the game.

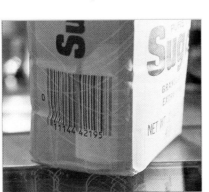

FIGURE 1B.15

A bar code reader projects a web of laser beams onto a package's bar code, then measures the pattern of the reflected light.

How an image is scanned.

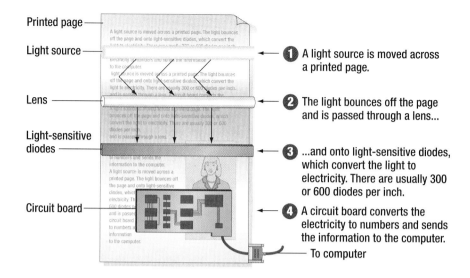

Printed page

Light source — ➊ A light source is moved across a printed page.

Lens — ➋ The light bounces off the page and is passed through a lens...

Light-sensitive diodes — ➌ ...and onto light-sensitive diodes, which convert the light to electricity. There are usually 300 or 600 diodes per inch.

Circuit board — ➍ A circuit board converts the electricity to numbers and sends the information to the computer.

To computer

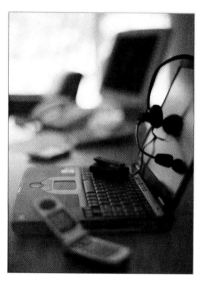

Microphones are becoming increasingly popular input devices.

Norton
ONLINE

For more information on alternative input devices, visit **http://www.mhhe.com/ peternorton**.

you might want to use optical character recognition (OCR) software to translate the image into text that you can edit. When a scanner first creates an image from a page, the image is stored in the computer's memory as a bitmap. A bitmap is a grid of dots, each dot represented by one or more bits. The job of OCR software is to translate that array of dots into text that the computer can interpret as letters and numbers.

» **Microphones** Microphones are becoming increasingly important as input devices to record speech (see Figure 1B.17). Spoken input is used often in multimedia, especially when the presentation can benefit from narration. Most PCs now have phone-dialing capabilities. If you have a microphone and speakers (or a headset microphone with an earphone), you can use your PC to make telephone calls.

Microphones also make the PC useful for audio and videoconferencing over the Internet. For this type of sound input, you need a microphone and a sound card. A sound card is a special device inside the computer that translates analog audio signals (that is, sound waves) from the microphone into digital codes the computer can store and process. This process is called digitizing. Sound cards also can translate digital sounds back into analog signals that can then be sent to the speakers.

There is also a demand for translating spoken words into text, much as there is a demand for translating handwriting into text. Translating voice to text is a capability known as speech recognition (or voice recognition). With it, you can dictate to the computer instead of typing, and you can control the computer with simple commands, such as Open or Cancel.

» **Video Cameras** With the growth of multimedia and the Internet, computer users are adding video input capabilities to their systems in great numbers. Applications such as videoconferencing enable people to use full-motion video images, which are captured by a PC video camera, and transmit them to a limited number of recipients on a network or to the world on the Internet. Videos are commonly used in presentations and on Web pages where the viewer can start, stop, and control various aspects of the playback.

A popular and inexpensive type of PC video camera—called a Webcam— can sit on top of a PC monitor or be placed on a stand, so the user can "capture" images of himself or herself while working at the computer. This arrangement is handy for videoconferencing, where multiple users see and talk to one another in real time over a network or Internet connection (see Figure 1B.18).

Using a video capture card, the user also can connect other video devices, such as VCRs and camcorders, to the PC. This enables the user to transfer images from the video equipment to the PC, and vice versa. Affordable video capture cards enable home users to edit their videotapes like professionals.

» **Digital Cameras** Digital cameras work much like PC video cameras, except that digital cameras are portable, handheld devices that capture still images (see Figure 1B.19). Whereas normal film cameras capture images on a specially coated film, digital cameras capture images electronically. The digital camera digitizes the image, compresses it, and stores it on a special memory card. The user can then copy the image to a PC, where it can be edited, copied, printed, embedded in a document, or transmitted to another user.

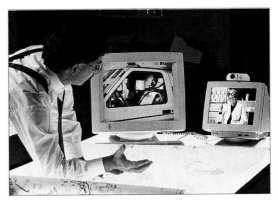

FIGURE 1B.18

PC video cameras enable you to conduct video phone calls.

Common Output Devices

Early computers made it difficult to see the results of their processing. They might display their results on a panel of flashing lights or punch holes on a long stream of tape. Today, output devices are an essential part of every computer, making it easy to see and hear the results of your work.

Monitors

The keyboard is the most commonly used input device and the monitor is the most commonly used output device on most personal computer systems. The monitor is a device that shows you the results of your work on the computer as you do it. As you use your computer—whether you are typing a letter, copying files, or surfing the Internet—hardly a moment goes by when you are not looking at your monitor.

In general, two types of monitors are used with PCs (see Figure 1B.20). The first is the typical monitor that comes with most desktop computers; it looks a lot like a television screen and works in much the same way. This type of monitor uses a large vacuum tube, called a cathode ray tube (CRT). The second type, known as a flat-panel display, was used primarily with portable computers in the past but is now a popular feature with desktop computers.

FIGURE 1B.19

Although most digital cameras look like traditional film cameras, they work in a very different way.

CRT Monitors

Figure 1B.21 shows how a typical CRT monitor works. Near the back of a monitor's housing is an electron gun. The gun shoots a beam of electrons through a magnetic coil, which aims the beam at the front of the monitor. The back of the monitor's screen is coated with phosphors, chemicals that glow when they are struck by the electron beam. The screen's phosphor coating is organized into a grid of dots. The smallest number of phosphor dots that the gun can focus on is called a pixel, a contraction of the term *pic*ture *el*ement. Each pixel has a unique address, which the computer uses to locate the pixel and control its appearance. Some electron guns can focus on pixels as small as a single phosphor dot.

Norton Notebook

Speech Recognition

The youngest daughter of an associate recently entered graduate studies at MIT. She's already received a BS in Engineering and an MA in Mathematics. So what has drawn her to Cambridge? "The speech-recognition railroad," she says. When I asked her how long she plans to stay on that train—"All the way to retirement!"

That answer speaks about more than just her smart sense of humor and the lucrative prospects of an MIT doctorate. It also reveals the nearly glacial pace of movement toward achieving that "holy grail" of human interface. Science has explored this idea—talk to machines and they do what we tell them—for nearly a century, and simulations of success have been in the public eye for almost as long. A popular sight at the 1939–1940 New York World's Fair was Westinghouse's "Elektro," a 10-foot-tall "robot" (the word was coined just 18 years prior) that could walk, dance, speak, and smoke a cigarette, all in apparent obedience to spoken commands. Of course, Elektro had a lot of human help, and there wasn't much progress in the world of speech recognition during the subsequent 50 years. Meanwhile Gene Roddenberry's *Star Trek* and George Lucas's *Star Wars* made commonplace the fantasy of machines that could, at the least, understand anything spoken by anyone and, at best, carry on conversations that expressed their own personalities. But, in the words of some forgotten sage, our own real future isn't what it used to be.

It's not for want of trying. Serious research has been done on the subject of voice recognition and control since the earliest days of computing. It turns out that what is such an innate skill for us humans is far from easy for computers. And this was something of a surprise because of how we humans hierarchically rate our own five senses. When we have thought about those senses in the past—sight, hearing, taste, smell, and touch—we've tended to order them with our precious and delicate binocular, full-color sight at the pinnacle. The eye and our entire vision mechanism are so complex—as I'm writing this, it remains one of very few organs of the body that we cannot transplant with impressive success. This complexity led many to assume that we would have computers listening to our voices long before they could see us. Wrong, again.

Computers can recognize individual human faces, machine parts, and components with accuracy and a precision far greater than our organic vision. Computers do this by using very sophisticated software to compare live video images with massive databases of, say, faces and facial features. Just like people, then, a computer needs to be taught what you look like before it can recognize you. Once the software records certain characteristics of your face, it can still recognize you even if you change your hair, grow a beard, even pretend to be of the opposite sex.

Voice recognition isn't nearly as successful. Part of the problem resides in the nature of sound. There are recognizable edges to your face, a line to the angle of your nose, and so forth, but there are no obvious "lines" to separate the sound waves of your voice from the background noise of, say, a loud party. As human beings, we rely tremendously on the context of a conversation to help understand what is

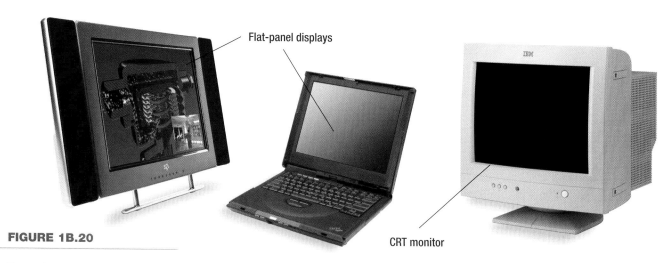

Flat-panel displays

CRT monitor

FIGURE 1B.20

The most common types of monitors used with personal computers.

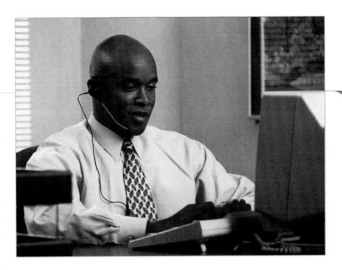

said to us in a noisy environment. Computers can be programmed to work with context, but they have to be able to distinguish our voices *first*. So, while facial recognition systems can pick out an individual walking along a busy street, speech recognition requires a carefully controlled environment from the start. A reasonably quiet office can allay this problem, but others are in queue. Good voice recognition systems can be trained to recognize and associate certain sounds with human words. Training usually involves spending several hours reading passages of text into a microphone while the computer "listens" and learns how the speaker pronounces certain sounds. Once the computer recognizes these phonemes, it can combine them together—usually in conjunction with a dictionary—to make whole words from the sounds.

But what happens when those sounds don't sound like those sounds? When I say, "Print a letter," it sounds like me—not like you, or like someone with a different regional accent. In fact, when I say, "Print a letter," with a bad sinus infection, even *I* no longer sound like myself. How is a computer to know that "pibbta lebrah" means anything at all? Given today's technology, it can't. Each voice recognition system needs to be trained to recognize the voice of each user, and if a user's voice changes significantly—or if the noise environment of the speaker changes—the computer must be retrained. Most of the best-trained systems provide better than 99 percent accuracy, which sounds excellent, until you consider that means that the computer makes as many as one recognition mistake for every 100

sounds—not words, *sounds*—it hears. (A few "no-training" systems are beginning to appear, but these have had limited applications, such as speaking numbers to choose from a telephone menu of options.)

Thousands of human hours have gone into the research and development of computer speech recognition to bring us to where we are today. Has it been worth it? Absolutely! Speech recognition holds untold promise for millions of people with different abilities, some of which have limited their freedom of creativity with modern technology. As personal computers continue to benefit from advances in processor power, it will be increasingly possible to make ever-more complex analyses of sound. This, in turn, will push recognition capabilities closer and closer to a level of perfection that has remained so elusive. It's also possible, even likely, that a new group of thinkers will conceive of an entirely new way to look at the problem. It may be *you* who finally unlocks speech recognition for generations to come.

---

① Electron guns shoot streams of electrons toward the screen.

② Magnetic yoke guides the streams of electrons across and down the screen.

③ Phosphor dots on the back of the screen glow when the electron beams hit them.

FIGURE 1B.21

How a CRT monitor creates an image.

Norton
ONLINE

For more information on monitors, visit
**http://www.mhhe.com/
peternorton**.

FIGURE 1B.22

Most mobile computers feature a color LCD monitor.

Flat-Panel Monitors

There are several types of flat-panel monitors, but the most common is the liquid crystal display (LCD) monitor (see Figure 1B.22). The LCD monitor creates images with a special kind of liquid crystal that is normally transparent but becomes opaque when charged with electricity.

One disadvantage of LCD monitors is that their images can be difficult to see in bright light. For this reason, laptop computer users often look for shady places to sit when working outdoors or near windows. A bigger disadvantage of LCD monitors, however, is their limited viewing angle—that is, the angle from which the display's image can be viewed clearly. With most CRT monitors, you can see the image clearly even when standing at an angle to the screen. In LCD monitors, however, the viewing angle shrinks; as you increase your angle to the screen, the image becomes fuzzy quickly. In many older flat-panel systems, the user must face the screen nearly straight on to see the image clearly. Technological improvements have extended the viewing angles of flat-panel monitors while causing their prices to increase.

There are two main categories of liquid crystal displays:

>> The passive matrix LCD relies on transistors for each row and each column of pixels, thus creating a grid that defines the location of each pixel. The color displayed by a pixel is determined by the electricity coming from the transistors at the end of the row and the top of the column. Although passive matrix monitors are inexpensive to manufacture, they have a narrow viewing angle. Another disadvantage is that they don't "refresh" the pixels very quickly. (Refresh rate is described in more detail later in this lesson.) If you move the pointer too quickly, it seems to disappear, an effect known as submarining. Animated graphics can blur on a passive matrix monitor.

Most passive matrix screens now use dual-scan LCD technology, which scans the pixels twice as often. Submarining and blurry graphics are less troublesome than they were before the dual-scan technique was developed.

>> Active matrix LCD technology assigns a transistor to each pixel, and each pixel is turned on and off individually. This enhancement allows the pixels to be refreshed much more rapidly, so submarining is not a problem. Active matrix screens have a wider viewing angle than passive matrix screens. Active matrix displays use thin-film transistor (TFT) technology, which employs as many as four transistors per pixel. Today, most notebook computers feature TFT displays.

Comparing Monitors

If you need to buy a monitor, go comparison shopping before making a purchase. Look for a monitor that displays graphics nicely and is easy on your eyes, allowing you to work longer and more comfortably. A poor monitor can reduce your productivity and may even contribute to eyestrain. Even if the monitor looks good (or if you are buying it through the mail), you need to check several specifications. The most important are

>> **Size** A monitor's size affects how well you can see images. With a larger monitor, you can make the objects on the screen appear bigger, or you can fit more of them on the screen (see Figure 1B.23). Monitors are measured diagonally, in inches, across the front of the screen. A 17-inch monitor measures 17 inches from the lower-left to the upper-right corner. However, a CRT monitor's actual viewing area—that is, the portion of the monitor that actually displays images—is smaller than the monitor's overall size. The viewing area of a flat-panel display will be somewhat larger than the viewing area of a comparably sized CRT monitor. As a rule of thumb, buy the largest monitor you can afford.

FIGURE 1B.23

The larger your monitor, the more easily you can see text and graphics.

» **Resolution** The term resolution refers to the sharpness or clarity of an image. A monitor's resolution is determined by the number of pixels on the screen, expressed as a matrix. The more pixels a monitor can display, the higher its resolution and the clearer its images appear. For example, a resolution of 640 × 480 means that there are 640 pixels horizontally across the screen and 480 pixels vertically down the screen. Because the actual resolution is determined by the video controller—not by the monitor itself—most monitors can operate at several different resolutions. Figure 1B.24 shows five commonly used resolution settings: (a) 640 × 480, (b) 800 × 600, (c) 1024 × 768, (d) 1152 × 864, and (e) 1280 × 1024. Note that, as the resolution increases, the image on the screen gets smaller.

There are various standards for monitor resolution. The Video Graphics Array (VGA) standard is 640 × 480 pixels. The Super VGA (SVGA) standard expanded the resolutions to 800 × 600 and 1024 × 768. Today, nearly any color monitor can be set to even higher resolutions. Higher settings are not always better, however, because they can cause objects on the screen to appear too small, resulting in eyestrain and squinting. Compare the two screens shown in Figure 1B.25. Both were taken from the same 17-inch monitor. The first image is displayed at 640 × 480 resolution; the second image shows the same screen at 1280 × 1024.

FIGURE 1B.24

Most monitors can operate at different resolutions, as shown here.

>> **Refresh Rate** A monitor's refresh rate is the number of times per second that the electron guns scan every pixel on the screen. Refresh rate is important because phosphor dots fade quickly after the electron gun charges them with electrons. If the screen is not refreshed often enough, it appears to flicker, and flicker is one of the main causes of eyestrain. Refresh rate is measured in hertz (Hz), or in cycles per second. This means that if a monitor's refresh rate is 100 Hz, it refreshes its pixels 100 times every second. When purchasing a monitor, look for one with a refresh rate of 72 Hz or higher.

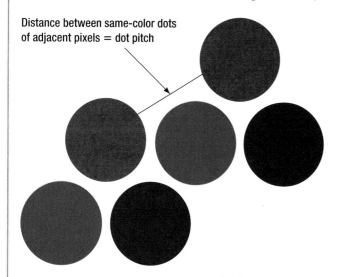

Distance between same-color dots of adjacent pixels = dot pitch

>> **Dot Pitch** The last critical specification of a color monitor is the dot pitch, the distance between the like-colored phosphor dots of adjacent pixels (see Figure 1B.26). In other words, if you measure the distance between the red dots of two adjacent pixels, you are measuring the monitor's dot pitch. Dot pitch is measured as a fraction of a millimeter (mm), and dot pitches can range from .15 mm (very fine) to .40 mm or higher (coarse). As a general rule, the smaller the dot pitch, the finer and more detailed images will appear on the monitor. Most experts agree that, when shopping for a color monitor, you should look for a dot pitch no greater than 0.28 millimeter (.28 mm). That number generally applies to 15-inch monitors. If you want a larger monitor, look for an even finer dot pitch, such as .22 mm or less.

Video Cards

The quality of the images that a monitor can display is defined as much by the video card (also called the *video controller* or the *video adapter*) as by the monitor itself. The video controller is an intermediary device between the CPU and the monitor. It contains the video-dedicated memory and other circuitry necessary to send information to the monitor for display on the screen. Within the monitor's constraints, the video controller determines the refresh rate, resolution, and number of colors that can be displayed.

Video controllers also feature their own built-in video RAM, or VRAM (which is separate from the RAM that is connected to the CPU). VRAM is dual-ported, meaning that it can send a screen full of data to the monitor and at the same time receive the next screen full of data from the CPU. Today's most sophisticated video controllers, which are fine-tuned for multimedia, video, and 3-D graphics, may have as much as 256 MB or more of video RAM.

Sound Systems

Microphones are now important input devices, and speakers and their associated technologies are key output systems (see Figure 1B.27). Today, nearly any new multimedia-capable PC includes a complete sound system, with a microphone, speakers, a sound card, and a CD-ROM or DVD drive. Sound systems are especially useful to people who use their computer to create or use multimedia products, watch videos or listen to music, or participate in online activities such as videoconferences or distance learning.

The most complicated part of a computer's sound system is the sound card. A computer's sound card is a circuit board that converts sound from analog to digital form, and vice versa, for recording or playback. A sound card actually has both input and output functions. If you want to use your computer's microphone to record your voice, for instance, you connect the microphone to the sound card's input jack. Other audio input devices connect to the sound card as well, such as the computer's CD-ROM or DVD drive. You may be able to attach other kinds of audio devices to your sound card, such as tape players, record players, and others.

Printers

Besides the monitor, the other important output device is the printer. A printer is a device that prints the results of your computing work on paper. Generally, printers fall into two categories: impact and nonimpact. An impact printer creates an image by using pins or hammers to press an inked ribbon against the paper. Nonimpact printers use other means to create an image. Ink jet printers, for example, use tiny nozzles to spray droplets of ink onto the page. Laser printers work like photocopiers, using heat to bond microscopic particles of dry toner to specific parts of the page.

Dot Matrix Printers

Dot matrix printers are commonly used in workplaces where physical impact with the paper is important, such as when the user is printing to carbon-copy or pressure-sensitive forms. These printers can produce sheets of plain text very quickly.

A dot matrix printer creates an image by using a mechanism called a print head, which contains a cluster (or *matrix*) of short pins arranged in one or more columns. On receiving instructions from the PC, the printer can push any of the pins out in any combination. By pushing out pins in various combinations, the print head can create alphanumeric characters (see Figure 1B.28).

When pushed out from the cluster, the protruding pins' ends strike a ribbon, which is held in place between the print head and the paper. When the pins strike the ribbon, they press ink from the ribbon onto a piece of paper.

The more pins that a print head contains, the higher the printer's resolution. The lowest-resolution dot matrix printers have only nine pins; the highest-resolution

FIGURE 1B.27

Speakers are common features on today's multimedia PCs. Top-of-the-line PC audio systems include premium sound cards and tweeters, midrange speakers, and subwoofers for sound quality that rivals home stereo systems.

ONLINE

For more information on printers, visit **http://www.mhhe.com/peternorton**.

How a dot matrix printer creates an image.

In a 9-pin print head, the pins are aligned in a single row.

In a 24-pin print head, the pins are "staggered" in two rows. This enables it to print over-lapping dots, creating finer characters and lines.

The bottom pins are used for the portions of lowercase letters that extend below the line, such as *g* or *q*.

PRINT HEAD

PRINT HEAD

Direction of print head

printers have 24 pins. The speed of dot matrix printers is measured in characters per second (cps). The slowest dot matrix printers create 50 to 70 cps; the fastest print more than 500 cps.

Ink Jet Printers

Ink jet printers create an image directly on the paper by spraying ink through tiny nozzles (see Figure 1B.29). The popularity of ink jet printers jumped around 1990 when the speed and quality improved and prices plummeted. Today, good ink jet printers are available for less than $100. These models typically attain print resolutions of at least 300 dots per inch. These same models can print from two to four pages per minute (only slightly slower than the slowest laser printers).

Laser Printers

Laser printers are more expensive than ink jet printers, their print quality is higher, and most are faster. As their name implies, a laser is at the heart of these printers. A CPU and memory are built into the printer to interpret the data that it receives from the computer and to control the laser. The result is a complicated piece of equipment that uses technology similar to that in photocopiers. Figure 1B.30 shows how a laser printer works. The quality and speed of laser printers make them ideal for office environments, where several users can easily share the same printer via a network.

Just as the electron gun in a monitor can target any pixel, the laser in a laser printer can aim at any point on a drum, creating an electrical charge. Toner, which is composed of tiny particles of ink, sticks to the drum in the places the laser has charged. Then, with pressure and heat, the toner is transferred off the drum onto the paper. The amount of memory that laser printers contain determines the speed at which documents are printed.

Comparing Printers

When you are ready to buy a printer, you must consider how you plan to use it. Do you need to print only text, or are graphics capabilities also important? Do you need to print in color? Will you need to print a wide variety of fonts in many sizes? How quickly do you want your documents to be printed?

Paper

Sprayed ink forms character

Ink droplets

Horizontal plates

Nozzle

Vertical plates

Ink fountain

Electrically charged plates control direction of ink jet spray.

FIGURE 1B.30

How a laser printer creates a printed page.

4 Toner is transferred to the charged paper by the drum.

5 Hot roller bonds toner to paper.

Output tray

Roller

Rotating mirror

1 Stack of paper in input tray

Paper path

Laser

Drum

Toner

Magnetic roller

2 Paper is given a static charge.

3 Rotating mirror reflects laser, which projects image of the page onto the rotating drum.

When evaluating printers, four additional criteria are important:

>> **Image Quality** Image quality, also known as print resolution, is usually measured in dots per inch (dpi). The more dots per inch a printer can produce, the higher its image quality. For example, most medium-quality ink jet and laser printers can print 300 or 600 dots per inch, which is fine for most daily business applications. If a printer's resolution is 600 dpi, this means it can

Computers In Your Career
Using Computers Outside of the IT Industry

Few hardwood products manufacturers can boast an e-commerce-enabled Web site where customers view catalogs, place orders, track orders, and review their account history 24 hours a day, seven days a week. Even fewer can offer customers a solution that uses computer modeling and simulation techniques to recreate "real world" projects in a virtual environment.

Thanks to the efforts of Richard Enriquez, Enkeboll Designs of Carson, California, can boast that and more in an industry where manufacturing and related processes remain largely manual and labor-intensive. "No one else offers e-commerce capabilities in our category," said Richard Enriquez, director of marketing, who envisions a time when the firm's woodcarvers will be able to use a computer to go from concept to finished product without ever having to touch a piece of wood or a chisel.

Having worked in the software development industry for 15 years, Enriquez aspires to use technology to bring more value to the customers while also making Enkeboll Designs' architectural woodcarving manufacturing process more efficient and productive. In 2003, for example, he spearheaded the conversion of the entire product line into three-dimensional formats that can be used in conjunction with commercial and residential previsualization applications to minimize specification errors.

Enriquez, who earned a Bachelor of Science degree from DeVry University, handles myriad tasks at Enkeboll Designs, including managing internal and external staff associated with marketing and new product development, evaluating technologies, reviewing strategic relationships, and overseeing the development of the company's Web site. He works 50 to 55 hours a week and enjoys the challenge of incorporating technology into a company that has traditionally conducted business utilizing traditional methods.

"When the company wanted to start leveraging technology, they hired me," says Enriquez. "Before I came on board, the company was very traditional and didn't believe, for example, in putting e-commerce capabilities on the Web site." One year later, Enriquez says the naysayers wouldn't have it any other way. "It all boils down to results."

---

print 600 columns of dots and 600 rows of dots in each square inch of the page, a total of 360,000 dots ($600 \times 600 = 360,000$) per inch, as shown in Figure 1B.31. Professional-quality printers, used for creating colorful presentations, posters, or renderings, offer resolutions of 1,800 dpi or even higher.

» **Speed** Printer speed is measured in the number of pages per minute (ppm) the device can print. (As you learned earlier, however, the speed of dot matrix printers is measured in characters per second.) Most printers have different ppm ratings for text and graphics because graphics generally take longer to print. As print speed goes up, so does cost. Most consumer-level laser printers offer print speeds of 6 or 8 ppm, but high-volume professional laser printers can exceed 50 ppm.

FIGURE 1B.31

The image quality of laser and ink jet printers is measured in dots per inch.

600 dots
across

600 dots
down

1 square
inch:
360,000
dots

Enriquez says opportunities for IT professionals in the non-IT space are plentiful. One need only look around the business world to see how technology is making an impact in the most unlikely occupations, such as

>> **Restaurant and Grocery Store Managers** Restaurants, grocery stores, and retail outlet managers use computer systems of all kinds—from handheld units to mainframes—to monitor inventories, track transactions, and manage product pricing.

>> **Courier Dispatchers** Courier services of all types use computerized terminals to help dispatchers schedule deliveries, locate pickup and drop-off points, generate invoices, and track the location of packages.

>> **Construction Managers** Construction managers and estimators use specialized software to analyze construction documents and to calculate the amount of materials and time required to complete a job.

>> **Automotive Mechanics** Automotive mechanics and technicians use computer systems to measure vehicle performance, diagnose mechanical problems, and determine maintenance or repair strategies.

Each of the following chapters in this textbook features a discussion of computers in the professional world. Each discussion focuses on the type of technology introduced in that unit and is designed to help you understand how that particular technology is used in one or more professions.

>> **Initial Cost** The cost of new printers has fallen dramatically in recent years, while their capabilities and speed have improved just as dramatically. It is possible to buy a good-quality ink jet printer for personal use for less than $100; low-end laser printers can be found for less than $200. Professional-quality, high-output systems can range in price from $1,000 to tens of thousands of dollars. Color printers always cost more than black-and-white printers, and this is especially true of laser printers.

>> **Cost of Operation** The cost of ink or toner and maintenance varies with the type of printer. Many different types of printer paper are available, too, and the choice can affect the cost of operation. Low-quality recycled paper, for example, is fine for printing draft-quality documents and costs less than a penny per sheet. Glossy, thick, photo-quality stock, used for printing photographs, can cost several dollars per sheet depending on size.

Summary ::

>> A standard computer keyboard has about 100 keys.

>> Most keyboards follow a similar layout, with their keys arranged in five groups. Those groups include the alphanumeric keys, numeric keypad, function keys, modifier keys, and cursor-movement keys.

>> The mouse is a pointing device that lets you control the position of a graphical pointer on the screen without using the keyboard. The trackball and trackpad are variants of the mouse.

>> Many kinds of alternative input devices exist, each with special uses. These include pens, touch screens, game controllers, bar code readers, image scanners, microphones, PC video cameras, and digital cameras.

>> Computer monitors are roughly divided into two categories: CRT and flat-panel displays.

>> A CRT monitor uses an electron gun that systematically aims a beam of electrons at every pixel on the screen.

>> Most LCD displays are either active matrix or passive matrix.

>> When purchasing a monitor, you should consider its size, resolution, refresh rate, and dot pitch.

>> The video controller is an interface between the monitor and the CPU. The video controller determines many aspects of a monitor's performance.

>> Multimedia PCs generally come with sound systems, which include a sound card and speakers.

>> Printers fall into two general categories: impact and nonimpact.

>> Impact printers create an image on paper by using a device to strike an inked ribbon, pressing ink from the ribbon onto the paper. Nonimpact printers use various methods to place ink (or another colored substance) on the page.

>> When evaluating printers for purchase, you should consider four criteria: image quality, speed, initial cost, and cost of operation.

>> A dot matrix printer is an impact printer. It uses a print head that contains a cluster of pins. The printer can push the pins out in rapid sequence to form patterns. The pins are used to press an inked ribbon against paper, creating an image.

>> An ink jet printer is an example of a nonimpact printer. It creates an image by spraying tiny droplets of ink onto the paper.

>> Laser printers are nonimpact printers. They use heat and pressure to bond tiny particles of toner (a dry ink) to paper.

Key Terms ::

active matrix LCD, 34
alphanumeric key, 25
bar code, 29
bar code reader, 29
cathode ray tube (CRT), 31
characters per second (cps), 38
cursor, 26
cursor-movement key, 26
digital camera, 31
digitize, 30
dot matrix printer, 37
dot pitch, 36
dots per inch (dpi), 39
dual-scan LCD, 34
flat-panel display, 31
function key, 26
game controller, 29
game pad, 29
hertz (Hz), 36
image scanner, 29
impact printer, 37
ink jet printer, 38

insertion point, 26
integrated pointing device, 28
joystick, 29
keyboard, 25
laser printer, 38
liquid crystal display (LCD), 34
mechanical mouse, 26
modifier key, 25
monitor, 31
mouse, 26
nonimpact printer, 37
numeric keypad, 25
optical character recognition (OCR)
    software, 30
optical mouse, 26
pages per minute (ppm), 40
passive matrix LCD, 34
PC video camera, 30
pixel, 31
pointer, 26
pointing device, 26
print head, 37

printer, 37
refresh rate, 36
resolution, 35
sound card, 30
speech recognition, 30
submarining, 34
Super VGA (SVGA), 35
thin-film transistor (TFT), 34
toner, 38
touch screen, 29
trackball, 27
trackpad, 27
TrackPoint, 28
video capture card, 31
video card, 36
Video Graphics Array (VGA), 35
video RAM (VRAM), 37
viewing angle, 34
viewing area, 34
voice recognition, 30
Webcam, 30

Key Term Quiz ::

Complete each statement by writing one of the terms listed under Key Terms in each blank.

1. IBM-compatible PCs have 12 _____ keys.

2. You use a mouse (or one of its variants) to position a(n) _____ on the screen.

3. Many laptop computers feature a small joystick between the G and H keys, which is called a(n) _____ or a(n) _____ .

4. You might not think of a(n) _____ as a true input device, but it is.

5. You can find _____ being used as input devices in supermarkets and department stores everywhere.

6. The process of translating voice into text or commands the computer can understand is called _____ .

7. Standard computer monitors work by using a large vacuum tube, which is called a(n) _____ .

8. In a CRT monitor, the electron gun can focus on a(n) _____ as small as a single phosphor dot.

9. A(n) _____ printer creates an image by using pins or hammers to press an inked ribbon against the paper.

10. The speed of dot matrix printers is measured in _____ .

Multiple Choice ::

Circle the word or phrase that best completes each statement.

1. These keys make up the part of the keyboard that looks like a typewriter's keys.

   a. special-purpose keys   **b.** function keys   **c.** typing keys   **d.** alphanumeric keys

2. Which of the following is *not* a modifier key?

   a. SHIFT   **b.** CTRL   **c.** ALT   **d.** BACKSPACE

3. This type of mouse uses reflected light to measure its movements.

   a. optical   **b.** laser   **c.** mechanical   **d.** wheel

4. With a pen-based system, you can use the pen as a(n) _____ , to select commands.

   a. keyboard   **b.** pointing device   **c.** antenna   **d.** microphone

5. A _____ is used to identify a product.

   a. price check   **b.** bar code   **c.** numeric digit   **d.** light-sensitive detector

6. Which type of software can translate scanned text into text that you can edit?

   a. OCS   **b.** ORC   **c.** OCR   **d.** ORS

7. Which type of monitor is most commonly used with portable computers?

   a. cathode ray tube   **b.** monochrome   **c.** flat-panel display   **d.** data projector

8. An LCD monitor uses crystals that become opaque when _____ is applied.

   a. pressure   **b.** force   **c.** phosphor   **d.** electricity

9. Most passive matrix LCD monitors now use _____ technology.

   a. thin-film   **b.** active matrix   **c.** dual-scan   **d.** flat-panel

10. A monitor's resolution is determined by the computer's _____ .

    a. monitor   **b.** video controller   **c.** CPU   **d.** system unit

Review Questions ::

In your own words, briefly answer the following questions.

1. Most standard keyboards include five major groups of keys. List them.
2. What does the CTRL key do?
3. Describe two benefits of using a mouse.
4. How do most touch-screen systems work?
5. There are two basic types of monitors used with PCs. List them.
6. List the four factors you should consider when comparing monitors.
7. As it relates to monitors, what does the term "resolution" refer to?
8. What is dot pitch?
9. What is the difference between an impact printer and a nonimpact printer?
10. What four factors should you consider when evaluating printers?

Lesson Labs ::

Complete the following exercises as directed by your instructor. (These exercises assume you use Windows XP. If you use a different operating system, ask your instructor for assistance.)

1. Test your typing skills in Notepad. Click the START button, point to All Programs, click Accessories, and then click Notepad to open the Notepad text-editing program. Notepad opens in a window. Have a classmate time you as you type a paragraph of text. The paragraph should be at least five lines long and should make sense. (For example, you could type a paragraph of text from any page in this book.) Do not stop to correct mistakes; keep typing until you are finished typing the selection.

2. Inspect your system's mouse settings. (Do not change any settings without your instructor's permission.) Use the following steps:
   a. Click the START button to open the Start menu; then click Control Panel. The Control Panel window opens.
   b. Double-click the Mouse icon to open the Mouse Properties dialog box. Click the tabs in this dialog box and inspect your settings.
   c. Experiment with the Pointer Speed and Show Pointer Trails tools. How do they affect your mouse's performance? When you are finished, click Cancel.

Chapter Labs

Complete the following exercises using a computer in your classroom, lab, or home.

1. Get some help. If you do not know how to perform a task on your computer, turn to its online help system for answers and assistance. Browse your operating system's help system to learn more about your computer. (This activity assumes you use Windows XP. If you use a different operating system, ask your instructor for assistance.)

   a. Click the START button on the Windows taskbar to open the Start menu.

   b. On the Start menu, click Help and Support. The Help and Support Center window opens.

   c. Under Pick a Help Topic, click the Windows Basics link. When the list of basic Windows topics appears in the next window, click any two of the topics and read the information that appears on your screen.

   d. Close the Help window by clicking the CLOSE button (with an X on it) in the upper-right corner of the window.

2. Explore your disk. Once you are familiar with your computer's hardware, it is time to see the folders and files that reside on its hard disk. To see what is on your disk, take these steps:

   a. Minimize or close all running program windows, so you can see the Windows desktop.

   b. On the desktop, double-click the My Computer icon. The My Computer window opens, listing all the disks on your computer.

   c. Double-click the icon labeled Local Disk (C:) to open a window displaying that disk's contents.

   d. Double-click at least five of the folders and review the contents of each one. Can you tell which files are data files and which are program files?

   e. When you finish exploring your disk, close all open windows.

3. Change your display's color settings. By experimenting with your PC's color settings, you can determine the settings that work best for you. Before you take the following steps, close any running programs and make sure there is no disk in your system's floppy disk drive.

   a. Click the START button to open the Start menu. Next, click Control Panel. The Control Panel window opens.

   b. Double-click the Display icon. The Display Properties dialog box opens.

   c. Click the Settings tab. Note the setting in the Color quality box and write it down.

   d. Click the Color quality drop-down list arrow and choose the lowest color setting. Then click Apply. Follow any instructions that appear on your screen. (Your computer may restart.)

   e. Open a program or two and look at the screen. How does it look? Note your impressions.

   f. Repeat steps A through E, this time choosing the highest color setting. Again, note your impressions.

   g. Repeat steps A through E, and select the system's original color setting.

Discussion Questions

As directed by your instructor, discuss the following questions in class or in groups.

1. Describe your experience with computers so far. Have you worked with (or played with) computers before? If so, why? Has your past experience with computers influenced your decision to study them?

2. Despite the rapid advancements being made with handwriting-recognition software, do you think that the keyboard will continue to be the preferred input device for generating text? Which alternative—speech recognition or handwriting recognition—do you think has a better chance of ultimately replacing the keyboard as the primary means of input?

Research and Report

Using your own choice of resources (such as the Internet, books, magazines, and newspaper articles), research and write a short paper discussing one of the following topics:

>> The use of supercomputers in mapping the human genome.

>> The availability and use of screen-reading technologies for computer users who are sight-impaired.

>> The DVORAK keyboard (an alternative to the standard QWERTY keyboard).

When you are finished, proofread and print your paper, and give it to your instructor.

ETHICAL ISSUES

Computer skills can make a difference in a person's employability. With this thought in mind, discuss the following questions in class.

1. A factory is buying computerized systems and robots to handle many tasks, meaning fewer laborers will be needed. The company needs people to run the new equipment but wants to hire new workers who already have computer skills. Is the company obligated to keep the workers with no computer skills and to train them to use the equipment? Are workers obligated to learn these new skills if they want to keep their jobs?

2. You are a skilled drafter with 15 years of experience. You have always done your drafting work using traditional methods (using pen and paper). Now you want to move to a different city and have sent resumes to several drafting firms there. You learn, however, that none of those firms will consider you for employment because you have no experience drafting on a computer. Is that fair? Why or why not? What would you do?

2

CHAPTER

Presenting the Internet

CHAPTER CONTENTS ::

This chapter contains the following lessons:

Lesson **2A:**
The Internet and the World Wide Web

>> The Internet's History
>> The Internet's Major Services
>> Understanding the World Wide Web
>> Using Your Browser and the World Wide Web
>> Searching the Web

Lesson **2B:**
E-Mail and Other Internet Services

>> Using E-Mail
>> More Features of the Internet

01 02 03 04 05 06 07 08 09 10 11 12 13 14

The Internet and the World Wide Web

Overview: What Is the Internet?

Even if you have not had a lot of experience with computers, it wouldn't be surprising to learn that you have been on the Internet.

In the past few years, millions of people have gone online—and some of them probably thought they would never have a use for a computer. Indeed, many Internet enthusiasts buy computers just so they can go online, and for no other reason.

But what is the Internet? Simply put, the Internet is a network of networks—a global communications system that links together thousands of individual networks. As a result, virtually any computer on any network can communicate with any other computer on any other network. These connections allow users to exchange messages, to communicate in real time (seeing messages and responses immediately), to share data and programs, and to access limitless stores of information.

The Internet has become so important that its use is considered an essential part of computer use. In other words, mastering the Internet is one of the first things you should do, if you want to get the most from your computing experience. In this lesson, you will get an overview of the Internet by reviewing its history, the basics of the World Wide Web, and browser use.

OBJECTIVES ::

>> List two reasons for the Internet's creation.

>> Identify six major services you can access through the Internet.

>> Name three ways in which people commonly use the Internet.

>> Use a Web browser to navigate the World Wide Web.

>> Find content on the Web, using standard search tools.

The Internet's History

No introduction to the Internet is complete without a short review of its history. Even though today's Internet bears little resemblance to its forebear of 30-plus years ago, it still functions in basically the same way.

The Beginning: A "Network of Networks"

The seeds of the Internet were planted in 1969, when the Advanced Research Projects Agency (ARPA) of the U.S. Department of Defense began connecting computers at different universities and defense contractors (see Figure 2A.1). The resulting network was called ARPANET. The goal of this early project was to create a large computer network with multiple paths—in the form of telephone lines—that could survive a nuclear attack or a natural disaster such as an earthquake. If one part of the network were destroyed, other parts of the network would remain functional and data could continue to flow through the surviving lines.

ARPA had a second important reason for creating such a network. That is, it would allow people in remote locations to share scarce computing resources. By being part of the network, these users could access faraway systems—such as governmental mainframes or university-owned supercomputers—and conduct research or communicate with other users.

At first, ARPANET was basically a large network serving only a handful of users, but it expanded rapidly. Initially, the network included four primary host computers. A host is like a network server, providing services to other computers that connect to it. ARPANET's host computers (like those on today's Internet) provided file transfer and communications services and gave connected systems access to the network's high-speed data lines. The system grew quickly and spread widely as the number of hosts grew (see Figure 2A.2).

The network jumped across the Atlantic to Europe in 1973, and it never stopped growing. In the mid-1980s, another federal agency, the National Science Foundation (NSF), joined the project after the Defense Department stopped funding the network. NSF established five "supercomputing centers" that were available to anyone who wanted to use them for academic research purposes.

FIGURE 2A.1

Before it became known as the Internet, ARPA's network served universities, defense contractors, and a few government agencies.

FIGURE 2A.2

This map shows the extent of the ARPANET in September 1971.

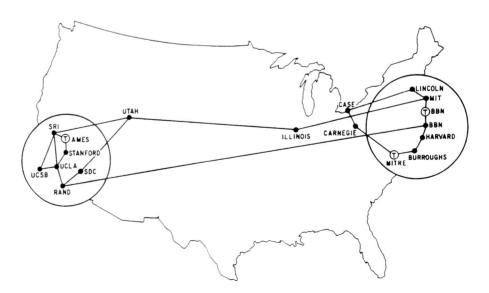

The NSF expected the supercomputers' users to use ARPANET to obtain access, but the agency quickly discovered that the existing network could not handle the load. In response, the NSF created a new, higher-capacity network, called NSFnet, to complement the older, and by then overloaded, ARPANET. The link between ARPANET, NSFnet, and other networks was called the Internet. (The process of connecting separate networks is called internetworking. A collection of "networked networks" is described as being internetworked, which is where the Internet—a worldwide network of networks—gets its name.)

NSFnet made Internet connections widely available for academic research, but the NSF did not permit users to conduct private business over the system. Therefore, several private telecommunications companies built their own network backbones that used the same set of networking protocols as NSFnet. Like a tree's trunk or an animal's spine, a network backbone is the central structure that connects other elements of the network (see Figure 2A.3). These private portions of the Internet were not limited by NSFnet's "appropriate use" restrictions, so it became possible to use the Internet to distribute business and commercial information.

The original ARPANET was shut down in 1990, and government funding for NSFnet was discontinued in 1995, but the commercial Internet backbone services replaced them. By the early 1990s, interest in the Internet began to expand dramatically. The system that had been created as a tool for surviving a nuclear war found its way into businesses and homes. Now, advertisements for movies are far more common online than collaborations on physics research.

Today: Still Growing

Today, the Internet connects thousands of networks and hundreds of millions of users around the world. It is a huge, cooperative community with no central ownership. This lack of ownership is an important feature of the Internet, because it means that no single person or group controls the network. Although there are several organizations (such as The Internet Society and the World Wide Web Consortium) that propose standards for Internet-related technologies and guidelines for its appropriate use, these organizations almost universally support the Internet's openness and lack of centralized control.

As a result, the Internet is open to anyone who can access it. If you can use a computer and if the computer is connected to the Internet, you are free not only to use the resources posted by others, but to create resources of your own; that is, you can publish documents on the World Wide Web, exchange e-mail messages, and perform many other tasks.

This openness has attracted millions of users to the Internet. Internet access was available to nearly one-half billion people worldwide in 2001. The number of actual users continues to climb dramatically, as shown in Figure 2A.4.

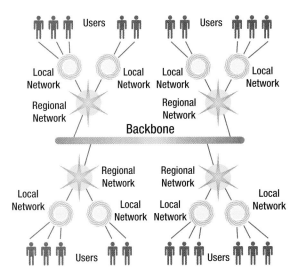

FIGURE 2A.3

At its heart, the Internet uses high-speed data lines, called backbones, to carry huge volumes of traffic. Regional and local networks connect to these backbones, enabling any user on any network to exchange data with any other user on any other network.

FIGURE 2A.4

The number of Internet users is expected to continue its dramatic increase for the foreseeable future.

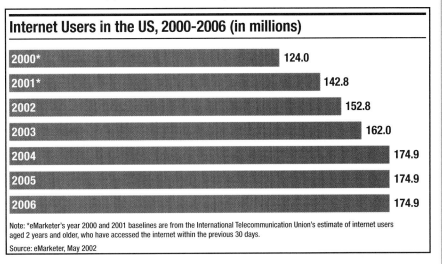

Internet Users in the US, 2000-2006 (in millions)

Year	Users
2000*	124.0
2001*	142.8
2002	152.8
2003	162.0
2004	174.9
2005	174.9
2006	174.9

Note: *eMarketer's year 2000 and 2001 baselines are from the International Telecommunication Union's estimate of internet users aged 2 years and older, who have accessed the internet within the previous 30 days.

Source: eMarketer, May 2002

The Internet's Major Services

The Internet acts as a carrier for several different services, each with its own distinct features and purposes (see Figure 2A.5). The most commonly used Internet services are

>> The World Wide Web

>> Electronic mail

>> News

>> File Transfer Protocol

>> Chat

>> Instant messaging

>> Online services

>> Peer-to-peer services

To use any of these services, you need a computer that is connected to the Internet in some way. Most individual users connect their computer's modem to a telephone line (or use a high-speed connection such as DSL or a cable modem) and set up an account with an Internet service provider (ISP), a company that provides local or regional access to the Internet backbone. Many other users connect to the Internet through a school or business network. To use a specific service, you also need the right type of software. Some programs enable you to use multiple Internet services, so you do not necessarily need separate applications for each service.

FIGURE 2A.5

The Internet's services differ in the way they look and function, but each one has a unique set of uses and its own special appeal to different users.

Understanding the World Wide Web

The World Wide Web (also known as the Web or WWW) was created in 1989 at the European Particle Physics Laboratory in Geneva, Switzerland, as a method for incorporating footnotes, figures, and cross-references into online documents. The Web's creators wanted to create a simple way to access any document that was stored on a network, without having to search through indexes or directories of files, and without having to manually copy documents from one computer to another before viewing them. To do this, they established a way to "link" documents that were stored in different locations on a single computer, or on different computers on a network.

If you imagine a collection of billions of documents, all stored in different places, but all linked together in some manner, you might imagine them creating a

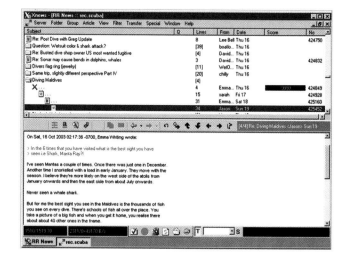

"web" of interconnected information (see Figure 2A.6). If you extend that collection of documents and their links to cover the entire globe, you have a "world-wide web" of information. This concept is where the Web gets its name.

Many people believe that the Web and the Internet are the same thing, but this is not correct. In fact, they are two different things. The Web is a service (a system for accessing documents) that is supported by the Internet (a gigantic network).

How the Web Works

Web documents can be linked together because they are created in a format known as hypertext. Hypertext systems provide an easy way to manage large collections of data, which can include text files, pictures, sounds, movies, and more. In a hypertext system, when you view a document on your computer's screen, you also can access all the data that might be linked to it. So, if the document is a discussion of honey bees, you might be able to click a hypertext link and see a photo of a beehive, or a movie of bees gathering pollen from flowers (see Figure 2A.7).

To support hypertext documents, the Web uses a special protocol, called the hypertext transfer protocol, or HTTP. (You will learn more about protocols in Chapter 9, "Networks.") A hypertext document is a specially encoded file that uses the hypertext markup language, or HTML. This language allows a document's author to embed hypertext links—also called hyperlinks or just links—in the document. HTTP and hypertext links are the foundations of the World Wide Web.

As you read a hypertext document—more commonly called a Web page—on screen, you can click a word or picture encoded as a hypertext link and immediately jump to another location within the same document or to a different Web page (see Figure 2A.8). The second page may be located on the same computer as the original page, or anywhere else on the Internet. Because you do not have to learn separate commands and addresses to jump to a new location, the World Wide Web organizes widely scattered resources into a seamless whole.

A collection of related Web pages is called a Web site. Web sites are housed on Web servers, Internet host computers that often store thousands of individual

FIGURE 2A.6

Billions of documents and their links create a web of information that reaches around the world.

FIGURE 2A.7

Hypertext systems, such as the Web, let you view a document and other data that might be linked to that document. Here, a Web page is being viewed in a browser and a video is being viewed in a media player. The video started playing automatically when the user clicked a link on the Web page.

This an example of a typical Web site. The user can click one of the hyperlinked text lines or images to jump to a different location in the same site, or to a different site.

Hyperlinks

When the user clicks the "About the Supreme Court" hyperlink, a new Web page opens in the browser window.

pages. Copying a page onto a server is called publishing the page, but the process also is called posting or uploading.

Web pages are used to distribute news, interactive educational services, product information, catalogs, highway traffic reports, and live audio and video, and other kinds of information. Web pages permit readers to consult databases, order products and information, and submit payment with a credit card or an account number.

Web Browsers and HTML Tags

For several years, the Web remained an interesting but not particularly exciting tool used by scientific researchers. But in 1993, developers at the National Center for Supercomputing Applications (NCSA) created Mosaic, a point-and-click Web browser. A Web browser (or browser) is a software application designed to find hypertext documents on the Web and then open the documents on the user's computer. A point-and-click browser provides a graphical user interface that enables the user to click hyperlinked text and images to jump to other documents or view other data. Several text-based Web browsers are also available and are used in nongraphical operating systems, such as certain versions of UNIX. Mosaic and Web browsers that evolved from it have changed the way people use the Internet. Today, the most popular graphical Web browsers are Microsoft's Internet Explorer (see Figure 2A.9) and Netscape Navigator (see Figure 2A.10).

Later in this chapter, you will learn about using a browser to navigate the Web and find content.

Norton
ONLINE

For more information on Web browsers, visit
http://www.mhhe.com/ peternorton.

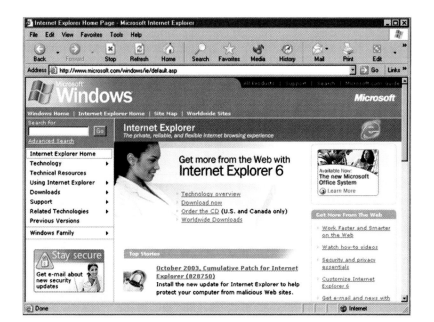

This is Microsoft Internet Explorer version 6, the most popular of all available Web browsers. It is available at no cost from Microsoft Corporation and is included with the Windows operating system.

FIGURE 2A.10

This is Netscape Navigator version 7, which is available for free from Netscape Corporation and many other sources.

URLs

The hypertext transfer protocol uses Internet addresses in a special format, called a uniform resource locator, or URL. (The acronym is usually pronounced by spelling its letters out, as in "U-R-L.") URLs look like this:

type://address/path

In a URL, *type* specifies the type of server in which the file is located, *address* is the address of the server, and *path* is the location within the file structure of the server. The path includes the list of folders where the desired file (the Web page itself or some other piece of data) is located. Consider the URL for a page at the Library of Congress Web site, which contains information about the Library's collection of permanent exhibits (see Figure 2A.11).

This address is for an
Internet server that uses
the hypertext transfer
protocol (HTTP).

This site is run by a
government agency—the
Library of Congress (LOC).

http://www.loc.gov/exhibits/treasures

This site is on the part of
the Internet known as the
World Wide Web (WWW).

To find specific Web pages
about ongoing exhibits at the
Library of Congress, your
browser follows the URL's path
to a folder named "exhibits,"
then to a subfolder named
"treasures."

::: **FIGURE 2A.12**

This is an example of a typical Web site.
The user can click one of the hyperlinked
text lines or images to jump to a different
location in the same site, or to a different
site.

URL   The browser's address box displays
the URL of the current page.

This is the document that
the URL identifies.

If you were looking for an HTML document (that is, a Web page) named "Ex-
hibition Overview" at this Web site, its URL would look like this:

http://www.loc.gov/exhibits/treasures/tr66.html

Because URLs lead to specific documents on a server's disk, they can be extremely long; however, every single document on the World Wide Web has its
own unique URL (see Figure 2A.12).

Helper Applications and Multimedia Content

As versatile as they are, Web browsers alone cannot display every type of content—
especially multimedia content—now available on the Web. Many Web sites feature
audio and video content, including full-motion animation and movies. These large
files require special applications in order to be played in real time across the Web.
Because these applications help the browser by being "plugged in" at the right moment, they are called helper applications or plug-in applications.

Norton
ONLINE

For more information on helper
applications for browsers, visit
**http://www.mhhe.com/
peternorton**.

Plug-ins are used to support several types of content, including streaming audio and streaming video. Streaming technology works by sending the audio or video content in a continuous stream from the Web server to your browser. The plug-in application receives the first portion of the stream and stores it temporarily in a buffer (an area in memory or on disk). After that portion of the stream has been buffered, it is played while the next portion of the stream is stored in the buffer (see Figure 2A.13). After the stream has been played, it is deleted. The buffer-and-play technique is an effective method for playing a large file quickly without waiting for the entire file to download—that is, to be transmitted in its entirety from the Web server to your computer.

There is a tremendous variety of multimedia content available on the Web. For example, if you visit Launch (http://www.launch.com), you can listen to CD-quality audio, watch music videos, and much more. At Apple's QuickTime Web site (http://www.apple.com/quicktime), you can listen to high-quality streaming music or watch the latest movie trailers. Television channels such as CNN (http://www.cnn.com) and The Weather Channel (http://www.weather.com) also deliver their audio and video content over the Web. Using a plug-in application—such as Microsoft's Windows Media Player, Apple's QuickTime Player, or Real-Networks' RealOne Player—you can play any of these sources on your computer (see Figure 2A.14).

FIGURE 2A.13

By streaming audio and video content to your PC in "chunks," multimedia Web sites let you watch movies and listen to high-quality audio.

Part 6
Part 5
Part 4
Part 3
Part 2

The server sends multimedia content in pieces to be buffered by the client PC.

The first piece of streaming content is buffered, then played as the next piece arrives.

SELF-CHECK ::

Circle the correct answer for each question.

1. This early version of the Internet was available for academic research, but not for business use.
   a. ARPAnet   b. NSFnet   c. INTRAnet

2. The World Wide Web is a service that lets users access documents, but the Internet is this.
   a. a gigantic network   b. a gigantic computer   c. a gigantic database

3. In a URL, the _____ is the location within the file structure of the server where a desired file can be found.
   a. type   b. address   c. path

Norton
ONLINE

For more information on streaming media, visit **http://www.mhhe.com/ peternorton**.

FIGURE 2A.14

This is the RealOne Player, displaying streaming content from CNN's Web site.

Internet Time Travel: The Wayback Machine

For roughly four millennia, if you were a scholar and needed—or simply wanted—access to some piece of your culture's knowledge, heritage, or history, you could enter a library and obtain what you needed. At least, that's how it worked in theory. Certainly there have always been private, religious, and royal libraries with limited access to materials. (Thousands of these still exist today—probably millions, if you include private corporate archives.) And, naturally, if you were a scholar in Tibet around 245 B.C.E. and the document you required was in Alexandria, access to materials once you were *in* the library was the least of your worries.

It would be, frankly, a gross overstatement to say that the Internet "has changed all of that," by making the world a smaller place, collapsing distances, providing ubiquitous access to everything ever known . . . and all of those other wonderful things the Internet was supposed to do. Even for those of us fortunate enough to *have* access to the Internet, finding useful resources can seem a monumental task. Sometimes the difficulty lies in the act of searching and the tools we use to find materials online. In many cases, however—and the more specialized the information you need, the more often this happens—even the most skilled searching simply produces one of the many Web browser error messages that mean "what you want is no longer available." To understand why this happens, it's useful to reconsider briefly both the history and nature of the Internet itself.

As you have already seen in this chapter, what we now call the Internet is actually a vast collection of computer networks that interoperate through the use of common standards and protocols. Originally, a much smaller collection of these networks allowed researchers and scientists to share documents (by which I mean text) across distances by file transfer and e-mail. Which documents were shared—what information was *available online*, as we say now—depended entirely on the individual people who were using the net-

works. This was information-on-demand in the strictest possible sense: Until someone knew that another person needed a particular document, it just wasn't available. Given that storage used to be phenomenally expensive, and data communications comparably slow, this was a need-driven environment, and often when a document was no longer needed, it was removed. New documents appeared, and so forth. From the start, we should think of the early Internet not as a library so much as a magazine rack.

As economy and technology began to cooperate, more people shared documents and kept them around. In 1990–1991, Tim Berners-Lee and others invented the World Wide Web, and the Internet, collectively, went through a real qualitative change. The Web made it possible to combine text documents, images, hypertext, and other media; store and share them practically across the growing Internet; and access them by using one of a number of different browser tools. This multimedia quality dramatically increased both the appeal and practical usefulness of the Internet to average computer users. As in the economics of supply and demand, more people online made it reasonable (indeed, necessary, as each person had his or her own interests) for ever-increasing amounts of information to be available online. In time, scholars, researchers, and traditional librarians and archivists began to store what we might call "traditional" documents online. One of the oldest and most significant of these efforts is The Gutenberg Project (http://www.gutenberg.net), the point of which is to provide free online access to significant and historical texts. While The Gutenberg Project is not aligned with a particular subject or field, unnumbered specialty sites, usually called "archives," have sprouted that provide similar access to more finely tuned collections, like the Confucian Etext Project, hosted at Wesleyan University (http://sangle.web.wesleyan.edu/etext), and the Classics Archive, hosted by

One of the most commonly used multimedia design tools is made by Macromedia, Inc. This tool—called Flash—enables Web page designers to create high-quality animation or video, complete with audio, that plays directly within the browser window. These types of animation do not require the browser to spawn (launch) an external application for viewing. In fact, many Web sites use this approach with all their multimedia content. For example, if you go to the Apple QuickTime Web site to watch movie trailers, they will run directly within your browser window instead of appearing in a separate QuickTime Player window—as long as you have the QuickTime plug-in installed.

products that are for sale. These online resources are more transient. Individuals stop paying for online space to host their creations; companies update their sites at least daily to showcase the latest products. Thus, bookmarks and indexed Web page links "break" and fail. A wealth of information seems in just as much danger of disappearing now as it was before our online world evolved.

In an attempt to prevent this from happening, the Internet Archive (www.waybackmachine.org) was formed in 1996. Its purpose: to permanently collect and make available

MIT (http://classics.mit.edu). Established institutions and museums, like the Louvre, are also increasingly providing multimedia access to their collections (http://www.louvre.fr). These large, institutional resources aren't in much danger of suddenly disappearing, either. It now costs only pennies to store gargantuan amounts of data, and user demand for these famous and "significant" media continues to grow.

So much for *significant* and historical resources. (As in the past, what qualifies today as *significant* media continues to be determined by the individuals—or institutions—that create and manage these resources.) But the Internet gathers a lot more than just Shakespeare, Michelangelo, and the Smithsonian Institution. Millions of individuals have spent as many hours making their own collections and interests available. These aren't collections of "significant" or "traditional" documents; they're personal expressions put forth for the joy of sharing interests with others. Still others are professional sites, either created specifically to earn money or to promote

everything on the World Wide Web, starting from its 1996 inception. To date, the Internet Archive has saved over 10 billion Web pages, using over 100 terabytes of storage. (A terabyte is roughly 1,000 gigabytes.) All these pages have been catalogued and are searchable; many of them have been culled together into specific collections of their own, such as a September 11, 2001, collection. You can go back and see what was on the Web back in 1998 exactly as it was. Both personal and corporate sites are archived and search capabilities are impressive. The Internet Archive is a surprisingly unknown resource, but I've found it invaluable. The next time you use a search engine and think you've found the perfect resource—only to discover that it's no longer online—switch over to the Internet Archive and take a look. With so much effort being made to share and preserve knowledge by means of the Internet, the Internet Archive's Wayback Machine satisfies a tremendous need: the Internet sharing and preserving *itself*.

Using Your Browser and the World Wide Web

Throughout this book, you will find many Internet-related discussions, as well as exercises and review questions that require you to use the Web. As you learned earlier, the Web enables users to view specially formatted documents, called Web pages, which can contain text, graphics, and multimedia objects such as video, audio, or animations. (Remember that a collection of related Web pages is called a Web site.) Web pages also can display navigational tools to help you move around within a Web page, from one page to another within a Web site, or among different sites.

ONLINE

For more information on using a browser, visit
http://www.mhhe.com/ peternorton.

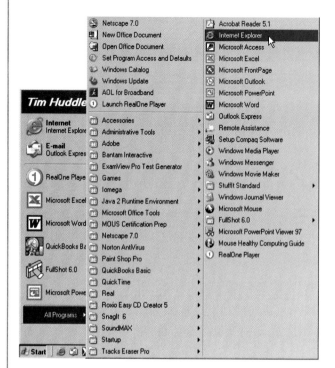

FIGURE 2A.15

Launching a Web browser from the
Windows Start menu.

To access the Web, you need a special software program called a Web browser. This section shows you the basic steps required for using a browser and navigating the Web. You should complete the following steps and become familiar with your browser before going any further in this book.

Note that the following discussions assume that you are using a personal computer running Windows XP Professional. If you use a different version of Windows, the actual steps you take may differ slightly from those discussed in the following sections. Ask your instructor for help, if necessary.

Launching Your Browser

Your browser is an application stored on your computer's disk. You must launch the program before you can view any Web pages. You may need to connect to the Internet before launching the browser. (If so, ask your instructor for directions on connecting to the Internet.) Once you have established a connection, launch your browser by following these steps:

1. Click the Start button on the Windows taskbar. The Start menu opens.

2. Point to All Programs to open the Programs submenu. When the Programs submenu opens, find the name of your browser and click it, as shown in Figure 2A.15.

Your browser will open on your screen, as shown in Figure 2A.16. The browser shown here is Microsoft Internet Explorer version 6.0. If you are using a different browser (or a different version of Internet Explorer), you will notice that your screen looks different.

Depending on how your browser is configured, a Web page may open in the browser window as soon as you launch the program. This page is called the start page. You can set the browser to open any page (either from a Web site or from your computer's disk) when it launches. In Figure 2A.16, the Excite home page is the start page.

Navigating the Web

Navigating the Web means moving from one Web page to another or from one Web site to another. Your browser provides several different ways to navigate the Web. Once you are familiar with your browser's interface, you can select the navigational tools and techniques that work best for you.

Using URLs

As you learned previously, every Web page has a unique address, called a uniform resource locator, or URL. URLs are the key to navigating the Web. When you provide a URL for the browser, the browser finds that URL's page and then transfers the page to your PC. The page's content then appears on your screen, in the browser window.

FIGURE 2A.16

The Internet Explorer browser.

You can specify a URL in several ways, but three methods are most commonly used:

>> Type the URL in the browser's Address box.

>> Click a hyperlink that is linked to that URL.

>> Store the URL in your browser's Favorites list, then select the URL from the list. (If you use Netscape Navigator, this list is called Bookmarks.)

For example, suppose you want to visit the Web site of the National Football League (NFL). To do this, you can click in the Address box, type **http://www.nfl.com**, and then press ENTER. The home page of the NFL Web site appears in the browser window (see Figure 2A.17).

Using Hyperlinks

A hyperlink is simply a part of the Web page that is linked to a URL. A hyperlink can appear as text, an image, or a navigational tool such as a button or an arrow. You can click a hyperlink and "jump" from your present location to the URL specified by the hyperlink. Hyperlinked text usually looks different from normal text in a Web page: it is often underlined, but can be formatted in any number of ways (see Figure 2A.18). When your mouse pointer touches hyperlinked text, the hyperlink's URL appears in the browser's status bar, and the pointer changes shape to resemble a hand with a pointing index finger.

Many Web pages also provide hyperlinked pictures or graphical buttons—called navigation tools—that direct you to different pages, making it easier to find

Type a URL here, and then press ENTER.

The URL's page appears in the browser window.

FIGURE 2A.17

Navigating the Web by typing a URL.

FIGURE 2A.18

Using hyperlinked text on a Web page.

The mouse pointer is resting on hyperlinked text.

If you click the hyperlinked text, the browser will open the page with the URL shown on the status bar.

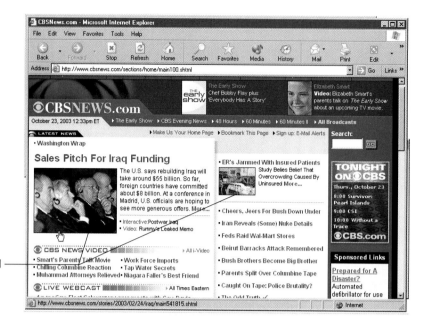

These graphics are hyperlinked
and act as navigation tools.

the information you need (see Figure 2A.19). Another common navigation tool is
the image map, a single image that provides multiple hyperlinks. You can click on
different parts of the image map to jump to different pages. When your mouse
pointer touches a navigation tool or image map, it turns into a hand pointer, and
the hyperlink's URL appears in your browser's status bar.

Using the Browser's Navigation Tools

Web browsers offer a variety of tools to help you move around the Web. These
tools can save you the trouble of typing URLs or searching for links, and they allow you to quickly go back to pages that you have already visited.

The Back and Forward buttons return you to recently viewed pages, similar to
flipping through a magazine (see Figure 2A.20). The Back button returns you to
the previously opened Web page. After using the Back button, you can click Forward to move forward again, returning to the last page you opened before you
clicked the Back button.

FIGURE 2A.20

The Back and Forward buttons in Internet
Explorer.

The opened list of
bookmarks

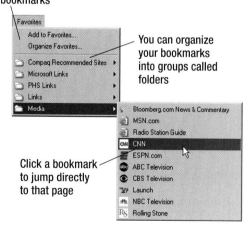

You can organize
your bookmarks
into groups called
folders

Click a bookmark
to jump directly
to that page

Most browsers allow you to "bookmark" Web pages that you visit
frequently. Instead of typing the page's URL, you simply select the
page's title from your list of bookmarks. Depending on the browser you
use, your bookmarks may be stored in a list called Bookmarks, Favorites, or something similar (see Figure 2A.21). Simply select a bookmark from that list, and the browser returns to that page.

When you type URLs into the Address bar, your browser saves
them, creating a history list for the current session (see Figure 2A.22).
You can choose a URL from this list and return to a previously opened
page without having to use the Back button or any other tools.

Closing Your Browser

To close your browser, open the File menu and choose Close. You also
can close the browser by clicking the Close button on the title bar. It
may be necessary to close your Internet connection, too.

FIGURE 2A.21

Selecting a bookmark from Internet
Explorer's Favorites list.

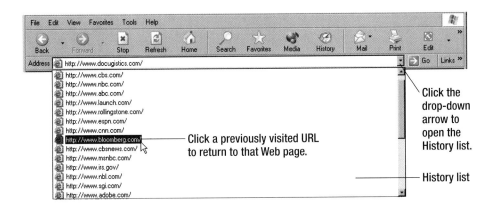

Click a previously visited URL
to return to that Web page.

Click the
drop-down
arrow to
open the
History list.

History list

Getting Help with Your Browser

Although most browsers are easy to use, you
may need help at some point. Browsers provide comprehensive Help systems, which can
answer many of your questions about
browsing and the World Wide Web.

Open the browser's Help menu, and then
choose Contents and Index. (Depending on
your browser, this option may be called Contents, Help Contents, or something similar.)

A Help window appears, listing all the
topics for which help or information is available (see Figure 2A.23). Look through the
list of topics and choose the one that matches
your interest. When you are done, click the
Close button on the window's title bar.

To get help from your browser maker's
Web site, open your browser's Help menu

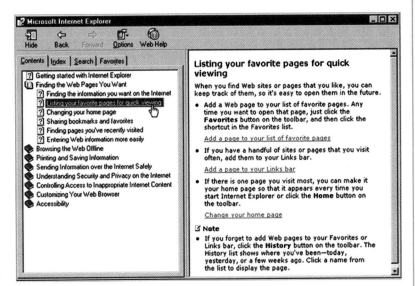

and look for an option that leads you to the product's Web site. The resulting
Web page will provide access to lists of frequently asked questions, links to help
topics, and methods for getting in-depth technical support.

FIGURE 2A.23

Internet Explorer's Help window.

Searching the Web

It is not always easy to find what you want on the Web. That is because there are
tens of millions of unique Web sites, which include billions of unique pages! This
section explains the basics of Web search tools and their use. However, there are
many more specific search tools available than can be listed here. To search the
Web successfully, you should use this section as a starting point; then spend some
time experimenting with a variety of search tools.

The two most basic and commonly used Web-based search tools are

>> **Directories.** A directory enables you to search for information by selecting cat-
egories of subject matter. The directory separates subjects into general categories (such as "companies"), which are broken into increasingly specific
subcategories (such as "companies—construction—contractors—builders and
designers"). After you select a category or subcategory, the directory displays
a list of Web sites that provide content related to that subject. The LookSmart
directory at http://www.looksmart.com is shown in Figure 2A.24.

>> **Search Engines.** A search engine lets you search for information by typing
one or more words. The engine then displays a list of Web pages that contain

ONLINE

For more information on
searching the Web, visit
**http://www.mhhe.com/
peternorton**.

The LookSmart home page. You can use the site's directory to search for Web sites relating to many topics.

information related to your words. (This type of look-up is called a keyword search.) Any search engine lets you conduct a search based on a single word. Most also let you search for multiple words, such as "scanner AND printer." Many search engines accept "plain English" phrases or questions as the basis for your search, such as "movies starring Cary Grant" or "How do cells divide?" The Google search engine at http://www.google.com is shown in Figure 2A.25.

FIGURE 2A.25

Google has become one of the Web's most popular search engines.

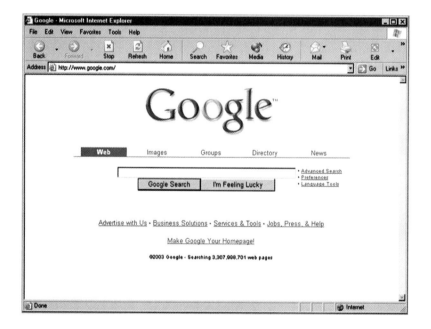

Note that both types of search tools are commonly called search engines. While this terminology is not technically correct, the differences between the two types are blurring; most Web-based search tools provide both directories and keyword search engines. In fact, if you look back at Figure 2A.24, you will see that LookSmart provides a box for performing keyword searches as well as its list of categories for performing directory-style searches.

Using a Directory

Suppose you want to find some Web sites that provide information about the latest digital cameras. Perhaps you want to buy a camera, or you just want to read about the technology before deciding whether to buy one. In the following exercise, you will use the LookSmart directory to find Web sites that provide "buyers guide" information.

1. Launch your Web browser.

2. In the Address box, type **http://www.looksmart.com** and press ENTER. The LookSmart home page opens in your browser window.

3. On the LookSmart home page, click the Computing category. A new page opens, displaying a list of subcategories under Computing.

4. Click the Hardware subcategory. A third page appears, displaying a list of subcategories under Hardware.

5. Choose Peripherals | Input Devices | Digital Cameras | Guides & Directories. A new page appears listing sites that provide information about buying digital cameras (see Figure 2A.26).

6. Browse through the list of Web sites and click one. The new site opens in your browser window. After reviewing it, you can use your browser's Back button to navigate back to the list of buyers' guides to choose another Web site.

FIGURE 2A.26

After you select the final subcategory, LookSmart displays a list of Web sites that provide information related to your topic.

Using a Search Engine

Suppose you want to find some information about ink jet printers. You know there are many different types of printers that are available at a wide range of prices. You also know that you want a printer that prints in color rather than in black and white only. In the following exercise, you will use a search engine to help you find the information you need.

1. Launch your Web browser.

2. In the Location/Address bar, type **http://www.lycos.com** and press ENTER. The Lycos home page opens in your browser window, as shown in Figure 2A.27. (Lycos is just one example of a Web search engine.)

3. In the Search text box, type **"ink jet printer"** (include the quotation marks) and click the Search button. A new page appears, listing Web pages that contain information relating to ink jet printers. Note, however, that the list includes hundreds of thousands of pages (see Figure 2A.28). This happens because a search engine assumes that a Web site is relevant to your needs if it contains terms that match the keywords you provide.

4. To narrow the search results, you must provide more specific search criteria. Click in the Search text box and type **"ink jet printer" "color"** (again, including the quotation marks); then click the Search button. Another page appears, listing a new selection of Web sites that match your keywords. Note that this list is shorter than the original one, by thousands of matches.

This search produced more
than 240,000 matches.

WEB RESULTS: Showing Results **1 thru 10** of 242,913 (info)

1. Bulk **ink jet printer ink** refill kit 24 hour super store - Refill your... *Sidesearch* »
    For your Inkjet **Printer** Cartridge Refill needs...<P>. More on Inkjet **Printer** Cartridge Refill ...
    www.printerfillingstation.com   September 22, 2003 - 22 KB

2. InkCartridge.com - InkJet Cartridges and **Ink Jet Printer** Supplies *Sidesearch* »
    Source for inkjet cartridges and **printer** supplies.
    www.inkcartridge.com   January 8, 2003 - 5 KB

3. **Printer** Cartridges Onn-Line - Original and Compatible **Ink Jet Printer**... *Sidesearch* »
    I-shops' ORIGINAL **PRINTER** CARTRIDGE store
 Accept no imitations. Suppliers of Original and Compatible **Printer Ink Jet** Cartridges
    www.printercartridges-onnline.co.uk   October 16, 2003 - 25 KB

FIGURE 2A.28

Search engines commonly produce thousands (even hundreds of thousands) of matches, depending on your search criteria. To narrow your list of results, you need to provide more specific keywords.

5. Scroll through the list and notice if it contains any duplicate entries. How many of the suggested pages actually seem irrelevant to your search criteria? Duplicate and useless entries are two significant problems users encounter when working with search engines.

The preceding examples showed quotation marks ("") surrounding some keywords. Many search engines require you to place quotation marks around multiple-word phrases. The marks tell the engine to treat the words as a phrase ("ink jet printer"), rather than as individual words ("ink," "jet," "printer"). You can use quotation marks to separate parts of a multiple-part keyword ("ink jet printer" "color"). Here, the marks tell the engine that the word "color" is separate from the phrase "ink jet printer."

Fortunately, most search engines provide other tools to help you search more accurately and find Web pages that are more relevant to your interests. These include Boolean operators and advanced search tools, which are discussed in the following sections.

Using Boolean Operators in Your Searches

Many—but not all—search engines accept special words, called Boolean operators, to modify your search criteria. Boolean operators are named after George Boole, a 19th century British mathematician.

Three basic Boolean operators are sometimes used in Web searches: AND, OR, and NOT. To use an operator, simply include it in the text box where you type your keywords. The following table shows simple examples of keyword searches that include the operators, and it explains how the operator affects each search.

A few search engines also support a fourth operator, NEAR. This operator determines the proximity, or closeness, of your specified keywords. For example, you may specify "printer NEAR color," with a closeness of 10 words. This tells the search engine to look for pages that include both terms, where the terms are no more than 10 words apart.

A good way to determine whether you need to use operators is to phrase your interest in the form of a sentence, and then use the important parts of the sentence as your keywords along with the appropriate operators.

A few (but not all) search engines will let you use multiple operators and set the order in which they are used. Suppose, for example, that you want to want to find information about cancer in dogs. You might set up your search criteria like this:

(dog OR canine) AND cancer

This tells the engine to look for pages that include either "dog," "canine," or both, and then to search those pages for ones that also include "cancer."

A few search engines accept symbols to represent operators. For example, you may be able to use a plus sign (+) to represent the AND operator, and a minus sign (−) to represent NOT.

Many search engines use implied Boolean logic by default, meaning you may not need to include an operator in some searches. For example, if you type the following search criteria:

dog canine

some search engines will assume that you want to find pages that include either term (using the OR operator by default). Others will assume you want pages that include both terms (using the AND operator by default), as was the case in your Lycos searches.

When dealing with implied logic, remember that each search engine operates in a slightly different way. For example, in some engines, you should use quotation marks when searching for a phrase or when you want all words to be included, as in

"ink jet printer"

Without the quotation marks, some engines will return pages that include the word "ink," others that include "jet," and others that include "printer," as well as pages that include all three.

The best way to determine how any search engine works is to study its Help-related pages (see Figure 2A.29). The Help section will tell you whether or how you can use operators with that particular engine.

Note, however, that all search engines do not support Boolean searches and multiple-word searches in the same way. Some engines will not even accept Boolean operators. In these cases, a better approach is to use the engine's advanced search tools, which are explored next.

Using Advanced Search Options

To overcome the problems of duplicate and irrelevant results, many search engines provide a set of advanced search options, sometimes called advanced tools.

Operator	Search Criteria	Effect
AND	printer AND color	The search engine looks only for pages that include both terms and ignores pages that include only one of them.
OR	printer OR color	The search engine looks for pages that include either or both of the terms.
NOT	printer NOT color	The search engine looks for pages that include the term *printer*, but do not also include the term *color*. The engine ignores any pages that include both terms.

Interest	Search
I need information about cancer in children.	cancer AND children
I need information about dogs, which are sometimes called canines.	dog OR canine
I need information about acoustic guitars, but not electric guitars.	guitar NOT electric

Productivity Tip

Evaluating the Reliability of Search Results and Web Sites

Once you master the science of searching the Web, you need to determine whether the information you find is accurate and useable. This may sound strange, but remember: the Web is not like a magazine that is published by a single group that takes responsibility for its accuracy and honesty.

By contrast, *anyone* can publish documents on the Web, and millions of people do. While many Web publishers work hard to post accurate, authoritative information, many others do not. In fact, lots of people use the Internet as a way to distribute misinformation or try to mislead others.

The Web is also rife with plagiarism, which is the act of copying someone else's work and using it as your own. This practice enables unscrupulous Webmasters to appear authoritative on a subject when they really know little about it.

These are important points when you are conducting serious research online—whether you are looking for movie reviews, shopping for a computer, or gathering data for a term paper. Relying on the wrong information source can lead to mistakes, or even land you in trouble.

How do you evaluate a Web site to make sure that the information it offers is accurate, honest, and useful? Here are some tips:

>> Try to identify the author of the information, and remember that the writer may not be the same person as the Web site's owner or manager. Check the site for information about the author and see if it is possible to contact that person directly. If you cannot find out anything about the author, then there is a chance that the site's material is not original or the author wishes to remain anonymous.

>> Look for copyright information on the site. If someone has gone to the trouble of researching, writing, and publishing information on a serious topic, then that person will probably try to protect it by posting a copyright notice. If the site is posting material authored by someone else, then there should be a notice stating that the material has been used with permission from the original

FIGURE 2A.29

The Help links at the Google search engine site. This Help section provides a basic overview of Google and how it conducts searches. You also can find information about Google's support for Boolean operators, basic and advanced search techniques, and more. The Help section is the best place to start when working with a search engine for the first time.

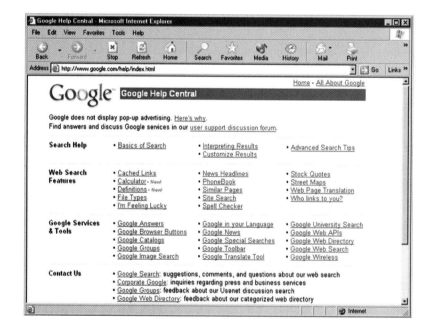

It is important to remember that each engine's advanced tool set is somewhat different from the tool set of another, but they all have the same goal of helping you refine your search criteria to get the best results.

In some engines, advanced search options include support for phrase-based searching or Boolean operators, as already discussed. In other engines, an advanced search provides you with customized tools. At Yahoo!, for example, if you

Unlike the printed resources you can find at your library, many Web sites cannot be trusted to provide accurate information.

author or publisher. If you cannot find such a notice, then the site's owner or writer may not hold a copyright and may have failed to acknowledge the material's source. In other words, it may have been plagiarized.

>> Look for signs of bias in the information. Authoritative information is normally written in an objective, unbiased manner, but this is not necessarily the case. Still, if you find a document that reflects an obvious bias, then it probably is not trustworthy. Ask yourself if the author seems to be promoting a certain viewpoint, theory, practice, or product over others. If so, look at the material skeptically.

>> Make sure the material is current. Credible Web designers place a date on each page of their site, noting when it was last updated. Authoritative articles are often dated. Otherwise, look for signs that the information is old or outdated by reading it closely. If the page contains non-working hyperlinks, the publisher has probably neglected it, and this may indicate that the information has been lying around for some time.

select the Advanced link, you can work in a special form to structure your search criteria (see Figure 2A.30). The form lets you use multiple words and phrases and specify whether any or all of the terms should be included in or omitted from the results. The form also provides tools that let you filter adult-oriented content (such as pornographic Web sites) from your results and search for information in a different language or from a given country.

FIGURE 2A.30

The advanced search form at Yahoo!.

While some advanced tool sets allow you to use Boolean operators in their search forms, some do not. This is because some advanced search forms are based on Boolean logic and are designed to help you create complex Boolean-based searches without deciding which operators to use or where to use them.

Using a Metasearch Engine

In addition to the tools described in the preceding sections, another type of Web-based search engine is also popular. These sites, called metasearch engines, use multiple search engines simultaneously to look up sites that match your keywords, phrase, or question.

Examples of metasearch engines include Mamma (http://www.mamma.com) and Dogpile (http://www.dogpile.com), as shown in Figure 2A.31. Metasearch engines are helpful if you are not certain which keywords to use or if you want to get a very long list of Web sites that meet your search criteria.

Sponsored versus Nonsponsored Links

A growing number of Web search engines allow Web sites to pay for preferential listings. In other words, a Web site's owner can pay a search engine to place the site at the top of the list of search results. These purchased listings are called sponsored links, and they have become the subject of some controversy.

Suppose, for example, that you need information about a specific kind of printer, so you use a search engine and conduct a search on the term "printer." The search engine displays a list of Web sites that match the term, but you notice that the first dozen sites in the list are all retailers—not printer manufacturers, reviewers, or technical experts. In this case, it's a good bet that some or all of these retailers paid the search engine to place their sites at the top of the list.

Norton ONLINE

For more information on metasearch engines, visit **http://www.mhhe.com/ peternorton**.

FIGURE 2A.31

Metasearch engines, such as Dogpile, use multiple search engines at one time to give you exhaustive results.

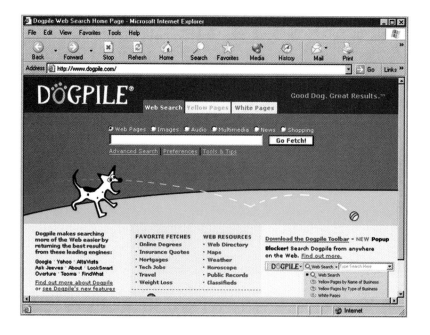

Sponsored links have become controversial because they are not always most relevant to the user's needs. Instead, they are a way for search engines to generate revenues. Some search engines display sponsored links in a special way—putting them in boxes or separate lists—so users can identify them.

Should you avoid sponsored links? No, especially if they are relevant and helpful to you. Be aware, however, that some search engine results may be sponsored; take care to look through search results carefully to find the sites that are most useful. If your favorite search engine does not highlight sponsored links in some way, consider using an engine that does.

Using Site-Specific Search Tools

Many high-volume Web sites feature built-in search tools of their own, enabling you to look for information on the Web site you are currently visiting. Sites such as Microsoft Corporation (http://www.microsoft.com), CNN (http://www.cnn.com), Netscape Communications (http://www.netscape.com), and many others feature such tools.

Suppose, for example, you are visiting the Microsoft Web site and want to find information about Flight Simulator, which is a popular Microsoft game. Instead of jumping from one page to another looking for information, you can click in the Search box, type the words **Flight Simulator**, and click the Go button. The site's search engine displays a list of pages on the Microsoft site that are related to Flight Simulator.

Some site-specific search tools also let you search outside that particular site. At ZDNet's site (http://www.zdnet.com), for example, you can type one or more keywords in the Search box and then decide whether you want to search only the ZDNet site or the entire Web for related information before clicking the Search button (see Figure 2A.32).

FIGURE 2A.32

You can search only the ZDNet site or the entire Web.

Summary ::

>> The Internet was created for the U.S. Department of Defense as a tool for communications. Today the Internet is a global network of interconnected networks.

>> The Internet carries messages, documents, programs, and data files that contain every imaginable kind of information for businesses, educational institutions, government agencies, and individuals.

>> One of the services available through the Internet is the World Wide Web (or Web). To access the Web, you need an Internet connection and a Web browser.

>> Navigating the Web means moving from one Web page or Web site to another.

>> Web pages can contain navigational tools, in the form of hyperlinks, which help the user move from page to page.

>> Most Web browsers allow the user to navigate the Web in various ways by using toolbar buttons, hyperlinks, bookmarks, and a history list.

>> Web browsers, like other application programs, feature online Help systems.

>> To search for content on the Web, you can use a directory, a search engine, or a metasearch engine.

>> A directory is a categorized list of links. Users can find the information they need by selecting categories and subcategories of topics.

>> A search engine lets users search for content by using keywords. The engine lists any Web sites it finds that match the keywords.

>> Users can refine their Web searches by using tools such as Boolean operators or advanced search tools.

>> Metasearch engines use multiple search engines simultaneously to look up sites that match your keywords, phrase, or question.

Key Terms ::

ARPANET, 50
backbone, 51
Boolean operator, 66
browser, 54
directory, 63
helper application, 56
host, 50
hyperlink, 53
hypertext, 53
hypertext link, 53
hypertext markup language
  (HTML), 53

hypertext transfer protocol (HTTP), 53
Internet, 49
Internet service provider (ISP), 52
internetworking, 51
keyword, 64
link, 53
metasearch engine, 70
NSFnet, 51
plug-in application, 56
publish, 54
search engine, 63
spawn, 58

sponsored link, 70
start page, 60
streaming audio, 57
streaming video, 57
uniform resource locator (URL), 55
Web browser, 54
Web page, 53
Web site, 53
World Wide Web (Web, WWW), 52

Key Term Quiz ::

Complete each statement by writing one of the terms listed under Key Terms in each blank.

1. On the Internet, a(n) _____ computer works like a network server computer.

2. To access the Internet, you need the right software and an account with a(n) _____ .

3. A Web page is a document formatted with the _____ language.

4. A(n) _____ is software you can use to navigate the World Wide Web.

5. AND, OR, and NOT are examples of _____ .

6. To allow you to view some kinds of content, your Web browser may need to spawn a(n) _____ application.

7. A(n) _____ uses multiple search engines simultaneously to look up sites that match your keywords, phrase, or question.

8. The process of connecting separate networks together is called _____ .

9. A(n) _____ helps you find content on the Web by allowing you to choose categories and subcategories of topics.

10. A(n) _____ is the Web page that appears in your browser window as soon as you launch the program.

Multiple Choice ::

Circle the word or phrase that best completes each statement.

1. Construction of the network now known as the Internet began in _____ .
   - **a.** 1949
   - **b.** 1959
   - **c.** 1969
   - **d.** 1979

2. The Internet is open to _____ .
   - **a.** members
   - **b.** government agencies
   - **c.** university researchers
   - **d.** anyone who can access it

3. A collection of related Web pages is called a _____ .
   - **a.** Web book
   - **b.** Web site
   - **c.** Web directory
   - **d.** Web engine

4. Every Web page has a unique address, called a _____ .
   - **a.** hyperlink
   - **b.** uniform resource locator
   - **c.** HTTP
   - **d.** map

5. When you use a search engine, you specify one or more _____ .
   - **a.** keywords
   - **b.** Web pages
   - **c.** sites
   - **d.** URLs

6. The Internet acts as a(n) _____ for services such as the World Wide Web and e-mail.
   - **a.** provider
   - **b.** host
   - **c.** carrier
   - **d.** server

7. Because it uses HTTP, the Web supports _____ documents.
   - **a.** electronic
   - **b.** hypertext
   - **c.** colorful
   - **d.** overlapping

8. The first point-and-click Web browser was named _____ .
   - **a.** Mosaic
   - **b.** Moselle
   - **c.** Moseying
   - **d.** Mostly

9. After streaming content is played in your browser, it is _____ .
   - **a.** returned
   - **b.** saved
   - **c.** copied
   - **d.** deleted

10. Before you launch your browser and view a Web page, you may need to _____ .
    - **a.** get permission
    - **b.** connect to the Internet
    - **c.** call your ISP
    - **d.** launch a helper application

Review Questions ::

In your own words, briefly answer the following questions.

1. How was ARPANET created, and what was its goal?
2. Why is the Internet sometimes described as a "network of networks"?
3. What is a backbone?
4. List eight of the Internet's major services.
5. What happens when you provide a URL for your Web browser?
6. List three ways you can specify a URL in your Web browser.
7. What is a bookmark in a Web browser and what do bookmarks allow you to do?
8. How does a search engine let you search for information on the Web?
9. List four Boolean operators that are sometimes used in Web searches.
10. The advanced tools of some search engines do not allow you to use Boolean operators. Why?

Lesson Labs ::

Complete the following exercises as directed by your instructor.

1. Practice using your browser. Launch your browser and practice navigating the Web. Try using URLs based on the names of people or companies you want to learn more about. For example, if you type **http://www.cheerios.com** in your Address box, what happens? Make up five different URLs from company, product, or individual names and see where they lead your browser. As you visit different sites, look for hyperlinked text and graphics; click them, and see where they lead.

2. Search, search, search. Pick a topic and search the Web for information about it. Pick a keyword to use in your search, then visit three search engines and use each of them to conduct a search using your chosen keyword. Use Yahoo! (http://www.yahoo.com), AltaVista (http://www.altavista.com), and Google (http://www.google.com) for your searches. Do the results differ from one search engine to another?

E-Mail and Other Internet Services

Overview: Communicating through the Internet

With its graphics-rich pages and streaming multimedia content, the World Wide Web belies the Internet's original purpose—to serve as a means of communication. As you have already seen, millions of people use the Internet to exchange e-mail. In fact, e-mail is now a more common means of communication than telephone calls.

The Internet's other services, though lesser known and used, provide users with other unique and interesting ways to communicate. While e-mail and news enable people to exchange "delayed" messages, services such as chat and instant messaging allow users to send and respond to message in real time. Other services, such as FTP and peer-to-peer systems, are used mainly for exchanging different types of files through the Internet—a practice that is now an essential part of electronic communications.

This lesson introduces you to each of these important Internet-based services. You will learn how each one is used and the types of software you will need to communicate or send information through them.

OBJECTIVES ::

>> Explain how e-mail technologies allow users to exchange messages.

>> Describe the parts of a typical e-mail address.

>> Explain how Internet newsgroups function.

>> Describe the process of transferring a file via FTP.

>> Differentiate between Internet relay chat and instant messaging.

>> Identify two ways in which Internet-based peer-to-peer services are used.

Using E-Mail

The only Internet service that is more frequently used than the Web is electronic mail. Electronic mail, or e-mail, is a system for exchanging messages through a computer network. People most commonly use e-mail to send and receive text messages, but depending on the software you use, you may be able to exchange audio or video messages with someone else.

E-mail was one of the first uses of the Internet, and quickly became a popular feature because it lets users exchange messages from anywhere in the world. Further, e-mail is less expensive than using the telephone because there is no charge for using it, beyond the regular fees you pay your ISP. E-mail is also a faster way to communicate than postal mail because e-mail messages typically reach their destination in seconds rather than days.

E-mail services are very easy to access, and this is another reason for e-mail's popularity. You can manage e-mail through a typical ISP account and a desktop computer, or use a Web-based e-mail service, which lets you check your messages wherever you have Web access. Many cellular telephones and pagers provide e-mail features, too (see Figure 2B.1). Some e-mail systems can even interact with any telephone and actually "read" your messages to you.

Another advantage of e-mail is the ability to attach data files and program files to messages. For example, you can send a message to a friend and attach a digital photograph or some other file to the message. The recipient then can open and use the document on his or her computer.

E-mail, however, is not a real-time communications system. This means that once you send a message to someone, you must wait until he or she reads it and sends you a reply. This delay, however, doesn't stop people from exchanging billions of messages each year.

Understanding E-Mail

The most common way to create, send, and receive e-mail is by using an e-mail program (also called an e-mail client) and an Internet connection through an ISP or LAN. Popular Internet e-mail programs include Eudora, Microsoft Outlook, Microsoft Outlook Express, Netscape Messenger, and others.

(There are many Web-based e-mail services that allow you to send and receive e-mail by using your Web browser. Those services will be discussed later in this lesson.)

E-Mail Addresses

If you have an account with an ISP or if you are a user on a corporate or school LAN, then you can establish an e-mail address. This unique address enables other users to send messages to you and enables you to send messages to others.

You can set up an e-mail account by creating a unique user name for yourself, which identifies your postal mailbox on the Internet. If your name is John Smith, for example, your user name might be "jsmith" or "john_smith." In an e-mail address, the user name usually appears before the ISP host computer's name. The user name and the host computer's name are separated by the @ symbol (commonly called the "at" symbol). So, if your ISP is America Online (AOL), your e-mail address might look like this:

jsmith@aol.com

You read this address as "J Smith at a-o-l dot com." Figure 2B.2 shows an e-mail address being used in a message.

Norton
ONLINE

For more information on Internet e-mail, visit
http://www.mhhe.com/ peternorton.

simnet™

FIGURE 2B.1

Portable devices, such as this BlackBerry® Wireless Handheld™ handheld system, let you send and receive e-mail messages wirelessly, from virtually any location.

E-mail addresses enable people to send and receive e-mail messages over the Internet.

Recipient's address

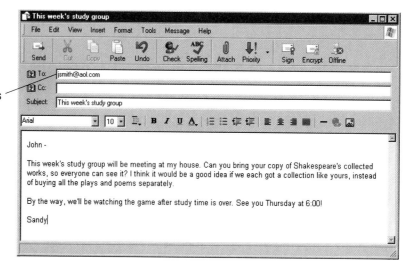

When you send an e-mail message, the message is stored on a server until the recipient can retrieve it. This type of server is called a mail server. Many mail servers use the post office protocol (POP) and are called POP servers. Nearly all ISPs and corporate networks maintain one or more mail servers for storing and forwarding e-mail messages.

Listserv Systems

The most common use for e-mail is when one person sends a message to someone else, or to a small group. However, e-mail systems can be used to distribute messages to thousands of people at the same time. These electronic, automated mailing lists are commonly used to distribute electronic newsletters or bulletin board–style messages to a group. For example, you might join a mailing list for people who are interested in antiques or a particular type of music and receive the group's bulletin with your regular e-mail. Members can contribute messages to the group, too.

One type of mailing list is the automated list server, or listserv. Listserv systems allow users on the list to post their own messages, so the result is an ongoing discussion that the entire group can see and join. Hundreds of mailing-list discussions are in progress all the time, on a huge variety of topics.

Using an E-Mail Program

Standard e-mail programs are free and easy to use. If you have purchased a computer in the last few years, it probably came with an e-mail program already installed. Microsoft Outlook Express is commonly installed on Windows-based computers.

The following sections briefly show you how to create and send an e-mail message using Outlook Express running under Windows XP. If you use a different e-mail program or operating system, the steps will be similar, but your screen will look different and the tools may have different names.

Creating a Message

To create a new e-mail message in Outlook Express, follow these steps:

1. Launch the program by choosing Start | All Programs | Outlook Express.
2. When the Outlook Express window appears, click the Create Mail button. A new window appears, where you can compose the message (see Figure 2B.3).
3. Click in the To: box and type the recipient's e-mail address. You can specify more than one recipient. (If the recipients' addresses are already stored in the

FIGURE 2B.3

Creating a message.

Click here to create a new message.

Click here to send the message.

Click here to attach a file to the message.

Type the recipient's address here.

Type the subject of your message here.

Type your message here.

program's address book, you can open it by clicking the To: button and selecting the addresses there.)

4. Click in the Subject: box and type the message's subject. This will let the recipient know what your message is about.

5. Click in the big text box at the bottom of the window and type your message.

6. When the message is ready, click the Send button to deliver the message.

Receiving and Reading a Message

When someone sends you a message, it will appear in your Inbox folder in Outlook Express (see Figure 2B.4), unless you have set the program to receive messages in a different folder. If you select the Inbox folder in the Folders list (in the left-hand pane of the Outlook Express window), a list of messages you have received will appear in the right side of the window. Double-click any message in the list to open and read it.

Once you receive a message, you can do several things with it:

>> **Reply.** This means sending a response back to the person who sent you the message.

>> **Print.** This creates a paper copy of the message.

>> **Forward.** This means sending the message on to someone else—someone other than you or the person who sent it.

>> **Delete.** By deleting old or unneeded messages, you keep your Inbox and other folders from getting too full.

SELF-CHECK ::

Circle the correct answer for each question.

1. Your _____ is unique to you.
   a. ISP   b. e-mail address   c. e-mail software

2. A _____ is a computer that stores and forwards e-mail messages.
   a. mail server   b. mail center   c. mail system

3. Standard e-mail programs are _____.
   a. hard to use   b. Web-based   c. free

At Issue

In a society almost as dependent on e-mail as the U.S. Postal Service, junk e-mail—better known as "spam"—has become more than a mere annoyance. For Internet-connected individuals, it's an increasingly time-consuming and offensive aggravation. In the business world, it's a growing crisis, draining resources and bandwidth and laying networks vulnerable to numerous security hazards.

In the last several years, unsolicited e-mail has quadrupled. Today, spam makes up an estimated 20 percent of corporate e-mail traffic, and the Aberdeen Group predicts spam will soon double, accounting for up to 50 percent of all corporate e-mail.

For personal users, the forecast is even grimmer: More than half of all e-mail traffic is now junk, say experts, up from only 8 percent just two years ago. That's 15 billion spam messages crisscrossing the Internet daily, or 25 spam e-mails a day for every person online in the world. Even worse, spam could make up the majority of message traffic on the Internet by the end of 2002, according to data from the three largest e-mail service providers.

Among the many problems caused by unsolicited e-mail, spam consumes significant time and resources. For example, in one year alone, unwanted commercial e-mail cost U.S. corporations almost $10 billion. Loss was measured in terms of lost worker productivity (workers waste an average of 4.5 seconds on each spam message); use of technical support time; and consumption of bandwidth and other tech resources used to fight spam.

E-mail is the lifeblood of the Internet—hands down it's the most popular application. But thanks to spam, many are losing faith in this modern-day marvel. Because of spam, about three-fourths of e-mail users now avoid giving out their e-mail addresses, more than half say they trust it less, and one in four uses it less, according to a recent study by the Pew Internet and American Life Project. Some are even

FIGURE 2B.4

Reading a message.

This list shows all the messages in the folder.

Double-click a message in the list to open it.

The Inbox is one of the folders you can use for storing messages.

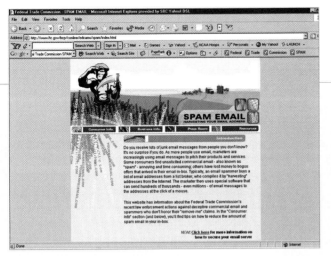

turning to more traditional forms of communication: the telephone and U.S. Postal Service.

So, what will it take to stem the tide? Many fork out big bucks for software blocking and filtering tools. Internet service providers spend hundreds of millions of dollars to improve their spam-blocking technology. Others are taking spammers to court, so far with limited success.

The Federal Trade Commission (FCC) has repeatedly warned that it will go after spammers in court, but the commission's threats have yet to be manifested in legal action (although the FTC does file complaints against spammers who run scams such as pyramid schemes and chain letters soliciting money).

Some feel only comprehensive federal legislation can effectively combat spam. In 2003, the U.S. House of Representatives gave final approval to the first federal anti-spam legislation, authorizing the creation of a Do Not Spam registry and imposing tough penalties for fraudulent e-mail.

Yet, most Internet experts agree. Spam will probably never be entirely eradicated. Ultimately, a consensus approach that coordinates legal and high-tech responses is likely to provide the best defense against the unrelenting flood of junk e-mail.

AT ISSUE

Using Web-Based E-Mail Services

You don't need to have a stand-alone e-mail program to send and receive messages. You can easily manage e-mail by using one of the many Web-based e-mail services. These services offer several advantages over standard e-mail programs:

>> **Cost.** Web-based e-mail services such as Hotmail and Mail.com offer free e-mail accounts, although storage space can be limited.

>> **Ease of Use.** Web-based e-mail services offer the same tools as standard e-mail programs, all within the familiar confines of your browser, so they are easy to use (see Figure 2B.5).

>> **Accessibility.** You can access a Web-based e-mail account from any computer that has Web access. You do not need to log into your ISP's account, which may be impossible if you are traveling.

More Features of the Internet

Because the Internet is a gigantic network, it can support many different types of services besides the Web and e-mail. In fact, some Internet services have been available for decades and are still widely used.

News

In addition to the messages distributed to mailing lists by e-mail, the Internet also supports a form of public bulletin board called news. There are tens of thousands of active Internet newsgroups, each devoted to discussion of a particular topic. Many of the most widely distributed newsgroups are part of a system called Usenet, but others are targeted to a particular region or to users connected to a specific network or institution, such as a university or a large corporation.

Norton **ONLINE**

For more information on Web-based e-mail services, visit **http://www.mhhe.com/ peternorton**.

simnet™

Norton **ONLINE**

For more information on Internet news, visit **http://www.mhhe.com/ peternorton**.

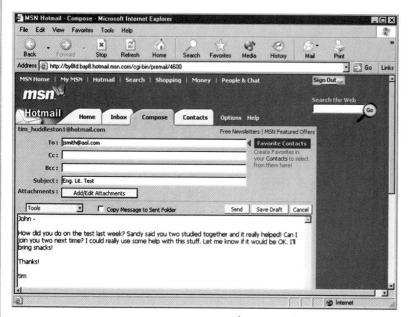

FIGURE 2B.5

Composing a message in Hotmail, a popular Web-based e-mail service.

TABLE 2B.1

Common Usenet Domains

Domain	Description
comp	Computer-related topics
sci	Science and technology (except computers)
soc	Social issues and politics
news	Topics related to Usenet
rec	Hobbies, arts, and recreational activities
misc	Topics that do not fit into one of the other domains

The most important alternative topics include the following:

alt	Alternative newsgroups
bionet	Biological sciences
biz	Business topics, including advertisements
clari	News from the Associated Press and Reuters, supplied through a service called Clarinet
K12	Newsgroups for primary and secondary schools

To participate in a newsgroup, users post articles (short messages) about the newsgroup's main topic. As users read and respond to one another's articles, they create a thread of linked articles. By reading the articles in a thread, you can see the message that initiated the discussion and all the messages that have been posted in response to it.

The most popular way to participate in newsgroups is by using a newsreader program. Popular newsreaders include News Rover, Xnews, and NewsPro, and there are many others. Some free e-mail programs, such as Microsoft Outlook Express and Netscape's Messenger, also have built-in newsreaders. A newsreader program obtains articles from a news server, a host computer that exchanges articles with other servers through the Internet. Because these servers use the network news transfer protocol (NNTP), they are sometimes called NNTP servers. To participate in newsgroups, you can run a newsreader program to log on to a server. Most ISPs provide access to a news server as part of an Internet account. You also can use a Web browser to participate in newsgroups, by visiting a Web site—such as Google (http://groups.google.com) or Newsfeeds.com (http://www.newsfeeds.com)—that publishes newsgroup content.

To see articles that have been posted about a specific topic, you can subscribe to the newsgroup that addresses that topic. Newsgroups are organized into major categories, called domains, and categorized by individual topics within each domain. There are several major domains within the Usenet structure and many more alternative domains. Table 2B.1 lists the major Usenet domains.

The name of a newsgroup begins with the domain, followed by one or more words that describe the group's topic, such as alt.food. Some topics include separate newsgroups for related subtopics, such as alt.food.chocolate. Newsgroup names can be quite long. As Figure 2B.6 shows, subscribing to a newsgroup is a three-step process. Figure 2B.7 shows a series of articles and responses that make up a thread.

To subscribe, you must download a list of available newsgroups from the server, choose the groups that interest you, and select articles. In most newsreaders, you can choose to reply to an article by posting another article to the newsgroup or by sending a private e-mail message to the person who wrote the original article.

Newsgroups are a relatively fast way to distribute information to potentially interested readers, and they allow people to discuss topics of common interest. They also can be a convenient channel for finding answers to questions. Many questions are asked again and again, so it is always a good idea to read the articles that other people have posted before you jump in with your own questions. Members of many newsgroups post lists of frequently asked questions (FAQ) and their answers every month or two.

Step 1: Download a list of available newsgroups.

Step 2: Choose a group that interests you.

Step 3: Select the article you want to read.

This is the article.

FIGURE 2B.6

Subscribing to a newsgroup.

These messages form a thread.

FIGURE 2B.7

A series of articles and responses create a thread, or ongoing discussion, in a newsgroup.

FTP

File transfer protocol (FTP) is the Internet tool used to copy files from one computer to another.

An FTP site is a collection of files, including data files and/or programs, that are housed on an FTP server. FTP sites, which are often called *archives*, may contain thousands of individual programs and files. Public FTP archives permit anyone to make copies of their files by using special FTP client software (see Figure 2B.8). Because these public archives usually require visitors to use the word "anonymous" as an account name, they are known as anonymous FTP archives.

FIGURE 2B.8

Here is a popular FTP client program named WS_FTP LE, which is used to transfer files from an FTP site (the remote site) to the user's computer (the local system).

It is not always necessary to use an FTP client to download files from an FTP site. Web browsers also support FTP. In fact, if you visit a Web site such as Microsoft (http://www.microsoft.com) or Macromedia (http://www.macromedia. com), you can download programs and data files directly onto your computer through your Web browser. This type of file transfer usually is an FTP operation and is available through many different Web sites.

FTP sites provide access to many different types of files. You can find information of all kinds, from weather maps to magazine articles, housed on these systems. Computer hardware and software companies frequently host their own FTP sites, where you can copy program updates, bug solutions, and other types of software.

Although FTP is easy to use, it can be hard to find a file that you want to download. One way to find files is to use Archie, the searchable index of FTP archives maintained by McGill University in Montreal. (Archie is a nickname for archives.) The main Archie server at McGill gathers copies of the directories from more than 1,000 other public FTP archives every month and distributes copies of those directories to dozens of other servers around the world. When a server receives a request for a keyword search, it returns a list of files that match the search criteria and the location of each file. Many FTP client programs provide Archie search tools, and some Web sites enable you to conduct Archie searches through your Web browser (see Figure 2B.9).

Internet Relay Chat (IRC) and Web-Based Chat

Internet relay chat (IRC) , or just chat, is a popular way for Internet users to communicate in real time with other users. Real-time communication means communicating with other users in the immediate present. Unlike e-mail, chat does not require a waiting period between the time you send a message and the time the other person or group of people receives the message. IRC is often referred to as the "CB radio" of the Internet because it enables a few or many people to join a discussion.

Norton
ONLINE

For more information on Internet chat, visit
http://www.mhhe.com/ peternorton.

FIGURE 2B.9

Web sites like this one enable you to use Archie to search for files on the Internet. Here, the user is searching for files related to the keyword hypertext.

IRC is a multi-user system where people join channels to exchange these real-time messages. Channels are discussion groups where chat users convene to discuss a topic. Chat messages are typed on a user's computer and sent to the IRC channel, where all users who have joined that channel receive the message. Users can then read, reply to, or ignore that message or create their own message (see Figure 2B.10).

Chat rooms are also a popular addition to Web sites. Users can participate in chat sessions directly within a Web browser window without installing or running special chat software (see Figure 2B.11).

Instant Messaging

The popularity of public chat rooms created a huge demand for a way to chat privately, so that a limited number of invited people could exchange real-time messages on their screens without being seen or interrupted by anyone else online.

This demand led to the development of instant messaging (IM), a type of chat software that restricts participation to specific users. There are several popular IM services available, such as Windows Messenger, AOL Instant Messenger, and others (see Figure 2B.12).

Using one of these programs, you can create a buddy list—a list of other users with whom you would like to chat. Whenever your IM program is running and you are online, the software lets you know when your "buddies" are also online, so you can chat with them.

Online Services

An online service is a company that offers access, generally on a subscription basis, to e-mail, discussion groups, databases on various subjects (such as weather information, stock quotes, newspaper articles, and so on), and other services

Computers In Your Career

Documentation and Online Help System Designer

Five years ago, most of Mark Jensen's help documents were produced and distributed to customers as paper-based manuals. A technical writer with Epicor Software's Vista Development division in Minneapolis, Jensen says the process has changed dramatically since then, and that most of those documents are now published online. The trend has driven Jensen to learn new applications like HTML and XML, both of which help him design and update Vista Development's online help system.

A developer of software enterprise solutions for small manufacturers, Vista Development relies on tech-savvy professionals like Jensen to produce materials that the company's customers use for help with their applications. An English major, Jensen earned his Bachelor's degree from Concordia College and a Master's in Fine Arts from the University of Nevada, Las Vegas.

When he's not cramming to finish up a large project, Jensen works a 40-hour week and populates his agenda with tasks that need "immediate" attention (documenting the changes that users can expect from a new version of Epicor's software, for example); tasks that are "ongoing"

(updating and adding new features to the firm's online help system); and creating and distributing a monthly technical newsletter for customers.

Jensen says he likes the variety that his job provides, particularly when it comes to learning new things and helping customers make better use of their technology investments. "It's very gratifying to know that the customers really need the help, and that I can provide it," says Jensen. "There's a good feeling that comes from creating something that can be useful to others."

Calling job opportunities for documentation and online help designers "stable," Jensen says both the Internet and technology have created a steady demand for technically oriented individuals who can create help systems and populate them with content that users rely on to help them maximize their own technology infrastructures.

Online documentation isn't limited to the IT space. Whether it's a new toaster or the latest PC operating system, and whether the documentation is in a brochure or on a compact disk, all product documentation has one thing in common: Someone has to research, write, edit, design, and

---

FIGURE 2B.12

Microsoft Messenger, a popular instant messaging program.

Norton ONLINE

For more information on online services, visit
http://www.mhhe.com/peternorton.

Norton ONLINE

For more information on peer-to-peer services on the Internet, visit
http://www.mhhe.com/peternorton.

ranging from electronic banking and investing to online games. Online services also offer access to the Internet, functioning as an ISP to their subscribers. The most popular online services are America Online (see Figure 2B.13), CompuServe, and Prodigy.

In addition to Internet access, online services offer other features that typical ISPs do not. For example, America Online has become famous for its casual chat rooms, and CompuServe is probably best known for its discussion forums geared to technically oriented users. These activities do not take place on the Internet, where everyone can access them. Rather, these services are provided only for the subscribers of the online services. Discussion groups hosted by online services are often monitored by a system operator, or sysop, who ensures that participants follow the rules. Users typically pay by the month for a subscription that allows them to use the service for a limited number of hours per month; they may pay by the hour for additional time, if needed. Subscriptions with unlimited hours are also available.

Peer-to-Peer Services

Peer-to-peer (P2P) services are distributed networks (individual computers, which may be miles apart, that are connected by a network) that do not require a central technicians who take the manuscript and illustrations and use desktop publishing software to prepare a professional-looking document. Online help architects use software tools to compile hundreds or thousands of individual documents (each one dealing with a specific topic) and link them together into a seamless online help system.

Many products include printed documentation to help users master its features and troubleshoot problems, but today nearly all software products provide online help, and often in lieu of printed documentation. This is simply documentation in electronic format

publish it. These tasks are usually handled by professionals who have special skills and who use a variety of tools in their work.

Technical writers like Jensen create the documentation team's backbone, which is rounded out by technical illustrators who create the graphic components and page layout

and must be researched and written just like printed documentation. The Bureau of Labor Statistics reports median annual earnings for salaried technical writers at $47,790 in 2000, with the middle 50 percent earning between $37,280 and $60,000.

server, such as a Web server, to manage files. Instead, specialty software is created, allowing an individual's computer to communicate directly with another individual's computer and even have access to files or information on that computer. Instant messaging, which you read about earlier, is an example of a P2P service.

File-sharing services are another type of P2P service that you may know about already. Services such as gnutella, Kazaa, and others allow users to search for files on each others' computers via the Internet. These file-sharing systems are most commonly used by people who want to share or trade music files online.

Peer-to-peer services are popular because they allow people to share files of all types directly from the peer connections available via the peer software. Corporations have adopted P2P technology as a quick means of transporting information without having to have all the information stored in a centralized location.

FIGURE 2B.13

Users of online services can exchange e-mail messages not only with one another, but with anyone else who has an e-mail account on the Internet. This screen shows the mailbox of an AOL user.

Summary ::

>> Even though it is not a real-time communications medium, e-mail is more commonly used than the Web.

>> To send and receive e-mail messages, you need an e-mail account with an ISP or some other resource (such as your school or business) and an e-mail program. Otherwise, you can exchange e-mail through a Web-based mail service.

>> An e-mail address is a unique identifier that enables someone to send and receive e-mail messages. It includes a user name, the @ symbol, and the host computer's name, such as jsmith@aol.com.

>> A listserv system allows many people to exchange messages with one another, so that everyone in the group can see and respond to them.

>> Internet news consists of thousands of newsgroups, each devoted to a topic. Users can post messages and responses in the group, creating discussions.

>> File transfer protocol (FTP) is the Internet tool used to copy files from one computer to another.

>> Internet relay chat (IRC) enables users to communicate in real time, in special groups called channels. Web-based chatrooms are an alternative to the more traditional IRC.

>> Instant messaging (IM) is like chat, but is private. Users can create their own chatrooms, where invited guests (called buddies) can participate.

>> Online services provide Internet access in addition to other features, which are available only to their subscribers.

>> Peer-to-peer (P2P) services allow users to access one another's computers via the Internet. P2P services form the basis for popular file-sharing systems such as Kazaa.

Key Terms ::

anonymous FTP archive, 83
article, 82
buddy list, 85
channel, 85
chat, 84
electronic mail (e-mail), 77
e-mail address, 77
e-mail client, 77
e-mail program, 77
file transfer protocol (FTP), 83
frequently asked questions (FAQ), 82

FTP client software, 83
FTP server, 83
FTP site, 83
instant messaging (IM), 85
Internet relay chat (IRC), 84
listserv, 78
mail server, 78
network news transfer protocol
    (NNTP), 82
news, 81
news server, 82

newsgroup, 81
newsreader, 82
NNTP server, 82
online service, 85
peer-to-peer (P2P) service, 86
POP server, 78
post office protocol (POP), 78
subscribe, 82
system operator (sysop), 86
thread, 82
user name, 77

Key Term Quiz ::

Complete each statement by writing one of the terms listed under Key Terms in each blank.

1. _____ is more commonly used than the World Wide Web.

2. Outlook Express is an example of a(n) _____ .

3. An e-mail address typically includes a(n) _____ , followed by the @ symbol and the ISP's domain name.

4. Mail servers generally use the _____ protocol.

5. The _____ system is like a public message board that is based on e-mail.

6. alt.food.chocolate could be an example of an Internet _____ .

7. In a newsgroup, a string of related messages and responses is called a(n) _____ .

8. If you want to get a specific file via the Internet, you might use the _____ protocol.

9. IRC users hold discussions in special areas called _____ .

10. CompuServe is an example of a(n) _____ .

Multiple Choice ::

Circle the word or phrase that best completes each statement.

1. E-mail is a system for exchanging messages through a _____ .
   a. client   b. program   c. network   d. backbone

2. A disadvantage of e-mail is that it does not operate in _____ .
   a. real time   b. time lines   c. time outs   d. time zones

3. The @ character is typically called the _____ symbol.
   a. approximate   b. at   c. address   d. about

4. When you send an e-mail message, it is stored on a _____ until the recipient can retrieve it.
   a. protocol   b. backbone   c. mailbox   d. server

5. A _____ system lets you participate in discussion groups by using your regular e-mail software.
   a. groupserv   b. mailserv   c. softserv   d. listserv

6. When you receive an e-mail message, you can _____ it to someone else.
   a. serve   b. forward   c. store   d. copy

7. Many of the widely distributed Internet newsgroups are part of a system called _____ .
   a. NNTPnet   b. Newsnet   c. Usenet   d. Topicnet

8. To see newsgroup articles that have been posted about a specific topic, you can _____ to a newsgroup that addresses the topic.
   a. subscribe   b. transfer   c. submit   d. publish

9. FTP sites are often called _____ .
   a. channels   b. archives   c. groups   d. domains

10. _____ is a type of chat software that restricts participation to specific users.
    a. IRC   b. Usenet   c. Newsreader   d. Instant messaging

Review Questions ::

In your own words, briefly answer the following questions.

1. What is e-mail most commonly used for?
2. E-mail is not a real-time communications system. What does this mean?
3. What is the purpose of a user name, in an e-mail address?
4. What is a POP server?
5. In Outlook Express, what happens when you click the Create Mail button?
6. List four things you can do with an e-mail message, once you receive it.
7. How are Internet newsgroups organized?
8. What is a public FTP archive?
9. What is Archie?
10. What is a "buddy list"?

Lesson Labs ::

Complete the following exercises as directed by your instructor.

1. Identify your e-mail program. If you haven't already done so, check your computer to see what e-mail programs have been installed. Click the Start menu, then click All Programs. When the Programs submenu appears, search for the names of any programs that look like e-mail clients. With your instructor's permission, launch each of the programs to see if you were right.

2. Send a message. Once you locate and launch your e-mail program, send a message to a classmate. First, exchange e-mail addresses with a classmate. Then, use your e-mail software to compose and send a short message. (If you need guidance, follow the instructions given earlier in this lesson, or ask your instructor for assistance.) Then wait for your classmate to respond to the message. How long does the process take? When you are finished, close the e-mail program.

Chapter Labs

Complete the following exercises using a computer in your classroom, lab, or home.

1. Learn more about the Internet. One of the best places to learn about the Internet is on the Internet. Dozens of authoritative Web sites provide information on the history of the Internet and technical issues, as well as tutorials for using the Web, Internet software, and more. To find more basic information about the Internet, visit these Web sites:

   >> **Webmonkey Guides.** http://www.hotwired.lycos.com/webmonkey/guides
   >> **Newbie.** http://www.newbie.org
   >> **Internet 101.** http://www.internet101.org

2. Master your browser. Following the directions given earlier in this chapter, launch your Web browser and open its Help window. Search for help on each of the following topics and then read the information you find. Your instructor may ask you to demonstrate one or more of these tasks after you learn about it:

   >> Changing your browser's start page.
   >> Printing a Web page.
   >> Saving information from a Web page.
   >> Customizing your browser's toolbar.
   >> Turning Web page graphics off and on.

3. Set up a free e-mail account. Even if you don't have an ISP account, you can still send and receive e-mail if you can use a computer with access to the World Wide Web. Visit the following sites to learn more about free e-mail accounts. Pick a provider and then follow the directions on that site to set up an account. Remember to write down your user name and password, and then exchange an e-mail message with someone in your class.

   >> **Hotmail.** http://www.hotmail.com
   >> **Mail.com.** http://www.mail.com
   >> **E-Mail.com.** http://www.email.com
   >> **Yahoo!** http://mail.yahoo.com

Discussion Questions

As directed by your instructor, discuss the following questions in class or in groups.

1. Despite the promise that the Internet will someday be as universal as radio and television, how do you feel about the growing "commercialization" of the Internet? Do you think the motive to use the Internet as a vehicle for profit will have a negative or positive effect on it as a source of information?

2. What is your view of the Internet's value to individual people? How important do you think the Internet is in the daily life of average people? For example, could you live without Internet access and enjoy the same quality of life you enjoy today?

Research and Report

Using your own choice of resources (such as the Internet, books, magazines, and newspaper articles), research and write a short paper discussing one of the following topics:

» The Internet's growth.

» A survey of the costs of ISP accounts in your area.

» The dangers of using Internet chatrooms and instant messaging.

When you are finished, proofread and print your paper and give it to your instructor.

ETHICAL ISSUES

Despite all the conveniences it offers, the Internet is filled with pitfalls. With this thought in mind, discuss the following questions in class.

1. People can do many things online, and Web designers, Internet marketers, ISPs, and other companies encourage us to use the Internet as much as possible, for any reason. But can Internet use be bad? At what point do we become too dependent on the Internet? At what point does Internet use interfere with our normal routines, instead of enhancing them?

2. Imagine that a large company, such as a bank, discovers that several of its employees are using the company network to view pornography on the Web. These workers also are using the company's e-mail system to exchange images with one another and with people outside the company. In your view, what should the company do about such behavior? Is firing the employees too harsh a punishment? Support your position.

Computing Keynotes

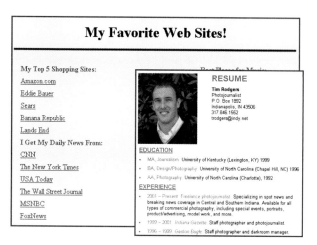

With the right tools, you can create simple Web pages—such as a list of your favorite links or a basic resume—in a snap.

Visit http://www.microsoft.com/frontpage/ for more information about FrontPage or to download a trial copy.

If you have put off creating a Web page because you think it's a long or difficult process, think again. Web design can be very easy, especially if you just want to build a simple personal Web page or a basic noncommerce Web site. Creating and publishing Web content is straightforward and does not have to be any more difficult than creating any other kind of digital document. You just need to understand the process.

Choosing Your Design Tools

When you set out to create a Web site, your first challenge is deciding which tools to use. Luckily, there are many Web design programs that let you create a site without mastering HTML or learning a scripting language. This means that you can design and lay out your pages as if you were using a word processing program; the software handles all the coding and formatting chores "behind the scenes," so you don't have to do it yourself. If you are enthusiastic about creating Web content but prefer to avoid a steep learning curve, these programs offer the easiest route to follow.

To that end, this *Computing Keynote* feature shows you how to create a Web page using Microsoft FrontPage—a popular Web page design program. Because FrontPage is intuitive and easy to use, it is a good choice for the first-time Web designer. What is more, it comes with templates that simplify the page-creation process. If you have Microsoft Office, then you may already have a copy of FrontPage installed on your PC. If not, you can get a trial copy of FrontPage by visiting Microsoft's Web site at http://www.microsoft.com/frontpage.

Of course, there are many other popular and easy-to-use Web design programs. The most popular programs for novice

designers work in much the same manner as FrontPage, by doing the "grunt work" of HTML coding automatically. You work in a graphical user interface, which lets you create text, import graphics, and format pages by clicking icons and menus. All of these programs, like FrontPage, also let you view and edit the HTML codes yourself, if you want to, and some offer detailed tutorials on the basics of HTML and Web-page design.

Some other popular Web design programs are

>> NetObjects Fusion, from Website Pros, Inc. For more information, visit http://www.netobjects.com.

>> Dreamweaver MX, from Macromedia, Inc. For more information, visit http://www.macromedia.com.

>> GoLive CS, from Adobe Systems, Inc. For more information, visit http://www.adobe.com.

If you want to add graphics to your Web page, you will need a graphics-editing program. A professional tool such as Adobe Photoshop can be used, or you can choose from a variety of affordable yet feature-rich graphics programs. Four low-cost favorites include the following:

>> Paint Shop Pro, from Jasc, Inc. For more information, visit http://www.jasc.com.

>> Fireworks MX, from Macromedia, Inc. For more information, visit http://www.macromedia.com.

>> LView Pro, from MMedia Research Corp. For more information, visit http://www.lview.com.

>> The GIMP, from The Free Software Foundation. For more information, visit http://www.gimp.org.

:: Graphics products like Paint Shop Pro offer professional imaging tools that are simple enough for beginners to master quickly.

Planning Your Page or Site

Before you design anything, you need to determine what your Web page (or site, if you want to publish several pages) is going to be about. For example, you may want to publish information about yourself or your family. Or you might want to create a page or small site for an organization, such as a synagogue, club, neighborhood association, or community center.

It is important to know each page's main topic before you start. The topic will help you decide what kind of information to prepare, and it will also help you keep the contents focused. Otherwise, visitors will quickly lose interest and leave your site. You need to engage your visitors right away and let them know why they should stay on your site, reading your content and visiting any other pages within the site.

Organizing Text The next step in planning is to arrange your site's information into sensible categories. Whether you are designing a single page or a site with many pages, you should organize your thoughts in order to help the site's visitors understand what you are trying to do. Get out a piece of paper and start organizing your ideas.

Some common topics for a personal page or site include the following:

>> About You (or your organization)
>> Photo Album
>> Friends and Family
>> Poems and Stories
>> Favorite Links
>> Resume

Be careful here, because many pages suffer from the "Too Much Stuff" syndrome. Clutter can turn visitors off. The best way to avoid this problem is to look carefully at the way you have organized the information you would like to have on your page. Keep written content short and to the point. If you have a lot of written content, such as information about your organization, break up the information by using headers and lists. This makes the information easier to read and more interesting.

Planning for Graphical Appeal Of course, a Web page can have much more than just words on it! You will want to create your own graphics or find suitable graphics for your Web site from popular graphic repositories.

Importing Graphics Graphics—such as scanned drawings or digital photos—can add a touch of your own personality and talent to your pages. To import graphics, you will need a graphics program, as mentioned earlier, as well

:: If your site is small, you can draw a basic layout on paper, as shown here. At this stage of the process you do not need too much detail; you just need an idea of the major topic or topics you want to include. And remember—limit your site to one topic per page.

CONTINUED >>>

If you have a scanner, you can use it to digitize your own snapshots or illustrations. However, you should not scan published images (such as photographs from a magazine), because they are protected by copyright law.

as the software that came with your scanner and/or digital camera.

If you want to import photos from your digital camera into your imaging software, you may need to resize them or touch them up to make them more suitable for Web use. Read the documentation that came with your digital camera and your image-editing program to learn about resizing, cropping, changing colors, and dealing with imperfections (such as "red eye" or poor lighting).

Scanning images demands a little more attention. If you scan your work improperly, the results will be disappointing. Follow these tips for successful scanning:

>> Clean your scanner's surface and the items to be scanned. Check your scanner's documentation for the best way to clean your scanner. To clean photos and art work, use canned air—available at most office and art supply stores—to blast away smudges and dust.

>> Scan and save your image files at 72 DPI (dots per inch), which is the standard resolution for images on the Web. If your images are fairly detailed or colorful, save them in JPEG (JPG) format; this format works best for photographs. If images do not have a lot of detail or contain only a few colors, save them in GIF format; this format works best for drawings and items such as backgrounds and buttons. You can find resolution settings and file formats in your imaging software.

>> Use your imaging software to crop and refine the scanned image.

Web graphics should be attractive, but it's just as important that they download quickly to the visitor's browser. This

means keeping your graphics at a reasonable size and resolution. What's reasonable? That depends on a lot of factors, but if an image is too large to fit on a single screen at 800 × 600 resolution without scrolling, or if it takes more than three or four seconds to download, then it's too large. There are no hard-and-fast rules for setting image sizes or resolutions, and you can find images of all sizes and quality on the Web. Generally speaking, however, smaller is better. Size your images so they look attractive on the page and work in harmony with other elements. Also, if you use an up-to-date version of an HTML editor such as FrontPage, the program can tell you how long your page will take to download over a standard modem connection. Pay attention to this information and use it as a guide to make sure that your pages aren't too big to download quickly. If you do not know how to work with Web graphics, you can learn from many helpful tutorials available online. One good place to start is Internet Eye's Paint Shop Pro Resources page, at http://the-internet-eye.com/resources/psp.htm. It provides articles and links to many other graphics-related sites.

Finding Graphics Online If you want to use clip art, photos, and animations—but you are not an artist—you may find free or inexpensive resources to use for your page by visiting these Web sites:

>> Barry's Clipart Server (http://www.barrysclipart.com) serves up a great big helping of clip art, animated GIFs, related links, and helpful software.

>> Jupiterimages (http://www.jupiterimages.com) is a clearinghouse of art, design samples and galleries, tuto-

Web sites like the Paint Shop Pro User Group Help Forum (at http://www.enigmasource.com/cgi-bin/pspizbeta2/pspug1.cgi) can help you learn how to add graphics to your Web site.

Look for license or usage agreements before you download an image from a clip-art service. This agreement appears on Barry's Clipart Server.

rials, and services for designers of all types and ability levels. The site features links to many other sites, where you can find graphics resources for your Web site. Some are free, others require a membership.

Before you download any kind of image from a Web site (or any other online source), however, be sure to read the licensing or usage agreement that governs its use. Reputable online clip-art services post these agreements on their Web sites, so you cannot miss them. Even free images can have some usage restrictions; for example, the image's owner may require you to acknowledge the owner or artist on your site or get written permission before you use the graphic.

You will find more information about borrowing images, text, and HTML code from other Web sites in the section titled "Web Content and Intellectual Property Rights," at the end of this *Computing Keynote*.

Building Your Site

So you have gathered your tools, organized your ideas, and gotten up to speed with Web graphics. Now it is time to roll up your sleeves and start building your Web site.

Start by launching FrontPage. To do this, open the Start menu, and then open the Programs menu (or the All Programs menu, if you use Windows XP). When you launch FrontPage, it creates a folder on your PC called My Webs. This folder contains a subfolder called Images. Before going any further, open Windows Explorer or My Computer and move all your images into the Images subfolder.

Now it is time to actually create a site, step by step.

Selecting a Template Since your goal is to create a site right away, you will work with a template and modify it to suit your needs. Follow these steps to select the template in FrontPage:

1. Open the File menu, click New | Page or Web. The New Page or Web task pane appears.

2. On the task pane, click Page Templates. The Page Templates dialog box opens.

3. In the dialog box, click the General tab, if necessary. Click the One-Column Body with Two Sidebars icon, and then click OK. The layout appears in FrontPage.

4. Open the File menu and click Save As. The Save As dialog box appears. Here, you need to do three things:

   a. Click the CHANGE TITLE button next to the Page title. When the Set Page Title dialog box appears, give the page a suitable title, such as Tiny Dancers' Home Page. Click OK to return to the Save As dialog box.

   b. Give the file a name, and then click SAVE. (If this is the site's first page, name it INDEX or HOME. The word *Index* is often used for a site's opening page because this page usually contains a list—or index—of links to other pages in the site.) The dialog box closes and FrontPage saves the file in the My Webs folder.

   c. Because this layout includes a picture, FrontPage displays the Save Embedded Files dialog box. For now, click OK. You'll replace the sample picture later.

Adding an Image Next, replace the placeholder image (on the right side of the page) with one of your own images:

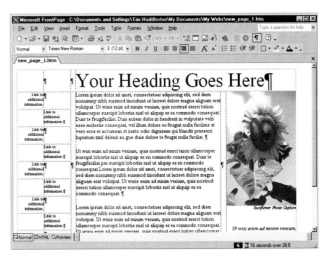

Using a FrontPage template to create an attractive home page.

CONTINUED >>>

Saving your first Web page, with a file name and a title.

Adding an image to a Web page.

1. Click the existing image and then right-click it. When the shortcut menu opens, click Cut. The image disappears from the template. Leave the cursor where it is.

2. Open the Insert menu, click Picture, and then click From File. The Picture dialog box appears. Navigate to the Images subfolder, if necessary, and then open the subfolder by double-clicking it.

3. When the Images subfolder opens, click the image you want to use. Click INSERT. The picture is now inserted into your design.

4. To change the picture caption, select the old text (by dragging across it with the mouse pointer) and type your own caption in its place.

Modifying a Heading and Adding Content Now you are ready to fill in all the template's text areas with your custom information:

1. To modify the heading, select it and type your new heading.

2. To add content to the main section, find the text you would like to use, and then copy and paste it right over the placeholder text. Or you can delete the placeholder text and type your own text in its place.

3. Continue replacing the placeholder text until you're happy with the results. You can modify font styles and sizes by using FrontPage's tools. Be careful to use these features lightly because using too many fonts and sizes can make reading difficult.

Adding Pages and Linking to Them Links are the most important part of a Web page. Luckily, the template you are using allows for a number of links. If you want to add other pages to your site—and the page you created

earlier is the site's index page—then you will probably want to add lines of text to this page and format them as hyperlinks that lead to the other pages. Here's how to do that:

1. To add new pages, follow the same steps you used earlier for working with the template. Be sure to name your files (they will be empty until you wish to edit them later) and save them in the My Web folder.

2. In the index page, highlight the placeholder text where you would like to add the link and rename the link as is appropriate for your needs. Then select the text.

3. Open the Insert menu and then click Hyperlink. The Insert Hyperlink dialog appears.

4. Select the page to which you want to link by clicking its name. Click OK.

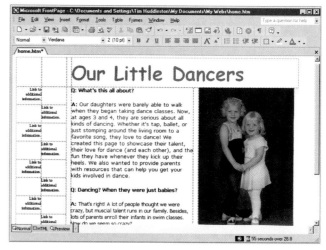

The template with a new image, heading, and content in place. Here, notice that the text is formatted differently than in the template.

Creating a hyperlink to another page on your site.

Continue adding links until you have added all the links you require. Save the page so your changes are updated. When you have finished (or whenever you want to see how your page will look online), you can click the Preview tab. Alternatively, if you prefer to see your page in an actual Web browser, open the File menu, and then click Preview in Browser.

Of course, there are many other modifications and additions you can make to this document, but you are off to a great start.

Web Design Tips

No matter what kind of content your Web page or site contains, you want it to look great. Just as important, you want your site's visitors to find your content easy to read and navigate. You can accomplish these goals and avoid common Web design pitfalls by following these tips:

» Use bold and italic sparingly. Bold and italic effects actually make text harder to read. Use bold and italic for emphasis only.

» Be sure to properly align body text. Centered body text (that is, paragraphs of body text centered between the margins, usually with "ragged" left and right edges) can be hard to read. It is better to adjust your margins than to center body text. You can center headers, footers, and accent text.

» Use a plain background that will not interfere with your text. Don't use complicated backgrounds (such as patterns or textures). Plain backgrounds are almost always best with any text.

» Use contrasting colors for backgrounds, text, and links. The higher the contrast, the better the readability. White text on a yellow background is just annoying.

» Keep body text at its default size.

» Look carefully at your page. Is there anything on it that is unnecessary? If so, get rid of it!

» Unless you update your pages regularly, do not post the date on which the page was last updated, and do not put time-sensitive information on it. If you are offering Christmas greetings to your visitors in July, for example, they will think your whole site is stale!

» Never put your home address or home phone number on a Web page, and always think carefully before putting very personal information on a page.

Finding a Host for Your Web Site

Once your page or site is ready to go, you will want to publish it online. This means finding a "host"—a person or company with a server computer that stores Web pages. A wide range of Web hosting options are available.

If you already have an account with an Internet service provider (ISP), you may have some free Web space available as part of your account. Check with your provider to see if this is true, and ask how to access your area on the ISP's Web server.

If your ISP does not provide Web space, there are plenty of other hosting options. The most popular options for enthusiasts are free hosting services and low-cost services.

Free Hosting Services   Free services can be a terrific option if you are just starting out. The big problem with using a free service, however, is that you may have no control over the advertisements that the service uses. This means your site might display pop-up advertisements (which "pop

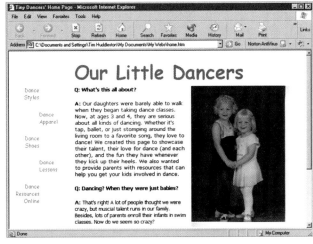

The final results: a simple but attractive home page, shown here in Microsoft Internet Explorer.

CONTINUED >>>

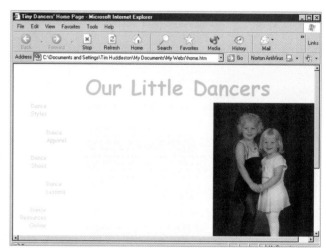

Complex backgrounds and poorly contrasting color schemes can make your Web pages hard to read.

up" in a small browser window) or banner ads (which appear as part of your page, in the form of a banner). This is the price you pay for the free hosting.

Some free hosting services include

>> **Free Servers.** This service offers ad-supported free Web hosting. If you upgrade to Free Servers' premium pay service, you can get rid of the advertising. For information, visit http://www.freeservers.com.

>> **FortuneCity.** Another service with ad-supported free home page publishing. There are low-cost and flex options as well, should you decide to upgrade. Visit http://www.fortunecity.com for information.

>> **AngelFire.** Particularly popular among young Web designers, AngelFire offers a variety of services including ways to connect to other home pages with similar interests. The service is free if you accept the display of advertisements on your page, and low-cost options are also available. To learn more, visit http://www.angelfire.lycos.com.

Fee-Based Hosting Services When you pay for hosting services, you can expect to receive other services along with storage for your Web site. Some fee-based hosts provide e-mail accounts, or even the ability to host your own domain name (such as www.yourname.com). Your choice of service depends on what you want to do and how much you can afford. Some pay services include the following:

>> **Hosting.Com.** This company offers a wide range of services to meet all kinds of needs from beginning to high-end professional. For information, visit http://www.hosting.com.

>> **Cedant Web Hosting.** Cedant provides a variety of services, ranging from low to medium cost. To learn more, visit http://www.cedant.com.

>> **TopHosts.com.** This portal site can help you find the best hosting service for you. Visit http://www.tophosts.com.

When you set up an account with a Web host, the service will set aside server space for your Web pages, and you will create a user name and password that allow you to access that space and store your content there. The next step is to publish your site.

Publishing Your Site

With your logon information to your Web host at the ready, you are prepared to publish.

Publishing your pages to a Web server requires you to have some form of file transfer software. If you create your site in FrontPage, open the File menu, then click Publish Web. A set of steps will appear, telling you how to publish your Web content to your host's server.

If you decide not to use FrontPage, or if you want to use a different means of transferring files, you need to use FTP client software. This type of program uses the File Transfer Protocol (FTP) to transfer your files over the Internet to the host's computer. Two very popular FTP client programs are WS_FTP (http://www.wsftp.com) and CuteFTP (http://www.cuteftp.com).

Additional Resources on Web Design

Building professional Web sites is quite different than creating personal sites. The reasons are many, but usually have to do with the amount of technology that must be learned

Publishing Web content with FrontPage.

in order to effectively create the many layers of complexity that today's professional sites entail.

There are many technologies and standards emerging, and as a result, the way professionals are working today is much different than the way an enthusiast will work. Still, the idea is essentially the same: create content and publish it on the Web.

If the process of creating a Web page excites you, and if you would like to learn more about professional Web design and development, consider a visit to these sites to see what a variety of resources are available to you.

>> The World Wide Web Consortium (W3C).
   http://www.w3.org

>> The HTML Writers Guild. http://www.hwg.org

>> WebReference.com. http://www.webreference.com

>> Webmonkey.com. http://hotwired.lycos.com/webmonkey

>> A List Apart. http://www.alistapart.com

>> Digital Web Magazine. http://www.digital-web.com

>> The Web Developer's Virtual Library.
   http://www.wdvl.com

>> Builder.com. http://www.builder.com

Web Content and Intellectual Property Rights

A lot of information sharing happens on the Web, but it is not always OK to use an item you happen to find online; you could be breaking the law. If you are not sure whether you should use a graphic, text, or code you find on a Web site, check the following list of questions and answers:

1. Can I swipe HTML code from a Web site I like?

   While many people use their browser's View Source feature to look at the way code is written, it is not necessarily helpful to simply swipe it! Be inspired by it, use it as an example to learn from, but do not just take it. Even though HTML code itself cannot be copyrighted, you should either learn how to work with it or use software that generates it for you.

2. Is it OK to "borrow" a graphic from someone else's page?

   Without express permission from the image's owner, you should not put other people's work on your Web site. Learn to create your own graphics, or use graphics that are royalty-free, such as those available from the Web sites mentioned earlier in this article.

3. Can I put quotes from articles, books, movies, and other sources on my page?

   If you use one paragraph or less, place it in quotes, and clearly state the source, you are following the general rules of what is known as "fair use." Be cautious and fair, however. Anything more than a paragraph can be considered infringement of copyright, and if you use someone else's work without referencing the source, you are guilty of plagiarism! Stay safe and honest—always ask for permission before using materials that are likely to be copyrighted.

It is also a good idea to protect your own work. If you have original art, writing, and music on your pages, it is a good idea to copyright it. You can learn more about copyright with a visit to these sites:

>> The United States Copyright Office. http://www.copyright.gov

>> The Canadian Intellectual Property Office.
   http://cipo.gc.ca

>> Ten Big Myths About Copyright Explained.
   http://www.templetons.com/brad/copymyths.html

>> An Intellectual Property Law Primer for Multimedia and Web Developers. http://www.eff.org/pub/CAF/law/ip-primer

CHAPTER

Computing Alone and in Groups

CHAPTER CONTENTS ::

This chapter contains the following lessons:

Lesson **3A:**
Transforming Data into Information

>> How Computers Represent Data
>> How Computers Process Data
>> Factors Affecting Processing Speed
>> A Look inside the Processor
>> Microcomputer Processors
>> Extending the Processor's Power to Other Devices
>> Storage Devices

Lesson **3B:**
Networking Basics

>> The Uses of a Network
>> Common Types of Networks
>> Hybrid Networks
>> How Networks Are Structured
>> Network Topologies and Protocols

01 02 03 04 05 06 07 08 09 10 11 12 13 14

Transforming Data into Information

Overview: The Process of Processing Data

It often seems as though computers must understand us because we understand the information they produce. However, computers cannot understand anything. Computers recognize two distinct physical states produced by electricity, magnetic polarity, or reflected light. Essentially, they understand whether a switch is on or off.

In fact, the CPU, which acts like the "brain" of the computer, consists of several million tiny electronic switches, called transistors. A computer appears to understand information only because it operates at such phenomenal speeds, grouping its individual on/off switches into patterns that become meaningful to us.

This lesson takes you deep inside the personal computer to show you how it processes data, stores it, and moves it from one component to another.

OBJECTIVES ::

>> Explain why computers use the binary number system.

>> Identify the two main parts of the CPU and explain how they work together.

>> List three hardware factors that affect processing speed.

>> Name the best-known families of CPUs.

>> Identify four connections used to attach devices to a PC.

>> List at least three types of magnetic storage device and four types of optical storage device.

Norton
ONLINE

For more information on number systems, visit

http://www.mhhe.com/peternorton.

FIGURE 3A.1

These 1s and 0s represent a sentence. The decimal system uses 10 symbols and multiple digits for the numbers 9 and higher.

H	0100 1000
e	0110 0101
r	0111 0010
e	0110 0101
	0010 0000
a	0110 0001
r	0111 0010
e	0110 0101
	0010 0000
s	0111 0011
o	0110 1111
m	0110 1101
e	0110 0101
	0010 0000
w	0111 0111
o	0110 1111
r	0111 0010
d	0110 0100
s	0111 0011
.	0010 1110

simnet™

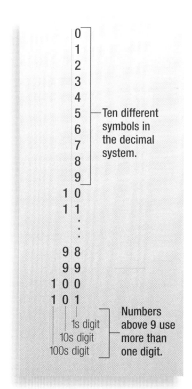

ON = 1   OFF = 0

FIGURE 3A.2

Places in the binary number system. In a computer, data is represented by the state of electronic switches. If a switch is on, it represents a 1. If a switch is off, it represents a 0.

How Computers Represent Data

As you learned in Chapter 1, computers are called "digital" because they use numbers (digits) to represent data. To do this, computers use a very simple number system. People use a number system too, but it is actually more sophisticated than the one used by computers! When you understand how computers represent data, you'll understand how they work and why they can operate so rapidly.

Number Systems

To a computer, everything is a number. Numbers are numbers; letters and punctuation marks are numbers; sounds and pictures are numbers. Even the computer's own instructions are numbers. When you see letters of the alphabet on a computer screen, you are seeing just one of the computer's ways of representing numbers. For example, consider the sentence *Here are some words*. This sentence may look like a string of alphabetic characters to you, but to a computer it looks like the string of ones and zeros shown in Figure 3A.1.

Computer data looks especially strange because people normally use base 10 to represent numbers. The decimal number system (*deci* means "10" in Latin) is called "base 10" because 10 symbols are available: 0, 1, 2, 3, 4, 5, 6, 7, 8, and 9. When you need to represent a number greater than 9, you use two symbols together, as in 9 + 1 = 10. Each symbol in a number is called a "digit," so 10 is a two-digit number. To build all the two-digit numbers (10–99) in the decimal number system, you use up all the possible pairings of the system's 10 symbols. After all 90 of the two-digit numbers are built, then you begin using three-digit numbers (100–999), and so on. This pattern can continue indefinitely, using only the 10 symbols you started with.

In a computer, however, all data is represented by the state of the computer's electronic switches. A switch has only two possible states—on and off—so it can represent only two numeric values. To a computer, when a switch is off, it represents a 0; when a switch is on, it represents a 1 (see Figure 3A.2). Because there are only two values, computers are said to function in base 2, which is known as the binary number system (*bi* means "2" in Latin).

When a computer needs to represent a quantity greater than one, it does the same thing you do when you need to represent a quantity greater than nine: it uses two (or more) digits.

Bits and Bytes

When referring to computerized data, the value represented by each switch's state—whether the switch is turned on or off—is called a bit (a combination of *binary digit*). A bit is the smallest possible unit of data a computer can recognize or use. To represent anything meaningful (in other words, to convey information), the computer uses bits in groups.

Figure 3A.1 text within figure:

0	
1	
2	
3	
4	
5	Ten different symbols in the decimal system.
6	
7	
8	
9	
1 0	
1 1	
. . .	
9 8	
9 9	
1 0 0	
1 0 1	

1s digit / 10s digit / 100s digit — Numbers above 9 use more than one digit.

1 bit

ON | OFF | ON | ON | OFF | OFF | ON | OFF

8 bits = 1 byte

FIGURE 3A.3

One byte is composed of eight bits. A nibble is four bits.

A group of eight bits is called a byte (see Figure 3A.3). Half of a byte is called a nibble. With one byte, the computer can represent one of 256 different symbols or characters because the eight 1s and 0s in a byte can be combined in 256 different ways.

The byte is an extremely important unit because there are enough different eight-bit combinations to represent all the characters on the keyboard, including all the letters (uppercase and lowercase), numbers, punctuation marks, and other symbols. If you look back at Figure 3A.1, you will notice that each of the characters (or letters) in the sentence *Here are some words.* is represented by one byte (eight bits) of data.

Text Codes

Early programmers realized that they needed a standard text code that was agreeable to all of them. In this system, the numbers represented the letters of the alphabet, punctuation marks, and other symbols. This standard code system would enable any programmer or program to use the same combinations of numbers to represent the same individual pieces of data. The four most popular text code systems invented are the following:

>> **EBCDIC** EBCDIC (pronounced EB-si-dic) stands for Extended Binary Coded Decimal Interchange Code. EBCDIC is an eight-bit code that defines 256 symbols. It is still used in IBM mainframe and midrange systems, but it is rarely encountered in PCs.

>> **ASCII** ASCII (pronounced AS-key) stands for the American Standard Code for Information Interchange. Today, the ASCII character set is by far the most commonly used in computers of all types. Table 3A.1 shows the 128 ASCII codes. ASCII is an eight-bit code that specifies characters for values from 0 to 127.

>> **Extended ASCII** Extended ASCII is an eight-bit code that specifies the characters for values from 128 to 255. The first 40 symbols represent pronunciation and special punctuation. The remaining symbols are graphic symbols.

>> **Unicode** The Unicode Worldwide Character Standard provides up to four bytes—32 bits—to represent each letter, number, or symbol. With four bytes, enough Unicode codes can be created to represent more than 4 billion different characters or symbols. This total is enough for every unique character and symbol in the world, including the vast Chinese, Korean, and Japanese character sets and those found in known classical and historical texts. In addition to world letters, special mathematical and scientific symbols are represented in Unicode. One major advantage that Unicode has over other text code systems is its compatibility with ASCII codes. The first 256 codes in Unicode are identical to the 256 codes used by the ASCII and Extended ASCII systems.

Norton
ONLINE

For more information on text codes, visit
http://www.mhhe.com/ peternorton.

ASCII Codes

ASCII Code	Decimal Equivalent	Character	ASCII Code	Decimal Equivalent	Character	ASCII Code	Decimal Equivalent	Character
0000 0000	0	Null prompt	0010 1011	43	+	0101 0110	86	V
0000 0001	1	Start of heading	0010 1100	44	,	0101 0111	87	W
0000 0010	2	Start of text	0010 1101	45	-	0101 1000	88	X
0000 0011	3	End of text	0010 1110	46	.	0101 1001	89	Y
0000 0100	4	End of transmit	0010 1111	47	/	0101 1010	90	Z
0000 0101	5	Enquiry	0011 0000	48	0	0101 1011	91	[
0000 0110	6	Acknowledge	0011 0001	49	1	0101 1100	92	\
0000 0111	7	Audible bell	0011 0010	50	2	0101 1101	93	]
0000 1000	8	Backspace	0011 0011	51	3	0101 1110	94	^
0000 1001	9	Horizontal tab	0011 0100	52	4	0101 1111	95	_
0000 1010	10	Line feed	0011 0101	53	5	0110 0000	96	`
0000 1011	11	Vertical tab	0011 0110	54	6	0110 0001	97	a
0000 1100	12	Form feed	0011 0111	55	7	0110 0010	98	b
0000 1101	13	Carriage return	0011 1000	56	8	0110 0011	99	c
0000 1110	14	Shift out	0011 1001	57	9	0110 0100	100	d
0000 1111	15	Shift in	0011 1010	58	:	0110 0101	101	e
0001 0000	16	Data link escape	0011 1011	59	;	0110 0110	102	f
0001 0001	17	Device control 1	0011 1100	60	<	0110 0111	103	g
0001 0010	18	Device control 2	0011 1101	61	=	0110 1000	104	h
0001 0011	19	Device control 3	0011 1110	62	>	0110 1001	105	i
0001 0100	20	Device control 4	0011 1111	63	?	0110 1010	106	j
0001 0101	21	Neg. acknowledge	0100 0000	64	@	0110 1011	107	k
0001 0110	22	Synchronous idle	0100 0001	65	A	0110 1100	108	l
0001 0111	23	End trans. block	0100 0010	66	B	0110 1101	109	m
0001 1000	24	Cancel	0100 0011	67	C	0110 1110	110	n
0001 1001	25	End of medium	0100 0100	68	D	0110 1111	111	o
0001 1010	26	Substitution	0100 0101	69	E	0111 0000	112	p
0001 1011	27	Escape	0100 0110	70	F	0111 0001	113	q
0001 1100	28	File separator	0100 0111	71	G	0111 0010	114	r
0001 1101	29	Group separator	0100 1000	72	H	0111 0011	115	s
0001 1110	30	Record separator	0100 1001	73	I	0111 0100	116	t
0001 1111	31	Unit separator	0100 1010	74	J	0111 0101	117	u
0010 0000	32	Blank space	0100 1011	75	K	0111 0110	118	v
0010 0001	33	!	0100 1100	76	L	0111 0111	119	w
0010 0010	34	"	0100 1101	77	M	0111 1000	120	x
0010 0011	35	#	0100 1110	78	N	0111 1001	121	y
0010 0100	36	$	0100 1111	79	O	0111 1010	122	z
0010 0101	37	%	0101 0000	80	P	0111 1011	123	{
0010 0110	38	&	0101 0001	81	Q	0111 1100	124		
0010 0111	39	'	0101 0010	82	R	0111 1101	125	}
0010 1000	40	(	0101 0011	83	S	0111 1110	126	~
0010 1001	41	)	0101 0100	84	T	0111 1111	127	Delete or rubout
0010 1010	42	*	0101 0101	85	U			

How Computers Process Data

Two components handle processing in a computer: the central processing unit, or CPU, and the memory. Both are located on the computer's motherboard (see Figure 3A.4), the circuit board that connects the CPU to the other hardware devices.

The CPU

The CPU is the "brain" of the computer, the place where data is manipulated. In large computer systems, such as supercomputers and mainframes, processing tasks may be handled by multiple processing chips. (Some powerful computer systems use hundreds or even thousands of processing units.) In the average microcomputer, the entire CPU is a single unit, called a microprocessor.

Most microprocessors are single chips mounted on a piece of plastic with metal wires attached to it. Some newer microprocessors include multiple chips and are encased in their own cover, which fits into a special socket on the motherboard. Regardless of its construction, every CPU has at least two basic parts: the control unit and the arithmetic logic unit.

All the computer's resources are managed from the control unit. Think of the control unit as a traffic signal directing the flow of data through the CPU, as well as to and from other devices. The control unit is the logical hub of the computer.

The CPU's instructions for carrying out commands are built into the control unit. The instructions, or instruction set, list all the operations that the CPU can perform. Each instruction in the instruction set is expressed in microcode—a series of basic directions that tell the CPU how to execute more complex operations.

Because all computer data is stored as numbers, much of the processing that takes place involves comparing numbers or carrying out mathematical operations. In addition to establishing ordered sequences and changing those sequences, the computer can perform two types of operations: arithmetic operations and logical operations. Arithmetic operations include addition, subtraction, multiplication, and division. Logical operations include comparisons such as determining whether one number is equal to, greater than, or less than another number. Also, every logical operation has an opposite. For example, in addition to "equal to" there is "not equal to." Table 3A.2 shows the symbols for all the arithmetic and logical operations.

Many instructions carried out by the control unit involve simply moving data from one place to another—from memory to storage, from memory to the printer, and so forth. When the control unit encounters an instruction that involves arithmetic or logic, however, it passes that instruction to the second component of the CPU, the arithmetic logic unit, or ALU. The ALU actually performs the arithmetic and logical operations described earlier.

The ALU includes a group of registers—high-speed memory locations built directly into the CPU that are used to hold the data currently being processed. You can think of the register as

FIGURE 3A.4

Processing devices.

For more information on CPUs, visit **http://www.mhhe.com/ peternorton**.

TABLE 3A.2

Operations Performed by the Arithmetic Logic Unit

Arithmetic Operations		Logical Operations	
+	add	=, ≠	equal to, not equal to
−	subtract	>, ≯	greater than, not greater than
×	multiply	<, ≮	less than, not less than
÷	divide	≧, ≩	greater than or equal to, not greater than or equal to
∧	raise by a power	≦, ≨	less than or equal to, not less than or equal to

a scratchpad. The ALU will use the register to hold the data currently being used for a calculation. For example, the control unit might load two numbers from memory into the registers. Then it might tell the ALU to divide the two numbers (an arithmetic operation) or to see whether the numbers are equal (a logical operation). The answer to this calculation is stored in another register before being sent out of the CPU.

Memory

The CPU contains the basic instructions needed to operate the computer, but it cannot store entire programs or large sets of data permanently. The CPU needs to have millions (or even trillions, in some computers) of bytes of space where it can quickly read or write programs and data while they are being used. This area is called memory, and it consists of chips either on the motherboard or on a small circuit board attached to the motherboard. This electronic memory allows the CPU to store and retrieve data quickly.

There are two types of built-in memory: permanent and nonpermanent (see Figure 3A.5). Some memory chips retain the data they hold, even when the computer is turned off. This type of permanent memory is called nonvolatile. Other chips—in fact, most of the memory in a microcomputer—lose their contents when the computer's power is shut off. Nonpermanent memory is called volatile.

FIGURE 3A.5

The CPU is attached to two kinds of memory: RAM, which is volatile, and ROM, which is nonvolatile.

Nonvolatile Memory

Nonvolatile chips hold data even when the computer is unplugged. In fact, putting data permanently into this kind of memory is called "burning in the data," and it is usually done at the factory. During normal use, the data in these chips is only read and used—not changed—so the memory is called read-only memory.

When a computer is turned on, it must know how to start. ROM contains a set of start-up instructions called the basic input output system (BIOS) for a computer. In addition to booting the machine, BIOS contains another set of routines, which ensure that the system is functioning properly and all expected hardware devices are present. This routine is called the power on self test (POST).

Flash Memory

Flash memory is a special type of nonvolatile memory. It is often used in portable digital devices for storage. Digital cameras, portable MP3 players, USB "key-chain" storage devices, and game consoles all use flash memory. The flash memory works by having actual switches store the binary values that make up the data. Thus, on a camera with a flash card, the picture is stored on the card by turning millions of tiny switches on and off. The card can store the picture indefinitely. Figure 3A.6 shows a typical flash memory card.

FIGURE 3A.6

A 512MB CompactFlash card for a digital camera.

Volatile Memory

Volatile memory requires power to store data. The volatile memory in a computer is called random access memory (RAM). When people talk about computer memory in connection with microcomputers, they usually mean the RAM. RAM's job is to hold programs and data while they are in use. Physically, RAM consists of chips on a small circuit board (see Figure 3A.7). Single in-line memory module (SIMM) and dual in-line memory module (DIMM) chips are found in desktop

FIGURE 3A.7

In modern personal computers, RAM chips are either DIMM or SO-DIMM chips.

computers, while the smaller, small outline DIMM (SO-DIMM) chips are found in laptop computers.

RAM is designed to be instantly accessible by the CPU or programs. The "random" in RAM implies that any portion of RAM can be accessed at any time. This helps make RAM very fast. Without the random abilities of RAM, the computer would be very slow.

A computer does not have to search its entire memory each time it needs to find data because the CPU uses a memory address to store and retrieve each piece of data. A memory address is a number that indicates a location on the memory chips, just as a post office box number indicates a slot into which mail is placed. Memory addresses start at zero and go up to one less than the number of bytes of memory in the computer.

Factors Affecting Processing Speed

A CPU's design determines its basic speed, but other factors can make chips already designed for speed work even faster. You already have been introduced to some of these, such as the CPU's registers and memory. In this section, you will see how other factors—such as the cache memory, the clock speed, and the data bus—affect a computer's speed. Figure 3A.8 shows how these components might be arranged on the computer's motherboard.

Registers

The registers in the first PCs could hold two bytes—16 bits—each. Most CPUs sold today, for both PCs and Macintosh computers, have 32-bit registers. Many newer PCs, as well as minicomputers and high-end workstations, have 64-bit registers.

Norton
ONLINE

For more information on processing speeds, visit **http://www.mhhe.com/ peternorton**.

FIGURE 3A.8

Devices affecting processing speed.

Motherboard

Data bus

RAM

Cache

Clock

CPU

ROM

The size of the registers, which is sometimes called the word size, indicates the amount of data with which the computer can work at any given time. The bigger the word size, the more quickly the computer can process a set of data. Occasionally, you will hear people refer to "32-bit processors" or "64-bit processors" or even "64-bit computers." This terminology refers to the size of the registers in the processor. If all other factors are kept equal, a CPU with 32-bit registers can process data twice as fast as one with 16-bit registers.

Memory and Computing Power

The amount of RAM in a computer can have a profound effect on the computer's power. More RAM means the computer can use bigger, more powerful programs, and those programs can access bigger data files.

More RAM also can make the computer run faster. The computer does not necessarily have to load an entire program into memory to run it. However, the greater the amount of the program that fits into memory, the faster the program runs. To run Windows, for example, the computer usually does not need to load all its files into memory to run properly; it loads only the most essential parts into memory.

When the computer needs access to other parts of an operating system or a program on the disk, it can unload, or swap out, nonessential parts from RAM to the hard disk. Then the computer can load, or swap in, the program code or data it needs. While this is an effective method for managing a limited amount of memory, the computer's system performance is slower because the CPU, memory, and disk are continuously occupied with the swapping process. Swapping unused portions of RAM to hard disk is known as virtual memory. As shown in Figure 3A.9,

FIGURE 3A.9

How RAM affects speed.

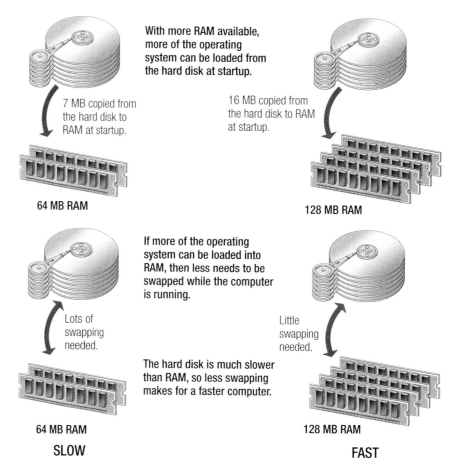

With more RAM available, more of the operating system can be loaded from the hard disk at startup.

7 MB copied from the hard disk to RAM at startup.

16 MB copied from the hard disk to RAM at startup.

64 MB RAM

128 MB RAM

If more of the operating system can be loaded into RAM, then less needs to be swapped while the computer is running.

Lots of swapping needed.

Little swapping needed.

The hard disk is much slower than RAM, so less swapping makes for a faster computer.

64 MB RAM

SLOW

128 MB RAM

FAST

if your PC has 128 MB of RAM (or more), you will notice a dramatic difference in how fast Windows runs because the CPU will need to swap program instructions between RAM and the hard disk much less often.

If you purchase a new computer system, it will probably come with at least 256 MB of RAM. Microsoft suggests 256 as the minimum recommended configuration for Windows XP. If you plan to play graphic-intensive games or develop complex graphics, you will need more RAM. The cost of upgrading the memory of a computer is very low, so upgrading RAM is the simplest and most cost-effective way to get more speed from your computer.

The Computer's Internal Clock

Every microcomputer has a system clock, but the clock's primary purpose is not to keep the time of day. Like most modern wristwatches, the clock is driven by a quartz crystal. When electricity is applied, the molecules in the crystal vibrate millions of times per second, a rate that never changes. The speed of the vibrations is determined by the thickness of the crystal. The computer uses the vibrations of the quartz in the system clock to time its processing operations.

Over the years, system clocks have become steadily faster. For example, the first PC operated at 4.77 megahertz. Hertz (Hz) is a measure of cycles per second. Megahertz (MHz) means "millions of cycles per second." Gigahertz (GHz) means "billions of cycles per second."

The computer's operating speed is tied to the speed of the system clock. For example, if a computer's clock speed is 800 MHz, it "ticks" 800 million times per second. A clock cycle is a single tick, or the time it takes to turn a transistor off and back on again. A processor can execute an instruction in a given number of clock cycles. As the system's clock speed increases, so does the number of instructions it can carry out each second.

Clock speeds of 1 GHz and higher are now common, and processor speeds are increasing rapidly. At the time this book was written, processor speeds had eclipsed 3 GHz.

The Bus

A bus is a path between the components of a computer. There are two main buses in a computer: the internal (or system) bus and the external (or expansion) bus. The system bus resides on the motherboard and connects the CPU to other devices that reside on the motherboard. An expansion bus connects external devices, such as the keyboard, mouse, modem, printer, and so on, to the CPU. Cables from disk drives and other internal devices are plugged into the bus. The system bus has two parts: the data bus and the address bus (see Figure 3A.10).

The data bus is an electrical path that connects the CPU, memory, and the other hardware devices on the motherboard. Actually, the bus is a group of parallel wires. The number of wires in the bus affects the speed at which data can travel between hardware components, just as the number of lanes on a highway affects how long it takes people to reach their destinations. Because each wire can transfer

❶ Please send the data in slot number
1001110110000100111101100101.

CPU

Address bus

RAM

Data bus

❷ OK, here it comes.
01001100

FIGURE 3A.10

The system bus includes an address bus and a data bus. The address bus leads from the CPU to RAM. The data bus connects the CPU to memory, and to all the storage, input/output, and communications devices that are attached to the motherboard.

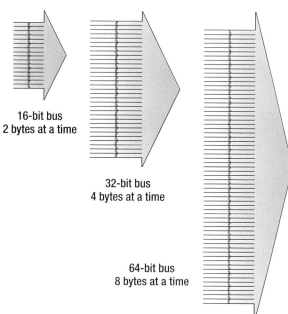

16-bit bus
2 bytes at a time

32-bit bus
4 bytes at a time

64-bit bus
8 bytes at a time

With a wider bus, the computer can move more data in the same amount of time, or the same amount of data in less time.

Requests for data are sent from the CPU to RAM along the address bus. The request consists of a memory address. The data returns to the CPU via the data bus.

one bit of data at a time, an eight-wire bus can move eight bits at a time, which is a full byte (see Figure 3A.11). A 16-bit bus can transfer two bytes, and a 32-bit bus can transfer four bytes at a time. Newer-model computers have a 64-bit data bus called the FrontSide Bus that transfers eight bytes at a time.

Like the processor, the bus's speed is measured in megahertz (MHz) because it has its own clock speed. As you would imagine, the faster a bus's clock speed, the faster it can transfer data between parts of the computer. The majority of today's PCs have a bus speed of either 100 MHz or 133 MHz, but speeds of 800 MHz and higher are becoming more common.

The bus speed is directly tied into the CPU speed. All processors use a multiplier to make the CPU run faster. Here is how it works. Consider a system bus that runs at 400 MHz supporting a 1.6 GHz processor. The fastest the CPU can talk to external devices is 400 MHz. However, internally the processor runs at 1.6 GHz, or four times the bus speed. The multiplier in this system is four. Since the processor is so much faster than the bus, the processor spends most of the time idle.

The address bus is a set of wires similar to the data bus (see Figure 3A.12). The address bus connects only the CPU and RAM and carries only memory addresses. (Remember, each byte in RAM is associated with a number, which is its memory address.)

Cache Memory

Moving data between RAM and the CPU's registers is one of the most time-consuming operations a CPU must perform, simply because RAM is much slower than the CPU. A partial solution to this problem is to include a cache memory in the CPU. Cache (pronounced *cash*) memory is similar to RAM except that it is extremely fast compared to normal memory and it is used in a different way.

Figure 3A.13 shows how cache memory works with the CPU and RAM. When a program is running and the CPU needs to read a piece of data or program instructions from RAM, the CPU checks first to see whether the data is in cache

RAM

Data bus

ROM

Address bus

Motherboard

CPU

Disk drives

FIGURE 3A.13

The cache speeds processing by storing frequently used data or instructions in its high-speed memory. External (Level-2) cache is shown here, but most computers also have memory circuitry built directly into the CPU.

memory. If the data is not there, the CPU reads the data from RAM into its registers, but it also loads a copy of the data into cache memory. The next time the CPU needs that same data, it finds it in the cache memory and saves the time needed to load the data from RAM.

Cache is present in several places in a computer. Most hard drives and network cards have cache present to speed up data access. Internet connections cache recently visited pages for quicker loading. Database utilities cache recently accessed data. Without cache, your computer would be a much slower device.

Since the late 1980s, most PC CPUs have had cache memory built into them. This CPU-resident cache is often called Level-1 (L1) cache. Today, many CPUs have as much as 256 KB built in.

To add even more speed to modern CPUs, an additional cache is added to CPUs. This cache is called Level-2 (L2) cache. This cache used to be found on the motherboard. However, Intel and AMD found that placing the L2 cache on the CPU greatly increased CPU response. Many PCs being sold today have 512 KB or 1024 KB of motherboard cache memory; higher-end systems can have as much as 2 MB of L2 cache.

In addition to the cache memory built into the CPU, cache also is added to the motherboard. This motherboard-resident cache is now called Level-3 (L3) cache. L3 cache is found on very-high-end computers. It is not necessary for a computer to have L3 cache.

L1, L2, and L3 all speed up the CPU, although in different ways. L1 cache holds instructions that have recently run. L2 cache holds potential upcoming instructions. L3 holds many of the possible instructions. In all cases, the cache memory is faster for the CPU to access, resulting in a quicker program execution.

A Look inside the Processor

You have already seen how a PC processes and moves data. For most people, the great mystery of the PC is what takes place inside its circuitry. How can this box of chips, wires, and other parts—most of which don't even move—do its work?

A processor's performance—even its capability to function—is dictated by its internal design, or architecture. A chip's architecture determines where its parts are located and connected, how it connects with other parts of the computer, and much more. It also determines the path that electricity (in the form of moving electrons) takes as it moves through the processor, turning its transistors on and off. There are many different chip architectures in use today, and each family of PC processors is based on its own unique architecture.

Different processors have different architectures. In some cases, architectures are so different that processors cannot run the same software. For this reason, software must be written especially for Windows PCs, Macintosh computers, and workstations.

In fact, processors are differentiated by their architecture (see Figure 3A.14). The processors of IBM PCs and Macintosh computers have such different architectures, for example, that they cannot even run the same software; operating systems and software must be written to run on each processor's specific architecture, to meet its requirements.

A processor's architecture determines how many transistors it has, and therefore the processor's power. Simply stated, the more transistors in a processor, the more powerful it is. The earliest microprocessors had a few thousand transistors. The processors in today's PCs contain tens of millions. In the most powerful workstation and server computers, a processor may contain hundreds of millions of transistors. When a computer is configured to use multiple processors, it can ultimately contain billions of transistors.

A processor includes many other features that affect its performance. For example, a processor's performance is affected by the number of bits of data it can process at any one time. Currently, nearly all standard PC processors move data in 32-bit chunks; they are called "32-bit processors." In 2003 American Micro Devices (AMD) released a new generation of desktop PC processor that can handle 64 bits of data. (High-end workstations and many minicomputer systems have used 64-bit processors for about a decade.)

Microcomputer Processors

simnet™

Norton
ONLINE

For more information on CPUs used in today's PCs, visit
**http://www.mhhe.com/
peternorton**.

For two decades after the birth of the personal computer, the biggest player in the PC CPU market was Intel Corporation. This dominance began to change in 1998 when several leading computer makers began offering lower-priced systems using chips made by AMD and other chip manufacturers. Initially, these microprocessors offered less performance at a lower price. That situation has changed, however, as AMD made rapid advances in its products' capabilities. Today, Intel and AMD chips compete head to head, not only in performance, but also in price.

Intel and AMD are not the only manufacturers on the block. Motorola, now known as Freescale, manufactured the processors for all Macintosh computers up to and including the G4. They still make chips for communication devices. The newer Macintosh G5 boasts a chip made by IBM. Many other companies make specialized processors for workstations, minicomputers, handheld devices, automobile electronics, and kitchen appliances.

As you read the following sections, remember that performance specifications and features can change rapidly. Chip manufacturers make constant improvements to their products; as a result, the most popular PC processors now operate at speeds higher than 3 GHz, and they continue to be faster every month. By continuously refining chip designs and manufacturing processes, chip makers are always finding ways to add more transistors to chips.

FIGURE 3A.15

The Pentium III Xeon and Itanium processors.

Intel Processors

Intel is historically the leading provider of chips for PCs. In 1971, Intel invented the microprocessor—the so-called computer on a chip—with the 4004 model. This invention led to the first microcomputers that began appearing in 1975. Even so, Intel's success in this market was not guaranteed until 1981 when IBM released the first IBM PC, which was based on an Intel microprocessor.

A list of current Intel chips (see Figure 3A.15), along with their clock speeds and numbers of transistors, is shown in Table 3A.3.

TABLE 3A.3

Current Intel Processors

Model	Primary Use	Clock Speed	Number of Transistors
Itanium 2	Server	1.3 GHz and up	410 million
Pentium 4	PC	1.4 GHz and up	42–55 million
Pentium III Xeon	Server/Workstation	700 MHz and up	42–55 million
Pentium III	PC	650 MHz and up	28–44 million
Celeron	Budget PC	500 MHz and up	28–44 million

Advanced Micro Devices (AMD) Processors

In 1998, Advanced Micro Devices (AMD) emerged as a primary competitor to Intel's dominance in the IBM-compatible PC market. Until that time, AMD processors were typically found in lower-performance, low-priced home and small business computers selling for less than $1,000. With the release of the K6 and Athlon processor series, AMD proved that it could compete feature for feature with many of Intel's best-selling products. AMD even began a new race for the fastest PC processor.

A list of current AMD chips (see Figure 3A.16), along with their clock speeds and numbers of transistors, is shown in Table 3A.4.

TABLE 3A.4

AMD Processors Used in Today's Personal Computers

Model	Clock Speed	Number of Transistors
Athlon FX 64	2.2 GHz and up	105.9 million
Athlon XP	2.2 GHz and up	54.3 million
Opteron for servers	1.4 GHz and up	106 million
Athlon	1.0 GHz and up	37 million
Duron	600 MHz and up	25 million

Freescale Processors

Freescale Semiconductor, Inc., (www.freescale.com) a subsidiary of Motorola, Inc., has a 50-year history in microelectronics. As mentioned earlier, many Apple computers use Freescale processors. Freescale processors were also an early favorite among companies that built larger, UNIX-based computers.

Through the years, Freescale offered two processor architectures that were used in Macintosh computers. The first is known as the 680x0 family. A

What *Is* a Computer Chip?

Throughout this book (and in any other information you read about computers), you see references to chips. Processors reside on chips, as do memory and other types of computer circuitry. But what does this mean? What is a computer chip?

To understand how chips work, you have to think small . . . very, very small. That's because the transistors, circuits, and connections that exist on a computer chip are so tiny that their dimensions are sometimes measured in terms of atoms rather than millimeters or inches.

Most computer chips are created on very thin wafers, which are made of nearly pure silicon. (Silicon is a mineral that is purified and refined for use in chips. It is used in many other products, too.) Some chips may be made from other materials, such as various types of plastic, but the chips commonly found in personal computers are silicon-based.

The Making of a Chip

Transistors and circuits exist as tiny channels on the surface of a chip, which means they must be carved out of the silicon. To do this, chip manufacturers use a process called photolithography to physically etch out the tiny grooves and notches that make up the chip's circuits. In the first step of this process, the silicon wafer's surface is covered with a gooey substance called photoresist, which is sensitive to certain types of light.

Next, a glass pattern (called a mask) is placed over the wafer. This pattern is marked with the precise lines where each transistor and circuit will lie on the chip's surface. The manufacturer then shines ultraviolet light through the pattern; the pattern's dark lines "mask" the silicon wafer from the light, protecting it. The exposed photoresist reacts to the light that touches it, softening the silicon beneath it. The exposed silicon is washed away, leaving a pattern of fine tracings on its surface.

The manufacturer then coats the wafer's surface with ions. This coating changes the way the silicon conducts electricity, making it more efficient at moving electrons through its circuits. (Moving electrons represent the binary 1s and 0s that make up data for the computer.) Because electrons are so small, the chip's circuitry can be very fine.

FIGURE 3A.16

The Athlon and Duron processors.

new type of processor, which was developed by Freescale, Apple, and IBM, has replaced this family of processors. This new processor architecture, called the PowerPC architecture, is the basis for all new computers made by Apple. Freescale's MPC74xx processors can be found in Apple's G4 computers. PowerPC processors from Freescale are also ideal platforms for Linux operating system implementations, which are growing in popularity among desktop users.

TABLE 3A.5

CPUs' Performance Specifications

Specification	AMD Athlon 64 FX	Intel Pentium IV	PowerMac G5
Number of registers	16	16	80
Word size	64	32	64
FrontSide or system bus speed	1.6 GHz	800 MHz	1 GHz
L1 cache	128 KB	na	na
L2 cache	1024 KB	512	512

In the next step of the process, atoms of metal (such as aluminum or copper) are placed in the etched channels on the wafer's surface. These connections will conduct electrons as they move through the chip.

So Many Transistors, So Little Space

Today's manufacturing processes are so precise that they can squeeze millions of transistors onto a single chip not much larger than a person's thumbnail. One way to achieve this is by etching the chip's surface in separate layers, literally stacking sets of circuits on top of one another.

Another way is to place those circuits closer and closer together. Currently, chipmakers can place transistors so close that they are separated by less than a micron. (A micron is one-millionth of a meter.) Production technologies are constantly being refined. Today's popular PC processors contain tens of millions of transistors; in a few years, there may be as many as one billion transistors on a single processor chip.

Chip designs are constantly evolving, making processors ever faster and more powerful.

IBM Processors

In addition to working with Apple and Freescale on the PowerPC line, IBM makes high-performance mainframe and workstation CPUs. In 2003, IBM partnered with Apple and released the G5, advertised as the "fastest desktop processor ever." While most new chips can make this claim, the G5 delivered. The G5 delivered true workstation power at the cost of a standard desktop. As a demonstration, Pixar studios were provided with several G5-equipped computers. The Disney/Pixar movie *Finding Nemo* was created entirely on the G5 desktop computers. Previous releases from Pixar, including *Toy Story*, required high-end workstations.

Comparing Processors

Most non–computer people only use the clock speed to compare two processors. This is a good comparison, but it is akin to comparing cars only by their top speed. There are many features of a car that are as important as rated speed. When comparing processors, many factors come into play. Larger cache and faster system bus speeds usually indicate better processors. Table 3A.5 contrasts three powerful desktop processors. Common performance specifications are listed.

SELF-CHECK ::

Complete each statement by filling in the blanks.

1. The smallest unit of data a computer can use is called a _____ .
   a. bit   b. nibble   c. byte

2. _____ is a special type of nonvolatilve memory, often used in digital cameras.
   a. RAM   b. Flash memory   c. Binary memory

3. The Itanium 2 processor has _____ transistors.
   a. 45 million   b. 105.9 million   c. 410 million

Extending the Processor's Power to Other Devices

You have already learned that all the components of a computer tie into the computer's CPU by way of the bus. When you need to add a new piece of hardware to your computer, you need to know how to connect it to the bus. In some cases, you can plug the device into an existing socket, or port, on the back of the computer. Most computers have several types of ports, each with different capabilities and uses. Older computers feature only three or four distinct types of ports, but new systems provide a wide array of specialized ports. When a port is not available, you need to install a circuit board that includes the port you need.

Standard Computer Ports

All modern computers come with the same basic set of ports. These allow you to connect common devices to your computer. Without these ports, your computer would not boot properly and if it did, you would be unable to interact with the software on the system.

Figure 3A.17 shows the back of a new computer. It contains several color-coded ports. At first glance, it can be overwhelming. However, remember that most plugs only fit where they belong and a mistake is never catastrophic. The most commonly used ports are

>> **Mouse and Keyboard Ports.** Accepts the keyboard and mouse plugs. The mouse is always the top port. If you make a mistake and plug the mouse into the keyboard port, the computer will not boot properly.

>> **Two Universal Serial Bus (USB) ports.** These accept any number of devices including cameras and joysticks.

>> **Serial port.** Serial ports are connected to external modems.

>> **Parallel port.** This port is most commonly used to connect older printers to the computer.

>> **Audio ports.** There are typically three audio ports on modern computers. The green speaker port is for your headphones or desktop speakers. The pink microphone port is for a small microphone. The yellow speaker port allows serious audiophiles to connect their computer to a home stereo system. Intense gamers or PC movie viewers may employ this option.

>> **Network Port.** This port allows your computer to plug into a network or use a high-speed Internet connection.

>> **Modem Port.** It connects your computer to a phone line. The most common use for a modem is Internet access. You learned about the Internet in Chapter 2, "Presenting the Internet."

>> **Monitor Port.** Most monitors connect to the three-row port on the right side of the computer. This can be found either by the serial port or with the expansion cards. Other monitor options may include connections for a TV.

Mouse
Keyboard
USB
Serial
Parallel
Modem
Network
Microphone
Speaker
TV/S-Video Output
VGA Output

Serial and Parallel Ports

A PC's internal components communicate through the data bus, which consists of parallel wires. Similarly, a parallel interface is a connection of eight or more wires through which data bits can flow simultaneously. Most computer buses transfer 32 bits simultaneously. However, the standard parallel interface for external devices such as printers usually transfers eight bits (one byte) at a time over eight separate wires.

With a serial interface, data bits are transmitted one at a time through a single wire (however, the interface includes additional wires for the bits that control the flow of data). Inside the computer, a chip called a universal asynchronous receiver-transmitter (UART) converts parallel data from the bus into serial data that flows through a serial cable.

Specialized Expansion Ports

In addition to the standard collection of expansion ports, many PCs include specialized ports. These ports allow the connection of special devices, which extends the computer's bus in unique ways.

SCSI

The Small Computer System Interface (SCSI, pronounced *scuzzy*) takes a different approach from standard parallel or serial ports. Instead of forcing the user to plug multiple cards into the computer's expansion slots, a single SCSI adapter extends the bus outside the computer by way of a cable. Thus, SCSI is like an extension cord for the data bus. Like plugging one extension cord into another to lengthen a circuit, you can plug one SCSI device into another to form a chain, as shown in Figure 3A.18. When devices are connected together this way and plugged into a single port, they are called a "daisy chain." Many devices use the SCSI interface. Fast, high-end hard disk drives often have SCSI interfaces, as do scanners, tape drives, and optical storage devices such as CD-ROM drives.

USB

The Universal Serial Bus (USB) has become the most popular external connection for PCs—both IBM-compatible and Macintosh systems. USB has several features that have led to its popularity. First, USB is a hot swappable bus. This means that users can switch USB devices without rebooting the PC. A second feature is its ease of use. Simply plugging the device in makes it ready to run. Finally, USB supports 127 devices daisy chained. Today, most new computers feature at least four USB ports, with two often in the front of the PC.

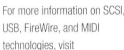

For more information on SCSI, USB, FireWire, and MIDI technologies, visit
http://www.mhhe.com/peternorton.

SCSI card

Scanner

External hard disk

Modem

FIGURE 3A.18

SCSI peripherals daisy-chained together.

IEEE 1394 (FireWire)

Like the USB standard, the IEEE 1394 (FireWire) standard extends the computer's bus to many peripheral devices through a single port. Because IEEE 1394–compliant technology is so expensive, however, it is not expected to become the dominant bus technology, although it may gain wide acceptance as a standard for plugging video and other high-data-throughput devices to the system bus.

Musical Instrument Digital Interface (MIDI)

The Musical Instrument Digital Interface (MIDI) has been in use since the early 1980s, when a group of musical instrument manufacturers developed the technology to enable electronic musical instruments to communicate. Since then, MIDI has been adapted to the personal computer. Many sound cards are MIDI-compliant and feature a special MIDI port. Using a MIDI port, you can plug a wide variety of musical instruments and other MIDI-controlled devices into the computer. MIDI systems are widely used in recording and performing music to control settings for electronic synthesizers, drum machines, light systems, amplification, and more.

Expansion Slots and Boards

PCs are designed so that users can adapt, or configure, the machines to their own particular needs. PC motherboards have two or more empty expansion slots, which are extensions of the computer's bus that provide a way to add new components to the computer. The slots accept expansion boards, also called cards, adapters, or sometimes just boards. Figure 3A.19 shows a PC expansion board being installed. The board is being attached to the motherboard—the main system board to which the CPU, memory, and other components are attached.

Adapters that serve input and output purposes provide a port to which devices can be attached and act as translators between the bus and the device itself. Some adapters also do a significant amount of data processing. For example, a video controller is a card that provides a port on the back of the PC into which you can plug the monitor. It also contains and manages the video memory and does the processing required to display images on the monitor. Similar devices include sound cards, internal modems or fax/modems, and network interface cards.

FIGURE 3A.19

An expansion board being inserted into an expansion slot.

PC Cards

Another type of expansion card is the PC Card (initially called a Personal Computer Memory Card International Association, or PCMCIA, card). It is a small device about the size of a credit card (see Figure 3A.20). This device was designed initially for use in notebook computers and other computers that are too small to accept a standard expansion card. A PC Card fits into a slot on the back or side of the notebook computer. PC Card adapters are also available for desktop computers, enabling them to accept PC Cards. Even some types of digital cameras accept PC Cards that store digital photographs. PC Cards are used for a wide

FIGURE 3A.20

Small PC Card devices provide memory, storage, communications, and other capabilities.

variety of purposes and can house modems, network cards, memory, and even fully functioning hard disk drives.

Storage Devices

The purpose of a storage device is to hold data—even when the computer is turned off—so the data can be used whenever it is needed. Storage involves two processes:

>> Writing, or recording, the data so it can be found later for use.

>> Reading the stored data, then transferring it into the computer's memory.

The physical materials on which data is stored are called storage media. The hardware components that write data to, and read data from, storage media are called storage devices (see Figure 3A.21). For example, a diskette is a storage medium (medium is the singular form of the word *media*); a diskette drive is a storage device.

The two main categories of storage technology used today are magnetic storage and optical storage. Although most storage devices and media employ one technology or the other, some use both.

Nearly every new PC comes with a diskette drive and a built-in hard disk, as shown in Figure 3A.21. Some PC makers now sell computers without built-in diskette drives, although they can be added to the system. Most new PCs also have a CD-ROM or DVD-ROM drive. For a little more expense, many consumers replace the optical drive with one that will let them record data onto an optical disc. A built-in drive for removable high-capacity floppy disks is another common feature in new PCs.

Magnetic Storage Devices

Because they all use the same medium (the material on which the data is stored), diskette drives, hard disk drives, high-capacity floppy disk drives, and tape drives use similar techniques for writing and reading data. The surfaces of diskettes, hard disks, high-capacity floppy disks, and magnetic tape are coated with a magnetically sensitive material, such as iron oxide, that reacts to a magnetic field.

Diskettes contain a single thin disk, usually made of plastic. This disk is flexible, which is why diskettes are often called floppy disks. A diskette stores data on both sides of its disk (numbered as side 0 and side 1), and each side has its own read/write head. High-capacity floppy disks contain a single disk, too, but their formatting enables them to store much more data than a normal floppy disk, as you will see later. Hard disks usually contain multiple disks, which are called platters because they are made of a rigid material such as aluminum.

How Data Is Stored on a Disk

You may remember from science projects that one magnet can be used to make another. For example, you can make a magnet by taking an iron bar and stroking it in one direction with a magnet. The iron bar becomes a magnet itself, because its iron molecules align themselves in one direction. Thus, the iron bar becomes polarized; that is, its ends have opposite magnetic polarity.

You also can create a magnet by using electrical current to polarize a piece of iron, as shown in Figure 3A.22. The process results in an electromagnet; you can control the polarity and strength of an electromagnet by changing the direction and strength of the current.

Magnetic storage devices use a similar principle to store data. Just as a transistor can represent binary data as "on" or "off," the orientation of a magnetic field

Norton
ONLINE

For more information on types of storage devices used in PCs, visit **http://www.mhhe.com/ peternorton**.

CD-ROM (or DVD) drive

Diskette drive

High-capacity floppy disk drive

FIGURE 3A.21

Common storage devices found in today's PCs.

Another way to make a magnet is to wrap a wire coil around an iron bar and send an electric current through the coil. This produces an electromagnet.

If you reverse the direction of the current, the polarity of the magnet also reverses.

If you place the electromagnet against a magnetic surface, such as the coating of a diskette...

...the electromagnet's pole induces a magnetic field on the diskette's surface.

FIGURE 3A.22

How an electromagnet creates a field on a magnetic surface.

Norton ONLINE

For more information on formatting disks, visit **http://www.mhhe.com/ peternorton**.

FIGURE 3A.23

A read/write head recording data on the surface of a magnetic disk.

can be used to represent data. A magnet has one important advantage over a transistor: that is, it can represent "on" and "off" without a continual source of electricity.

The surfaces of magnetic disks and tapes are coated with millions of tiny iron particles so that data can be stored on them. Each of these particles can act as a magnet, taking on a magnetic field when subjected to an electromagnet. The read/write heads of a magnetic disk or tape drive contain electromagnets that generate magnetic fields in the iron on the storage medium as the head passes over the disk or tape. As shown in Figure 3A.23, the read/write heads record strings of 1s and 0s by alternating the direction of the current in the electromagnets.

To read data from a magnetic surface, the process is reversed. The read/write head passes over the disk or tape while no current is flowing through the electromagnet. The head possesses no charge, but the storage medium is covered with magnetic fields, which represent bits of data. The storage medium charges the magnet in the head, which causes a small current to flow through the head in one direction or the other, depending on the field's polarity. The disk or tape drive senses the direction of the flow as the storage medium passes by the head, and the data is sent from the read/write head into memory.

How Data Is Organized on a Magnetic Disk

Before the computer can use a magnetic disk to store data, the disk's surface must be magnetically mapped so that the computer can go directly to a specific point on it without searching through data. (Because a magnetic disk drive's heads can go directly to any point on the disk's surface to read or write data, magnetic storage devices are also categorized as random access storage devices.) The process of mapping a disk is called formatting or initializing.

When you purchase new diskettes or high-capacity floppy disks, they should already be formatted and ready to use with your computer. In a new computer, the built-in hard disk is almost always already formatted and has software installed on it. If you buy a new hard disk by itself, however, you may need to format it yourself, but this is not difficult to do.

You may find it helpful to reformat diskettes from time to time, because the process ensures that all existing data is deleted from the disk. During the formatting process, you can determine whether the disk's surface has faulty spots, and you can copy important system files to the disk. You can format a floppy disk by using operating system commands (see Figure 3A.24).

When you format a magnetic disk, the disk drive creates a set of concentric rings, called tracks, on each side of the disk. The number of tracks required depends on the type of disk. Most diskettes have 80 tracks on each side of the disk. A hard disk may have several hundred tracks on each side of each platter. Each track is a separate circle, like the circles on a bull's-eye target. The tracks are numbered from the outermost circle to the innermost, starting with 0, as shown in Figure 3A.25.

In the next stage of formatting, the tracks are divided into smaller parts. Imagine slicing a disk the way you slice a pie. As shown in Figure 3A.26, each slice would cut across all the disk's tracks, resulting in short segments called sectors. Sectors are where data is physically stored on the disk. In all diskettes and most hard disks, a sector can store up to 512 bytes (0.5 KB). All the sectors on a disk are numbered in one long sequence, so that the computer can access each small area on the disk by using a unique number.

A sector is the smallest unit with which any magnetic disk drive can work; drives can read or write only whole sectors at a time. If the computer needs to change just one byte out of 512, it must rewrite the entire sector.

If a diskette has 80 tracks on each side, and each track contains 18 sectors, then the disk has 1,440 sectors (80 × 18) per side, for a total of 2,880 sectors. This configuration is true regardless of the length of the track. The disk's outermost track

FIGURE 3A.24

Formatting a diskette and a Zip disk (a high-capacity floppy disk).

FIGURE 3A.25

Tracks are concentric circles on a disk's surface.

FIGURE 3A.26

Sectors on a disk, each with a unique number.

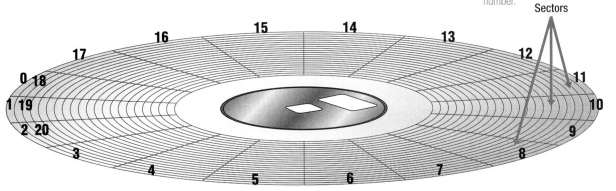

is longer than the innermost track, but each track is still divided into the same number of sectors. Regardless of physical size, all of a diskette's sectors hold the same number of bytes; that is, the shortest, innermost sectors hold the same amount of data as the longest, outermost sectors.

How the Operating System Finds Data on a Disk

A computer's operating system can locate data on a disk because each track and each sector are labeled, and the location of all data is kept in a special log on the disk. The labeling of tracks and sectors is called logical formatting.

Different operating systems can format disks in different ways. Each formatting method configures the disk's surface in a different manner, resulting in a different file system—a logical method for managing the storage of data on a disk's surface. A commonly used logical format performed by Windows is called the FAT file system because it relies on a standardized file allocation table (FAT) to keep track of file locations on the disk.

When a diskette is formatted with the FAT file system, four areas are created on the disk.

>> The boot sector contains a program that runs when you first start the computer. This program determines whether the disk has the basic components that are necessary to run the operating system successfully. If the program determines that the required files are present and the disk has a valid format, it transfers control to one of the operating system programs that continues the process of starting up. This process is called booting, because the boot program makes the computer "pull itself up by its own bootstraps." The boot sector also contains information that describes other disk characteristics, such as the number of bytes per sector and the number of sectors per track—information that the operating system needs to access data on the disk.

>> The file allocation table (FAT) is a log that records the location of each file and the status of each sector. When you write a file to a disk, the operating system checks the FAT to find an open area, stores the file, and then logs the file's identity and its location in the FAT. When a program needs to locate data on the disk, the operating system checks the FAT to see where that data is stored. During formatting, two copies of the FAT are created; both copies are always maintained to keep their information current.

>> The root folder is the "master folder" on any disk. A folder (also called a directory) is a tool for organizing files on a disk. Folders can contain files or other folders, so it is possible to set up a hierarchical system of folders on your computer, just as you can have folders within other folders in a file cabinet. The topmost folder is known as the *root*, but also may be called the *root folder* or *root directory*. This is the folder that holds all the information about all the other folders on the disk. When you use the operating system to view the contents of a folder, the operating system lists specific information about each file in the folder, such as the file's name, its size, the time and date that it was created or last modified, and so on. Figure 3A.27 shows a typical folder listing on a Windows XP system.

>> The data area is the part of the disk that remains free after the boot sector, the FAT, and the root folder have been created. This is where data and program files are actually stored on the disk.

During logical formatting, the operating system also groups sectors together, into storage units called clusters. A cluster,

ONLINE

For more information on file systems, visit

http://www.mhhe.com/ peternorton.

FIGURE 3A.27

A folder listing in Windows XP.

The folder named C: is the root; it contains all other folders on this disk.

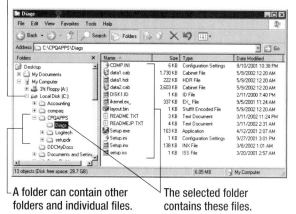

A folder can contain other folders and individual files.

The selected folder contains these files.

124   Chapter 3

therefore, is simply a group of sectors that the OS sees as a single unit. A cluster is the smallest space an OS will allocate to a single file, and a cluster may store an entire file or just part of a file. Cluster sizes vary, depending on the size and type of the disk, but they can range from four sectors for diskettes to 64 sectors for some hard disks. Cluster usage is tracked in the file allocation table.

Diskettes (Floppy Disks)

Figure 3A.28 shows a diskette and a diskette drive. The drive includes a motor that rotates the disk on a spindle and read/write heads that can move to any spot on the disk's surface as the disk spins. The heads can skip from one spot to another on the disk's surface to find any piece of data without having to scan through all of the data in between.

Diskettes spin at about 300 revolutions per minute. Therefore, the longest it can take to position a point on the diskette under the read/write heads is the amount of time required for one revolution—about 0.2 second.

A 3.5-inch diskette, as shown in Figure 3A.29, is encased in a hard plastic shell with a sliding shutter. When the disk is inserted into the drive, the shutter is slid back to expose the disk's surface to the read/write head.

Norton
ONLINE

For more information on floppy disks, visit
http://www.mhhe.com/ peternorton.

FIGURE 3A.28

Parts of a diskette and a diskette drive.

FIGURE 3A.29

A 3.5-inch diskette.

A disk's density is a measure of its capacity—the amount of data it can store. To determine a disk's density, you can multiply its total number of sectors by the number of bytes each sector can hold. For a standard floppy disk, the equation looks like this:

```
    2,880 sectors
 X    512 bytes per sector
1,474,560 total bytes
```

Not all this space is dedicated to storing data, so a floppy disk's actual capacity is a bit smaller—1.44 MB.

Hard Disks

A hard disk includes one or more platters mounted on a central spindle, like a stack of rigid diskettes. Each platter is covered with a magnetic coating, and the entire unit is encased in a sealed chamber. Unlike diskettes, where the disk and drive are separate, the hard disk and drive are a single unit. It includes the hard disk, the motor that spins the platters, and a set of read/write heads (see Figure 3A.30). Because you cannot remove the disk from its drive (unless it is a removable hard disk), the terms *hard disk* and *hard drive* are used interchangeably.

The smallest hard disks available today can store several hundred megabytes; the largest store 200 GB or even more. Most entry-level consumer PCs now come with hard disks of at least 40 GB, but minimum capacities are continually increasing.

The hard disks found in most PCs spin at a speed of 3,600, 7,200, or 10,000 revolutions per minute (rpm). Very-high-performance disks found in workstations and servers can spin as fast as 15,000 rpm. (Compare these figures to a diskette's spin rate of 300 rpm.)

Hard disks pack data more closely together than floppy disks can, but they also hold more data because they include multiple platters. To the computer system, this configuration means that the disk has more than two sides: sides 0, 1, 2, 3, 4, and so on. Larger-capacity hard disks may use 12 or more platters.

Like diskettes, hard disks generally store 512 bytes of data in a sector, but hard disks can have more sectors per track—54, 63, or even more sectors per track are not uncommon.

Removable High-Capacity Magnetic Disks

Removable high-capacity disks and drives combine the speed and capacity of a hard disk with the portability of a diskette. A wide variety of devices fall into this category, and each device works with its own unique storage medium. There are basically two types of removable high-capacity magnetic disks:

>> **High-Capacity Floppy Disks** Many computer makers now offer built-in high-capacity floppy disk drives in addition to a standard diskette drive. You can easily add a high-capacity floppy disk drive to a system that doesn't already have one. These drives use disks that are about the same size as a 3.5-inch diskette but have a much greater capacity than a standard diskette. The most commonly used high-capacity floppy disk system is the Zip drive and disks, made by Iomega Corp. (see Figure 3A.31). Zip disks come in capacities ranging from 100 MB to 750 MB.

Norton
ONLINE

For more information on hard disks, visit
http://www.mhhe.com/peternorton.

Read/write head

Access arm

Spindle

Aluminum platters with magnetic coating

FIGURE 3A.30

Parts of a hard disk.

Norton
ONLINE

For more information on removable high-capacity magnetic disks, visit
http://www.mhhe.com/peternorton.

> » **Hot-Swappable Hard Disks** At the high end in terms of price and performance are hot-swappable hard disks, also called removable hard disks. These disks are sometimes used on high-end workstations or servers that require large amounts of storage. They allow the user to remove (swap out) a hard disk and insert (swap in) another while the computer is still running (hot). Hot-swappable hard disks are like removable versions of normal hard disks. The removable box includes the disk, drive, and read/write heads in a sealed container.

Tape Drives

Tape drives read and write data to the surface of a tape the same way an audio-cassette recorder does. The difference is that a computer tape drive writes digital data rather than analog data—discrete 1s and 0s rather than finely graduated signals created by sounds in an audio recorder.

Tape storage is best used for data that you do not use often, such as backup copies of your hard disk's contents. Businesses use tape drives for this purpose because they are inexpensive and reliable, and have capacities as high as 200 GB and greater (see Figure 3A.32).

Tapes, however, are slow when it comes to accessing data. Because a tape is a long strip of magnetic material, the tape drive has to write data to it serially—one byte after another. To find a piece of data on a tape, the drive must scan through all the data in sequence until it finds the right item. For this reason, tape drives are often called sequential access devices. They locate data much more slowly than a random access storage device such as a hard disk.

Optical Storage Devices

The most popular alternatives to magnetic storage systems are optical systems, including CD-ROM, DVD-ROM, and their variants. These devices fall into the category of optical storage because they store data on a reflective surface so it can be read by a beam of laser light. A laser uses a concentrated, narrow beam of light, focused and directed with lenses, prisms, and mirrors.

CD-ROM

The familiar audio compact disc is a popular medium for storing music. In the computer world, however, the medium is called *compact disc–read-only memory* (*CD-ROM*). CD-ROM uses the same technology used to produce music CDs. If your computer has a CD-ROM drive, a sound card, and speakers, you can play audio CDs on your PC.

A CD-ROM drive reads digital data (whether computer data or audio) from a spinning disc by focusing a laser on the disc's surface. Some areas of the disc reflect the laser light into a sensor, and other areas scatter the light. A spot that reflects the laser beam into the sensor is interpreted as a 1, and the absence of a reflection is interpreted as a 0.

Data is laid out on a CD-ROM disc in a long, continuous spiral. Data is stored in the form of lands, which are flat areas on the metal surface, and pits, which are depressions or hollows. As Figure 3A.33 shows, a land reflects the laser light into the sensor (indicating a data bit of 1) and a pit scatters the light (indicating a data bit of 0). A standard compact disc can store 650 MB of data or about 70 minutes of audio. A newer generation of compact discs, however, can hold 700 MB of data or 80 minutes of audio.

FIGURE 3A.31

The Iomega Zip system.

FIGURE 3A.32

New-generation tape drives feature data capacities of 200 GB and higher, and can transfer several megabytes of data per second.

Norton
ONLINE

For more information on optical storage technologies and CD-ROM, visit **http://www.mhhe.com/ peternorton**.

At Issue

Cyborgs among Us: Wearable Technology

Cyborg: the melding of man and machine, organism and circuitry. Though no Robocop, metaphoric cyborgs are more than the stuff of media sci-fi. They are reality for the thousands who utilize a new generation of wearable computing device making intimate human–machine interaction now possible.

The term *wearable computer* refers to a wireless computer system worn on the user's body, either in a backpack, on a belt, or sewn into a piece of clothing such as a jacket or vest. Some are small enough to fit in the user's shirt pocket or have monitors worn as eyeglasses.

Wearable computers are designed specifically for mobile and mostly hands-free operations, often incorporating head-mounted displays and vocal recognition software. Most variations of wearable PCs are always on and always accessible. In this way, this new computing framework dif-

fers from that of other existing wireless technologies, such as laptop computers and personal digital assistants.

It is this "always ready" feature that is the true hallmark of wearables. Unlike other personal computers or handheld devices, a wearable computer is subsumed into the personal space of the user, becoming almost a part of him or her. This leads to a new form of synergy between human and computer, brought about by long-term adaptation through constancy of the user–computer interface. Over time, the user adapts to the computer to the point he or she no longer feels as if it is a separate entity. Often users report feeling uncomfortable—even "naked"—without their devices.

Also unlike other portable devices, wearable PCs are full-featured computers, with all of the functionality of a traditional desktop or mainframe computer.

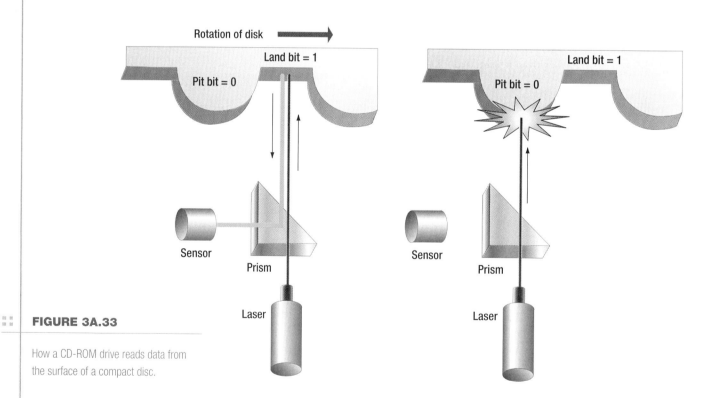

FIGURE 3A.33

How a CD-ROM drive reads data from the surface of a compact disc.

The first CD-ROM drives could read data at 150 KBps (kilobytes per second) and were known as *single-speed* drives. Today, a CD-ROM drive's speed is expressed as a multiple of the original drive's speed—2x, 4x, 8x, and so on. A 2x drive reads data at a rate of 300 KBps (2 × 150). At the time this book was published, the fastest available CD-ROM drive was listed at a speed of 75x; it could read data at a rate of 11,250 KBps (or slightly more than 11 MBps).

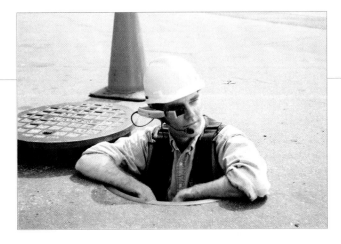

One company leading the way in the wearables space is Hitachi. The Hitachi wearable PC unit is small and lightweight enough to be carried in a pocket. It includes a head-mounted display that gives users the illusion that there is a 13-inch color screen in front of them. Users operate the machine via a tiny handheld optical mouse.

The Hitachi wearable PC runs on Microsoft's Windows CE operating system and contains a Hitachi 128 MHz RISC processor and 32 MB of RAM. It also comes with a Flash card and a USB slot. According to the firm, the unit measures 140 × 90 × 26 mm, and the whole device weighs a slight 500 g.

Though still on the cutting edge, many experts believe that wearables will someday soon supersede technologies such as mobile phones and PDAs, holding out the promise that wearable computers will improve the quality of day-to-day life for their Cyborg users.

DVD-ROM

Many of today's new PCs feature a built-in digital video disc–read-only memory (DVD-ROM) drive rather than a standard CD-ROM drive. DVD-ROM is a high-density medium capable of storing a full-length movie on a single disk the size of a CD. DVD-ROM achieves such high storage capacities by using both sides of the disc and special data-compression technologies and by using extremely small tracks for storing data. (Standard compact discs store data on only one side of the disc.)

The latest generation of DVD-ROM disc actually uses layers of data tracks, effectively doubling their capacity. The device's laser beam can read data from the first layer and then look through it to read data from the second layer.

DVDs look like CDs. DVD-ROM drives can play ordinary CD-ROM discs. A slightly different player, the DVD movie player, connects to your television and plays movies like a VCR. The DVD movie player also will play audio CDs as well as many types of data CDs, such as home-recorded audio discs, video CDs, and others.

Since each side of a standard DVD-ROM disc can hold 4.7 GB, these discs can contain as much as 9.4 GB of data. Dual-layer DVD-ROM discs can hold 17 GB of data.

Recordable Optical Technologies

The latest innovations in consumer-grade optical technologies allow home users to create their own DVDs, filled with audio and video, music, or computer data. Here are some popular "writable" CD and DVD technologies:

>> **CD-Recordable** A CD-Recordable (CD-R) drive allows you to create your own data or audio discs on special recordable discs (called CD-R discs) that can be read by most CD-ROM drives. Most CD-R discs can be played in audio CD players, too. After information has been written to part of the CD-R disc, that information cannot be changed. With most CD-R drives, you can continue to record information to other parts of the disc until it is full.

ONLINE

For more information on DVD-ROM, visit
http://www.mhhe.com/ peternorton.

ONLINE

For more information on recordable optical technologies, visit **http://www.mhhe.com/ peternorton**.

» **CD-ReWritable (CD-RW)** Using a CD-ReWritable (CD-RW) drive, you can write data onto special rewritable compact discs (called CD-RW discs), then overwrite it with new data. In other words, you can change the contents of a CD-RW disc in the same manner as a floppy disk. CD-RW discs have the same capacity as standard compact discs, and most can be overwritten up to 100 times. CD-RW discs, however, will not play on every CD-ROM drive, and most CD-RW discs cannot store audio data.

» **PhotoCD** Kodak developed the PhotoCD system to store digitized photographs on a recordable compact disc. Many film developing stores have PhotoCD drives that can record your photos on a CD. You can then put the PhotoCD in your computer's CD-ROM drive (assuming that it supports PhotoCD, and most do) and view the images on your computer as shown in Figure 3A.34. You also can paste them into other documents. With a PhotoCD, you can continue to add images until the disc is full. After an image has been written to the disc, however, it cannot be erased or changed.

» **DVD-Recordable (DVD-R)** After PC makers began adding DVD-ROM drives to computers, it did not take long for user demand to build for a recordable DVD system. The first to emerge is called DVD-Recordable (DVD-R). Like CD-R, a DVD-R system lets you record data onto a special recordable digital video disc, using a special drive. Once you record data onto a DVD-R disc, you cannot change it.

» **DVD-RAM** The newest optical technology to reach consumers, sophisticated DVD-RAM drives let you record, erase, and re-record data on a special disc. Using video editing software, you can record your own digitized videos onto a DVD-RAM disc, then play them back in any DVD player. DVD-RAM drives can read DVDs, DVD-R discs, CD-R discs, CD-RW discs, and standard CDs.

FIGURE 3A.34

After your pictures have been processed and stored on a PhotoCD, you can see them on your computer screen and copy them into documents.

Summary ::

>> Computer data is reduced to binary numbers because computer processing is performed by transistors that have only two possible states: on and off.

>> The binary number system works the same way as the decimal system, except that it has only two available symbols (0 and 1) rather than ten (0, 1, 2, 3, 4, 5, 6, 7, 8, and 9).

>> A single unit of data is called a bit; eight bits make up one byte.

>> In the most common text-code set, ASCII, each character consists of one byte of data. In the Unicode text-code set, each character consists of two bytes of data.

>> A microcomputer's processing takes place in the central processing unit, the two main parts of which are the control unit and the arithmetic logic unit (ALU).

>> The actual manipulation of data takes place in the ALU, which is connected to the registers that hold data and program instructions while they are being processed.

>> Random access memory (RAM) is volatile (or temporary). Programs and data can be written to and erased from RAM as needed.

>> Read-only memory (ROM) is nonvolatile (or permanent). It holds instructions that run the computer when the power is first turned on.

>> The size of the registers, also called word size, determines the amount of data with which the computer can work at one time.

>> The amount of RAM can affect speed because the CPU can keep more of the active program and data in memory, which is faster than storage on disk.

>> The computer's system clock sets the pace for the CPU by using a vibrating quartz crystal. The faster the clock, the more instructions the CPU can process per second.

>> The system bus has two parts—the data bus and the address bus—both of which are located on the motherboard.

>> Cache memory is a type of high-speed memory that contains the most recent data and instructions that have been loaded by the CPU. The amount of cache memory has a tremendous impact on the computer's speed.

>> A key to a processor's performance is the number of transistors it contains. Chip designers constantly look for new ways to place more transistors on microprocessor chips. Today's PC processors contain tens of millions of processors.

>> External devices, such as those used for input and output, are connected to the system by ports on the back or front of the computer.

>> Most computers come with a serial port and a parallel port. A serial port transmits one bit of data at a time; a parallel port transmits one byte (eight bits) of data at a time.

>> Bus technologies such as Small Computer System Interface (SCSI), Universal Serial Bus (USB), and IEEE 1394 (FireWire) enable the user to connect many devices through a single port.

>> Common storage devices can be categorized as magnetic or optical.

>> The most common magnetic storage media are diskettes, hard disks, high-capacity floppy disks, and magnetic tape.

>> The primary types of optical storage are compact disc–read-only memory (CD-ROM), digital video disc–read-only memory (DVD-ROM), CD-Recordable (CD-R), CD-ReWritable (CD-RW), DVD-Recordable (DVD-R), DVD-RAM, and PhotoCD.

>> Magnetic storage devices work by polarizing tiny pieces of iron on the magnetic medium. Read/write heads contain electromagnets that create magnetic charges on the medium.

>> CD-ROM uses the same technology as a music CD does: a laser reads lands and pits on the surface of the disc.

Key Terms ::

adapter, 120
address bus, 112
Advanced Micro Devices (AMD), 115
American Standard Code for
    Information Interchange
    (ASCII), 105
architecture, 113
arithmetic logic unit (ALU), 107
arithmetic operation, 107
audio port, 118
basic input output system (BIOS), 108
binary number system, 104
bit, 104
board, 120
boot, 124
boot sector, 124
bus, 111
cache memory, 112
card, 120
clock cycle, 111
clock speed, 111
cluster, 124
configure, 120
control unit, 107
data area, 124
data bus, 111
decimal number system, 104
density, 126
directory, 124
dual in-line memory module
    (DIMM), 108
DVD-RAM, 130

DVD-Recordable (DVD-R), 130
expansion board, 120
expansion slot, 120
Extended ASCII, 105
Extended Binary Coded Decimal
    Interchange Code (EBCDIC), 105
file allocation table (FAT), 124
file system, 124
folder, 124
format, 122
Freescale, 115
gigahertz (GHz), 111
hertz (Hz), 111
high-capacity floppy disk, 126
hot-swappable hard disk, 127
IBM, 117
IEEE 1394 (FireWire), 120
initialize, 122
instruction set, 107
Intel, 115
land, 127
Level-1 (L1) cache, 113
Level-2 (L2) cache, 113
Level-3 (L3) cache, 113
logical formatting, 124
logical operation, 107
magnetic storage, 121
megahertz (MHz), 111
memory address, 109
microcode, 107
Musical Instrument Digital
    Interface (MIDI), 120

optical storage, 121
parallel interface, 119
PC Card, 120
PhotoCD, 130
pit, 127
power on self test (POST), 108
random access storage device, 122
register, 107
root folder, 124
sector, 123
sequential access device, 127
serial interface, 119
single in-line memory module
    (SIMM), 108
Small Computer System Interface
    (SCSI), 119
small outline DIMM (SO-DIMM), 109
storage device, 121
storage media, 121
swap in, 110
swap out, 110
system clock, 111
text code, 105
track, 123
transistor, 103
Unicode Worldwide Character
    Standard, 105
universal asynchronous receiver-
    transmitter (UART), 119
Universal Serial Bus (USB), 119
virtual memory, 110
word size, 110

Key Term Quiz ::

Complete each statement by writing one of the terms listed under Key Terms in each blank.

1. People use the _____ number system, but computers use the _____ number system.

2. The most widely used text code system among personal computers is _____ .

3. _____ are high-speed memory locations built directly into the CPU that hold data while they are being processed.

4. The computer uses _____ when it runs out of RAM, swapping programs out to the hard drive.

5. With a(n) _____ interface, data bits are transmitted one at a time through a single wire.

6. An expansion _____ is plugged into a computer to provide additional connectivity or functionality.

7. Floppy disks and compact discs are examples of _____ .

8. When formatting a magnetic disk, the disk drive creates a set of concentric rings, called _____ , on its surface.

9. On the surface of an optical disc, data is stored as a series of _____ and _____ .

10. The _____ is the part of a magnetic disk that actually stores data and program files.

Multiple Choice ::

Circle the word or phrase that best completes each statement.

1. The _____ standard promises to provide enough characters to cover all the world's languages.
   - **a.** ASCII
   - **b.** Unicode
   - **c.** RAM
   - **d.** EBCDIC

2. The CPU uses a _____ to store and retrieve each piece of data in memory.
   - **a.** control unit
   - **b.** cache
   - **c.** memory address
   - **d.** POST

3. The computer can move data and instructions between storage and memory, as needed, in a process called _____ .
   - **a.** swapping
   - **b.** volatility
   - **c.** pipelining
   - **d.** exchanging

4. This cache holds the most recently used data or instructions.
   - **a.** L1
   - **b.** L2
   - **c.** L3
   - **d.** L4

5. FireWire is another name for the _____ interface.
   - **a.** parallel
   - **b.** IEEE 1394
   - **c.** MIDI
   - **d.** USB

6. The more _____ a processor has, the more powerful it is.
   - **a.** microns
   - **b.** transistors
   - **c.** connections
   - **d.** neurons

7. Older printers are likely to be connected through the _____ interface.
   - **a.** COM
   - **b.** parallel
   - **c.** modem
   - **d.** network

8. A(n) _____ is an example of a magnetic storage device.
   - **a.** flash memory drive
   - **b.** CD-ROM drive
   - **c.** hard disk drive
   - **d.** optical drive

9. In a magnetic disk drive, the read/write heads generate _____ in the iron particles on the storage medium.
   - **a.** polarized magnets
   - **b.** electromagnetic pulses
   - **c.** magnetic waves
   - **d.** magnetic fields

10. A _____ is a tool for organizing the files on a disk.
    - **a.** disk
    - **b.** folder
    - **c.** cluster
    - **d.** record

Review Questions ::

In your own words, briefly answer the following questions.

1. How many characters or symbols can be represented by one eight-bit byte?
2. What is meant by "word size"?
3. What is the difference between arithmetic operations and logical operations?
4. What is a data bus?
5. What is the purpose of the UART?
6. List four types of magnetic storage media commonly used with PCs.
7. List eight types of optical storage devices that can be used with PCs.
8. Why is a hard disk called a random access storage device?
9. What is the purpose of formatting a magnetic disk?
10. Describe the function of lands and pits on the surface of a compact disc.

Lesson Labs ::

Complete the following exercises as directed by your instructor.

1. Format a blank floppy disk:
   a. Make sure the disk's write-protect tab is closed. Place the disk in the diskette drive.
   b. Launch Windows Explorer. (The steps to launch Windows Explorer depend on the version of Windows you use. Ask your instructor for specific directions.)
   c. Right-click the floppy disk icon in the left pane. Click Format on the shortcut menu.
   d. In the Format dialog box, choose a capacity for the disk. Click the Quick (Erase) option. Make sure the Display Summary When Finished option is checked. Click START.
   e. Click CLOSE twice. Remove the disk from the drive. Leave the Exploring window open.

2. Explore the contents of your hard disk. In the Exploring window's left pane, click the system's hard disk icon labeled (C:). Look at the status bar at the bottom of the window. How many "objects" (folders) are stored on the hard disk? How much free space is available? Click several folders and review their contents in the right pane. When finished, close the Exploring window.

Networking Basics

Overview: Sharing Data Anywhere, Anytime

When PCs first appeared in businesses, software programs were designed for a single user. There were few obvious advantages to connecting PCs, and the technology was not adequate for doing so. As computers spread throughout business, developers began offering complex software designed for multiple users. Many organizations quickly learned the importance of connecting PCs. Data communications—the electronic transfer of information between computers—became a major focus of the computer industry. During the past decade, networking technology has become the most explosive area of growth in the entire computer industry. The demand for larger and faster high-capacity networks has increased as businesses have realized the value of networking their computer systems.

Networks come in many varieties. When most people think of a network, they imagine several computers in a single location sharing documents and devices such as printers. But a network can include all the computers and devices in a department, a building, or multiple buildings spread over a wide geographic area, such as a city or even a country. By interconnecting many individual networks into a massive single network, people around the world can share information as though they were across the hall from one another. The information they share can be much more than text documents. Many networks carry voice,

OBJECTIVES ::

>> Identify at least three benefits of using a network.

>> Differentiate between LANs and WANs.

>> Identify at least three common network topologies.

>> Name two common network media.

>> Identify network hardware and linking devices.

audio, and video traffic, enabling videoconferencing and types of collaboration that were not possible just a few years ago. The Internet is an example of one such network and is possibly the single largest network in existence today.

The Uses of a Network

A network is a set of technologies—including hardware, software, and media—that can be used to connect computers together, enabling them to communicate, exchange information, and share resources in real time (see Figure 3B.1).

Networks allow many users to access shared data and programs almost instantly. When data and programs are stored on a network and are shared, individual users can substantially reduce the need for programs on their own computers. Networks open up new ways to communicate, such as e-mail and instant messaging. By allowing users to share expensive hardware resources such as printers, networks reduce the cost of running an organization.

FIGURE 3B.1

Most office PCs are connected together to form a network.

Norton
ONLINE

For more information on networks, visit
http://www.mhhe.com/ peternorton.

Simultaneous Access

There are moments in any business when several workers may need to use the same data at the same time. A good example is a company's quarterly sales report, which needs to be viewed and updated by several managers. Without a network that allows workers to share files, workers must keep separate copies of data stored on different disks by each worker who accesses the data. When the data is modified on one computer, data on the other computers becomes outdated. It becomes difficult to determine which copy of the data is the most current.

Companies can solve this problem by storing commonly used data at a central location, usually on a network server (also called a server). A network server is a central computer with a large storage device and other resources that all users can share.

If the server stores data files for users to access, it is commonly called a file server. The business can store a single copy of a data file on the server that employees can access whenever they want (see Figure 3B.2). Then, if one user makes a change to the file, other users will see the change when they use the file, and no one needs to figure out who has the latest copy of the data. Advanced software is needed to allow simultaneous access to the same file.

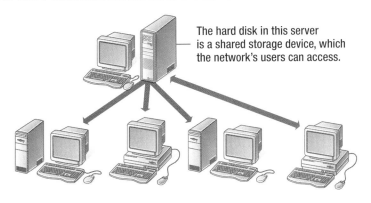

The hard disk in this server is a shared storage device, which the network's users can access.

FIGURE 3B.2

Users can share data stored on a central file server.

In addition to using many of the same data files, most office workers also use the same programs. In an environment where PCs are not networked, a separate copy of each program must be installed on every computer. This setup can be costly for two reasons. First, software can be expensive, especially when you must buy many dozens or hundreds of copies. Second, installing and configuring a program on many different computers can take a lot of time and labor, and maintaining many separate installations of a program is an ongoing expense. There are two basic solutions to this problem:

>> **Site Licenses** One solution to this problem is to purchase a site license for an application. Under a site license, a business buys a single copy (or a few copies) of an application and then pays the developer for a license to copy the application onto a specified number of computers. Under a site license, each user has a complete, individual copy of the program running on his or her PC, but the business generally pays less money than it would by purchasing a complete copy of the software for each user.

>> **Network Versions** Another solution is to connect users' computers to a central network server and enable users to share a network version of a program. In a network version, only one copy of the application is stored on the server, with a minimum number of supporting files copied to each user's PC. When workers need to use a program, they simply load it from the server into the RAM of their own desktop computers, as shown in Figure 3B.3.

There are trade-offs with placing applications on a centrally located server. In some networks, and with certain types of programs, the user's computer handles all the processing tasks required by the application, even though the application's core files are stored on the network. In other cases, the network server also handles some or all of the processing tasks. In these cases, the network server may be called an application server because it handles some application processing as well as storage.

Shared Peripheral Devices

The ability to share peripheral devices (especially expensive ones such as high-volume laser printers, which can cost thousands of dollars) is one of the best reasons for small businesses to set up a network. Although printers are more affordable than they were a few years ago, it is still too expensive to provide every worker with a personal printer. Aside from the cost of buying multiple printers, maintenance contracts and supplies increase the total cost of ownership. When several people can share a printer on a network, printing becomes less expensive and easier to manage.

FIGURE 3B.3

Using a network version of an application.

The hard disk in this computer is a shared storage device. A network version of an application can be installed here and shared by the users of the network.

With the application stored on the server, there is no need to store an individual copy on each user's machine.

There are two common ways to share a printer. A printer can connect directly to the network or it can be attached to a print server, which is a computer that manages one or more printers. Either way, users on desktop PCs will be able to submit documents across a network to a printer.

Personal Communications

One of the most far-reaching applications of data communications is electronic mail (e-mail), a system for exchanging written messages (and, increasingly, voice and video messages) through a network.

In Chapter 2, you learned how e-mail travels over the Internet. An e-mail system in a company's network functions in much the same way (see Figure 3B.4). Such systems may be purely internal, but many companies connect their private networks to the Internet so workers can send messages to and receive messages across the Internet from people outside the company's network.

In addition to e-mail, the spread of networking technology is adding to the popularity of teleconferencing. A teleconference is any kind of multiway communication carried out in real time using telecommunications or computer networks and equipment. In a teleconference, audio and video signals travel across a local area through the use of cables and switches or across the network's Internet connections to remote sites located throughout the world.

Another developing area of integrated communication is Voice over Internet Protocol (VoIP). VoIP systems bypass the need for the cost of regular telephone service by using the company's internal network to send and receive phone calls. VoIP transmits the sound of your voice over a computer network using the Internet Protocol (IP) rather than sending the signal over traditional phone wires. The PC that sits on a user's desk will share the same wire as a VoIP phone. This can work on a private network for interoffice calls or over the Internet.

Easier Data Backup

In business, data is extremely valuable, so it is important that employees back up their data. One way to assure that data is backed up is to keep it on a shared storage device that employees can access through a network. Often the network manager makes regular backups of the data on the shared storage device (see Figure 3B.5).

Managers also can use special software to back up files stored on employees' hard drives from a central location. With this method, files do not have to be copied to the server before they can be backed up.

Norton
ONLINE

For more information on e-mail and network conferencing technologies, visit **http://www.mhhe.com/ peternorton**.

FIGURE 3B.4

Sending and receiving e-mail over a typical network.

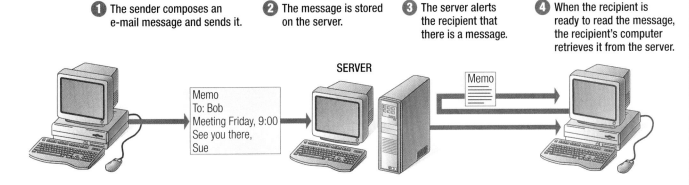

1 The sender composes an e-mail message and sends it.

2 The message is stored on the server.

3 The server alerts the recipient that there is a message.

4 When the recipient is ready to read the message, the recipient's computer retrieves it from the server.

SERVER

Memo
To: Bob
Meeting Friday, 9:00
See you there,
Sue

Memo

Backup systems like this one can be used to back up a server and individual personal computers on the network.

Common Types of Networks

If you want to understand the different types of networks and how they operate, you need to know how networks are structured. There are two main types of networks: local area networks (LANs) and wide area networks (WANs).

Local Area Networks (LANs)

A local area network (LAN) is a data communication system consisting of several devices such as computers and printers. This type of network contains computers that are relatively near each other and are physically connected using cables or wireless links. A LAN can consist of just two or three PCs connected together to share resources, or it can include hundreds of computers of different kinds. Any network that exists within a single building, or even a group of adjacent buildings, is considered a LAN. A LAN is not a system that connects to the public environment (such as the Internet) using phone or data lines.

Wide Area Networks (WANs)

Typically, a wide area network (WAN) is two or more LANs connected together, generally across a wide geographical area. For example, a company may have its corporate headquarters and manufacturing plant in one city and its marketing office in another. Each site needs resources, data, and programs locally, but it also needs to share data with the other sites. To accomplish this feat of data communication, the company can attach devices that connect over public utilities to create a WAN. (Note, however, that a WAN does not have to include any LAN systems. For example, two distant mainframe computers can communicate through a WAN, even though neither is part of a local area network.)

These remote LANs are connected through a telecommunication network (a phone company) or via the Internet through an Internet service provider (ISP) that contracts with the telecommunication networks to gain access to the Internet's backbone.

Hybrid Networks

Between the LAN and WAN structures, you will find hybrid networks such as campus area networks (CANs) and metropolitan area networks (MANs). In addition, a new form of network type is emerging called home area networks (HANs). The following sections introduce these networks.

Campus Area Networks (CANs)

A campus area network (CAN) follows the same principles as a local area network, only on a larger and more diversified scale. With a CAN, different campus offices and organizations can be linked together. For example, in a typical university setting, a bursar's office might be linked to a registrar's office. In this manner, once a student has paid his or her tuition fees to the bursar, this information is transmitted to the registrar's system so the student can enroll for classes. Some university departments or organizations might be linked to the CAN even though they already have their own separate LANs.

Metropolitan Area Networks (MANs)

The metropolitan area network (MAN) is a large-scale network that connects multiple corporate LANs together. MANs usually are not owned by a single organization; their communication devices and equipment are usually maintained by a group or single network provider that sells its networking services to corporate customers. MANs often take the role of a high-speed network that allows for the sharing of regional resources. MANs also can provide a shared connection to other networks using a WAN link. Figure 3B.6 shows the relationship between LANs, MANs, and WANs.

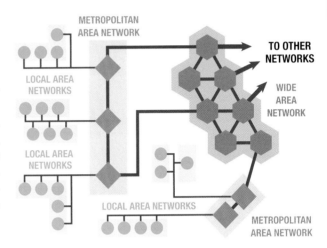

Home Area Networks (HANs)

A home area network (HAN) is a network contained within a user's home that connects a person's digital devices, from multiple computers and their peripheral devices, such as a printer, to telephones, VCRs, DVDs, televisions, video games, home security systems, "smart" appliances, fax machines, and other digital devices that are wired into the network.

FIGURE 3B.6

The relationship between LANs, MANs, and WANs.

How Networks Are Structured

Networks can be categorized by the roles the servers and PCs play in terms of hierarchical and security interaction. Some networks use servers (server-based networks) and some do not (peer-to-peer networks). These terms are defined in detail in the following sections.

Server-Based Networks

To understand a server-based network, it is important to know the meaning of the term *node*. In a network, a node is a processing location that can be a PC or some other device such as a networked printer. Usually, server-based networks include many nodes and one or more servers, which control user access to the network's resources.

As described earlier, this central computer is known as the file server, network server, application server, or just the server. Files and programs used by more than one user (at different nodes) are often stored on the server.

Norton
ONLINE

For more information on network structures, visit
http://www.mhhe.com/ peternorton.

Today, many people have the opportunity to work at home or on the road with the help of computers, telecommunications equipment, and the Internet. These workers are called *telecommuters* because they work at a remote location rather than their employer's office.

Companies are supporting efforts to allow employees from time to time to work from home. Some employees who travel often also are using home offices because it can be less expensive to equip a home worker than to pay for on-site office space. Employers also can reduce workplace-related hazards by minimizing the number of workers on site. Another benefit of telecommuting is that some workers are more productive in a home office where they can spend more time actually working on assignments and less time commuting.

To be effective, telecommuters must be just as well equipped as someone working in the company's office headquarters. The home offices need to be set up for creating and processing data, exchanging data with others, and communicating with colleagues and clients. A typical telecommuter's equipment checklist might look like this:

>> **Reliable Computer** Because of the remoteness from the main office, telecommuters may need more powerful computers, or at least more reliable equipment, to complete the necessary tasks. Often the telecommuter needs to have important programs and data files stored on a local disk. This is because the off-site worker may not always be able to access all programs and data files he or she needs by remotely logging into the company's network. In this case, the telecommuter needs to have important programs and data files stored on a local disk. Because the telecommuter's computer may need to perform additional tasks, such as remotely connecting to other systems, faxing, and printing to a local printer, the more power and storage space the computer system has, the better.

>> **Data Communications Media** Although most computers have a modem, dial-up connections are too slow and inefficient for many business uses. For this reason, many employers equip telecommuters' PCs with a network card, enabling them to use a cable modem or DSL connection. Oftentimes with these high-speed connections, multiple PC connections may be made using switches or hubs, or a wireless access point. Telecommuters usually use the Internet to connect with the office's network or they may dial up over a phone line that attaches directly to the company's private network. It is critical that the Internet connection be fast enough to meet all access demands needed for proper productivity.

A file server network (see Figure 3B.7) is a fairly simple example of this kind of nodes-and-server network. This arrangement gives each node access to the files on the server, but not necessarily to files on other nodes. When a node needs information from the server, it requests the file containing the information. The server simply stores files and forwards (sends) them to nodes that request them.

FIGURE 3B.7

A simple LAN with a file server.

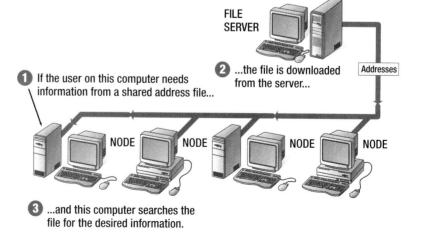

① If the user on this computer needs information from a shared address file...

② ...the file is downloaded from the server...

③ ...and this computer searches the file for the desired information.

>> **Faxing Alternatives** Rather than purchasing an expensive fax machine that takes up space and ties up a phone line, many telecommuters use the more affordable scanner instead. Using fax software, they can send and receive faxes directly from their PC. If they need to fax a document with a signature, they can scan the document first and then fax it. Multifunction "all-in-one" printer/copier/scanner/fax machines are ideal for telecommuters.

>> **Wireless Communications** With the use of access points offered by hotels and cafes, having a wireless network interface card (NIC) for a laptop can allow mobile users access to the company's private network via the Internet at any time. Today, handheld devices offer the same type of access. A farther-reaching technology is the use of various cellular phone devices that allow Internet connections via the cell phone connection.

>> **Service Accounts** Telecommuters are often responsible for setting up and maintaining their own accounts for communications and Internet services, especially when their home is in a different city than their employer's office. A conscientious employer will reimburse the worker for reasonable expenses, but the employee may be expected to seek out, set up, and maintain communication accounts and Internet services.

One way to identify a server-based network is the point at which network resources such as files are made available to users. In this environment, users gain access to files, printers, and other network-based objects by obtaining rights and permissions given through a centrally controlled server or groups of servers. Users must "log on" to the network to gain access to its resources.

Client/Server Networks

One popular type of server-based network is the client/server network, where individual computers share the processing and storage workload with a central server. This arrangement requires special software for the nodes and the server. It does not, however, require any specific type of network. Client/server software can be used on LANs or WANs, and a single client/server program can be used on a LAN where all the other software is based on a simple file server system.

The most common example of client/server computing involves a database that can be accessed by many different computers on the network. The database is stored on the network server, along with a portion of the database management system (DBMS)—the program that allows users to work with the database. The user's computer (which can be called the node, workstation, or client) stores and runs the client portion of the DBMS. When a user needs to find information in the database, he or she uses client software to send a query to the server, which searches the database and returns the information to the user's PC.

Peer-to-Peer Networks

In a peer-to-peer network (abbreviated as "P2PN" and sometimes called a work-group), all nodes on the network have equal relationships to all others, and all have similar types of software that support the sharing of resources (see Figure 3B.8). In a typical peer-to-peer network, each node has access to at least some of the resources on all other nodes. If they are set up correctly, many multi-user operating systems give users access to files on hard disks and to printers attached to other computers in the network. Many client operating systems, such as Windows and the Macintosh OS, feature built-in support for peer-to-peer networking. This enables users to set up a simple peer-to-peer network using no other software than their PCs' own operating systems.

One of the main distinguishing characteristics of the peer-to-peer network is the management and control point of access to shared resources such as files and printers. With peer-to-peer networks, access is controlled on the local PC by the user setting passwords on shared folders and printers. For example, if a user wants to gain access to a shared resource such as a Word document stored on another user's PC, the requesting user must ask the user with the document to share the file. The user sharing the Word document also may require that the requesting user utilize a password to access it.

A peer-to-peer network also can include a network server. In this case, a peer-to-peer LAN is similar to a file server network. The only difference between them is that the peer-to-peer network gives users greater access to the other nodes than a file server network does.

Some high-end peer-to-peer networks allow distributed computing, which enables users to draw on the processing power of other computers in the network. For example, a user can transfer tasks that take a lot of CPU power—such as creating computer software or rendering a 3-D illustration—to other computers on the network. This leaves the user's machines free for other work.

SELF-CHECK ::

Circle the word or phrase that best completes each statement.

1. _____ is one of the benefits of using a network.

   a. File security   **b.** Peripheral sharing   **c.** Protection from viruses

2. If a server stores data files for users to access, it is commonly called a(n) _____ .

   a. file server   **b.** application server   **c.** folder server

3. A(n) _____ generally does not connect to the public environment using phone or data lines.

   a. WAN   **b.** Internet   **c.** LAN

FIGURE 3B.8

A peer-to-peer network.

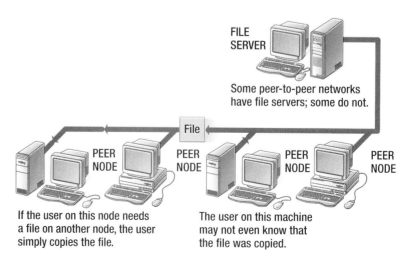

FILE SERVER

Some peer-to-peer networks have file servers; some do not.

File

PEER NODE   PEER NODE   PEER NODE   PEER NODE

If the user on this node needs a file on another node, the user simply copies the file.

The user on this machine may not even know that the file was copied.

Network Topologies and Protocols

An important feature of any LAN is its topology—the logical layout of the cables and devices that connect the nodes of the network. Network designers consider several factors when deciding which topology or combination of topologies to use: the type of computers and cabling (if any) in place, the distance between computers, the speed at which data must travel around the network, and the cost of setting up the network.

Data moves though the network in a structure called packets. Packets are pieces of a message broken down into small units by the sending PC and reassembled by the receiving PC. Different networks format packets in different ways, but most packets have two parts: the header and the payload. The header is the first part of the packet, which contains information needed by the network. The header identifies the node that sent the packet (the source) and provides the address of the node that will receive the packet (the destination). The network reads each packet's header to determine where to send the packet and, in some cases, to determine the best way to get it to its destination. The header also holds control data that helps the receiving node reassemble a message's packets in the right order. The payload is the actual data that is being transmitted between the two nodes. (In the Internet environment, packets are called datagrams.)

A network's topology and related technologies are important for two reasons. First, a correctly designed network, using the most appropriate topology for the organization's needs, will move data packets as efficiently as possible. Second, the network's topology plays a role in preventing collisions, which is what happens when multiple nodes try to transmit data at the same time. Their packets can collide and destroy each other.

A bus topology network uses one cable (see Figure 3B.9). All the nodes and peripheral devices are connected in a series to that cable. A special device, called a terminator, is attached at the cable's start and end points to stop network signals so they do not bounce back down the cable. This topology's main advantage is that it uses the least amount of cabling of any topology. In a bus topology network, however, extra circuitry and software are used to keep data packets from colliding with one another. A broken connection can bring down all or part of the network.

The star topology (see Figure 3B.10) is probably the most common topology. In a star network, all nodes are connected to a device called a hub and communicate through it. Data packets travel through the hub and are sent to the attached nodes, eventually reaching their destinations. Some hubs—known as intelligent hubs—can monitor traffic and help prevent collisions. In a star topology, a broken connection between a node and the hub does not affect the rest of the network. If the hub is lost, however, all nodes connected to that hub are unable to communicate.

The ring topology (see Figure 3B.11) connects the network's nodes in a circular

This bus topology shows one cable connecting multiple devices.

The star topology connects all nodes to a hub or switch.

The ring topology is a linked circular chain.

Laser printer

Norton ONLINE

For more information on network topologies and protocols, visit
http://www.mhhe.com/ peternorton.

In a meshed topology, all nodes are connected to each other.

chain, with each node connected to the next. The last node connects to the first, completing the ring. Each node examines data as it travels through the ring. If the data—known as a token—is not addressed to the node examining it, that node passes it to the next node. There is no danger of collisions because only one packet of data travels the ring at a time. If the ring is broken, however, the entire network is unable to communicate.

The mesh topology (see Figure 3B.12) is the least-used network topology and the most expensive to implement. In a mesh environment, a cable runs from every computer to every other computer. If you have four computers, you must have six cables—three coming from each computer to the other computers. The big advantage to this arrangement is that data can never fail to be delivered; if one connection goes down, there are other ways to route the data to its destination.

Network Media

With computer networks, *media* refers to the means used to link a network's nodes together. There are many different types of transmission media, the most popular being twisted-pair wire (normal electrical wire), coaxial cable (the type of cable used for cable television), and fiber-optic cable (cables made out of glass). In wireless networks, the atmosphere itself acts as the medium because it carries the wireless signals that nodes and servers use to communicate. The following sections examine wire-based and wireless media.

Wire-Based Media

Twisted-pair cable (see Figure 3B.13) normally consists of four pairs of wires. The individual pairs have two wires that are separately insulated in plastic, then twisted around each other and bound together in a layer of plastic.

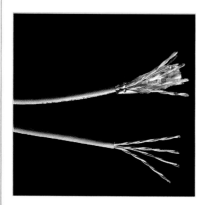

Twisted-pair cable wires are insulated and twisted around each other. They are usually used to connect hubs/switches to PCs in a star topology.

Like the cabling used in cable television systems, coaxial cable (see Figure 3B.14) has two conductors. One is a single wire in the center of the cable, and the other is a wire mesh shield that surrounds the first wire, with an insulator between.

A fiber-optic cable (see Figure 3B.15) is a thin strand of glass that transmits pulsating beams of light rather than electric current.

Wireless Media

Wireless networks use radio or infrared signals that travel through the air (called *ether*) for transmitting data. Office LANs can use radio signals to transmit data between nodes in a building. Laptops equipped with cellular modems allow users to connect to the office network when they travel. Corporate WANs often use microwave transmission to connect LANs within the same metropolitan area (see Figure 3B.16). WANs that cover long distances often use satellites and microwave communication.

Central wire

Insulator

Wire mesh

One-inch coaxial cables are usually found in older networks. The large cables shown here are used for crossing greater distances such as the ocean.

Network Hardware

As data moves between PCs, it needs to be channeled properly to reach its final destination. To make this possible, the proper hardware must be attached to and between all PCs.

Network Interface Cards (NICs)

Regardless of the wiring and topology used, each computer on the network needs a hardware component to control the flow of data. The device that performs this function is the network interface card (NIC), also known as a network adapter card or network card. This printed circuit board fits into one of the computer's expansion slots and provides a port where the network cable is attached.

In the case of a wireless NIC, there will not be a port, an antenna will be showing, or a light will indicate that an internal antenna is activated. Network software works with the operating system and tells the computer how to use the NIC. Both the network software and the NIC must adhere to the same network protocols, which are explored later in this chapter.

Network Linking Devices and Technologies

To create a network, some type of linking mechanism is needed to interconnect at least two computers. Most servers, nodes, and printers are attached by a linking device or a series of linking devices. Linking devices have ports where cables connect them to the nodes, printers, or other devices that have ports or NICs installed. The various linking devices that are available include

>> **Hubs**   A hub is an affordable connection point for different types of devices on a network. This is not a particularly fast connection because it broadcasts the packets it receives to all nodes attached to its ports.

>> **Bridges**   A bridge is a device that connects two LANs or two segments of the same LAN. A bridge looks at the information in each packet header and forwards data that is traveling from one LAN to another.

>> **Switches**   A switch is a device that learns which machine is connected to its port by using the PC, printer, or other devices' IP address. This is a very popular and sought-after device used to connect a LAN. A switch substantially reduces the amount of broadcast traffic and is currently the most popular network-linking device. Modern switches can even function as routers (see below), allowing multiple LANs to be interconnected by linking the LAN's switches together. This is called an uplink.

>> **Routers**   A router is a complicated device that stores the routing information for networks (see Figure 3B.17). A router looks at each packet's header to determine where the packet should go and then determines the best route for the packet to take toward its destination.

To create a connection between different types of networks, you need a gateway. In its simplest form, a gateway is a node on a network that serves as an entrance to another network. In the small business or home network, the gateway is the device that routes data from a local PC to an outside network such as the

FIGURE 3B.15

Although very fast, fiber-optic cables are not easy to cut and cannot be bent to accommodate sharp angles.

Strands of glass

FIGURE 3B.16

This wireless network is using line-of-site dishes to link locations together.

simnet™

Norton
ONLINE

For more information on network media and linking devices, visit
http://www.mhhe.com/peternorton.

FIGURE 3B.17

A router.

Internet. The router intercepts then redirects and filters (if necessary) any data packets passing through. Packets from different types of networks have different kinds of information in their headers, and the information can be in various formats. The gateway can take a packet from one type of network, read its header, and then add a second header that is understood by the second network. When configuring your internal network to allow an Internet connection, you need to point the PC to the gateway's IP address.

Tying together the linking devices, servers, nodes, printers, and other network equipment into an actual LAN is the cabling equipment. Cabling equipment is designed to work with a certain kind of network topology, and each one has certain standard features.

The most common types of network technologies include

>> **Ethernet** The most common network technology in use. The original implementations of Ethernet used coaxial cable and were called 10Base-5 and 10Base-2. The most popular implementation of Ethernet—called 10Base-T—uses a star topology and twisted-pair wires and can achieve transmission speeds up to 10 Mbps (megabits per second). Most new network installations use an Ethernet star topology with either twisted-pair or fiber-optic cables as the medium. With Ethernet, if two nodes transmit data at the same instant, the collision is detected and the nodes retransmit one at a time.

>> **Fast Ethernet** (Also called 100Base-T) Fast Ethernet is available using the same media and topology as Ethernet, but different NICs are used to achieve speeds of up to 100 Mbps. This cable is called a Category 5 (Cat5), as shown in Figure 3B.18.

>> **Gigabit Ethernet** Gigabit Ethernet is a version of Ethernet technology that supports data transfer rates of one gigabit per second. It evolved from the same 10 Mbps Ethernet technology that was created in the 1970s. Although capable of transferring 10 Gbps, a standard that became more affordable and popular is 1000Base-T or 1 Gbps. Another standard that is popular is the 5 Gbps fiber-optic cable that is used to connect switches together. The Ethernet protocol can allow a network administrator to back up 2 TB (terabytes) of data in about 27 minutes. Gigabit Ethernet also can carry approximately 900 video signals at once, at about 1.5 Mbps of digital video. With advanced audio, video, and telephone applications coming into the market every day, it will not be long before the Gigabit Ethernet standard will become the norm for high-bandwidth tasks and processes.

>> **Token Ring** The controlling hardware in a Token Ring network transmits an electronic token—a small set of data—to each node on the network many times each second if the token is not already in use by a specific node. A computer can copy data into the token and set the address where the data should be sent. The token then continues around the ring, and each computer along the way looks at the address until the token reaches the computer with the address that was recorded in the token. The receiving computer then copies the contents of the token and sends an acknowledgment to the sending computer. When the sending computer receives the acknowledgment from the receiving computer, it resets the token's status to "empty" and transmits it to the next computer in the ring. The hardware for a Token Ring network is expensive; Token Ring adapter cards can cost as much as five times more than other types of network adapters. Token Ring networks once operated at 4 or 16 Mbps, but like Ethernet, new standards for Token Ring have increased the transmission rate, which is now up to 100 Mbps.

FIGURE 3B.18

A typical Cat5 cable.

Protocols

Each LAN is governed by a protocol, which is an agreed-upon format for transmitting data between two devices. There are many standard protocols. Each has particular advantages and disadvantages. Some protocols are simpler than others, some are more reliable, and some are faster. To effectively communicate, a user must have the same protocol installed on the local PC and the remote PC to make a connection.

Protocols, using their own methods, break data down into small packets in preparation for transportation. Linking devices pass these packets to the various pieces of equipment, including other computers and printers that are attached to the network. As discussed earlier in this chapter, a packet is a data segment that includes a header, payload, and control elements that are transmitted together (see Figure 3B.19). The receiving computer reconstructs the packets into their original structure.

A single LAN may utilize more than one protocol. Some of the most common protocols in use today include

» **TCP/IP** Originally associated with UNIX hosts, TCP/IP is the protocol of the Internet and is required on any computer that must communicate across the Internet. TCP/IP is now the default networking protocol of Windows 2000 Professional (client) and Server editions, Windows XP, Windows Server 2003, and many other operating systems.

» **IPX/SPX** A proprietary protocol of Novell, IPX/SPX has been used in most versions of the NetWare network operating system for networking offices throughout the world. Newer versions of NetWare also support TCP/IP.

» **NetBIOS/NetBEUI** A relatively simple protocol that has no real configurable parameters, NetBIOS/NetBEUI sends messages to every computer that can receive them. It is an excellent protocol for networking small offices or homes, but it does not expand well into larger environments.

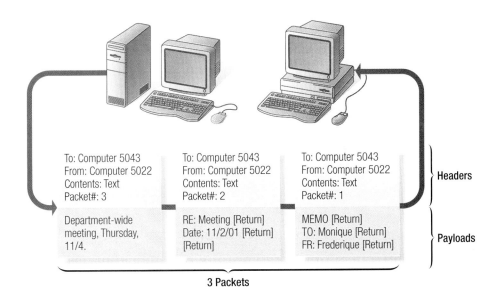

FIGURE 3B.19

An e-mail message is being divided up into packets.

Computers In Your Career

With the increased attention to national and corporate security in the United States, Michael French is well positioned for a long and successful career in computer networking, particularly when it comes to protecting those systems from hackers.

As a senior security consultant for IBM, French has conducted and managed projects for leading firms in the insurance, banking, investment, and educational industries. A typical workday will find him on the road at a client's location, working to improve security on company networks, SUN Solaris servers, or PCs running Microsoft Windows.

French is living proof that networking professionals have a wide range of career paths to choose from. Before joining IBM, for example, French ran his own consulting firm focused on mobile computing and voice/data networks and previously served as vice president of e-commerce for Bank of America.

A graduate of Brown University and Long Island University, where he earned a Master of Science in management science, French is IBM certified in IT security, was awarded two patents for electrical designs, and was a co-inventor on four other patents. He typically works a 10-hour day, with much of it spent assessing network security for individual IBM clients.

Keeping up to date on the latest developments in the networking space is French's biggest job challenge, and one he overcomes by reading, studying, and attending trade conferences and seminars. "There's a constant need to upgrade your knowledge," says French. "The current buzzword, for example, is Voice over IP and it's unleashing a flood of new products and problems that we never knew we had."

Most rewarding about the IT networking field, says French, is that it's always interesting and never boring. The job also comes with a degree of autonomy, since many networking professionals manage their own projects and are considered competent and capable of making decisions and attaining goals. He sees future prospects in networking as "exciting" and doesn't predict any drop-off in demand for good networking professionals. "It's a fast-growing and fast-changing field," he adds.

Other careers relating to networking and data communications include

>> **Customer Service Support** Many entry-level jobs are coming from the customer support areas of software, operating systems, and telecommunication systems industries. This involves troubleshooting issues with customers over the phone or sometimes providing mobile

on-site support. Customer support comes in various levels. Frontline support is usually called level 1. The support levels can go all the way back to the developers of the software or hardware. Support at this level is usually very technical and the salaries are high.

» **Network Administrators** These individuals are responsible for managing a company's network infrastructure. Some of the jobs in this field include designing and implementing networks, setting up and managing users' accounts, installing and updating network software and applications, and backing up the network.

» **Information Systems (IS) Managers** IS managers are responsible for managing a team of information professionals, including network administrators, software developers, project managers, and other staff. Jobs in the IS management field differ according to the needs of the company.

» **Data Communications Managers** These managers are responsible for setting up and maintaining Internet, intranet, and extranet sites. Often they are also responsible for designing and establishing an organization's telecommuting initiative.

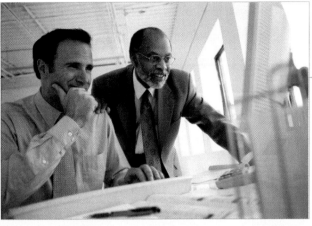

Although the networking fields are facing a slight economic downturn for upper-level jobs, the industry is expected to grow faster than other industries, especially at the skilled support or entry levels.

The Bureau of Labor Statistics calls networking one of the most rapidly growing fields in the computing industry. Median annual earnings of network and computer systems administrators were $51,280 in 2000, with the middle 50 percent earning between $40,450 and $65,140.

Summary ::

>> A network is a way to connect computers for communication, data exchange, and resource sharing.

>> Many networks are built around a central computer called a server, which provides storage and other resources that users can share.

>> A local area network (LAN) consists of computers that are relatively close to one another. A LAN can have a few PCs or hundreds of them in a single building or several buildings.

>> A wide area network (WAN) results when multiple LANs are connected through public utilities such as phone lines or microwave systems.

>> Many networks are built around a central server. The PCs that connect to the server are called nodes.

>> In a file server network, the server provides storage and file-sharing services for the nodes.

>> An application server is a server that is used to run applications from a centralized location on the network to free up resources on the nodes.

>> In a client/server network, nodes and the server share the storage and processing tasks.

>> A peer-to-peer network is a small network that usually does not include a central server. In a peer-to-peer network, users can share files and resources on all the network's nodes.

>> A topology is the physical layout of the cables and devices that connect the nodes of a network. Topologies get their names—such as bus, star, or ring—from the shape of the network they create.

>> The most common media for data communications are twisted-pair wire, coaxial cable, fiber-optic cable, and wireless links.

>> The performance of network media is measured by the amount of data they can transmit each second. This value is called bandwidth. The higher a network's bandwidth, the more data it can carry.

>> A protocol is an agreed-upon format for transmitting data between two devices. Some popular protocols include TCP/IP (the Internet protocol), IPX/SPX, and Net-BIOS/NetBEUI.

Key Terms ::

10Base-T, 148
application server, 138
bridge, 147
bus topology, 145
campus area network (CAN), 141
client/server network, 143
coaxial cable, 146
datagrams, 145
distributed computing, 144
Ethernet, 148
Fast Ethernet (100Base-T), 148
fiber-optic cable, 146
file server, 137
file server network, 142
gateway, 147
Gigabit Ethernet, 148

header, 145
home area network (HAN), 141
hub, 147
local area network (LAN), 140
mesh topology, 146
metropolitan area network (MAN), 141
network, 137
network interface card (NIC), 147
network version, 138
node, 141
packet, 145
payload, 145
peer-to-peer network, 144
print server, 139
protocol, 149
ring topology, 145

router, 147
server, 137
site license, 138
star topology, 145
switch, 147
teleconference, 139
terminator, 145
token, 146
Token Ring, 148
topology, 145
twisted-pair cable, 146
Voice over Internet Protocol
 (VoIP), 139
wide area network (WAN), 140
wireless networks, 146
wireless NIC, 147

Key Term Quiz ::

Complete each statement by writing one of the terms listed under Key Terms in each blank.

1. A(n) _____ is a network of computers that serves users located relatively near each other.

2. If you connect computers together to communicate and exchange information, the result is called a(n) _____ .

3. The physical layout of wires and devices that connect the network's nodes is called the network's _____ .

4. In a bus topology network, a special device called a(n) _____ is placed on each end of the cable.

5. A(n) _____ is a thin strand of glass that transmits pulsating beams of light.

6. A(n) _____ is the device that is added to a PC that allows it to connect to a LAN.

7. A centralized computer that allows multiple remote users to share the same printing device is referred to as a _____ .

8. _____ cables have two conductors: one is a single wire in the center and the other is a wire mesh shield that surrounds the first wire.

9. You can use a device called a(n) _____ to connect two different types of networks together.

10. High-end peer-to-peer networks allow for _____ . This lets users access the power of multiple computers to process programs such as 3-D illustration software.

Multiple Choice ::

Circle the word or phrase that best completes each sentence.

1. Companies store data on a network server because it is _____ .
   - **a.** easier to track changes made to important data
   - **b.** less convenient for the user to access the data from home
   - **c.** easier to download or retrieve large video files
   - **d.** more difficult for users to access programs

2. In a _____ network, all devices are connected to a device called a hub and communicate through it.
   - **a.** bus
   - **b.** star
   - **c.** ring
   - **d.** mesh

3. A solution that connects users' computers to a central network server that enables them to share programs is called _____ .
   - **a.** single-user version programs
   - **b.** PC license programs
   - **c.** site license programs
   - **d.** network version programs

4. When software is stored and run from a centralized location, the computer containing such software is called a(n) _____ .
   - **a.** file server
   - **b.** print server
   - **c.** application server
   - **d.** CD server

5. A _____ is an agreed-upon format for transmitting data between two devices.
   - **a.** protopology
   - **b.** protoplasm
   - **c.** prototype
   - **d.** protocol

6. _____ means any kind of multiway communication carried out in real time using telecommunications or computer network equipment.
   - **a.** Television
   - **b.** Telemarketing
   - **c.** Teleconferencing
   - **d.** Telecasting

7. A _____ is two or more LANs connected together, generally across a large geographical area.
   - **a.** WAN
   - **b.** SAN
   - **c.** CAN
   - **d.** HAN

8. The _____ topology is the least-used network topology.
   - **a.** star
   - **b.** mesh
   - **c.** ring
   - **d.** bus

9. A _____ is a type of network usually found where students and school administrators have a need to share files across several buildings.
   - **a.** wide area network (WAN)
   - **b.** metropolitan area network (MAN)
   - **c.** campus area network (CAN)
   - **d.** local area network (LAN)

10. An arrangement where user accounts are centralized on a server and PCs gain access to network resources by accessing this server is called a _____.
    - **a.** client/server network
    - **b.** peer-to-peer network
    - **c.** server-to-server network
    - **d.** client/client network

Review Questions ::

In your own words, briefly answer the following questions.

1. List four benefits that networks provide to their users.
2. How can a network help a small business save money on printing?
3. Name four types of media used to link networks.
4. List four types of network topologies used in wire-based networks.
5. Name three common LAN protocols.
6. A network is a set of technologies that can be used to connect computers together. What three general components are needed to set up a network?
7. What is a packet?
8. What distinguishes a peer-to-peer network?
9. What is a network server?
10. What are two common ways to share a printer via a network?

Lesson Labs ::

Complete the following exercise as directed by your instructor. (Note: These exercises assume you are using Windows XP or Windows 2000. If you have a different version of Windows, ask your instructor for specific directions.)

1. Explore your network.
   a. On your Windows desktop, double-click the My Network Places icon. The My Network Places window opens. This window lets you access all the computers, folders, files, and devices on the network.
   b. Find the icon named Entire Network and double-click it. What do you see? Because every network is unique, the contents of this window will vary from network to network.
   c. Following your instructor's directions, click icons and open new windows to explore your network. How many network resources can you access?
   d. When you finish exploring, close all open windows.

Chapter Labs

Complete the following exercises using a computer in your classroom, lab, or home.

1. **Plug it in.** With your instructor observing, turn your computer and monitor off and unplug them from their power source. Then take these steps:

   a. Move to the back of the computer and inspect all the cables plugged into it. Which devices are connected to the PC and by which cables? Which port is connected to each device? Make a chart of these connections.

   b. Unplug each connection. After all students have unplugged their devices from their computers, switch places with someone and reconnect all the devices to the computer. Does the other student's system have the same connections as yours? If not, can you reconnect all its devices correctly?

   c. Return to your PC. Use your chart to see whether your system has been reconnected correctly. If not, correct any connecting errors. When you are sure all devices are plugged into the right ports, reconnect the PC and monitor to the power source. Turn the PC on and make sure everything is working correctly.

2. **Watch those files grow.** The concept of bits and bytes may seem unimportant until you begin creating files on your computer. Then you can begin to understand how much memory and storage space your files take up (in bytes, of course). Create a file in Notepad, save it to disk, and take the following steps to add to the file to see how it grows:

   a. Launch Notepad. The steps to launch the program vary, depending on which version of Windows you use. If you need help, ask your instructor for directions.

   b. Type two or three short paragraphs of text. When you are done, click the File menu, and then click the Save As command.

   c. In the Save As dialog box, choose a drive and folder in which to save the new file, and give the file a short name you can remember easily, such as SIZE-TEST.TXT.

   d. With Notepad running, launch Windows Explorer. If you need help, ask your instructor for directions.

   e. Navigate to the drive and folder where you saved your Notepad file. When you find the file, look for its size in the Size column and write down the size. Close the Exploring window.

   f. Return to the Notepad window and add two or three more paragraphs of text. Then click the File menu and click the Save command to resave the file under the same name.

   g. Reopen Windows Explorer and look at the file's size again. Has it changed? By how much?

Discussion Questions

As directed by your instructor, discuss the following questions in class or in groups.

1. Do you think the international interchange of data provided by the Unicode character set is a worthwhile goal for computing technology? Do you see any other benefits to Unicode's widespread implementation?

2. Why is the CPU commonly referred to as the computer's "brain"? Do you think it is a good idea to use this term to describe the CPU? Why?

Research and Report

Using your own choice of resources (such as the Internet, books, magazines, and newspaper articles), research and write a short paper discussing one of the following topics:

>> The history of the Pentium family of processors.

>> The uses of parallel processing computer systems in business.

>> The USB and FireWire bus standards.

When you are finished, proofread and print your paper, and give it to your instructor.

ETHICAL ISSUES

Computers are becoming more powerful all the time. Many people see this capability as a source of limitless benefits, but others view it as a threat. With this thought in mind, discuss the following questions in class.

1. As technology improves, processing becomes faster. It can be argued that computer technology has made Americans less patient than they were a decade ago. Do you agree? If so, do you see it as a benefit of our technological progress or a drawback? Should we restrain our urge to increase the pace of life? Be prepared to explain your position.

2. Computers are not only getting faster, but they also are becoming exponentially more powerful all the time. For example, many think that in the next decade artificial intelligence will be developed to the point that computers can begin reasoning—weighing facts, solving problems, perhaps even making decisions. Will people relinquish even a tiny bit of control to computers? If so, what kinds of decisions will we allow them to make for us? What risks do we run by enabling computers to become "smart" enough to solve problems or ultimately to think?

CHAPTER 4

Introduction to Software

01 02 03 04 05 06 07 08 09 10 11 12 13 14

CHAPTER CONTENTS ::

This chapter contains the following lessons:

Lesson **4A:**
Operating System Basics

>> Types of Operating Systems
>> Providing a User Interface
>> Running Programs
>> Managing Hardware
>> PC Operating Systems
>> Network Operating Systems
>> Embedded Operating Systems

Lesson **4B:**
Productivity Software

>> Word Processing Programs
>> Spreadsheet Programs
>> Presentation Programs
>> Personal Information Managers

Overview: The Purpose of Operating Systems

An operating system (OS) is a software program, but it is different from word processing programs, spreadsheets, and all the other software programs on your computer. As you may recall from Chapter 1, the OS is an example of system software—software that controls the system's hardware and that interacts with the user and application software. In short, the operating system is the computer's master control program. The OS provides you with the tools (commands) that enable you to interact with the PC. When you issue a command, the OS translates it into code that the machine can use. The OS ensures that the results of your actions are displayed on screen, printed, and so on. The operating system also acts as the primary controlling mechanism for the computer's hardware.

The operating system performs the following functions:

>> Displays the on-screen elements with which you interact—the user interface.

>> Loads programs (such as word processing and spreadsheet programs) into the computer's memory so that you can use them.

>> Coordinates how programs work with the computer's hardware and other software.

>> Manages the way information is stored on and retrieved from disks.

In this lesson you will learn about the types of operating systems and the services they provide.

Operating System Basics

OBJECTIVES ::

>> List the four primary functions of an operating system.

>> List the four types of operating systems.

>> Identify four components found in most graphical user interfaces.

>> Describe the operating system's role in running software programs.

>> List all the current PC operating systems.

>> Describe the role of network operating systems.

Types of Operating Systems

Operating systems can be organized into four major types:

» **Real-Time Operating Systems** A real-time operating system is a very fast, relatively small OS. Real-time OSs are often also embedded OSs, when they are built into the circuitry of a device and are not loaded from a disk drive. A real-time OS is needed to run real-time applications; it may support multiple simultaneous tasks, or it may only support single-tasking. A real-time application is an application that responds to certain inputs extremely quickly—thousandths or millionths of a second (milliseconds or microseconds, respectively). Real-time applications are needed to run medical diagnostics equipment, life-support systems, machinery, scientific instruments, and industrial systems.

FIGURE 4A.1

A single user can only run a single program in a single-user/single-tasking operating system.

» **Single-User/Single-Tasking Operating Systems** An operating system that allows a single user to perform one task at a time is a single-user/single-tasking operating system (see Figure 4A.1). To a user, a "task" is a function such as printing a document, writing a file to disk, editing a file, or downloading a file from a network server. To the operating system, a task is a process, and small and simple OSs can only manage a single task at a time.

» **Single-User/Multitasking Operating System** A single-user/multitasking operating system is one that allows a single user to perform two or more functions at once. It takes a special operating system to keep two or more tasks running at once. The most commonly used personal computers usually run such OSs, including Microsoft Windows and the Macintosh Operating System (see Figure 4A.2). The multitasking features of these OSs have greatly increased the productivity of people in a large variety of jobs because they can accomplish more in a shorter period of time. For instance, to an office worker, it is important to be able to send a large document to a printer and be able to do other work on his or her computer while it is being printed. It is also helpful for many types of workers to be able to have two or more programs open, to share the data between the two programs, and to be able to switch between the programs.

FIGURE 4A.2

In many types of jobs, a single user can be more productive when working in a multitasking operating system.

» **Multi-User/Multitasking Operating Systems** A multi-user/multitasking operating system is an operating system that allows multiple users to run programs that are simultaneously running on a single network server, called a terminal server. This is not at all the same as connecting to a network server for the sake of accessing files and printers. When a computer is connected to a typical network server to access document files to edit, the client com-

Terminal Server

User 1 Session

User 2 Session

Terminal Client

Terminal Client

User 1

User 2

FIGURE 4A.3

A multi-user/multitasking operating system runs on a computer to which many users connect; each user can run his or her own session on the server.

puter performs the processing work locally. Not so with a multi-user OS, which gives each user a complete environment, called a user session, on the server. Each user's applications run within their user session on the server separate from all other user sessions. The software that makes this possible is called a terminal client. In a multi-user/multitasking operating system environment, all or most of the computing occurs at the server. (See Figure 4A.3.) Examples of multi-user OSs include UNIX, VMS, and mainframe operating systems such as MVS.

Providing a User Interface

When you work on a computer, you see and use a set of items on the screen. Taken together, these items are called the user interface. The two most common types of user interfaces are graphical and command line.

Graphical User Interfaces

Most current operating systems, including all versions of Windows, the Macintosh operating system, OS/2, and some versions of UNIX and Linux, provide a graphical user interface (GUI, pronounced GOO-ee). Graphical user interfaces are so called because you use a mouse (or some other pointing device) to work with graphical objects such as windows, menus, icons, buttons, and other tools. These graphical tools all represent different types of commands; the GUI enables you to issue commands to the computer by using visual objects instead of typing

Norton
ONLINE

For more information on user interfaces, visit
http://www.mhhe.com/ peternorton.

Introduction to Software 161

commands. This is one of the key advantages of a graphical user interface; it frees you from memorizing and typing text commands.

Windows is one of several GUIs that use the desktop metaphor in which the background of the GUI is said to be a desktop on which you have your graphical tools and within which you can store your work. Figure 4A.4 shows the Windows XP desktop. The small pictures on the desktop—called shortcuts—represent links to resources on the PC or network. Although shortcuts are often called icons, an icon actually is only the tiny graphic that represents an object, such as programs, folders, files, printers, and shortcuts. Using your mouse or other pointing device, you can move the pointer (a small graphic that moves in reaction to mouse movements) and choose (or activate) a shortcut, telling Windows you want to use the resource that the shortcut represents. For example, you can choose the Microsoft Word shortcut to launch that program. The items that appear on the desktop depend on the contents of the computer's disks, the resources it can access, and the user's preferences; therefore, any two Windows desktops can look different.

Certain elements always appear on the Windows desktop. As shown in Figure 4A.4, the taskbar appears at the bottom of the Windows desktop; it is used to launch and manage programs. The START button is a permanent feature of the taskbar; click it to open the Start menu. The Start menu contains shortcuts for launching programs and opening folders on a computer (see Figure 4A.5). Shortcuts can be added to the desktop, the Start menu, and other areas. When you start a program in Windows, a button representing it appears on the taskbar.

When you launch a program, it is loaded into memory and begins to run. A running program may take up the whole screen, it may appear in a rectangular frame called a window, or it may appear only as a shortcut on the taskbar.

Desktop Shortcuts

The background is called the Desktop

Start Button

Taskbar

Quick Launch Area   Notification Area

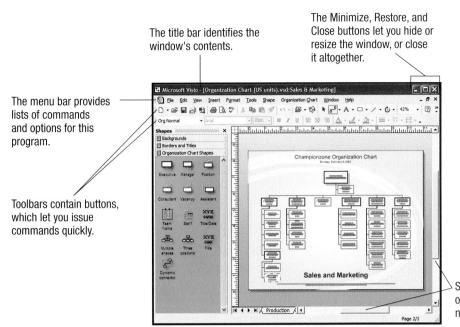

The title bar identifies the window's contents.

The Minimize, Restore, and Close buttons let you hide or resize the window, or close it altogether.

The menu bar provides lists of commands and options for this program.

Toolbars contain buttons, which let you issue commands quickly.

Scroll bars let you view parts of the program or file that do not fit in the window.

FIGURE 4A.6

Most Windows applications feature the tools shown here.

You access all the resources on your computer through windows. For example, you can view the contents of a disk in a window, run a program and edit a document in a window, view a Web page in a window, or change system settings in a window. A different window appears for each resource you want to use. Figure 4A.6 shows Microsoft Visio running in a window. Some menus and buttons, such as the ones shown here, appear in nearly every window you open. In the Windows GUI, programs share many of the same features, so you see a familiar interface no matter what program you are using. Among the common GUI features are the title bar, menu bar, toolbars, scroll bars, and various buttons. The **title bar** identifies the windows' contents and it also contains the MINIMIZE, RESTORE, and CLOSE buttons, which let you hide the window, resize it, or close it altogether. The **menu bar** provides lists of commands and options for this specific program. **Toolbars** contain buttons that let you issue commands quickly. **Scroll bars** let you view parts of the program or file that do not fit in the window.

You initiate many tasks by clicking icons and toolbar buttons, but you also can perform tasks by choosing commands from lists called **menus**. In most program windows, you open menus from a horizontal list called the menu bar. As shown in Figure 4A.7, many programs feature a File menu, which typically contains commands for opening, closing, saving, and printing files. To execute or run one of the menu commands, you click it. In many cases, you can issue menu commands by using keyboard shortcuts instead of the mouse.

Dialog boxes are special-purpose windows that appear when the OS or application needs to give you some status and possible choice of actions or you need to tell a program (or the operating system) what to do next. A dialog box is so named because it conducts a "dialogue" with you as it seeks the information it needs to perform a task. A dialog box can even have more than one

FIGURE 4A.7

A typical File menu

You can open a menu by clicking its name on the menu bar.

The underlined F indicates that you can press Alt+F to open the File menu, instead of clicking.

With the File menu open, you can press P to execute the Print command.

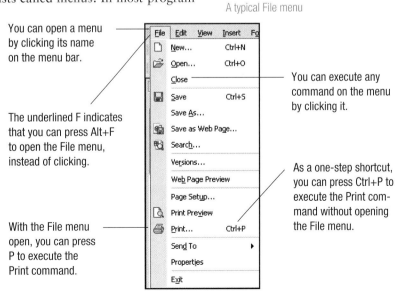

You can execute any command on the menu by clicking it.

As a one-step shortcut, you can press Ctrl+P to execute the Print command without opening the File menu.

This dialog box includes multiple tabs and a variety of methods for selecting options.

Click a tab to display different "pages" of the dialog box.

Option buttons let you select one option from a set of choices.

The Help button provides information about the tools in the dialog box.

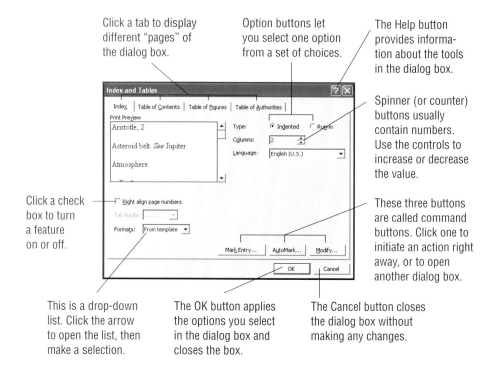

Spinner (or counter) buttons usually contain numbers. Use the controls to increase or decrease the value.

Click a check box to turn a feature on or off.

These three buttons are called command buttons. Click one to initiate an action right away, or to open another dialog box.

This is a drop-down list. Click the arrow to open the list, then make a selection.

The OK button applies the options you select in the dialog box and closes the box.

The Cancel button closes the dialog box without making any changes.

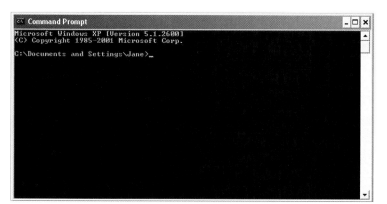

FIGURE 4A.9

The Windows XP Command Prompt can be used to launch any program that will run in Windows, even a GUI program that will open its own window.

page, in which case the pages are made available through tabs and look like a stack of tabbed pages. Figure 4A.8 shows a dialog box from Microsoft Word and describes some of the most common dialog box features.

Command-Line Interfaces

Some older operating systems (such as MS-DOS) and some current versions of UNIX and Linux feature a command-line interface, which uses typewritten commands—rather than graphical objects—to execute tasks. A command-line interface displays in character mode—using only equal-sized alphanumeric and other simple symbols. Users interact with a command-line interface by typing strings of characters at a prompt on the screen. As much as people prefer to work in a GUI, a command-line interface gives you a quick way to enter commands, and even now Windows has an optional command-line interface, called the Command Prompt (see Figure 4A.9).

Running Programs

The operating system provides a consistent interface between application programs and the user. It is also the interface between those programs and other computer resources such as memory, a printer, or another program.

For example, when you want your word processing program to retrieve a file, you use the Open dialog box to list the files in the folder that you specify (see Figure 4A.10). To provide the list, the program calls on the operating system. The OS goes through the same process to build a list of files whether it receives its instructions from you (via the desktop) or from an application. The difference is that when the request comes from an application, the operating system sends the results of its work to the application rather than to the desktop.

Some other services that an operating system provides to programs, in addition to listing files, include

>> Saving the contents of files to a disk.

>> Reading the contents of a file from disk into memory.

>> Sending a document to the printer and activating the printer.

>> Providing resources that let you copy or move data from one document to another, or from one program to another.

>> Allocating RAM among the running programs.

>> Recognizing keystrokes or mouse clicks and displaying characters or graphics on the screen.

Sharing Information

Many types of applications let you move chunks of data from one place to another. For example, you may want to copy a chart from a spreadsheet program and place the copy in a document in a word processing program (see Figure 4A.11). Some operating systems accomplish this feat with a feature known as the Clipboard. The Clipboard is a temporary holding space (in the computer's memory) for data that

FIGURE 4A.10

The Open dialog box in Microsoft Word.

FIGURE 4A.11

Using the Clipboard to copy a chart from an Excel document to a Word document.

1. Select the desired data—in this case, a chart in Excel.

2. Issue the Copy command.

3. A copy of the data is placed on the Windows Clipboard

4. Go to the destination document and issue the Paste command. The chart is placed in the Word document.

is being copied or moved. The Clipboard is available for use by applications running under the operating system. For example, if you want to move a paragraph in a word processor document, select the paragraph, then choose the Cut command; the data is removed from the document and placed on the Clipboard. (If you want to leave the original data in place, you can use the Copy command; a copy is made of the data, and it is stored on the Clipboard but is not removed from the document.) After placing the insertion point in the document where you want to place the paragraph, you choose the Paste command; the data on the Clipboard is placed into the document.

The Clipboard also can be used to move data from one document to another. For example, you can copy an address from one letter to another and thereby avoid rekeying the address. The real versatility of the Clipboard, however, stems from the fact that it is actually a part of the operating system and not a particular application. As a result, you can use the Clipboard to move data from one program to another.

The versatility of the Clipboard has been extended further with a feature known in Windows as OLE, which stands for Object Linking and Embedding. A simple cut and paste between applications results in object embedding. The data, which is known as an object in programming terms, is embedded in a new type of document. It retains the formatting that was applied to it in the original application, but its relationship with the original file is destroyed; that is, it is simply part of the new file. Furthermore, the data may be of a type that the open application cannot change. Therefore, if you want to edit embedded data, simply double-click the embedded object, and the original application that created the data is opened to allow editing of the embedded data.

Object linking adds another layer to the relationship: The data that is copied to and from the Clipboard retains a link to the original document so that a change in the original document also appears in the linked data. For example, suppose that the spreadsheet and memo shown in Figure 4A.11 are generated quarterly. They always contain the same chart updated with the most recent numbers. With object linking, when the numbers in the spreadsheet are changed, the chart in the report will automatically reflect the new figures. Of course, object linking is not automatic; you need to use special commands in your applications to create the link.

Managing Hardware

When programs run, they need to use the computer's memory, monitor, disk drives, and other devices, such as a printer. The operating system is the intermediary between programs and hardware. In a computer network, the operating system also mediates between your computer and other devices on the network.

The operating system responds to requests to use memory and other devices, keeps track of which programs have access to which devices, and coordinates everything the hardware does so that various activities do not overlap causing the computer to become confused and stop working. The operating system uses interrupt requests (IRQs) to help the CPU coordinate processes. For example, Figure 4A.12 shows what happens if you tell the operating system to list the files in a folder.

In addition to using interrupts, the operating system often provides complete programs for working with special devices such as printers. These programs are called drivers because they allow the operating system and other programs to activate and use—that is, "drive"—the hardware device. Most of the software you buy will work with your printer, monitor, and other equipment without requiring you to install any special drivers.

① When you click on a folder, the OS interprets the action as a command to list the files in that folder.

OPERATING SYSTEM

④ The OS tells the CPU to go to the disk drive and retrieve the names of the files in the folder.

② The OS sends an interrupt request to the CPU.

③ When doable, the CPU pauses any other processing and checks with the OS to see what new processing job is being requested.

HARD DISK

⑤ The CPU retrieves the names of the files in the folder.

⑥ The OS intercepts the list of file names returned from the disk drive and displays it on the screen.

⑦ The folder's contents are now shown on the screen.

FIGURE 4A.12

How the operating system communicates with the CPU.

PC Operating Systems

Microsoft's Windows operating system continues to thrive on PCs all over the world and has the largest market share of any competitor. At this writing, even management at Apple Computers admits that the Macintosh has just 5 percent of the desktop OS market share, but Linux is making inroads on the desktop.

The following sections provide a brief survey of the many operating systems being used on desktop computers. Although some of these OSs—such as DOS and Windows 95—may seem out of date, they are still widely used and deserve to be included in this discussion.

SELF-CHECK ::

Circle the correct answer for each question.

1. An operating system is an example of this type of software.

   a. multitasking   **b.** system   **c.** utility

2. Which of the following is most likely to use a real-time OS?

   a. computerized life-support system   **b.** Macintosh computer   **c.** desktop PC

3. The "desktop" of a GUI operating system is not a real desktop, but simply a _____.

   a. simile   **b.** metaphor   **c.** analogy

DOS

Even though it has been around for decades, DOS (which stands for *disk operating system*) is still in use today for a variety of reasons. DOS originally came into widespread use in the 1980s with the appearance of the IBM PC, which was the first personal computer to catch on with consumers and businesses.

Two versions of DOS reigned as the desktop operating system of choice throughout the 1980s. The first was PC DOS, which IBM released with its computers. The other was Microsoft's version of DOS, known as MS-DOS (Microsoft DOS), which was used on millions of "IBM-compatible" PCs, or "clones." (These terms describe any PC that is based on the same architecture used by IBM's personal computers.)

Despite its dominance in the PC market for more than a decade, DOS suffered some weaknesses. For example, it supported only one user at a time, and could run only one program at a time. It had no built-in support for networking, and users had to manually install drivers any time they added a new hardware component to their PC. DOS also was limited in the amount of RAM and storage space it could support. Finally, even today, DOS supports only 16-bit programs,

Norton
ONLINE

For more information on PC operating systems, visit
http://www.mhhe.com/ peternorton.

Productivity Tip

If you want to learn a new feature or need help solving a problem, the answers may be on your hard disk or the Internet.

Using Local Online Help

Most commercial operating systems and applications include an online help system that is installed on your computer along with the software. New-generation help systems include descriptions, tips, audio/video demonstrations, hyperlinks, and links to Internet-based resources.

To find help on your hard disk, open the help system and look for answers. To get help with the Windows XP operating system, for example, click the START button and choose Help and Support from the Start menu. In any Windows application, click the Help menu and choose Contents or Help Topics. A Help window appears, providing tools that let you search for help in different ways. Remember the following tips:

>> **Be Patient** You may not find your answer immediately. Be prepared to try again.

>> **Learn Different Search Options** Most Windows-based help systems provide different options for finding help.

For example, you may be able to browse a list of help topics that are organized by category. Or you may be able to search the help system for topics that contain certain terms or phrases. Some help systems let you type questions in plain English. If you need help printing a document, for example, you can type the question "How do I print a document?"

>> **Think of the Problem in Different Ways** For example, if you want help with setting up an Internet connection, the terms "Internet," "connection," "modem," and "Internet account" may bring up the right answers.

>> **Use Bookmarks and Annotations** Most help systems let you bookmark specific help topics so you can find them again quickly. You also can add your own notes to specific topics.

Using Remote Online Help

Many software makers provide help resources that you can access over the Internet.

>> **Web-Based Technical Support** Many software companies have a Support or Help link on their Web home page.

---

so it does not take full advantage of the power of modern 32-bit (and 64-bit) processors. Finally, DOS used a command-line interface that forced users to remember cryptic command names.

So, why is DOS still in use? Two reasons are its size and simplicity. It does not require much memory or storage space for the system, and it does not require a powerful computer. Therefore, it is sometimes used as an embedded OS for devices that run very simple, single-tasking applications. Another reason for its continued use is that many businesses still have custom applications either written as a one-of-a-kind application for their business or written for their special needs and marketed to similar businesses. A restaurant may still be using the employee scheduling applications written for them 10 or 15 years ago (see Figure 4A.13), or a small picture framing business may still use the same program to calculate the cost of the frames they build and sell.

Windows NT Workstation

Microsoft released Windows NT, a 32-bit operating system for PCs, in 1993. Windows NT (New Technology) was originally designed as the successor to DOS, but by the time it was ready for release, it had become too large to run on most of the PCs used by consumers at the time. As a result, Microsoft repositioned Windows NT to be a high-end operating system for powerful workstations and network servers used in business. (After releasing Windows NT, Microsoft went back to the drawing board to create a more consumer-oriented version of Windows to

>> **FAQs** Most software companies have Web sites with lists of frequently asked questions (FAQs).

>> **E-Mail Help** At the company's Web site, you may find an option that lets you describe a problem and submit a request for help. A support technician will investigate the problem, or an automated system will send you a list of possible solutions.

>> **Knowledge Bases** A knowledge base is a sophisticated database containing detailed information about specific topics. To use a knowledge base, you type a term or phrase or describe a problem. After your text is matched against a database, you are presented with a list of possible solutions.

>> **Newsgroups** Large software companies sponsor newsgroups on the Internet. Using your newsreader, you can access these newsgroups, post questions for other users to answer, or participate in discussions about specific products and technical issues.

Before you use any remote online help resource, read all the information the company provides about it. Look for notices about fees, registration, and proof of product ownership.

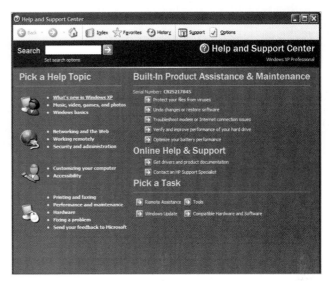

A program's help system is often the last place users turn for help, when it should be the first place.

FIGURE 4A.13

DOS applications, like this one for employee scheduling, are still in use today. They are often custom applications written years ago for a certain industry or company.

replace DOS on home and office PCs. Windows 95, which is discussed later, was the result.)

Because high-end networked computers fall into two primary categories, Microsoft separated Windows NT into two products: Windows NT Workstation and the first Windows versions for network servers, Windows NT Server. The

FIGURE 4A.14

The interface for Windows NT Workstation 4.0, the last version of Windows to use "NT" in its name.

server product was optimized to run on dedicated network servers (see the discussion later in this chapter on NT Server).

Although Windows NT Workstation looks almost identical to Windows 95 (see Figure 4A.14), its underlying operating system is different; it's almost completely devoid of MS-DOS code that had been present in earlier versions of Windows. Windows NT Workstation is typically used on standalone PCs that may or may not be part of a network. While Windows NT Workstation supports networking and can be used as a server in peer-to-peer networks, it generally is not used on network servers. At first, "power users" made up a large part of the market for Windows NT Workstation. As a result, it can be found in such varied places as architectural firms, audio and video production studios, and graphics studios. Windows NT Workstation continues to be on desktops in large organizations, but it is being replaced by newer versions of Windows or by Linux.

Windows 9x

The term *Windows 9*x is used when referring to any member of the closely related threesome: Windows 95, Windows 98, and Windows Me. Although these versions of Windows are considered obsolete by many experts in the computer industry, they are still widely used, especially by consumers with older PCs. In fact, many businesses still run Windows 9x on their desktop PCs.

In 1995, Microsoft released Windows 95, a complete operating system that did not require MS-DOS to be installed separately before it was installed, unlike its predecessors (Windows 3.0, 3.1, and 3.11—collectively known as Windows 3.x). Windows 95 installs the necessary MS-DOS operating system components that it needs and has additional programming code that takes advantage of the more advanced capabilities of newer CPUs and maintains a GUI. Windows 3.x, by contrast, was an operating environment that ran on top of DOS to provide a GUI and additional capabilities.

In addition to some MS-DOS program code that allows it to run DOS applications, Windows 95 contains 16-bit code that enables it to run programs originally designed for Windows 3.x (see Figure 4A.15). If a company had already invested in many such programs, it could continue to use its familiar programs while migrating to the new operating system.

Windows 95 has several other attractions as well. First, for programs designed with 32-bit processing, it can exchange information with printers, networks, and files in 32-bit pieces instead of 16-bit pieces (as in Windows 3.x and DOS). For moving information around in the computer, the effect was like doubling the number of lanes on an expressway. Windows 95 has improved multitasking, compared to previous versions of Windows, and it is the first version of Windows that supports the Plug and Play standard for connecting new hardware. With integrated networking support and improvements to the GUI, such as the taskbar and START button, Windows 95 remains popular with individual users, in spite of newer versions with even more improvements.

Many experts considered Windows 98 (so-named for the year it was introduced—1998) to be an update to Windows 95 rather than a major Windows

FIGURE 4A.15

Windows 95 runs 32-bit applications, but it can run older 16-bit applications designed for Windows 3.x and DOS.

DOS, running
in a window

A 16-bit application
written for Windows 3.x

operating system upgrade. In other words, the differences from Windows 95 to Windows 98 are not as significant as the differences from Windows 3.x to Windows 95. However, one key change in Windows 98 is the inclusion of the Internet Explorer Web browser with a new feature, the Active Desktop, that lets users browse the Internet and local computer in a similar manner (see Figure 4A.16). Active Desktop enables users to integrate Internet resources such as stock tickers and news information services directly on the Windows desktop.

In 2000, Microsoft released Windows Me (Millennium Edition), the last member of the Windows 9x family of consumer-grade operating systems. Windows Me offers several notable enhancements over its predecessors, such as improved multimedia capabilities, built-in support for digital video editing, and enhanced Internet features. But like Windows 95 and 98, Windows Me still contains a lot of 16-bit code that supports old DOS and Windows 3.x applications. As a result, Windows Me was not much more stable or robust than Windows 95 or 98, and it was subject to frequent crashes.

FIGURE 4A.16

The Windows 98 Active Desktop lets the operating system function like a Web browser.

Windows 2000 Professional

Released in 2000, Windows 2000 combines the user-friendly interface and features of Windows 98 with the file system, networking, power, and stability of Windows NT and some new and improved features. This combination of features makes Windows 2000 both powerful and easy to use. Microsoft developed four versions of Windows 2000: Windows 2000 Professional for the desktop and three versions especially for network servers, discussed later in this chapter.

Windows XP

Windows XP, released in October 2001, is the latest in the Windows suite of PC operating system families. The desktop has a more three-dimensional look, with

FIGURE 4A.17

The Windows XP desktop, shown here in its colorful default mode.

rounded corners and more shading. It also offers some brighter color choices (see Figure 4A.17). Windows XP is available in several different products: Windows XP Professional, Windows XP Home, Windows XP Media Center Edition, and Windows XP Embedded. Microsoft also created 64-bit Windows XP for use with AMD's Opteron and Athlon 64 CPUs. With Windows XP, Microsoft consolidated its consumer-grade and enterprise desktop operating systems into one environment. For home users, this means added security and an operating system that is far less likely to stall or crash than Windows 9x. Here are some of the features that have been upgraded in Windows XP:

>> **Digital Media Support** Through the use of Windows Media Player 9, users of XP can take advantage of digital broadcast support, as well as video and audio rendering for multimedia projects.

>> **Advanced Networking and Communications** Windows XP takes advantage of universal Plug and Play support, which enables the PC to find and use hardware connected via a network, without forcing the user to configure the system or install drivers. It also makes use of Internet Connection Sharing, which allows users to connect multiple computers to the Internet via a single connection.

>> **Advanced Mobile Computing** Through the use of features like Automatic Configuration, you can connect an XP-based laptop to a desktop PC without needing to know different types of network settings. XP's IrComm modem support lets you use a cellular telephone to connect to the Internet.

The Macintosh Operating System

The fact that the Macintosh operating system (or Mac OS) works only on Macintosh computers has long been considered one of the operating system's biggest drawbacks. Although it has a very small market share, the Mac remains the first choice of many publishers, multimedia developers, graphic artists, and schools. The current version is called the Mac OS System X (ten), which has had four major releases. The latest release is Mac OS X Panther, also called version 10.3. It

FIGURE 4A.18

The Mac OS System X desktop has remained basically the same through the major releases to the OS.

has the same desktop, with upgrades to the OS and various components, such as the Finder, Mail, and Address Book. Figure 4A.18 shows the Mac OS X Panther desktop, customized by a user.

UNIX for the Desktop

It is difficult to pin UNIX down to one class of computer, because it runs on such a wide range, including supercomputers, notebook PCs, and everything in between. Although UNIX does not have an important place in the market for desktop operating systems, thanks to its power and its appeal to engineers and other users of CAD and CAM software, UNIX has been popular for high-powered workstations such as those from Sun Microsystems, Hewlett-Packard, and Silicon Graphics.

UNIX is not for the faint of heart because of its command-line interface, cryptic instructions, and the fact that it requires many commands to do even simple tasks. Most versions of UNIX are case-sensitive: they can differentiate between upper- and lowercase letters typed at the command prompt. However, those who have worked with UNIX have found the power and stability of this OS worth the effort to learn the commands.

Linux for the Desktop

Even though Linux is considered a "freeware" operating system, industry experts have been impressed by its power, capabilities, and rich feature set. Linux is a full 32-bit, multitasking operating system that supports multiple users and multiple processors. Linux can run on nearly any computer and can support almost any type of application. Linux uses a command-line interface, but windows-based GUI environments, called shells, are available.

The biggest nontechnical difference between UNIX and Linux is price. Anyone can get a free copy of Linux on the Internet, and disk-based copies are often inserted in popular computer books and magazines. Commercial versions of Linux, which are inexpensive when compared to the cost of other powerful operating systems, are also available from a variety of vendors who provide the Linux code for free and charge for the extras, such as utilities, GUI shells, and documentation. At this writing, the most popular Linux vendors are Red Hat and Novell, who both offer special Linux bundles for desktop computers as well as for servers.

Figure 4A.19 shows the version of Linux released by Red Hat, with the KDE Desktop environment.

Network Operating Systems

A network operating system (NOS) is an OS that is designed to run on a network server dedicated to providing various services to other computers on the network. The "other" computers are called client computers, and each computer that connects to a network server must be running client software designed to request a specific service. If you are connecting to a server to store and retrieve files, your computer must have the client software that allows it to connect to that server for that purpose. Further, the specific client software needed varies based on the NOS running on the server.

FIGURE 4A.19

Linux with an optional GUI desktop.

Network operating systems are optimized to provide network services, with support for multiple processors and for redundancy such as schemes in which one network server is a "mirror" of another server and is available immediately if the first server fails. There are many other "under-the-hood" enhancements that enable a NOS to provide reliable service. The most commonly used network operating systems are

>> **Windows NT Server** While it shares the same core as Windows NT Workstation, Windows NT Server has additional capabilities. Microsoft fine-tuned Windows NT Server so it would function as an operating system for servers. It has security features for grouping and authenticating users and controlling their access to network resources. It supports the use of many hard disks, working together to store huge amounts of data. It also can be configured to provide redundancy of data, writing the same data to multiple disks, so it is preserved in case one disk fails. All these features make it possible for Windows NT Server to ensure disk and data security even in the event of a catastrophic failure of a hard disk.

>> **Windows 2000 Server** Introduced in 2000, Microsoft Windows 2000 Server is available as three products (Standard Edition, Advanced Server, and Data Center Server), all of which support managing very large stores of data about the users of the network and the computer resources of the network. A generic term for such a specialized database is enterprise directory (not to be confused with the term *directory* sometimes used when talking about disk folders). One of the many things Windows 2000 Server can do that Windows 2000 Professional cannot is to manage a directory with a specialized service called Active Directory. All three server products have the same user interface as Windows 2000 Professional, as shown in Figure 4A.20.

>> **Windows Server 2003** Microsoft extended their Windows Server system line with Windows Server 2003, introduced in April 2003 as two products: Windows Server 2003 Standard Edition and Data Center Server. Windows Server 2003 has a Windows XP–style interface that hides a very beefed-up server OS that they hope will compete with UNIX, which dominates the very high-end enterprise network servers. This server OS was designed to support a set of technologies Microsoft dubbed the .NET Framework. In a nutshell, this means it is designed to support Web-based applications, large databases, e-commerce servers, and distributed applications, which are applications with parts that run on different computers, *distributing* the work and data across

FIGURE 4A.20

The Windows 2000 Server GUI is
identical to that of the Professional
version.

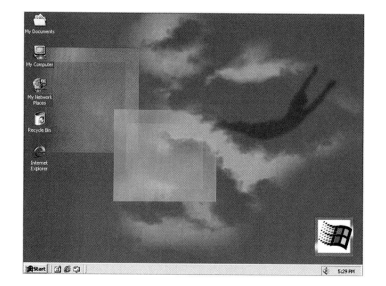

the network. The network, in this case, can be the Internet or a corporate intranet, or an extranet. (Intranets and extranets are discussed in Chapter 2.)

>> **Novell NetWare** NetWare (developed by Novell, Inc.) was one of the earliest and most popular network operating systems in terms of number of installations through the 1980s and into the 1990s. Although their market share has declined in recent years, Novell still has a strong following and continues to bring out new network products. NetWare server is now just one server operating system offered by Novell. Since their purchase of SuSE Linux in 2004, Novell offers two Linux Server products, SuSE Enterprise and SuSE Standard, in addition to the Novell NetWare server product. The benefit of the NetWare server product is the long-term reliability of the product and the loyal network administrators of its installed base of servers that have been running earlier versions of NetWare servers for many years. The SuSE Linux products offer both a basic, department/small business NOS in SuSE Standard and in SuSE Enterprise, a powerful operating system that can run on a broad range of computers, up to mainframes. The NetWare and SuSE Enterprise products support distributed applications.

>> **UNIX for Servers** Because of its ability to work with so many kinds of hardware and its reliability (it rarely crashes), UNIX remains a very frequently chosen operating system for Internet host computers. In the business world, UNIX remains a popular network operating system, especially among organizations that manage large databases shared by hundreds or thousands of users. Many types of specialized database-specific software programs have been developed for the UNIX platform and are deeply entrenched in industries such as insurance, medicine, banking, and manufacturing. The various versions of UNIX have collectively "owned" the market for very large, mission-critical servers in the largest of enterprises. UNIX is also widely used on Web servers, especially those that support online transactions and make heavy use of databases. In addition, UNIX has long been the OS of choice for the most critical servers of the Internet, such as those that maintain the lists of Internet domain names.

>> **Linux** Linux has garnered a large share of the small business and home market as a server OS for providing Internet and networking services. An open operating system, it is a cost-effective alternative to other operating systems for sharing files, applications, printers, modems, and Internet services. There are a large number of Linux servers hosting Web sites and performing other roles on the Internet. In the last few years, more and more vendors have brought out products bundled with Linux targeting large (enterprise) organizations; among them are Red Hat and Novell. Novell's venture into Linux products is expected to help bring about the eventual dominance of Linux on a wide range of servers, competing with both Microsoft and UNIX NOSs.

Embedded Operating Systems

An embedded operating system is one that is built into the circuitry of an electronic device, unlike a PC's operating system, which resides on a magnetic disk. Embedded operating systems are now found in a wide variety of devices, including appliances, automobiles, bar-code scanners, cell phones, medical equipment, and personal digital assistants (PDAs) such as the Palm Pilot and the Compaq iPaq. The most popular embedded operating systems for consumer products such as PDAs include the following:

>> **Windows XP Embedded** One of two embedded OSs currently available from Microsoft, Windows XP Embedded is based on the Windows XP Professional

At Issue

Who Really Owns the Software on Your PC?

Once you start using a computer, it does not take long to learn that software can be very expensive. If you use your PC a lot, especially if you use it for work, you can spend hundreds or even thousands of dollars on software in a very short time.

But even though you pay a lot for software, you do not necessarily *own* the programs on your PC. This fact surprises a lot of people, but it is true just the same.

What happens, then, when you pay for a piece of software? That depends on the software maker, but very few developers grant you actual ownership of a program, even after you "purchase" it. Instead of buying the software itself, you really pay for a license that grants you permission to install and use the software.

Why a License?

In very simple terms, a license is an agreement between you and the software's maker. Under most software license agreements, the developer grants you a few rights to the program, but keeps all the remaining rights.

Most licenses allow the user to install the program on a single computer and to make one backup copy of the in-

stallation disk(s). If you want to install the software on a different computer, the agreement may state that you must uninstall it from the first computer. If you install the program on multiple PCs or make multiple duplicates of it, you may be violating the terms of the license. If the software developer catches you, it can take the software away from you and even press charges under applicable laws.

Software developers have good reasons for licensing software instead of selling it outright:

>> **Piracy** Software piracy is the act of copying software without the developer's consent (and, more important, without paying the developer), then selling or giving away the copies. If you use the original installation disks to install the program on multiple computers at the same time, that is piracy too. Software developers lose billions of dollars every year because of piracy. By licensing their products and maintaining some ownership of them, however, developers can take action against pirates. If a developer actually sold the software itself, it might be giving away all its rights to it, and piracy would be an even greater problem.

FIGURE 4A.21

Like many other handheld computing devices, the Palm line of personal digital assistants uses the Palm OS.

OS, but it is not an off-the-shelf operating system so much as it is a do-it-yourself kit for device manufacturers who wish to pick and choose the parts of the Windows XP Professional OS their products need.

>> **Windows CE .NET** The second Windows embedded product is Windows CE .NET. Also provided as a kit to manufacturers, it is not based on the Windows desktop products but is the latest version of Windows CE, which was designed especially for embedded devices requiring a real-time OS. Although a small OS, it supports wireless communications, multimedia, and Web browsing. It also allows for the use of smaller versions of Microsoft Word, Excel, and Outlook. Microsoft is positioning a version of Windows CE for the automotive market, calling it Windows Automotive.

>> **Palm OS** Palm OS is the standard operating system for Palm-brand PDAs as well as other proprietary handheld devices (see Figure 4A.21). For several years the Palm OS was the more popular option for handheld devices and there were many manufacturers offering PDAs with the Palm OS. More recently, only Palm and Sony continue to make PDAs that run the Palm OS, but they have a significant market share and, as a result, users have a large degree of choice in terms of software that can be used with this embedded system. The Palm OS continues to be used in other systems, such as cell phones and other small devices.

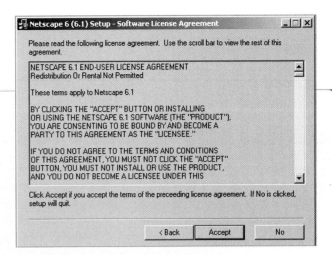

Modifications Most license agreements state that you cannot make modifications to a program's source code. If developers allowed this, it would be an easy matter for others to make changes to a program, then try to claim the modified program as their own.

Even though the developer keeps most rights to a program, however, you still have some rights, too. If the program does not perform as you expected, you have the right to return or exchange it. You also should be able to expect reasonable customer support from the developer.

Where Will I Find the License?

In many cases, the license agreement and its terms are printed on the software's packaging; when you open the package and install the program, you are bound by the license's terms. More and more developers, however, are adding the agreement to the software installation process. This means that when you install the program, the agreement appears on the screen so you can read it. You then can click a button to indicate whether you accept or decline the agreement. If you accept, the installation continues. If you decline, the installation aborts.

Either way, you should always read the license agreement carefully and decide if you want to accept it. If you do not accept the license agreement, you may be able to return the software. (Note, however, that many stores may not accept opened software packages for a refund, although you may be able to exchange it for a store credit or a different program.) If you accept a license agreement, however, you should honor its terms.

>> **Pocket PC OS** Pocket PC OS is a specific type of operating system that Microsoft developed to use in direct competition with the Palm OS on PDAs. These devices are targeted at the business and corporate market rather than consumers. The latest version gives users the ability to securely access data from a business network via a handheld device, and it gives system administrators the ability to manage and control a PC or server via a wireless network connection.

>> **Symbian** Symbian is an OS found in "smart" cell phones from Nokia and Sony Ericsson that features options such as touch screens, games, multimedia functions, and Internet connectivity. In addition to the conventional cell phone functions, you can play games and view Web pages (in color) with a full browser over a high-speed mobile network.

Summary ::

>> An operating system is system software that acts as a master control program, controlling the hardware and interacting with the user and application software.

>> The four major types of operating systems are real-time operating systems, single-user/single-tasking operating systems, single-user/multitasking operating systems, and multi-user/multitasking operating systems.

>> Most modern operating systems feature a graphical user interface (GUI). You control a GUI-based system by pointing and clicking graphical objects on the screen. In a typical GUI, all objects and resources appear on a background called the desktop.

>> Some older operating systems use a command-line interface, which the user controls by typing commands at a prompt.

>> The operating system manages all the other programs that run on the PC, and it provides services such as file management, memory management, and printing to those programs.

>> Some operating systems enable programs to share information using a feature known as the Clipboard. This lets you create data in one program and use it again in other programs.

>> The Object Linking and Embedding feature in Windows extends its data-sharing capabilities, allowing you to embed data into a document while working in an application that cannot, on its own, manipulate the data.

>> Network operating systems are optimized to provide network services—with support for multiple processors and support for redundancy. This redundancy support occurs both locally in the form of data redundancy on drives and specialized network redundancy such as schemes in which one network server is a "mirror" of another server and is available immediately if the first server fails.

>> Popular network OSs include Microsoft server products, UNIX, Novell NetWare, and Linux.

>> Embedded operating systems such as the Palm OS, Symbian OS, and the Microsoft products—Windows XP Embedded, Windows CE .NET, and Pocket PC OS—are miniaturized OSs designed to run on small computing devices such as handheld computers.

Key Terms ::

activate, 162
choose, 162
Clipboard, 165
command-line interface, 164
Copy command, 166
Cut command, 166
desktop, 162
dialog box, 163
distributed application, 174
DOS, 167
driver, 166
embedded operating system, 175
enterprise directory, 174
graphical user interface (GUI), 161
icon, 162
Linux, 173
Macintosh operating system
   (Mac OS), 172

menu, 163
menu bar, 163
multitasking, 160
multi-user/multitasking operating
   system, 160
.NET Framework, 174
network operating system (NOS), 173
Object Linking and Embedding
   (OLE), 166
Paste command, 166
prompt, 164
real-time application, 160
real-time operating system, 160
scroll bar, 163
shell, 173
shortcut, 162
single-user/multitasking operating
   system, 160

single-user/single-tasking operating
   system, 160
START button, 162
Start menu, 162
taskbar, 162
terminal client, 161
terminal server, 160
title bar, 163
toolbar, 163
UNIX, 173
user interface, 161
user session, 161
window, 162
Windows, 167

Key Term Quiz ::

Complete each statement by writing one of the terms listed under Key Terms in each blank.

1. The small pictures on the desktop—called _____—represent links to resources on the PC or network.

2. _____ is the ability to perform two or more tasks at the same time.

3. You interact with a command-line interface by typing strings of characters at a(n) _____ .

4. A running program may take up the whole screen or it may appear in a rectangular frame, called a(n) _____ .

5. A(n) _____ supports an application that responds to certain input very, very quickly.

6. In a GUI _____ let you view parts of a program or file that do not fit in the window.

7. The _____ operating system runs only on Macintosh computers.

8. A(n) _____ is an OS that is designed to run on a network server dedicated to providing various services to other computers on the network.

9. A(n) _____ is a specialized database that contains data about the users of a network and the computer resources of the network.

10. A(n) _____ application is a program with parts that run on different computers, distributing the work and data across the network.

Multiple Choice ::

Circle the word or phrase that best completes each statement.

1. A list of command choices in an operating system or application is called a _____.
   a. command line   b. check box   c. drop-down list   d. menu

2. DOS and some versions of UNIX are examples of _____ interfaces.
   a. old-fashioned   b. GUI   c. command-line   d. parallel

3. To remove data from one document and place it in another, you can use the _____ and _____ commands.
   a. Cut, Paste   b. Copy, Paste   c. File, Open   d. Delete, Paste

4. In many GUI-based programs, a _____ displays buttons that let you issue commands quickly.
   a. command bar   b. scroll bar   c. menu bar   d. toolbar

5. From what you learned in this chapter, select the type of operating system you would expect to be used in a computerized heart monitor.
   a. multi-user/ multitasking   b. real-time   c. single-user/ multitasking   d. single-user/single tasking

6. An operating system keeps track of which programs have access to which hardware devices and uses _____ to help the CPU coordinate processes.
   a. interrupt requests (IRQs)   b. disk drives   c. multitasking   d. user interface

7. What type of operating system allows multiple users to connect over the network to a special server and work with their programs in separate sessions, and allows each user to run multiple programs?
   a. single-user/multiple computers   b. real time   c. multi-user/ multitasking   d. single-user/ single-tasking

8. The acronym DOS stands for _____.
   a. distributed operating system   b. driver operating system   c. disk operating system   d. diskless operating system

9. One reason for the popularity of Windows 95 was its ability to run applications that were developed for this operating system.
   a. DOS   b. UNIX   c. Linux   d. Mac OS

10. Which network operating system has long been the OS of choice for the most critical servers of the Internet, such as those that maintain the lists of Internet domain names?
    a. DOS   b. UNIX   c. Windows NT Professional   d. Mac OS

Review Questions ::

In your own words, briefly answer the following questions.

1. What are the four primary functions that an operating system performs?
2. What device is used to work with graphical objects in a GUI?
3. What is the function of windows in a GUI?
4. What is a dialog box?
5. Describe the Clipboard and its use.
6. What is the difference between object linking and object embedding?
7. Explain what a driver does.
8. What is a "clone"?
9. Explain why DOS is still in use.
10. What purpose would a "shell" serve in Linux?

Lesson Labs ::

Complete the following exercises as directed by your instructor.

1. Use your online help system to learn more about Windows. Click the START button, and then choose Help and Support from the Start menu. Explore the Help window to learn more about the tools provided by the help system in your particular version of the operating system. (The exact features vary from one version of Windows to another.) When you are comfortable with the Help window, use any method you prefer to search for information on these topics: *operating system*, *GUI*, *command*, *dialog box*, *menu*, and *multitasking*. When you are finished, close the Help window.

2. Practice using the DOS command prompt:

   a. Click the START button.

   b. If you use Windows 9*x* or 2000, point to Programs, then click the MS-DOS prompt on the Programs menu. If you use Windows XP, choose All Programs | Accessories | Command Prompt. Either way, the command prompt appears in a new window.

   c. At the prompt, type **DIR** and press ENTER. Review the results. Then type the **VER** command, press ENTER, and review the results. Close the window.

Productivity Software

Overview: Software to Accomplish the Work of Life

You have seen that hardware alone doesn't do much of anything. PC hardware must work under the control of the operating system in order to accomplish work. The work that the hardware or operating system can do on its own is very limited, however. Their jobs are focused mostly on running the computer itself, not helping the user perform tasks.

Application software shifts this focus from the computer to humans. Application software is designed to help users be productive, which is why one class of it is called productivity software. There are as many different types of application software as there are different tasks to accomplish on a PC.

This lesson introduces you to some of the most commonly used types of application software—the programs that millions of people use each day to accomplish routine tasks. Although you might think of a computer as being a highly specialized machine, in fact it is most often used for basic, everyday tasks at home, school, and work. By applying computers and application programs to these mundane tasks, people can be more productive, creative, and efficient.

OBJECTIVES ::

>> List and differentiate four commonly used types of productivity software.

>> Name three kinds of formatting you can perform with word processing software.

>> Identify four types of data that can be used by spreadsheet programs.

>> Explain what presentation programs are used for.

>> List two key tasks that people perform with PIM applications.

Word Processing Programs

A word processing program (also called a word processor) provides tools for creating all kinds of text-based documents, as shown in Figures 4B.1 and 4B.2. Word processors are not limited to working with text; they enable you to add images to your documents and design documents that look like products of a professional print shop. Using a word processor, you can create long documents with separate chapters, a table of contents, an index, and other features.

A word processor can enhance documents in other ways; you can embed sounds, video clips, and animations into them. You can link different documents together—for example, link a chart from a spreadsheet into a word processing report—to create complex documents that update themselves automatically. Word processors can even create documents for publishing on the World Wide Web, complete with hyperlinked text and graphics.

The Word Processor's Interface

The word processor's main editing window displays a document and several tools, as illustrated in Figure 4B.3. In addition to a document area (or document window), which is where you view the document, a word processor provides several sets of tools, including

>> A menu bar, which displays titles of menus (lists of commands and options).

>> Toolbars, which display buttons that represent frequently used commands.

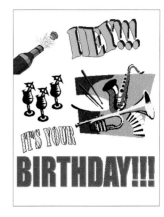

FIGURE 4B.1

This simple birthday card was created in a word processing program. It features colors, rotated text, and graphics.

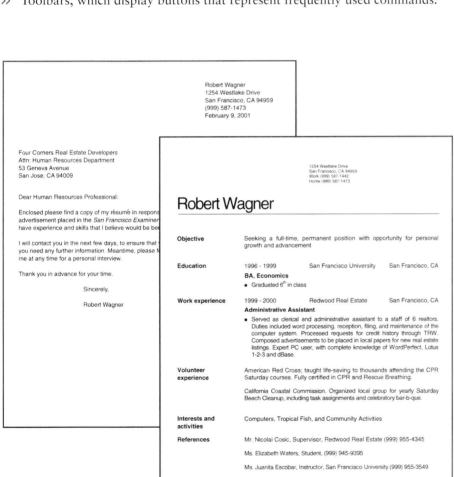

FIGURE 4B.2

Word processors are used frequently to create business letters and resumes. The formatting can be simple (as demonstrated by the cover letter) or more elaborate (as in the resume).

Norton
ONLINE

For more information on word processing programs, visit **http://www.mhhe.com/ peternorton**.

Microsoft Word's interface features tools that are commonly found in word processing programs.

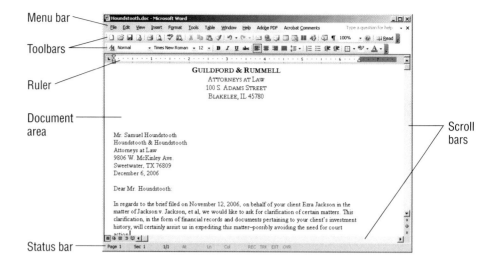

Menu bar

Toolbars

Ruler

Document area

Scroll bars

Status bar

>> Rulers, which show you the positions of text, tabs, margins, indents, and other elements on the page.

>> Scroll bars, which let you scroll through a document that is too large to fit inside the document area.

>> A status bar, which displays information related to your position in the document, the page count, and the status of keyboard keys.

Entering and Editing Text

You create a document by typing on the keyboard—a process known as entering text. In a new document, the program places a blinking insertion point (also called a cursor) in the upper-left corner of the document window. As you type, the insertion point advances across the screen, showing you where the next character will be placed (see Figure 4B.4).

Word processing software lets you change text without retyping the entire page; you retype only the text that needs to be changed. Changing an existing document is called editing the document.

The word processor's real beauty is its ability to work with blocks of text. A block is a contiguous group of characters, words, lines, sentences, or paragraphs in your document that you mark for editing or formatting. To mark text for editing or formatting, you select it. You can select text by using the mouse, the keyboard, or both. When you select text, it changes color—becoming highlighted, as shown in Figure 4B.5—to indicate that it is selected. You can erase an entire selected block by pressing the DELETE key or by typing other text over the selected block. You can change the formatting of the selection by making it bold or underlined, for example, or by changing the font or font size. To deselect a selected block of text, click the mouse anywhere on the screen or press any arrow key. The text is displayed again as it normally would be.

It's important to understand that these same data-entry and data-editing concepts apply to many other types of programs, including spreadsheets, databases, presentation programs, and others. If you can enter, edit, and select text in one program, then you know how to do it in other programs.

FIGURE 4B.4

The insertion point shows your place in a document as you type.

Now is the time for all good men to come to the aid of their country ——— Insertion point

> To help even out the sudden changes in a river, communities build reservoirs. If there is a drought or sudden demand for water, water from the reservoir supplements the river. As the river's water level rises with rain, the reservoir absorbs the extra water to prevent floods. If there is a sudden change in the rate of flow, or a burst of waves, the reservoir cushions the banks from changing forces. A UPS is like a reservoir for electricity. As your electricity fluctuates, the UPS absorbs and supplements the flow.
>
> To fully appreciate how helpful a UPS is, take the water analogy one step further and think of the plumbing in your home. If someone is drawing water when you start a shower, the other person notices a drop in the water pressure and you notice that the water pressure isn't as high as it should be. Then, if someone else flushes a toilet, you can expect the flow of cold water to momentarily drop even more. When the toilet finishes filling up, you can expect a sudden return of the cold water. And, when the original person drawing water stops, you notice a sudden increase in water pressure. Once you're through fiddling with the faucets, you appreciate how nice a personal reservoir could be. The electricity in your home works much the same way, so a UPS goes a long way to even out the flow as various appliances are turned on an off.
>
> **What Are the Most Common Electrical Problems?**
> Electrical problems come in all types, from the nearly harmless minor fluctuation in the voltage level, to

FIGURE 4B.5

The paragraph that appears as white text against a black background is highlighted. The user has selected the text for editing or formatting.

Formatting Text

Most word processing features are used to format the document. The process of formatting a document includes controlling the appearance of text, the layout of text on the page, and the use of pictures and other graphic elements. Most formatting features fall into one of three categories:

>> Character formatting includes settings that control the attributes of individual text characters such as fonts, font size, and type style. A font is a named set of characters that have the same characteristics. Popular fonts include Courier, Times New Roman, and Arial, but popular word processors feature dozens of different fonts (see Figure 4B.6). A font's size (its height) is measured in points. One point equals 1/72 of an inch, so 72 points equal one inch. Type styles are effects applied to characters such as boldface, underline, or italic.

In Word, this formatting tool lets you select a font.

This tool sets the font's size.

These tools apply styles— such as bold, italic, or underline—to selected characters.

FIGURE 4B.6

Basic character-formatting tools in Microsoft Word.

>> Paragraph formatting includes settings applied only to one or more entire paragraphs, such as line spacing, paragraph spacing, indents, alignment, tabs, borders, or shading. In a word processor, a paragraph is any text that ends with a special character called a paragraph mark. You create a paragraph mark when you press the ENTER key.

>> Document formatting includes the size of the page, its orientation, and headers or footers. Word processing software also lets you apply special formats, such as columns, to documents. You also can divide a document into sections and give each section its own unique format (see Figure 4B.7).

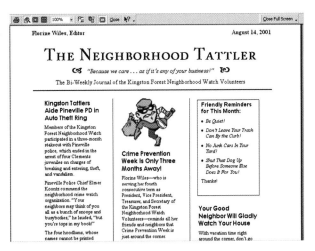

FIGURE 4B.7

A newsletter, such as this one, has many different formats, including sections, columns, fonts, borders, and others. This newsletter was created in a standard word processing program.

FIGURE 4B.8

Norton
ONLINE

For more information on spreadsheet programs, visit **http://www.mhhe.com/peternorton**.

Spreadsheet Programs

A spreadsheet program is a software tool for entering, calculating, manipulating, and analyzing sets of numbers. Spreadsheets have a wide range of uses—from family budgets to corporate earnings statements. As shown in Figure 4B.8, you can set up a spreadsheet to show information in different ways, such as the traditional row-and-column format (the format used in ledger books) or a slick report format with headings and charts.

The Spreadsheet's Interface

Like a word processor, spreadsheets provide a document area, which is where you view the document. In a spreadsheet program, you work in a document called a worksheet (or sheet, as it is also called), and you can collect related worksheets in a workbook (called a notebook in some programs). Worksheets can be named, and a workbook can contain as many individual worksheets as your system's resources will allow.

A typical spreadsheet interface provides a menu bar, toolbars, scroll bars, and a status bar. Spreadsheet programs also display a special formula bar, where you can create or edit data and formulas in the worksheet.

An empty worksheet (one without any data) looks like a grid of rows and columns. The intersection of any column and row is called a cell, as shown in Figure 4B.9. You interact with a spreadsheet primarily by entering data into individual cells. A typical worksheet contains thousands of individual cells.

Entering Data in a Worksheet

Entering data in a worksheet is simple. Using the mouse or arrow keys, you select a cell to make it active. The active cell is indicated by a cell pointer, a rectangle that makes the active cell's borders look bold (see Figure 4B.10).

To navigate the worksheet, you need to understand its system of cell addresses. All spreadsheets use row and column identifiers as the basis for their cell addresses. If you are working in the cell where column B intersects with row 3, for example, then cell B3 is the active cell.

When you have selected a cell, you simply type the data into it. When a cell is active, you also can type its data into the formula bar. The formula bar is handy because it displays much more data than the cell can. If a cell already contains data, you can edit it in the formula bar.

FIGURE 4B.9

Microsoft Excel's interface features tools common to nearly all Windows and Macintosh spreadsheets.

Menu bar

Toolbars

Formula bar

Document area

Row

Cell (intersection of a row and a column)

Status bar

Column

Scroll bars

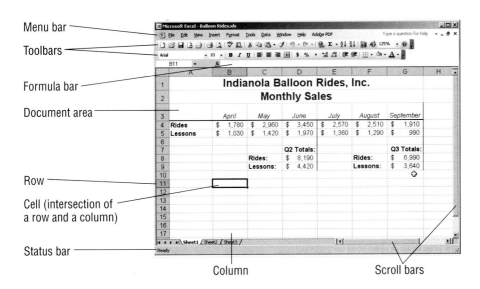

The active cell's address appears here. A cell's address is made up of its column letter and row number.

Each column is identified by a letter.

Each row is identified by a number.

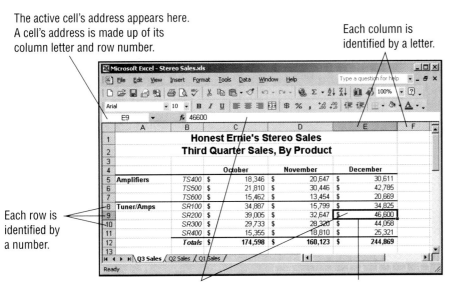

You can enter data in the cell or in the formula bar.

The cell pointer indicates which cell is active.

A worksheet's cells can hold several types of data, but the four most commonly used kinds of data are

>> **Labels** Worksheets can contain text—called labels (names for data values)—as well as numbers and other types of data. In spreadsheets, text is usually used to identify a value or series of values (as in a row or column heading) or to describe the contents of a specific cell (such as a total). Labels help you make sense of a worksheet's contents (see Figure 4B.11).

>> **Values** In a spreadsheet, a value is any number you enter or that results from a computation. You might enter a series of values in a column so that you can total them. Or you might enter several different numbers that are part of an elaborate calculation. Spreadsheets can work with whole numbers, decimals, negative numbers, currency, and other types of values, including scientific notation.

>> **Dates** Dates are a necessary part of most worksheets, and spreadsheet programs can work with date information in many ways. A date may be added

Norton Notebook

Why Own When You Can Rent?

At some point in the lives of many adults, someone older and in a position of supposed wisdom will ask, "Why rent an apartment when you can own a house?" While responsive answers to the question are usually forthcoming, the fact remains that the question is fundamentally rhetorical. The person speaking isn't seriously inquiring about anything; they're simply waiting for an opportunity to provide their young listener with a viewpoint. The question rings in the mind with that "used car salesman on television" intonation: *But wait! There's more!* The question has taken on real meaning, thanks to the development of broadband technologies that stand ready to turn the future into the past.

In the past, for almost all companies, owning a computer was simply out of the question. You've heard the history: Computers filled whole buildings, needed their own support staff, and so forth. What you may not know is that most, if not all, of the private companies that *did* purchase computers before the evolution of the PC leveraged the tremendous purchase and support cost by providing time-sharing computer services to other companies. For example, a small chain of grocery stores might have had no need for a computer of its own, but computational power would really help with weekly inventory, monthly financial reports, and so on. The store chain would rent time on a mainframe computer, during which time its inventories and so forth

would be run. This time-sharing scheme was so successful, it wasn't uncommon for a mainframe owner to not be the primary user of the computer.

All this changed with the development of the PC and, in time, the cheap availability of tremendous computing power on the desktop. (Based strictly on the number of instructions a computer can perform in one second, modern desktop PCs are well in excess of 7,000 times faster than mainframe computers from the 1980s. Relative to work accomplished, PCs are considerably faster still.) You've seen elsewhere in this chapter how application software, run on a local PC, changed the face of computing and the whole world. However, there are drawbacks to running programs and processing data in this way. Of the many problems we could talk about, the greatest has almost always been the nature of personal computers themselves. Programs and data stored on a PC are just that: on *a* PC. Simple sharing of files used to be anything but simple, and an entire genre of software used to exist to make it possible. Digital collaboration was simply out of the question.

Eventually, local area networks and Microsoft Windows made moving and sharing files simple, and collaboration became possible through special multi-user versions of application software. With all of this data being shared successfully across high-speed networks, one of the remain-

to a worksheet simply to indicate when it was created. Spreadsheets also can use dates in performing calculations, as when calculating late payments on a loan. If the spreadsheet knows the payment's due date, it can calculate late fees based on that date.

>> **Formulas** The power of the spreadsheet lies in formulas, which calculate numbers based on values or formulas in other cells. You can create many kinds of

FIGURE 4B.11

Labels help organize the information in a worksheet.

These labels are column headings that describe the contents of the cells below them.

These labels identify the data in the cells to their right.

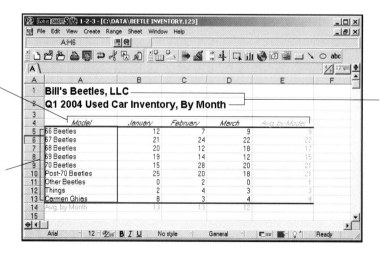

These labels are used as titles for the sheet.

ing major drawbacks to companywide computing (often called "enterprise" computing) was the cost of installing all the necessary applications on each desktop. In order for employees all over the world to work together on a project, each employee needed the creator application for the project. Even if a particular user only worked with a particular program twice a year, the company had to purchase a full-cost user license for the product. A possible solution to this rather central concern may be a new twist on the old idea of time-shared computing: application service providers, or ASPs. As the name implies, ASPs are for application software what ISPs are for the Internet itself.

ASPs provide access to an application over a network connection to a central application server. On an as-needed basis, application components are downloaded to user workstations. Companies can subscribe to specific applications and, in most cases, pay fees based on actual employee usage. In principle, access to an application through an ASP program should be dramatically less expensive than purchasing a full user license for each employee who has occasional need for the software. Additionally, companies receive customer and technical support from the ASP, not from the application manufacturer and not through the costly maintenance of in-house technical support staff. Since the customer company doesn't own the application software—the ASP does—the direct cost of software updates is included in the subscription fees, and the indirect update costs, such as unproductive downtimes and the aforementioned technical support staff, are borne by the ASP as part of its own costs of doing business. The most significant difference between time-sharing and ASP use, of course, is that all of the actual computing—except in the case of database servers—is done on the user's desktop. This means that online applications run much the same as do locally installed ones. Applications need not be installed on every PC, so many desktop units need only minimal internal storage. The ASP business model is a new idea for the 21st century, but its basis lies in time-tested efficient use of resources—money, time, bandwidth, and people.

formulas to do basic arithmetic operations, calculus or trigonometric operations, and so on. Suppose, for example, that the manager of a real estate office wants to calculate the commissions paid to agents over a specific time period. Figures 4B.12 and 4B.13 show a simple formula that takes the total sales for each agent and calculates the commission for that total. If any part of the formula (either the sales total or the commission percentage) changes, the formula can automatically recalculate the resulting commission.

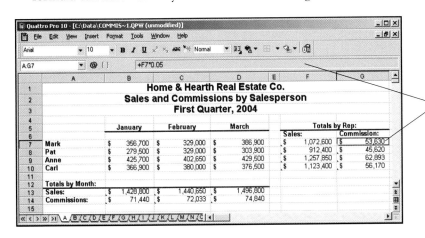

FIGURE 4B.12

An example of a formula used to calculate simple percentages.

This cell contains a simple formula that multiplies total sales by a commission percentage. Notice that the cell displays the results of the formula, rather than the formula itself.

Spreadsheet formulas can recalculate automatically if any of their base data changes.

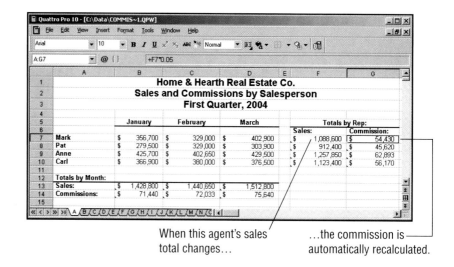

When this agent's sales total changes...

...the commission is automatically recalculated.

Norton
ONLINE

For more information on presentation programs, visit **http://www.mhhe.com/ peternorton**.

Cells also can hold graphics, audio files, and video or animation files. To the spreadsheet program, each type of data has a particular use and is handled in a unique manner.

Presentation Programs

If you have ever attended a seminar or lecture that included slides or overhead transparencies that were projected on a wall screen or displayed on a computer screen or video monitor, then you probably have seen the product of a modern presentation program. Presentation programs enable the user to create and edit colorful, compelling presentations that can be displayed in various ways and used to support any type of discussion.

Presentation programs allow the user to design slides—single-screen images that contain a combination of text, numbers, and graphics (such as charts, clip art, or pictures) often on a colorful background. A series of slides, displayed in a specific order to an audience, is called a presentation. Usually, the person showing the slides (the presenter) speaks to the audience while the slides are being displayed. The slides themselves show unique, specific pieces of information; the presenter fills in the details with his or her speech.

Slides can be simple or sophisticated. Depending on your needs, you can turn a basic slide show into a multimedia event using the built-in features of many presentation programs.

The Presentation Program's Interface

The typical presentation program displays a slide in a large document window and provides tools for designing and editing slides. Presentation programs provide many of the features found in word processors (for working with text), spreadsheets (for creating charts), and graphics programs (for creating and editing simple graphics). You can add elements to the slide simply by typing, making menu or toolbar choices, and dragging. As you work on the slide, you see exactly how it will look when it is shown to an audience.

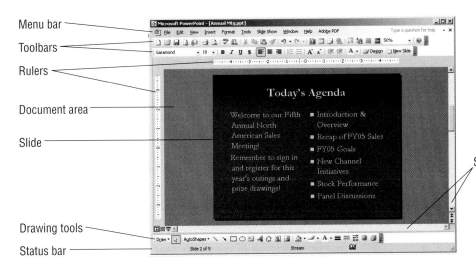

Menu bar
Toolbars
Rulers
Document area
Slide
Drawing tools
Status bar

Scroll bars

FIGURE 4B.14

Interface features of Microsoft
PowerPoint, a popular presentation
program.

Figure 4B.14 shows a slide in Microsoft PowerPoint, a popular presentation program. Note that the status bar says that the presentation contains five slides. A presentation can contain a single slide or hundreds. Presentation programs let you save a group of slides in one file so that you can open the related slides and work with them together.

A presentation program includes a menu bar, one or more toolbars (for managing files, formatting, drawing, and doing other tasks), rulers, slide-viewing or navigation buttons that let you move from one slide to another, a status bar, and other tools.

Creating a Presentation

Creating a presentation is simple: just choose the type of slide you want to create and then start adding the content. A complete presentation usually includes multiple slides arranged in a logical order. As you go, you can insert new slides anywhere, copy slides from other presentations, and reorder the slides.

You can create slides from scratch (starting with a blank slide), but it is easier and faster to work with one of the presentation program's many templates. A **template** is a predesigned document that already has coordinating fonts, a layout, and a background. Your presentation program should provide dozens of built-in templates, as shown in Figure 4B.15.

After you select a template, you can quickly assemble a presentation by creating individual slides. To create a slide, you choose a layout for it, as shown in Figure 4B.16. Presentation programs provide many slide layouts that hold varying combinations of titles, text, charts, and graphics. You can choose a different layout for each slide in your presentation, if you want.

After you select a layout, the blank slide appears in the document window, ready for you to add text, charts, or graphics. The program provides special **text boxes** and **frames** (special resizable boxes for text and graphical elements, respectively) to contain specific types of content. These special boxes often contain instructions telling you exactly what to do. To add text to a text box, simply click in the box and type your text, as shown in Figure 4B.17. The text is formatted automatically, but you can easily reformat the text later, using many of the same formatting options that are available in word processors.

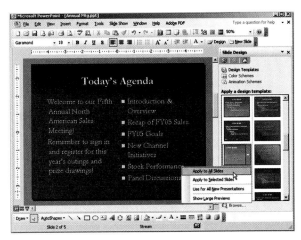

FIGURE 4B.15

Choosing a template in PowerPoint.

Choosing a layout for a new slide. The new slide will be inserted after the slide that is on the screen.

Adding text to a slide.

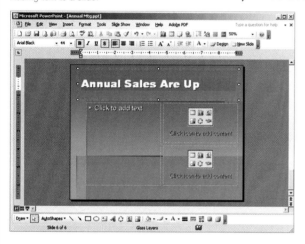

Adding charts, tables, clip art, or other graphics is nearly as easy (see Figure 4B.18). When you choose a slide layout that contains a chart, for example, you enter the chart's data in a separate window, called a *datasheet*. The program uses the data to create a chart.

To insert clip art or another type of graphic in a slide, you can select an image from your software's collection of graphics (as shown in Figure 4B.19) or import an image file such as a scanned photograph or clip art. Built-in paint tools also enable you to draw simple graphics and add them to your slides. These tools are handy if you want to add callouts to specific elements of a slide.

Presenting Slide Shows

You can present slides directly from your computer's disk, along with any audio or video files that you embed in your slides. Your audience can view slides in several ways:

>> **On the PC's Screen** If you are presenting slides to a few people, your PC's monitor might be adequate for an informal slide show. Of course, the larger the monitor, the better your audience can see the slides.

Creating a chart in PowerPoint. You type the chart's data in the datasheet window, which resembles a spreadsheet program. The program uses the data to create a chart, which appears on your slide.

FIGURE 4B.19

Selecting a graphic to insert into a slide.

>> **On a Large-Format Monitor** Large-format CRT and plasma monitors can display your slides at the proper resolution and large enough for a sizable audience to view comfortably (see Figure 4B.20). These devices are expensive and more difficult to transport than a standard monitor, but they may be the best solutions for some presentation settings.

>> **On a Television Screen** Using a PC-to-TV converter, you can connect your computer to a standard television and view the PC's video output on the television monitor. This solution may sound convenient, but compatibility issues must be considered (not all converters work with all televisions, for example), and televisions do not display images at the same resolution as a PC monitor. Image quality may suffer when a PC-to-TV converter is used.

>> **From a Data Projector** Portable, high-resolution data projectors are expensive, but they can display slides to a large audience. These projectors plug into one of the PC's ports and accept the system's video output.

FIGURE 4B.20

You can get the best results from your slide shows if you present them directly from the PC's disk using a display device that is appropriate for the audience and room size.

Regardless of the method you use to project your slides, navigating a slide show is a simple process. You can move from one slide to the next by clicking the mouse button or pressing ENTER. Or you can automate the presentation by setting a display time for each slide. Presentation programs make it easy to take slides out of sequence or rearrange slides during a presentation. You can even use the program's drawing tools to draw on a slide while it is being displayed.

Personal Information Managers

It's harder than ever to keep track of people. You probably know several people who have a home phone number, a cell phone number, one or two e-mail addresses, an instant messenger address, and a fax machine number, all in addition to their "snail mail" address. (The term snail mail refers to the U.S. Postal Service.) To make matters more difficult, some people also have a Web page, a special number for voice mail messages, a pager, and even a second mailing address!

ONLINE

For more information on PIMs, visit **http://www.mhhe.com/ peternorton**.

Computers In Your Career

Help Desk and Technical Support Specialists

Mark Barry knows that when he picks up a phone line in his office, there's a good chance that the caller will be edgy, and possibly even on the verge of tears, over the fact that his or her hardware or software may never work properly again. Part counselor, part computer technician, Barry asks questions about the problem itself, positions himself in front of the same application or piece of hardware in his own office, then helps the caller find a workable solution.

"It's always great to be able to help someone take care of a technology problem," says Barry, president and owner of Configured PC in Whitinsville, Massachusetts. "There's a lot of personal satisfaction in befriending someone, and making their day." A graduate of Clark University's Computer Career Institute, Barry holds his CompTIA A+ certification. Prior to starting his own firm, which specializes in technical sales and support, he was a technical trainer for CompUSA.

With the assistance of one technical support professional and an office manager, Barry has made a career out of helping people work through their technology problems. He fills

a gap in the industry where vendor technology support personnel often leave off: being able to communicate well with customers and walk them through diagnostic and repair steps via telephone. When he's not on the phone, Barry helps walk-in customers, makes house calls, and consults with clients in need of customized technology solutions.

Barry predicts a healthy demand for IT types who can communicate with customers—be they internal customers (those calling to an internal help desk) or outside customers (such as the ones he works with)—and walk them through technical problems with their hardware and software. Both help desk workers and technical support specialists share the same goal of helping others use their computers, but generally work in different environments:

>> Help desk professionals are usually employed by a company to help its other employees with the computer systems they use at work. Suppose, for example, that you work for a large retailer and use its specialized order management or customer relationship management (CRM)

It is very common for businesspersons to have multiple contact points. Of course, these many means of contacting people are supposed to make it easier to reach them. But keeping track of all those names, numbers, and addresses—called contact information—can be frustrating.

The explosion of contact information has given rise to a special type of software, called the personal information manager, or PIM. A personal information manager is designed to keep track of many different kinds of contact information, for many different people. PIMs are sometimes referred to as contact managers or contact-management software. One of the most popular PIMs is Microsoft Outlook, shown in Figure 4B.21.

FIGURE 4B.21

Microsoft Outlook lets you manage contact lists, your schedule, and other important information. It is also a powerful e-mail program.

software. If you need help using the program, you can call the company's internal help desk to ask for assistance.

>> Technical support specialists are usually employed by a company to help its customers use the products they have purchased from the company. If you have ever had trouble with a computer program and called the manufacturer for help, then you probably spoke with a technical support specialist.

According to the Bureau of Labor Statistics, computer support specialists are projected to be among the fastest-growing occupations over the 2000–2010 period, with job prospects being optimal for college graduates who are up to date with the latest skills and technologies; certifications and practical experience are essential for persons without degrees. Median annual earnings of computer support specialists were $36,460 in 2000, with the middle 50 percent earning between $27,680 and $48,440.

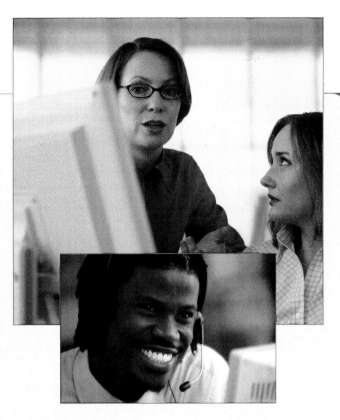

PIMs make contact management easy, because they provide special placeholders for all kinds of contact information—everything from phone numbers and e-mail addresses to Web pages and regular mail addresses. To manage contact information for a person, you add him or her to your contact list. (Most PIMs store and arrange contacts by first name or last name, according to your preference.) Then you simply type all the contact points into the appropriate boxes in that person's contact sheet (see Figure 4B.22).

Like many other PIMs, Outlook stores much more than just contact information. You also can use a PIM to manage your schedule, create reminders, and set up to-do lists. Outlook is also a powerful e-mail program that you can use to send

FIGURE 4B.22

Adding contact information for a person in Microsoft Outlook.

messages to anyone in your contact list (see Figure 4B.23). Contact lists are often called address books in e-mail programs and PIMs.

Many professionals, especially salespeople, use a PIM as their primary software tool. This is because they can manage their calendar and associate specific events with specific contacts. For example, if you schedule a meeting, you can place it in your PIM's calendar; note the time, place, and purpose of the meeting; and create a list of attendees from your contact list. This capability not only lets you manage your schedule down to the last detail, but gives you a permanent record of your activities. (See Figure 4B.24.)

FIGURE 4B.23

Sending an e-mail message in Outlook.

FIGURE 4B.24

A PIM's scheduling capabilities let you manage meetings, deadlines, appointments, and special events.

Summary ::

>> Word processing programs are used to create and format text-based documents, such as letters and reports.

>> Word processors feature on-screen tools found in most kinds of productivity applications. These tools include a menu bar, toolbars, rulers, scroll bars, and a status bar.

>> Most of a word processor's tools are used for formatting documents. You can format characters, paragraphs, and entire documents using these tools.

>> Spreadsheet programs are used to create numerically based documents, such as budgets.

>> Spreadsheets work with four basic kinds of data: labels, numbers, dates, and formulas. A spreadsheet can perform complex calculations on the numbers in its cells.

>> Presentation programs let you create presentations, which are collections of single-screen images called slides. A presentation also may be called a slide show.

>> Presentation programs include tools found in word processors, spreadsheets, and graphics programs, so you can combine all manner of text and images on your slides. You can present slides directly from your computer's disk.

>> Personal information managers (PIMs) are special programs designed to manage contact information, schedules, and other personal or business information.

>> Many PIMs also are e-mail programs, making it easy to send e-mail messages to anyone in the program's address book.

Key Terms ::

address book, 196	font, 185	ruler, 183
block, 184	format, 185	select, 184
cell, 186	formula, 188	slide, 190
cell address, 186	formula bar, 186	snail mail, 193
cell pointer, 186	frame, 191	spreadsheet, 186
character format, 185	label, 187	status bar, 183
contact information, 194	paragraph, 185	template, 191
contact-management software, 194	paragraph format, 185	text box, 191
contact manager, 194	PC-to-TV converter, 193	type style, 185
deselect, 184	personal information manager	value, 187
document area, 183	(PIM), 194	word processing program, 183
document format, 185	point, 185	word processor, 183
document window, 183	presentation, 190	workbook, 186
edit, 184	presentation program, 190	worksheet, 186

Key Term Quiz ::

Complete each statement by writing one of the terms listed under Key Terms in each blank.

1. A font's size is measured in _____ .

2. Changing an existing document is called _____ the document.

3. Word processors enable you to perform three basic types of formatting: _____ , _____ , and _____ .

4. In a spreadsheet program, you actually work in a document called a(n) _____ .

5. A column letter and a row number combine to form a(n) _____ .

6. A spreadsheet program uses _____ to calculate numbers based on the contents of a worksheet's cells.

7. You use a presentation program to design _____ , which are single-screen images containing a combination of text, numbers, and graphics.

8. In a slide, you enter text in a special placeholder, which is called a(n) _____ .

9. The term _____ refers to the U.S. Postal Service.

10. Contact lists are often called _____ in e-mail programs and PIMs.

Multiple Choice ::

Circle the word or phrase that best completes each statement.

1. In a word processor, you _____ text to mark it for editing or formatting.
   a. block   b. delete   c. move   d. select

2. In a word processor, a special tool called the _____ shows you the precise locations of items in a document.
   a. toolbar   b. menu bar   c. status bar   d. ruler

3. To navigate a worksheet, you should understand its system of _____ .
   a. cell addresses   b. spreadsheets   c. formulas   d. labels

4. _____ can help you make sense of a worksheet's contents.
   a. Cell pointers   b. Labels   c. Cell references   d. Values

5. In a spreadsheet program, a _____ is a set of worksheets in the same file.
   a. formula   b. label   c. workbook   d. value

6. In a worksheet, a _____ is the intersection of a row and a column.
   a. formula bar   b. cell   c. ruler   d. frame

7. To create a chart in a slide, you enter data in a separate window called a _____ .
   a. datasheet   b. spreadsheet   c. worksheet   d. rapsheet

8. A _____ is designed to keep track of many different kinds of contact information, for many different people.
   a. workbook   b. program   c. PIM   d. stand-alone program

9. Many PIMs, such as Outlook, let you manage _____ .
   a. fonts   b. formulas   c. charts   d. e-mail

10. Which of the following is not a way to display a presentation?
    a. computer screen   b. telephone   c. television   d. large-format monitor

Review Questions ::

In your own words, briefly answer the following questions.

1. In a word processor, what makes a block of text?
2. What happens when you press ENTER in a word processor?
3. What is the purpose of a formula bar in a spreadsheet program?
4. In a spreadsheet, what is a value?
5. What is the difference between a spreadsheet and a worksheet?
6. What does a formula do in a spreadsheet?
7. What is a presentation?
8. Describe two ways you can create slides in a presentation program.
9. List four ways you can display a slide show to an audience.
10. What is contact information?

Lesson Labs ::

Complete the following exercises as directed by your instructor.

1. Practice some basic formatting:
   a. In your word processor's document area, type a few lines of text, allowing the lines to wrap when they reach the right edge of the screen. Press ENTER and type a new paragraph. Create several more paragraphs. (If you have trouble thinking of text to type, just copy a few paragraphs of text from this book.)
   b. Using the mouse, select a word. (Double-click the word or drag the mouse pointer across it.) Click the Bold tool. Then deselect the word by pressing an arrow key on the keyboard. Select the word again and click the Bold tool to turn off the effect.
   c. Select different words, lines, and paragraphs and practice using other tools such as a Font tool, a Font size tool, Italic, and Underline.
   d. Close the program by clicking the CLOSE button (the button marked with an X on the title bar). If the program prompts you to save the file, choose NO.

2. Practice using a worksheet:
   a. In your worksheet's document area, type numbers in cells A1 through A5.
   b. Using the mouse, select all the values in this range. (Click in cell A1, and then drag the mouse pointer down through cell A5.)
   c. Click in cell A6 and type **=SUM(A1:A5)**. Press ENTER. The total of the values in cells A1 to A5 should appear in cell A6. If it does not, ask your instructor for help.
   d. Click in cell A3 and press DELETE. The value in the cell disappears and the total in cell A6 changes.
   e. Issue the Undo command. (There should be an Undo tool on the toolbar. If not, ask your instructor for assistance.) The value is returned to cell A3 and the total in cell A6 updates once more.
   f. Click in cell B6 and type **=A6*0.05**. Press ENTER. The formula's result appears in cell B6.
   g. Close the spreadsheet program by clicking the CLOSE button. If the program prompts you to save the worksheet, choose NO.

Chapter Labs

Complete the following exercises using a computer in your classroom, lab, or home.

1. Find some fonts. The Internet is a good place to find and acquire fonts. Some fonts can be downloaded from various Web sites at no cost. Other fonts can be purchased over the Web. Visit the following Web sites and study the available fonts, but do not download any fonts without your instructor's permission.

   Microsoft Typography http://www.microsoft.com/typography/default.asp. (You won't actually find fonts here, but you will find a tremendous amount of information about fonts and links to non-Microsoft sites where fonts can be downloaded.)

   CNet http://www.cnet.com. Use the Search tool to search on the term "fonts."

   ZDNet http://www.zdnet.com. Use the Search tool to search on the term "fonts."

2. Create a file system. Suppose that you work for a soft drink company. Your manager has asked you to create a business proposal for a new product—a fun, caffeine-free soda for kids under the age of eight. The proposal will be about 50 pages in length and will include several supporting documents, such as reports, memos, budgets, customer lists, research on the product's safety, focus group results, taste tests, and so on. These different documents will be created in several forms, including word processing documents, spreadsheet files, databases, presentations, and so on.

   Your first task is to create a file system on your computer's hard disk where you can store and manage all these files. Using a piece of paper, design a set of folders (and subfolders, if needed) to store all the files in a logical manner. Be prepared to share your file system with the class and to discuss the logic behind your file system.

3. Get the latest on Windows XP. If you do not have Windows XP yet, chances are good that you will be using it in the future. Get a jump on the OS by finding the latest information about it on the Web.

   Visit the following Web sites for more information:

   Microsoft Corporation Visit Microsoft's main Windows XP page at http://www.microsoft.com/windowsxp/default.asp.

   PC Magazine For a series of articles and reviews about Windows XP, visit http://www.pcmag.com/winxp.

Discussion Questions

As directed by your instructor, discuss the following questions in class or in groups.

1. What does multitasking mean to the average computer user?

2. Suppose that you were asked to give a presentation on a subject you understand well. To support your presentation, you must prepare a 20-minute slide show using presentation software. Describe the slide presentation you would create. How many slides would you use? How would you organize them? What types of content would you use in each? What features of the presentation program would you use to enhance the presentation?

Research and Report

Using your own choice of resources (such as the Internet, books, magazines, and newspaper articles), research and write a short paper discussing one of the following topics:

» The story behind the creation of the Linux operating system.

» A cost comparison of currently available desktop operating systems.

» The ways spreadsheet programs are used in business.

When you are finished, proofread and print your paper, and give it to your instructor.

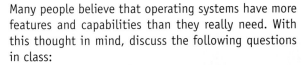

ETHICAL QUESTIONS

Many people believe that operating systems have more features and capabilities than they really need. With this thought in mind, discuss the following questions in class:

1. The Windows Update feature has been part of the Windows operating system since the release of Windows 98. This tool enables the operating system to notify the user when updated features are available for downloading on the Internet. Some observers think that future operating systems will be able to update themselves automatically without first noti-

fying the user. How do you feel about this possibility? What dangers could it pose to users?

2. Word processors make it easy to create documents. They also make it easy to copy documents created by others. Copying other people's work is a growing concern because more people are downloading others' creations from the Internet and disks and then using the documents as their own. Would you use this tactic, say, to create a term paper for school? Do you think it is legally or morally right? Why or why not?

Computing Keynotes

You may have seen the TV commercial: a bored-looking office worker sits in her cubicle, checking her e-mail. She perks up when she sees a message with an exciting subject line, then unthinkingly opens the message. Instantly, a menacing-looking character appears on her computer screen, "eats" the program icons on her desktop, and announces that she has just unleashed a virus. Within seconds, the same chaos erupts in the surrounding cubicles, and it becomes clear that the worker has made a horrible mistake.

In reality, computer viruses aren't so dramatic. In fact, most viruses are designed to hide, do their work quietly, and avoid detection for as long as possible. But a virus's damage can be dramatic in the extreme, causing untold losses to data and productivity.

Because of their ability to cause damage and disruption, viruses have been big news in recent years, especially with the outbreak of e-mail viruses beginning in the late 1990s. These viruses alone have accounted for billions of dollars in downtime and lost data in the past few years. Experts predict that virus attacks will only increase in the future.

Even so, many computer users are unaware of the dangers posed by viruses and make no effort to protect their computers and data from viruses. This is the primary reason viruses continue to be so successful.

What Is a Computer Virus?

A virus is a parasitic program that infects another legitimate program, which is sometimes called the host. To infect the host program, the virus modifies the host to store a copy of the virus. Many viruses are programmed to do harm once they infect the victim's system. As you will see later, a virus can be designed to do various kinds of damage. But the ability to do damage is not what defines a virus.

To qualify as a virus, a program must be able to replicate (make copies of) itself. This can mean copying itself to different places on the same computer or looking for ways to reach other computers, such as by infecting disks or traveling

across networks. Viruses can be programmed to replicate and travel in many ways.

Here are some common ways to pick up a virus:

>> Receiving an infected file attached to an e-mail message, or a virus hidden within the message itself. E-mail has become the single most common method for spreading viruses, especially now that so many people use the Internet to exchange messages and files. Viruses can even be spread through online chat rooms and instant messenger programs.

"Touch a key, and your data gets it!"

Viruses may not look menacing, but they can do all kinds of damage.

① The programmer creates a boot sector virus and stores it on a hard disk. The virus is copied to any floppy disk that is inserted into the same computer.

② The programmer distributes infected floppies to other users.

③ The hard disks of other users are infected by the infected floppy. Every floppy that is placed in an infected computer also becomes infected, and the number of infected computers grows exponentially.

Many viruses can spread by copying themselves to floppy disks or recordable CDs. As shown here, each time an infected machine's user gives someone else a disk, a copy of the virus goes with it.

>> Downloading an infected file to your computer across a network, an online service, or the Internet. Unless you have antivirus software that inspects each incoming file for viruses, you probably will not know if you have downloaded an infected file.

>> Receiving an infected disk (a diskette, a CD created by someone with a CD-R drive, a high-capacity floppy disk, and so on) from another user. In this case, the virus could be stored in the boot sector of the disk or in an executable file (a program) on the disk.

>> Copying to your disk a document file that is infected with a macro virus. An infected document might be copied from another disk or received as an attachment to an e-mail message.

What Can a Virus Do?

The majority of computer viruses are relatively harmless; their purpose is to annoy their victims rather than to cause specific damage. Such viruses are described as benign. Other viruses are indeed malicious, and they can do great damage to a computer system if permitted to run.

Viruses can be programmed to do many kinds of harm, including the following:

>> Copy themselves to other programs or areas of a disk.

>> Replicate as rapidly and frequently as possible, filling up the infected system's disks and memory, rendering the system useless.

>> Display information on the screen.

>> Modify, corrupt, or destroy selected files.

>> Erase the contents of entire disks.

>> Lie dormant for a specified time or until a given condition is met, and then become active.

>> Open a "back door" to the infected system that allows someone else to access and even take control of the system through a network or Internet connection. This type of virus may actually be a type of program called a Trojan Horse, and can be used to turn an infected system into a "zombie," which the virus's author can use to attack other systems. For example, by using viruses to create a large number of zombie systems, the author can use the zombies to send thousands of requests to a specific Web server, effectively shutting it down. Such an attack is sometimes called a "denial of service (DOS) attack" or a "distributed denial of service (DDOS) attack," because it prevents the server from providing services to users.

This list is by no means comprehensive. Virus programmers can be extremely creative, and many create viruses to perform a specific type of task, sometimes with a specific victim in mind. Regardless, you need to protect your system against all kinds of viruses, because nearly any one can strike at any time, given the right circumstances.

Viruses may seem like major problems for individual computer users. For corporations, however, viruses can be devastating in terms of lost data and productivity. U.S. companies lose billions of dollars every year to damage caused by viruses. Most of the expenses come from the time and effort required to locate and remove viruses, restore systems, rebuild lost or corrupted data, and ensure against future attacks. But companies also lose valuable work time—millions of person-hours each year—as workers sit idle, unable to use their computers.

1 This PC becomes infected by an e-mail virus.

2 The virus sends a copy of itself to other PCs on the network, through e-mail or simply by travelling across the network connections.

Server

3 Soon, every other computer on the network is infected. If the network is connected to the Internet or a WAN, the virus may be able to infect other systems through that connection.

Viruses also can spread through a network connection, as shown here. In this simple example, one PC has been infected by a virus, which quickly spreads to other computers on the network.

CONTINUED >>>

Categories of Viruses

Depending on your source of information, different types of viruses may be described in slightly different ways. Some specific categories of viruses include the following:

>> **Bimodal, Bipartite, or Multipartite Viruses.** This type of virus can infect both files and the boot sector of a disk.

>> **Bombs.** The two most prevalent types of bombs are time bombs and logic bombs. A time bomb hides on the victim's disk and waits until a specific date (or date and time) before running. A logic bomb may be activated by a date, a change to a file, or a particular action taken by a user or a program. Many experts do not classify bombs as viruses, but some do. Regardless, bombs are treated as viruses because they can cause damage or disruption to a system.

>> **Boot Sector Viruses.** Regarded as one of the most hostile types of virus, a boot sector virus infects the boot sector of a hard or floppy disk. This area of the disk stores essential files the computer accesses during startup. The virus moves the boot sector's data to a different part of the disk. When the computer is started, the virus copies itself into memory where it can hide and infect other disks. The virus allows the actual boot sector data to be read as though a normal start-up were occurring.

>> **Cluster Viruses.** This type of virus makes changes to a disk's file system. If any program is run from the infected disk, the program causes the virus to run as well. This technique creates the illusion that the virus has infected every program on the disk.

>> **E-mail Viruses.** E-mail viruses can be transmitted via e-mail messages sent across private networks or the Internet. Some e-mail viruses are transmitted as an infected attachment—a document file or program that is attached to the message. This type of virus is run when the victim opens the file that is attached to the message. Other types of e-mail viruses reside within the body of the message itself. To store a virus, the message must be encoded in HTML format. Once launched, many e-mail viruses attempt to spread by sending messages to everyone in the victim's address book; each of those messages contains a copy of the virus.

>> **File-Infecting Viruses.** This type of virus infects program files on a disk (such as .exe or .com files). When an infected program is launched, the virus's code is also executed.

>> **Joke Programs.** Joke programs are not viruses and do not inflict any damage. Their purpose is to frighten their victims into thinking that a virus has infected and dam-

An e-mail attachment may look harmless, but opening it could unleash a virus onto your PC.

aged their system. For example, a joke program may display a message warning the user not to touch any keys or the computer's hard disk will be formatted.

>> **Macro Viruses.** A macro virus is designed to infect a specific type of document file, such as Microsoft Word or Excel files. These documents can include macros, which are small programs that execute commands. (Macros are typically used to issue program-specific commands, but they also can issue certain operating-system commands.) A macro virus, disguised as a macro, is embedded in a document file and can do various levels of damage to data, from corrupting documents to deleting data.

>> **Polymorphic, Self-Garbling, Self-Encrypting, or Self-Changing Viruses.** This type of virus can change itself each time it is copied, making it difficult to isolate.

>> **Stealth Viruses.** These viruses take up residence in the computer's memory, making them hard to detect. They also can conceal changes they make to other files, hiding the damage from the user and the operating system.

>> **Trojan Horses.** A Trojan Horse is a malicious program that appears to be friendly. For example, some Trojan Horses appear to be games. Because Trojan Horses do not make duplicates of themselves on the victim's disk (or copy themselves to other disks), they are not technically viruses. But, because they can do harm, many experts consider them to be a type of virus. Trojan Horses are often used by hackers to create a "back door" to an infected system as described earlier.

>> **Worms.** A worm is a program whose purpose is to duplicate itself. An effective worm will fill entire disks with

Scanning a computer's memory and hard disk with Norton AntiVirus.

Macro viruses have become such a problem that many software programs now provide built-in security measures against them. This screen shows Microsoft Word's macro security settings, which can disable any macro to prevent it from running.

copies of itself and will take up as much space as possible in the host system's memory. Many worms are designed to spread to other computers. An entire LAN or corporate e-mail system can become totally clogged with copies of a worm, rendering it useless. Worms are commonly spread over the Internet via e-mail message attachments and through Internet Relay Chat (IRC) channels. Technically, a worm is not the same as a virus. Because worms have become so prevalent in recent years, however, and because they can do considerable damage, worms are treated as though they were viruses.

Preventing Infection

Safeguarding a system against viruses is not difficult if you have a little knowledge and some utility software.

Start by being aware that viruses can come from many sources—even sources you trust. For example, an e-mail virus may arrive in your inbox disguised as a message from a friend or colleague because it has already infected that person's computer. A homemade data CD or floppy disk can be infected, too. In fact, even programs purchased in shrink-wrapped packages from reputable stores have been known to harbor viruses on rare occasions. The best precaution is to treat all e-mail messages and disks as potential carriers of infection.

Checking for viruses requires antivirus software, which scans your computer's memory and disks for known viruses and eradicates them. After it is installed on your system and activated, a good antivirus program checks for infected

files automatically every time you insert any kind of disk or download a file via a network or Internet connection. Most antivirus utilities can also scan e-mail messages and attached files as you receive or send them. Sophisticated virus scanners can also alert you if a Web page attempts to load suspicious code onto your PC.

Some popular antivirus programs include

>> McAfee VirusScan
>> Norton AntiVirus
>> Virex
>> PC-cillin
>> Avast!

However, simply having antivirus software on your computer is not enough to keep viruses away. This is where many casual computer users slip up and allow their systems to be infected.

Once you install the software, be sure to read its documentation thoroughly and master all of its functions. Most antivirus programs allow you to make various settings, such as activating automatic e-mail scanning. All these options may not be active by default, so you may need to activate them yourself and choose settings to control their operation. Make sure that you understand all the program's options and set them to give you maximum protection. Once the program is in place, scan your computer's disks at least once every week to check for viruses; your program may include a scheduling function that can automate disk-scanning for you.

Because new viruses are released almost daily, no antivirus program can offer absolute protection against them all. Many antivirus software vendors allow users to download updated virus definitions or virus patterns (databases

CONTINUED >>>

Setting options in Norton AntiVirus.

Downloading updated virus definitions from the McAfee VirusScan Web site.

of information about viruses and code that can eradicate them) to their programs over the Internet. The newest-generation antivirus programs can find, download, and in-stall updated virus definitions by themselves, automatically, whenever your computer is connected to the Internet. Whether you choose to update your antivirus software man-ually or automatically, you should do it at least once a week, to make sure you are protected against the latest viruses.

It's also a good idea to stay up to date on the latest news about viruses. A good way to do that is to visit the Web site of your antivirus software program's developer. A few other sources of general virus-related information are

>> Computer Security Institute (CSI).
http://www.gocsi.com

>> IBM Antivirus Research.
http://www.research.ibm.com/antivirus

>> Vmyths.com. http://www.vmyths.com

>> Symantec Security Response.
http://www.symantec.com/avcenter

>> F-Secure Security Information Center.
http://www.f-secure.com/vir-info

>> CERT Coordination Center Computer Virus Resources.
http://www.cert.org/other_sources/viruses.html

Many reputable Web sites, such as the CERT Coordination Center, provide up-to-the-minute information on viruses and virus prevention.

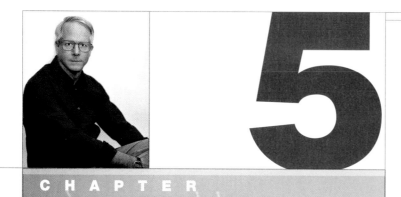

5

Living in the Online World

CHAPTER

01 02 03 04 05 06 07 08 09 10 11 12 13 14

CHAPTER CONTENTS ::

This chapter contains the following lessons:

Lesson **5A:**
Doing Business in the Online World

>> E-Commerce at the Consumer Level
>> E-Commerce at the Business Level
>> Security

Lesson **5B:**
Staying Safe in the Online World

>> Protecting Yourself
>> Keeping Your Data Secure
>> Safeguarding Your Hardware

Doing Business in the Online World

Overview: Commerce on the World Wide Web

The World Wide Web has become a global vehicle for electronic commerce (e-commerce), creating new ways for businesses to interact with one another and their customers. E-commerce means doing business online, such as when a consumer buys a product over the Web instead of going to a store to buy it.

E-commerce technologies are rapidly changing the way individuals and companies do business. You can go online to buy a book, lease a car, shop for groceries, or rent movies. You can even get a pizza delivered to your door without picking up the phone.

But these kinds of transactions are only the tip of the e-commerce iceberg. In fact, the vast majority of e-commerce activities do not involve consumers at all. They are conducted among businesses, which have developed complex networking systems dedicated to processing orders, managing inventories, and handling payments.

This lesson introduces you to the basics of e-commerce at the consumer and business levels. You will learn how to make sure your online shopping and browsing activities are secure, and how to protect your personal information when using the Internet.

OBJECTIVES ::

>> Explain, in basic terms, what *e-commerce* is.

>> Describe two e-commerce activities that are important to consumers.

>> Describe one important way businesses use e-commerce technologies.

>> Explain the role of intranets and extranets in business-to-business e-commerce.

>> List two ways to make sure you are shopping on a secure Web page.

simnet™

E-Commerce at the Consumer Level

Tens of thousands of online businesses cater to the needs of consumers. These companies' Web sites provide information about products and services, take orders, receive payments, and provide on-the-spot customer service. Consumer-oriented e-commerce Web sites take many forms and cover the gamut of products and services, but can be divided into two general categories: shopping sites and personal-finance sites.

Online Shopping

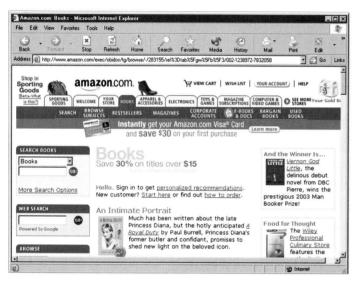

Online shopping means buying a product or service through a Web site. (Another term for online shopping is business-to-consumer (B2C) transaction.) Even if you have never shopped online, you probably have heard of Web sites such as Amazon.com and Buy.com (see Figure 5A.1). They are just two of the many popular Web sites where consumers can buy all sorts of things.

What can you buy online? The list is almost limitless—including everything from cars to appliances, electronics to jewelry, clothes to books, fine wines to old-fashioned candies. You can subscribe to your favorite newspaper or magazine online, hunt for antiques, and order complete holiday meals for delivery to your door. You can even buy and sell items of all kinds on auction sites like eBay—a one-time fad that has turned into a full-time business for thousands of eBay users (see Figure 5A.2)

FIGURE 5A.1

Like many e-commerce sites that target consumers, Amazon.com offers a catalog, extensive help, secure purchasing, customer service, and other features.

There are thousands of consumer Web sites and each has its own look, feel, and approach to customer satisfaction. But effective online shopping sites share a few essential features:

>> A catalog where you can search for information about products and services.

>> A "checkout" section where you can securely pay for the items you want to purchase.

>> A customer-service page, where you can contact the merchant for assistance.

FIGURE 5A.2

At auction sites like eBay, you can bid on just about any kind of item imaginable.

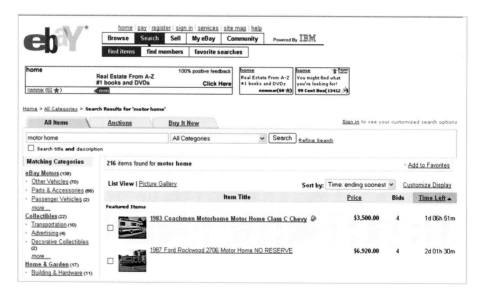

Online Stores versus Physical Locations

In a brick-and-mortar store (that is, a physical store that you can visit in person to do your shopping), you can wander the aisles and see the merchandise for yourself (see Figure 5A.3). If the store is too big or the layout too confusing, you can ask a clerk or a customer service representative for guidance. This is one big advantage of going to the store yourself.

In an online store (that is, a store that exists only on the Web, with no physical locations you can visit), you don't have that advantage. You can't walk the aisles, pick up the merchandise, or grab some free samples. You have to do all your shopping in your browser window. Amazon.com and PCConnection.com are examples of online stores, because they have no "real" store you can go to.

A hybrid merchant is called a click-and-mortar store—a physical store that also has a Web site where you can shop. Best Buy and Nordstrom are examples of click-and-mortar stores because they have physical locations in many cities, as well as Web sites where you can view and purchase their products (see Figure 5A.4). Some click-and-mortar retailers let customers buy items online, then pick them up or return them at the store. This arrangement offers the best of both worlds in convenience and customer service.

Using Online Catalogs

Online shopping would be very difficult if merchants did not provide easy-to-use catalogs on their Web sites. In the early days of e-commerce, many retailers struggled to come up with catalogs that were user-friendly for customers and easy to manage. Retail-oriented Web sites need to be maintained and updated on a continuing basis, so that prices and descriptions are always correct. Site managers and designers must be careful to balance their own needs against those of consumers, or they risk losing business.

Many e-commerce Web sites are set up like directories (see Figure 5A.5). These catalogs lump products or services into categories and subcategories. If you are shopping for an MP3 player at the Web site of an electronics vendor, for example,

FIGURE 5A.3

Sometimes there is no substitute for shopping in a real store.

FIGURE 5A.4

Nordstrom is an example of a "click-and-mortar" store, with physical locations and an online presence.

FIGURE 5A.5

Like many online merchants, Buy.com categorizes its products, making it easy to find anything in its online catalog.

you might click the Electronics category first, then the Personal Electronics subcategory, then Personal Audio, then Handheld Devices, and then MP3 Players.

Along with a directory of product categories, you may find a Search tool at your favorite online shopping site. Like any Web search engine, this tool lets you conduct a keyword search, but the search occurs only on the merchant's site instead of the entire Web. So, if you are shopping for boots on a site that sells clothes, you should be able to click in the Search box, type **boots**, and press ENTER. The site will then display a list of products or pages that match your interest (see Figure 5A.6).

Paying for Purchases

Online merchants usually try to make online shopping as similar as possible to shopping at a real store. One way they do this is by letting shoppers create a shopping cart—an electronic holding area that stores information about items that the customer has chosen for purchasing (see Figure 5A.7).

When you are ready to make your purchase, you can pay for it in several ways. Two of the most common payment methods include the following:

>> **One-Time Credit Card Purchase.** If you do not want to set up an account with the seller, you can provide your personal and credit card information each time you make a purchase.

>> **Set Up an Online Account.** If you think you will make other purchases from the online vendor, you can set up an account at the Web site (see Figure 5A.8). The vendor stores your personal and credit card information on a secure server, and then places a special file (called a cookie) on your computer's disk. Later, when you access your account again by typing a user ID and password, the site uses information in the cookie to access your account. Online accounts are required at some vendors' Web sites, such as brokerage sites that provide online investing services.

Getting Customer Service

Would you buy clothes at a department store that had no Customer Service counter? Probably not. When you spend your money, you want to make sure that someone will be available to help if you have a problem. This is just as true on the Web as in any store.

Before you buy anything from a Web site, check its customer service resources (see Figure 5A.9). Look for the following information:

>> **Contact Information.** You should be able to contact a customer service representative by telephone and by regular mail—not just by e-mail. If the site does not display at least one customer service number and one mailing address, consider shopping elsewhere.

>> **Return Policies.** If you want to return a product that you bought online, you will probably be responsible for packing it up and shipping it. You may need to get an authorization number or take other steps to ensure that the return is handled correctly.

FIGURE 5A.6

Searching for boots at the L.L. Bean Web site.

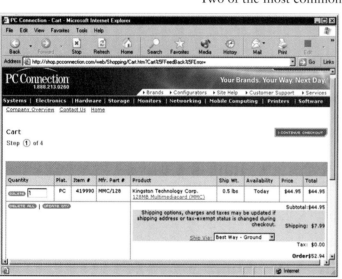

FIGURE 5A.7

An example of an electronic shopping cart at the PC Connection Web site. This user is preparing to purchase a memory upgrade for a computer. The cart shows the product, model information, price, quantity, in-stock status, shipping charges, and more.

FIGURE 5A.8

Setting up an account at the Best Buy Web site.

>> **Shipping Policies.** Before ordering, find out what your shipping options are. Many online vendors use the least expensive means of shipping unless you ask for something else. Always check the shipping charges before checking out, and make sure they are reasonable.

>> **Charges and Fees.** Some online vendors charge processing fees or other "hidden" fees, which may not be described when you purchase something. Look for signs that the seller charges such fees.

FIGURE 5A.9

Always look for customer service information before buying anything through a Web site. This is the main Help page at Target's Web site.

Online Banking and Finance

Retailers are not the only businesses reaching out to consumers over the Web. No matter where you live in the United States, there's a good chance that one of your local banks has a Web site where you can manage your accounts. If you are interested in investing, borrowing money, buying insurance, applying for a credit card, or doing some other task involving personal finance, you can do that online, too.

Online Banking

The term online banking refers to using a bank's Web site to handle banking-related tasks (see Figure 5A.10). Individuals and businesses alike can visit any bank's Web site and do the following:

>> Create an account.

>> Transfer funds.

>> Record or view transactions.

>> Reconcile statements.

>> Pay bills.

If you use a personal-finance program at home (such as Microsoft Money or Quicken), it can use your Internet connection to access your bank accounts online. This feature makes it easy to manage your accounts and keep your checkbook balanced.

Norton Notebook

Business, the Internet, and Everything

When the Internet was first developed by scientists and academics, its purpose was to share research and communication more effectively. At the time, fax machines and overnight express delivery were still years away, and moving data electronically across the country was a revolutionary opportunity. The problem with revolutions, as Maximilien Robespierre could certainly attest, is that, once you've got them started, they tend to take on a life of their own far beyond the imaginings and ideals of their founders. No one involved with the early development of Internet technologies started out thinking, "We're going to make a packet of money with this." It wasn't until nearly 20 years after initial work on what became the Internet that the World Wide Web was developed, and businesspeople suddenly came to the conclusion that the Internet was some kind of idealized television. That is to say, a new medium where, for the small cost of producing a little lowest-common-denominator entertainment or news, companies could get customers to willingly sit through endless streams of product advertisements—with the added bonus that you could actually *sell* your products directly over the Internet, and even get people to *pay you* to ship them out. On television, it was necessary to create engaging advertisements that motivated people out of their homes and into the stores. On the Web, everything available for sale could be turned into a high-profile impulse buy.

Riding high on this wave of idealistic consumerism, thousands of people with a little technical savvy—some of them, very little—created initial public offerings of stock (IPOs) for tech companies that were going to do amazing things. Nobody was sure what those amazing things would be, but everyone knew that someone else was doing the actual work, developing actual products to solve actual problems. All you had to do was put up a Web page with a cool animated logo and keep your eyes open for the right coattails to ride all the way to the bank. The stock market found itself littered—and I use that word with precision—with thousands of "dot com" companies. Even respectable, established corporations were taken in by the charade, investing their employees' 401(k) retirement plans in these promising newcomers with no products, no profits, but stratospheric stock prices: "So the word *must* be that they're about to come out with the next must-have thing!" But they weren't, and they didn't. In an atmosphere of general economic downturn, hundreds of thousands of jobs and billions of dollars simply evaporated. Magazines and books from 1995 to 2001 were stuffed with messages that the Internet had created a new economy in which old business methods and rules simply no longer applied. They were wrong. At the end of the day, by which I mean around the middle of 2001, it remained true that one must spend less than one makes, one must satisfy one's customers, and one must actually produce or provide something of value in order for one to make a profit. Business is still business-as-usual.

Or is it? Despite the disappearance of the majority of "Internet companies," the Internet remains, and online technology continues to evolve in areas of tangible products and services. That technology is real, and it has changed more about us than we may initially realize. Consider, by way of example, the motion picture industry. This century-old industry has spread from Thomas Edison's lab in

FIGURE 5A.10

Like many banks' Web sites, the Bank of America site lets customers create and manage accounts, pay bills, and do other banking.

New Jersey to Hollywood, and on to "Bollywood" in India. Thanks to the development of DVD technology, it's often no longer vital that a movie earn a profit at the box office. Films that are financial flops can be repackaged, repositioned, and sold on DVD to an ever-thriving movie rental industry and home purchasers. Profits from DVD sales are so great that motion picture studios have begun to instruct directors to think from the beginning in terms of the two movies she or he wants to make—the first to be shown in theatres, the second to be available exclusively on a multidisc DVD package including "never-before-seen" footage. At first, most of these never-before-seen add-ins were nothing more than scraps from the cutting room floor—material that the director had deemed of insufficient quality to be shown in the theatre. Now, however, additional viable footage is intentionally shot and budgeted, never to be shown in theatres . . . but you can purchase it for private viewing. The Internet comes into this equation with the realization that the same digital video and broadband technologies developed in the hope of creating profitable "interactive television" made it possible for consumers to copy and share DVD content without paying for it. That technology also enables small production houses to create, market, and sell their motion pictures, circumventing traditional distribution channels and, sometimes, retailers. And the open forum provided by the worldwide Internet has led to the dissemination of instructions and tools for defeating copy protection methodologies.

So, traditional businesses that weren't damaged in the vast failure of Internet companies may find themselves damaged by the vast success of the Internet itself. Most media companies have retaliated by wasting millions of taxpayer dollars clogging the courts with questions like "What is ownership?" and "What do we actually mean when we say 'purchase'?" These are desperate attempts to turn back time and undo what is already sitting in millions of offices and homes. To survive, these businesses will have to redefine themselves and move forward in a post-Internet world, embracing the individual's ownership of powerful technology. They must spend less than they make, satisfy their customers, and produce something of value in order to make a profit—business as usual!

Online Finance

The term online finance refers to any kind of personal financial transaction you can conduct online, other than managing your bank accounts (see Figure 5A.11). These activities include:

>> Investing.

>> Applying for loans.

>> Applying for credit cards.

>> Buying insurance.

>> Preparing tax returns and paying taxes.

>> Doing financial research or seeking financial advice.

At Prudential Financial's Web site, clients can investigate insurance options, make investments, get advice, and do other financial tasks.

SELF-CHECK ::

Circle the correct answer for each question.

1. Which of the following is not an essential feature of an effective e-commerce Web site?

   a. catalog   **b.** customer service   **c.** great graphics

2. You should avoid shopping at a Web site if its customer service department can be reached only by this means.

   a. e-mail   **b.** telephone   **c.** regular mail

3. Which of the following is making it easy for companies to handle huge volumes of transactions?

   a. protocols   **b.** Web-based technologies   **c.** online catalogs

Norton ONLINE

For more information on business-to-business e-commerce, visit **http://www.mhhe.com/ peternorton**.

E-Commerce at the Business Level

Beyond individual consumer transactions, e-commerce has given companies an entirely different way to conduct business. Using powerful Web sites and online databases, companies not only sell goods to individual customers, but also track inventory, order products, send invoices, and receive payments. Using e-commerce technologies (ranging from standard networks to supercomputers), companies are rapidly forming online partnerships to collaborate on product designs, sales and marketing campaigns, and more. By giving one another access to their private networks, corporate partners access vital information and work together more efficiently.

Business-to-Business (B2B) Transactions

Although millions of consumer transactions take place each day on the Web, business-to-business (B2B) transactions actually account for most of the money that is spent online. As its name implies, a business-to-business transaction is one that takes place between companies; consumers are not involved.

The concept of B2B transactions did not arrive with the Internet. In fact, companies were doing business electronically long before the rise of the Web, by using private networks and computer systems to handle transactions. But Internet technologies have made the process easier, more efficient, and available to virtually all businesses.

Any financial transaction between two companies can be considered a B2B transaction, and probably can be handled over the Internet (see Figure 5A.12). Consider some examples:

>> A store orders an out-of-stock product from a distributor.

>> A car manufacturer orders parts from a wide range of suppliers.

>> A stock broker buys shares for a client by using an electronic exchange.

>> A bank requests credit information from a major credit-reporting agency.

You can probably think of other examples, too. In any case, the transaction occurs whether it is handled on paper, through a private network, or via the Internet. It does not necessarily have to take place on the Web. However, Web-based technologies are making it easy for companies to handle huge volumes of transactions.

Intranets and Extranets

Businesses use many different means to handle transactions electronically. For example, two companies may have their own networks, but may link them together so they can share certain resources and exchange certain types of data. Using this kind of link, for example, a design firm and a building contractor can collaborate on designs, quickly make changes to shared documents, update schedules, conduct online meetings, and transmit invoices to one another.

But most companies do business with many other companies, not just one. For this reason, they need to have systems that are flexible enough to handle an ever-changing array of partners or customers. An effective way to do this is to create corporate networks that look and function like the Internet, and that grant access to authorized external users through the Internet. These specialized business networks are called intranets and extranets.

An intranet is a corporate network that uses the same protocols as the Internet, but which belongs exclusively to a corporation, school, or some other organization. The intranet is accessible only to the organization's workers. If the intranet is connected to the Internet, then it is secured by a special device called a firewall, which prevents external users from gaining access to it.

An extranet is an intranet that can be accessed by authorized outside users over the Internet. To gain entrance to the extranet's resources, an external user typically must log on to the network by providing a user name and a password.

Intranets and extranets are popular for several reasons:

>> Because they use the same protocols as the Internet, they are simpler and less expensive to install than many other kinds of networks.

>> Because they enable users to work in standard (and usually free) Web browsers, they provide a consistent, friendly interface (see Figure 5A.13).

>> Because they function with standard security technologies, they provide excellent security against unauthorized access.

Telecommuters

A telecommuter is someone who normally works in a location other than the company's office or factory (see Figure 5A.14). Most telecommuters work from their

FIGURE 5A.12

Ordering parts or products from a supplier is one of the most common types of B2B transaction.

Norton
ONLINE

For more information on intranets and extranets, visit **http://www.mhhe.com/ peternorton**.

At Issue

On the Beat with Techno-Cops

The newest addition to the Sacramento California Police Department (SACPD) just sits in the car all day, doesn't write tickets, and doesn't wear a badge. But the "new guy" might just be the most effective member of the force at catching the bad guy.

This rookie is Versadex, a wireless mobile computer and public safety software system, complete with mobile records management and linked to computer-aided dispatch and radio systems.

Mobile computer systems such as the Versadex Computer Aided Dispatch (CAD) and Records Management System (RMS) (created by Versaterm) are the latest weapon in law enforcement's high-tech arsenal. They result in reduced workload, better information, and increased safety for officers in the field.

These systems give in-the-field access to all of the records and information an officer back at a desk at headquarters has, allowing police officers to get down to their real job: fighting crime.

The Versaterm CAD and RMS, Northrop Grumman mobile computers, and other components of the solution save officers a significant amount of time and make them—and the public—safer because of the information that is now available and the speed at which it can be accessed. According to the SACPD, with the new integrated hardware and software in place, officers saw improvements almost immediately.

For example, under the new system, officers can query both the central and national police computers about questionable license plates or suspects directly from the safety of the patrol car. Access to the county's mainframe system, which hosts local warrant information and parolee probation status, is credited with saving officers time and equipping them with critical information about whom they are handling.

This type of information used to be accessed over the radio, often taking up to 20 minutes to get warrant informa-

FIGURE 5A.13

An intranet's interface can look and work like any other Web page, allowing users to access resources and perform tasks in a browser window.

simnet™

homes, while many are constantly moving from one location to another. Either way, telecommuters rely on computers and Internet connections to do their jobs.

Telecommuters usually use their home computer to access the Internet, which in turn lets them connect to their employers' private network. This connection may take place through an extranet, but other kinds of networking techniques can be used to give telecommuters access to the network while keeping everyone else out.

Security

Until 1998, e-commerce was slow to gain acceptance among consumers who were concerned about security. Many people feared that it was not safe to provide personal or credit card information over the Internet because it was possible for criminals to intercept the data and use it, or to steal it from unprotected Web servers. Those fears have largely been eliminated, however, with improved security measures and public perception of the Internet's safety.

It is actually very easy to make sure that you are surfing safely and keeping your personal information secure while online, even when you are giving credit card numbers to a Web merchant.

Reputable e-commerce Web sites (especially those run by well-known companies) use sophisticated measures to ensure that customer information cannot fall into the hands of criminals. Online merchants typically protect customers by pro-

218   Chapter 5

tion and from 60 to 90 minutes for data from parole officers. This data is now accessible almost instantly.

The NEC notebooks are used extensively out of the car as well. Officers take them into homes and businesses to take witness statements and incident reports.

Northrop Grumman Mission Systems (NGMS) provided the car-mounted mobile data computers used by Versaterm. In addition to the Sacramento installation, NGMS has successfully overseen the activation of E-911 systems in several other major cities, including Atlanta, Baltimore, Chicago

O'Hare Airport, and Los Angeles, as well as a statewide system in Ohio.

Radio IP's RadioRouter is the wireless network solution selected by the SACPD, offering TCP/IP connectivity from the base station to patrol cars. PC devices running a secure, encrypted wireless IP network are deployed through Radio Router, enabling officers access to any of the SACPD's local area network–based applications.

In the future, the department plans to integrate other useful technologies into the network, including automatic vehicle location (AVL) software and the ability to interface directly with a mug-shot system the Sacramento Police Department shares with Sacramento County. Eventually mug shots, identifying information, and fingerprints will be available in the patrol car, giving officers immediate access to a suspect's criminal history.

AT ISSUE

viding secure Web pages where customers can enter credit card and account numbers, passwords, and other personal information.

To secure the data you transmit to a Web site, online merchants can encode pages using secure sockets layer (SSL) technology, which encrypts data. (Encryption technology secures data by converting it into a code that is unusable by anyone who does not possess a key to the code.) If a Web page is protected by SSL, its URL will begin with https:// rather than http://.

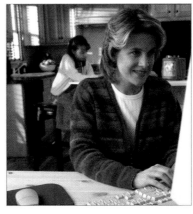

When using an e-commerce site, you can determine if the current page is secure in two ways (see Figure 5A.15):

>> **Check the URL.** If the page's URL begins with https://, the page is secure. The letter *s* indicates security measures.

>> **Check Your Browser's Status Bar.** If you use Microsoft Internet Explorer or Netscape Navigator, a closed padlock symbol will appear in the browser's status bar when a secure Web page is open.

Norton
ONLINE

For more information on online security, visit
http://www.mhhe.com/ peternorton.

FIGURE 5A.14

Today, many people work at home and use a PC to access their company's network through the Internet. Companies must take measures to ensure that this kind of access is secure.

FIGURE 5A.15

Verifying that a Web page is secure.

The https:// address indicates a secure Web site.

Browsers display special symbols (such as a closed padlock on the status bar) to indicate a secure Web site.

Summary ::

>> Electronic commerce (e-commerce) means doing business online, and can be conducted between consumers and businesses, or among businesses with no consumer involvement.

>> Two primary types of consumer-oriented e-commerce activities are online shopping and online banking and finance.

>> Businesses have been conducting transactions electronically for years, but the advent of Internet technologies has made the process easier and accessible to more businesses.

>> Businesses use many networking technologies to support e-commerce, but intranets and extranets make e-commerce easier by utilizing Internet technologies.

>> An intranet is a corporate network that works like the Internet, but belongs exclusively to an organization and allows no outside access.

>> An extranet is an intranet that allows access by some authorized external users, usually through the Internet.

>> Telecommuters are workers who work somewhere besides the company's central location, such as from home. They rely on computers and Internet technologies to access the company's network resources.

>> Security is an important aspect of e-commerce, and enhanced security measures have contributed to the explosion of e-commerce transactions in recent years.

>> Consumers can take steps to make sure they are using secure Web pages when doing business online.

Key Terms ::

brick-and-mortar store, 213
business-to-business (B2B)
    transaction, 216
business-to-consumer (B2C)
    transaction, 210
click-and-mortar store, 211
cookie, 212

electronic commerce
    (e-commerce), 209
encryption, 219
extranet, 217
intranet, 217
online banking, 213
online finance, 215

online shopping, 210
online store, 211
secure sockets layer (SSL), 219
secure Web page, 219
shopping cart, 212
telecommuter, 217

Key Term Quiz ::

Complete each statement by writing one of the terms listed under Key Terms in each blank.

1. _____ means doing business online.

2. _____ means buying a product or service through a Web site.

3. Another term for online shopping is _____ .

4. A(n) _____ is a store that exists only on the Web, with no physical location you can visit.

5. A(n) _____ is an electronic holding area, provided by an online merchant, that stores information about items the customer has chosen for purchasing.

6. The term _____ refers to any kind of personal financial transaction you can conduct online, other than managing your bank accounts.

7. A(n) _____ transaction is one that takes place between companies, and does not involve consumers.

8. A(n) _____ is an intranet that can be accessed by outside users over the Internet.

9. A(n) _____ is someone who normally works in a location other than the company's office or factory.

10. To secure the data you transmit to a Web site, online merchants can encode pages using _____ technology.

Multiple Choice ::

Circle the word or phrase that best completes each statement.

1. This one-time fad has turned into a full-time business for thousands of online shoppers.
   - **a.** buying groceries online
   - **b.** managing bank accounts online
   - **c.** buying and selling items through online auctions
   - **d.** paying taxes online

2. Which part of an online store's Web site can you use to contact the merchant for assistance?
   - **a.** catalog
   - **b.** customer-service page
   - **c.** checkout section
   - **d.** home page

3. This type of store lets you wander the aisles and see the merchandise for yourself.
   - **a.** catalog store
   - **b.** clicks-and-bricks store
   - **c.** online-only store
   - **d.** brick-and-mortar store

4. Many e-commerce Web sites' catalogs are set up like _____ , lumping products or services into categories and subcategories.
   - **a.** directories
   - **b.** search engines
   - **c.** brick-and-mortar stores
   - **d.** vendor

5. Online merchants usually try to make online shopping as similar as possible to this.
   - **a.** shopping by mail
   - **b.** shopping at a real store
   - **c.** shopping by phone
   - **d.** shopping in a different country

6. When you set up an account with an online merchant, the Web site may place one of these on your computer's disk.
   - **a.** catalog
   - **b.** shopping cart
   - **c.** cookie
   - **d.** encryption

7. Which of the following can*not* be done when banking online?
   - **a.** create an account
   - **b.** buy a sweater
   - **c.** view transactions
   - **d.** pay bills

8. Which type of transaction between companies can be considered a B2B transaction?
   - **a.** any financial transaction
   - **b.** buying parts
   - **c.** ordering products
   - **d.** purchasing stocks

9. This is a corporate network that uses the same protocols as the Internet, but which belongs to an organization, and which prohibits access by external users.
   - **a.** network
   - **b.** intranet
   - **c.** extranet
   - **d.** internalnet

10. This technology secures data by converting it into a code that is unusable by anyone who does not possess a key to the code.
    - **a.** shopping cart
    - **b.** B2B
    - **c.** user name
    - **d.** encryption

Review Questions ::

In your own words, briefly answer the following questions.

1. If an e-commerce Web site's catalog is set up like a search engine, how does it work?
2. What are the two most common payment methods used when making purchases from online merchants?
3. What purpose does a cookie serve, when you set up an online account with a merchant?
4. What is one advantage of using a personal-finance program, such as Microsoft Money or Quicken?
5. List two personal–financial transactions you can conduct online, other than managing your bank accounts.
6. Which type of transaction accounts for most of the money that is spent online?
7. What is the primary difference between an intranet and an extranet?
8. What is a telecommuter?
9. How do online merchants typically protect customers?
10. When using an e-commerce site, how can you determine if the current page is secure?

Lesson Labs ::

Complete the following exercises as directed by your instructor.

1. Do some shopping. Visit the Web site of one popular online merchant. (Your instructor may ask you to visit a specific site.) Without purchasing anything or providing any personal information, inspect the site. What products does it sell? How does its catalog function? Is it easy to navigate the site and find products? Check the site's customer-service and help options. Describe your findings in a one-page report, to share with the class.

2. Can you bank online? Visit the Web site of one of your local banks, or a site chosen by your instructor. Without setting up an account or providing any personal information, inspect the site. What kinds of banking-related tasks can you do at the site? How easy is it to find the services you need at the site? Does the site require you to visit a bank branch to conduct certain transactions? Describe your findings in a one-page report, to share with the class.

Staying Safe in the Online World

Overview: Keeping Your System Safe

Whether you use your PC and the Internet for work or pleasure, there are many threats that can affect you, your privacy, your data, and your computer. Although these threats range from mild to severe, you need to take each of them seriously. This means evaluating the chance that each one might strike you, prioritizing likely threats by severity, and taking the appropriate precautions.

In this lesson, you will learn about specific steps you can take to secure your computer system and your data from a variety of threats. You might be surprised to learn that computer security is not primarily a technical issue, and is not necessarily expensive. For the most part, keeping your system and data secure is a matter of common sense. By mastering a few basic principles and some easy-to-use software programs, you can virtually guarantee the safety of your hardware, software, data, and privacy.

OBJECTIVES ::

>> List three ways you can protect your identity from theft.

>> Name two precautions you can take to guard your personal information.

>> Identify seven federal laws designed to protect an individual's privacy and personal information.

>> Describe methods for managing spyware and cookies on your computer.

>> List three steps you can take to avoid spam.

>> Explain the purpose of a firewall and why you may need one.

>> Describe four ways to protect hardware and storage media.

Protecting Yourself

The only part of your computer system that needs protection more than your data is you. Remember that if an identity thief strikes or a malicious Webmaster gets hold of your personal information, your computer will keep right on working, but other aspects of your life will be affected.

The following sections revisit some of the threats that computer users face and tell you how to prevent them from becoming a reality.

Avoiding Identity Theft

Identity (ID) theft occurs when someone impersonates you by using your name, Social Security number, or other personal information to obtain documents or credit in your name. With the right information, an identity thief can virtually "become" the victim, obtaining a drivers license, bank accounts, mortgages, and other items in the victim's name.

Identity theft cost the U.S. economy $53 billion in 2002. That year alone, 10 million Americans became victims of ID theft. According to the Federal Trade Commission, identity theft rose by nearly 41 percent from 2001 to 2002 and shot up 81 percent between 2002 and 2003.

Beyond monetary losses, victims of ID theft pay in other ways, spending many hours trying to repair the financial damages and regain their good reputation.

Identity thieves can use several methods—low-tech as well as high-tech—to obtain the information they need:

>> **Shoulder Surfing.** A trick known as shoulder surfing is as simple as watching someone enter personal identification information for a private transaction, such as an ATM machine.

>> **Snagging.** In the right setting, a thief can try snagging information by listening in on a telephone extension, through a wiretap, or over a cubicle wall while the victim gives credit card or other personal information to a legitimate agent.

>> **Dumpster Diving.** Other techniques are as simple as stealing mail containing personal information—right out of the victim's own mailbox. A popular low-tech approach is dumpster diving. Thieves can go through garbage cans, dumpsters, or trash bins to obtain cancelled checks, credit card statements, or bank account informaiton that someone has carelessly thrown out.

>> **Social Engineering.** This method is not as sophisticated as it sounds, but can still be effective. In social engineering, the ID thief tricks victims into providing critical information under the pretext of something legitimate. The thief can call an unwary victim, for example, claim to be a system administrator at the Web site of the victim's bank, and ask for the victim's user ID and password for a system check. With this information in hand, the thief can go online and access the victim's account information directly through the bank's Web site.

>> **High-Tech Methods.** Sophisticated ID thieves can get information using a computer and Internet connection. For instance, Trojan horses can be planted on a system or a person's identity may be snagged from unecured Internet sites. Although not common, it happens. One reason it is not common is because of the general use of security technologies such as Secure Sockets Layer (SSL) and Secure HTTP (S-HTTP) to ensure the integrity and confidentiality of credit card and financial transactions. Because so much attention is paid to protecting transmitted data, social engineering and low-tech swindles are the predominant sources of ID theft.

Norton
ONLINE

For more information on avoiding ID theft, visit **http://www.mhhe.com/ peternorton**.

Victims of identity theft stand to lose large sums of money, suffer damage to their credit and reputation, and can possibly even lose possessions if the situation is not handled properly. It's important to remember that even if you don't make transactions yourself, you may still be held responsible for them unless you take action quickly.

Recall that ID thieves mainly use nontechnical methods to get the information they need to impersonate someone. Likewise, most of the precautions you can take against ID theft are "low-tech." Further, they all are matters of common sense; you should do these things anyway, even if ID theft were not even possible.

Managing Your Papers

From the moment they enter your mailbox until they reach the landfill, many of your most valuable documents are vulnerable. These include account statements, financial records, bills, credit card applications, and other documents that you receive and handle every week. By handling them wisely, you can keep them out of the hands of an ID thief:

>> **Guard Your Mail.** Pick up your mail as soon as possible after it arrives. Never allow mail to sit for a long time in your mailbox. If ID theft is a problem in your area, get a P.O. box and have sensitive documents delivered there. Also, put important outgoing mail in a public mailbox or take it to the post office, where no one can steal it.

>> **Check Your Statements Immediately.** Open and check your bank and credit card statements as soon as you get them. Look for suspicious charges, ATM transactions, or checks you did not write; if you find one, report it immediately. The sooner you report suspicious activity, the greater the chance that the company will be able to help you. Some financial institutions place a time limit on reporting unauthorized transactions; after the time limit, your bank or credit card company may ask you to pay for the charge.

>> **Discard Important Documents Wisely.** Some documents need to be kept on file for some time. For example, you should keep pay stubs and credit card statements for at least three years, in case you need them for tax purposes. But when you are ready to get rid of any important document, do it right. Shred any document that contains sensitive information such as your Social Security number, account numbers, or passwords (see Figure 5B.1).

Guarding Personal Information

In the course of a normal week, you probably give away all sorts of information about yourself without even thinking about it. It pays to be careful when sharing personal information, to make sure it doesn't fall into the wrong hands:

>> Never give anyone an account number over the phone unless you are sure he or she is a legitimate agent. Remember, a bank or legitimate business will never call you and ask for an account number. They should already have this information; if they need it, they will notify you by mail.

>> Never give out account numbers, passwords, or other personal information via e-mail. E-mail is not a secure way to transmit data. It can be intercepted, or the recipient can forward it to someone else. Banks and legitimate businesses won't ask you to provide such information via e-mail.

>> When buying something online, make sure the Web site is secure before entering any personal information into a form.

FIGURE 5B.1

Shredders are inexpensive and easy to use and render documents useless to an ID thief.

Looking at the Big Picture

You can take additional steps to protect your credit as well as your personal information:

>> Check your credit report at least once a year. A credit report is a document that lists all your financial accounts that can be a source of credit or that you can use for making purchases or for other transactions. These include bank accounts, mortgages, credit cards, and others. Under certain circumstances, you may be entitled to get a free copy of your credit report one or more times a year. Even if you need to pay for a copy of your credit report, you should get one from each of the three major credit reporting bureaus (Equifax, Experian, and Trans Union) at least once each year. Check each report not just to learn your overall credit rating but to find and report any errors they may contain.

>> Maintain a good filing system. Carefully file all important papers and keep them for at least three years. You may need them to dispute errors on a credit report or when reporting unauthorized activity to your credit card company or bank.

>> Check with your bank and credit card company to make sure you are protected against unauthorized charges (see Figure 5B.2). In most states, your liability is limited if someone else accesses your bank account or uses your credit card without your knowledge. But you may be required to report the incident quickly. Contact these agencies and ask what protections they offer against fraud and ID theft.

Protecting Your Privacy

Did you know that your buying habits are tracked electronically, in a range of commercial systems? This doesn't apply just to online transactions either. Any time you use a "store loyalty" card to rent movies or buy groceries, the purchases are logged in a database. Your medical, financial, and credit records are available to anybody authorized to view them.

Many of the companies you deal with every day—from your local supermarket to your insurance company—maintain databases filled with information about you. You might expect these firms to know your name and address, but you might be surprised to learn that they know how many times each month you

FIGURE 5B.2

This page, at the VISA Web site, explains the company's "zero liability" policy. Many credit cards carry similar protections, but you are generally responsible for reporting unauthorized activity on your card.

put gas in your car or buy a magazine. And a lot of companies do not keep this information confidential; they may sell it to other companies who are interested in knowing about you.

If you take precautions to guard against ID theft, you'll be going a long way toward protecting your privacy in general, but there are a few other steps you should take to keep your private information out of the wrong hands.

Keeping Marketers at Bay

One of the main reasons for guarding your personal information is to avoid the attention of marketers, who want to know as much about you as possible so they can target marketing campaigns to people of your demographic status or interests. The following tips can help you keep them off your back:

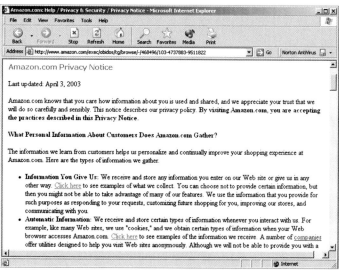

>> **Be Wary about Filling Out Forms.** Whenever you fill out a form on a Web page, send in a subscription card for a magazine, or submit a warranty card for a product, you give out information about yourself. Some of these forms ask for much more than your name and address. As a general rule, don't submit such forms (either online or by mail) unless you have read the company's privacy policy (see Figure 5B.3). This policy will tell you how the company handles private information and what they will do with your information. Many companies provide an opt-out option on their registration or warranty forms. If you select this option, the company promises either not to share your information with anyone else or not to send you advertisements.

FIGURE 5B.3

The privacy notice at Amazon.com.

>> **Guard Your Primary E-Mail Address.** As you will read later in this lesson, you can avoid spam by having two e-mail addresses. Give your primary address only to people you trust and use the second address for everything else. The secondary address will receive most of the spam, leaving your main inbox relatively clean.

Knowing Your Rights

You can protect yourself further by knowing your legal rights (see Figure 5B.4). Consumers have the right to control access to their information. The control is based on a set of laws that have evolved over the past 40 years, including

>> In 1966, the Freedom of Information Act (5 U.S.C. § 552) allowed each individual to view and amend personal information kept about them by any governmental entity.

>> The Privacy Act of 1974 (5 U.S.C. § 552a) places universal restrictions on sharing of information about you by federal agencies without written consent.

>> The Fair Credit Reporting Act (1970) mandates that personal information assembled by credit reporting agencies must be accurate, fair, and private. It allows you to review and update your credit record as well as dispute the entries.

>> The Electronic Communications Privacy Act (1986) prevents unlawful access to voice communications by wire. It originally regulated electronic wiretaps and provided the basis for laws defining illegal access to electronic communications, including computer information. It is the basis for protection against unreasonable governmental intrusion into Internet usage, stored electronic communications, and e-mail.

Norton ONLINE

For more information on laws that protect your privacy and personal information, visit **http://www.mhhe.com/ peternorton**.

>> The Right to Financial Privacy Act of 1978 and the Financial Modernization Act of 1999 (Gramm-Leach-Bliley) require companies to give consumers notice of their privacy and information-sharing practices.

In response to terrorist attacks on September 11, 2001, the federal government took actions aimed at modifying these protections. Specifically, the Uniting and Strengthening America by Providing Appropriate Tools Required to Intercept and Obstruct Terrorism Act was enacted. It is commonly known as the USA PATRIOT Act and extends the authority of law enforcement and intelligence agencies in monitoring private communications and access to your personal information.

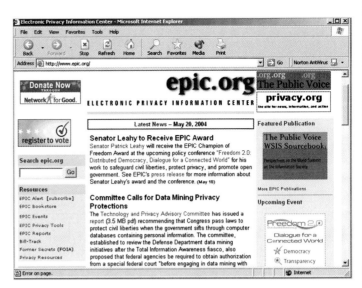

Managing Cookies, Spyware, and Other "Bugs"

When using the Internet, you should be aware that your interests and habits are being monitored automatically. The monitoring activity can be carried out by programs running on your own computer or a connected server. This might not seem to be a problem, especially if you aren't doing anything wrong. But the interpretation of why you visit a particular site is in the eye of the beholder. You may not be aware of how your browsing habits are interpreted by others. A single visit to one of the ubiquitous advertising banners at the top of your browser identifies you as someone with an interest in related products.

Software developers have created a number of ways to track your activities online. Although many of these tools were created for benign purposes—such as helping legitimate Webmasters determine who visits their sites most often—they are also being used in ways most consumers do not appreciate. These "online spying tools" include:

>> **Cookies.** A cookie is a small text file that a Web server places on your computer. The file contains information that identifies your computer (its IP address), you (your user name or e-mail address), and information about your visit to the Web site. For instance, the cookie might list the last time you visited the site, which pages you downloaded, and how long you were at the site before leaving. Despite their helpful purpose, cookies are now considered a significant threat to privacy. This is because they can be used to store and report many types of information. For example, a cookie can store a list of all the sites you visit; this data can be transferred back to the site that placed the cookie on your system. Ultimately, this information can be used against your wishes. Your PC may be storing hundreds or thousands of cookies at any given moment.

>> **Web Bugs.** A Web bug is a small GIF-format image file that can be embedded in a Web page or an HTML-format e-mail message. Behind the image lies code that functions in much the same way as a cookie, allowing the bug's creator to track many of your online activities. A bug can record what Web pages you view, keywords you type into a search engine, personal information you enter in a form on a Web page, and other data.

>> **Spyware.** The term spyware is used to refer to many different kinds of software that can track computer user's activities and report them to someone else. There is now a countless variety of spyware programs. Another common term for spyware is adware, because Internet advertising is a common

FIGURE 5B.4

You can learn more about the laws regarding public records by visiting Web sites such as the Electronic Privacy Information Center at http://www.epic.org.

Norton
ONLINE

For more information on cookie-management and anti-spyware utilities, visit **http://www.mhhe.com/ peternorton**.

source of spyware. Spyware is typically installed on a computer without the user's knowledge and collects information without the user's consent. Spyware can land on your PC from many sources, such as Web pages, e-mail messages, and pop-up ads.

High-tech methods are required to deal with threats such as cookies and spyware. Luckily, there are many options to choose from, including some that can find and eradicate just about any type of spyware that might find its way onto your system.

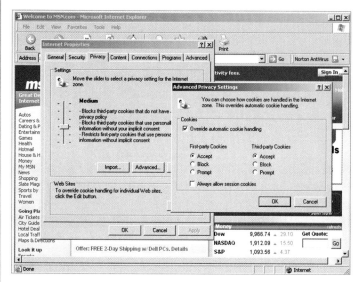

::

FIGURE 5B.5

Cookie-control settings in Microsoft Internet Explorer.

Dealing with Cookies

Most Web browsers feature built-in settings that give you some control over cookies (see Figure 5B.5). Internet Explorer, for example, gives you the option of refusing all cookies, accepting all cookies, or requiring notification before allowing a cookie onto your PC. If you actually use these tools, however, they can make browsing difficult. If you refuse all cookies, some Web sites simply won't function in your browser. If you set your browser to notify you before accepting a cookie, you can expect to see a notification (in the form of a pop-up message) every few seconds. This is because most Web sites use cookies in some manner.

Making things more difficult is the fact that there are multiple types of cookies, including the following:

>> Session cookies are temporary cookies that are automatically deleted when you close your browser (ending your browsing session). Session cookies can be essential for viewing some Web pages, and they generally are not used to store any type of personal information. Session cookies are also known as transient cookies.

>> Persistent cookies are stored on your computer's hard disk until they expire or you delete them. (Persistent cookies usually have expiration dates, at which time they are deleted.) Persistent cookies are used to store information about you or to remember settings you have made for a Web site you visit often. Persistent cookies are also called stored cookies.

>> First-party cookies come from the Web site you are currently viewing. First-party cookies are persistent and usually store preferences you have set for viewing the site. Some first-party cookies store information that can personally identify you.

>> Third-party cookies come from a different Web site than the one you are currently viewing. This is possible because some Web sites get content from other sites. Banner ads are an example. Third-party cookies are often used to track your browsing history for marketing purposes. These cookies are usually session cookies but can be persistent.

If you don't manage cookies, thousands can build up on your hard disk. Although persistent cookies are set to expire, their expiration date may be years away. Further, you may decide you just don't want all these cookies on your system gathering information about you. There are two ways to manage cookies:

>> **Manually Delete Them.** Your Web browser should have a tool that lets you erase cookies. Figure 5B.6 shows cookies being manually deleted in Internet Explorer.

>> **Use Cookie Management Software.** A cookie-management utility can locate and delete all the cookies on your PC, either automatically or when you tell

it to. Some utilities will let you decide which cookies to remove and which ones to keep. This is a good idea, because it lets you keep cookies for Web sites you trust while getting rid of the rest. Some programs, such as Cookie Crusher, focus primarily on handling cookies. More feature-filled programs such as Windows Washer can remove cookies and other types of files from your system, making it difficult for anyone to track your surfing habits.

Removing Web Bugs and Spyware

Most software developers classify Web bugs and spyware together. For this reason, most anti-spyware utilities (or anti-adware utilities, as they may be called) can detect both types of programs. The key to successfully dealing with these nuisances is to find an anti-spyware program you like, run it frequently, and keep it up-to-date according to the developer's directions. Popular anti-spyware programs include SpyGuard, NoAdware, and XoftSpy, but there are many others (see Figure 5B.7). Many antivirus programs can find and remove Web bugs and spyware in addition to viruses, worms, and other malicious files.

Another key to avoiding spyware is to be careful about downloading files and programs from the Internet. Shareware and freeware programs are popular sources of spyware, because many spyware developers pay other software developers to include spyware code in their programs.

Also, be sure to install a pop-up blocker on your PC (see Figure 5B.8). These small utilities prevent secondary browser windows (called pop-up windows, because they "pop up" on your screen) from appearing when you are on the Web. The majority of pop-ups are advertisements, many of which carry spyware.

Evading Spam

Although the availability of your private information might be troubling, the consequence for most users is something called spam. Spam is Internet "junk mail." After all, your e-mail address is often included in the personal information that companies collect and share. The correct term for spam is unsolicited commercial e-mail (UCE). Almost all spam is commercial advertising. According to reports

FIGURE 5B.6

Deleting cookies in Microsoft Internet Explorer.

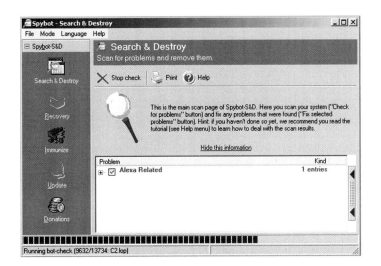

FIGURE 5B.7

Scanning for spyware with Spybot – Search & Destroy.

FIGURE 5B.8

Configuring the Google toolbar in
Microsoft Internet Explorer. This toolbar,
which you can download for free
from the Google Web site
(http:www.google.com), can block
pop-up windows.

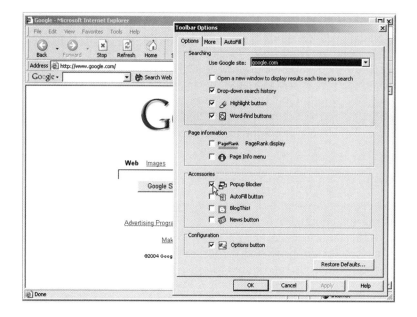

filed with Congress in early 2004, about two-thirds of all e-mail traffic was spam
messages. In the United States, nearly 80 percent of all e-mail was spam.

You can take several countermeasures against spam, all of which are simple.
First, if you receive a great deal of spam, contact your Internet service provider.
Have a list of messages ready and be prepared to give your ISP information about
the messages. Many ISPs have the ability to block messages from known spammers or messages that appear to be spam. Your ISP can tell you how to take advantage of these services, which are typically free.

As mentioned earlier, you should never give your primary e-mail address to any
person or business you don't know. (Your primary e-mail account is the one you
set up with your ISP as part of your Internet access package.) Instead, give that
address only to people and businesses you trust, and ask them not to give it to
anyone else. Then, set up a secondary e-mail account using a free, Web-based
e-mail service such as Hotmail or Yahoo (see Figure 5B.9). Use this address when
you must provide an e-mail address when making a purchase or registering for a

FIGURE 5B.9

Setting up a free e-mail account on the
Mail.com Web site. There are dozens of
free, Web-based e-mail services to
choose from.

Setting up an e-mail filter in Microsoft Outlook.

For more information on avoiding spam, visit **http://www.mhhe.com/ peternorton**.

service. The secondary address can collect the spam, while your primary address stays out of the hands of spammers.

You also can protect yourself by setting up filters in your e-mail program. A filter is a rule you establish that the program must follow when receiving mail. (For this reason, e-mail filters are sometimes called rules.) For example, you can tell the program to ignore messages from a specific sender or to automatically store certain messages in a specific folder. In Microsoft Outlook, filters are configured from the Tools menu (see Figure 5B.10).

Protection that is more robust is provided by special programs called spam blockers. These programs monitor e-mail messages as you receive them, can block messages from known spammers, and can mark suspicious messages. Spam-blocking software is available from many reputable vendors, such as McAfee and Symantec.

Finally, never respond to a spam message, even if it includes a link that purports to "remove you" from the sender's address list. Most such "remove me" options are phony. If you respond, the spammer knows that your e-mail account is active and you are a good target.

To get onto the Internet equivalent of a "do not spam" list, you may choose to opt out of any kind of targeted advertising by going to http://www.networkadvertising.org (see Figure 5B.11). This site is operated by the Network Advertising Initiative (NAI) and it is that industry's voluntary response to the objections to secretive tracking and spamming of Internet users.

Keeping Your Data Secure

Threats to your data are numerous, but the most ominous threat comes from malware in its various forms: viruses, worms, Trojan horses, and others. Viruses, in fact, are such a significant problem that an entire Computing Keynote feature, "Computer Viruses," is devoted to them following this chapter. Refer to that

The "opt out" page at the Network Advertising Initiative's Web site.

feature for detailed information on viruses of all types and the best methods for dealing with them.

The following sections discuss two important countermeasures you can take to protect your data from a variety of threats.

Restricting Access to Your System

Aside from viruses, disk failures, and natural disasters, the worst thing that can happen to your data is when someone else gains access to it. And it doesn't take a professional hacker to ruin all the data on your PC. A member of your own family can do it just as well, if unintentionally. This is why it's critical to restrict access to your system, to keep other people away from your data.

Limiting Physical Access

If other users have physical access to your PC, you still may be able to limit their ability to find your data. Most newer operating systems, such as Windows XP, allow users to set up "accounts" on a shared PC. In his or her account, each user can set up a unique set of preferences, such as the desktop's appearance, passwords, and more. Your operating system may allow you to hide folders and files, or make them private so that no one else can open them while using your computer.

Some applications can lock files so they can be opened only with a password (see Figure 5B.12). If others frequently use your computer, you may want to take advantage of these features. If your PC is part of a network, you can turn off sharing of entire disks or of individual files and folders. You also can encrypt data so no one else can use it via a network connection.

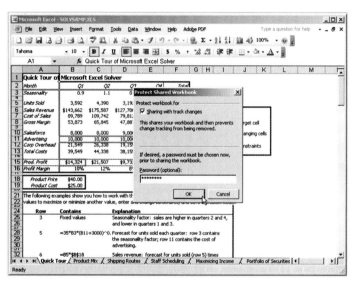

FIGURE 5B.12

Protecting a document in Microsoft Excel. The document cannot be edited unless the user provides a password.

If other people have physical access to your computer, but you don't want them to use it, configure your operating system to require a password when starting up. As an extra precaution, set up a password-protected screen saver. (A screen saver is a blank screen or a moving image that appears on the screen after the computer has gone unused for several minutes.) Configure the screen saver to ask for a password before going off; this way, no one will be able to use your system if you leave it running.

For specific instructions on configuring these privacy tools, refer to the help system or documentation for your operating system and applications.

Using a Firewall

You have seen the term *firewall* used several times already in this book. That's because firewalls have become an essential part of any network that is connected to the Internet. A firewall's main purpose is to prohibit unauthorized access to your computer via the Internet.

A functioning firewall is your best defense against hackers or anyone else who might try to reach your PC via the Internet. There are various kinds of firewalls—both hardware and software—and they can use different methods to keep intruders away from your system. Many firewalls work, for example, by effectively "hiding" your computer from other computers on the Internet. The only computers that can find your computer are the ones with which you have initiated communications.

 Norton ONLINE

For more information on personal firewalls, visit http://www.mhhe.com/peternorton.

If your PC connects to the Internet through an always-on connection—that is, a connection that is always active, such as a cable modem or DSL connection—then you should use a firewall. Without one, your computer is virtually unprotected from intruders, who can easily find your system and break into it.

If you do not yet have a firewall, you should get one. Many network hubs and hub/router units have firewalls built in and can be purchased for as little as $50 (see Figure 5B.13). Hardware firewalls are easy to use, especially those designed for home and small network use. Just connect it and you're done.

If you prefer a software firewall, there are plenty to choose from. In fact, Windows XP has a basic firewall built in that you can activate in less than a minute (see Figure 5B.14). For more sophisticated protection, you can purchase a full-featured firewall program such as ZoneAlarm, BlackICE PC Protection, or Norton Personal Firewall.

FIGURE 5B.13

Many routers, such as this one by Linksys, feature built-in firewalls.

Backing Up Data

You never know when or how data may be lost. A simple disk error can do just as much damage as a hacker might do. And even the most experienced computer user occasionally deletes a file or folder by accident. When such events happen, you'll be in the clear if you keep your data backed up (see Figure 5B.15).

You can use a backup copy of your data to restore lost files to your PC. Backups are useful for lots of reasons. If you save changes to a file, then decide the changes should not have been made, you can return to the previous version of the file by using the backup. If you buy a new computer, having a complete backup makes it easy to move your data and programs.

Safeguarding Your Hardware

Hardware is actually easy to secure. As mentioned already, you can limit physical access to your computer system. If necessary, you can even anchor it to a desk, making it difficult to steal.

FIGURE 5B.14

Activating the firewall in Windows XP Professional.

FIGURE 5B.15

Using the backup utility in Windows XP.

Norton
ONLINE

For more information on backing up data, visit **http://www.mhhe.com/ peternorton**.

Productivity Tip

Because PC hardware and software are becoming increasingly complex, it is becoming increasingly important to do regular maintenance on them. At the very minimum, this means defragmenting your hard disk, checking for viruses, and performing other basic housekeeping chores to keep your machine humming along. You learned several of these techniques in Chapter 6, "Storing Data." But routine system maintenance includes another step that many users ignore: updating important system and program files.

By making sure that your system software is kept up to date, you reduce the risk of system failures and keep your programs running as well as possible. Device drivers provide a good example. Suppose you update your operating system, then your CD-ROM drive begins functioning poorly. You might be able to fix this problem by installing an updated device driver that is more compatible with your new OS.

Fortunately, you don't need to call a PC technician (or become one yourself) to update critical system files. Thanks to a new breed of automated Web sites, you can sit back and let your PC update itself.

If you are a registered user of Microsoft Windows or Microsoft Office, for example, you can visit Microsoft's product update Web sites and download bug fixes, patches, updated system files, templates, security-related files, and much more. You can visit the Windows Update site at http://windowsupdate.microsoft.com. You can find the Office Update site at http://officeupdate.microsoft.com.

Users of Windows 2000 and Windows XP can configure their operating system to automatically update files. These versions of Windows can find and install updates in the background, whenever the PC is connected to the Internet.

Companies such as Symantec (http://www.symantec.com/downloads), McAfee (http://software.mcafee.com/centers/download/default.asp), and other makers of popular antivirus software and utility programs host product-update sites, too. At these sites, users can download up-to-the-minute versions of virus databases, utilities, drivers, and other products. This updating is extremely important; without the latest virus definitions, your antivirus software cannot protect your system against the latest viruses.

If you use any kind of high-capacity storage device—such as a Zip drive, a CD-RW drive, or a DVD-R/RW drive—you can probably visit the manufacturer's Web site for

---

SELF-CHECK ::

Circle the correct word or phrase that best completes each statement.

1. To avoid ID theft, you should _____ your mail as soon as it arrives.
   a. shred **b.** hide **c.** pick up

2. E-mail is not a _____ way to transmit data.
   a. secure **b.** legal **c.** practical

3. The _____ places restrictions on the sharing of information about you by federal agencies.
   a. Fair Credit Act **b.** Privacy Act of 1974 **c.** Freedom of Information Act

But even if theft is unlikely, there are still steps you should take to keep your PC hardware safe and functioning. These are countermeasures against hardware failures that not only can be costly, but can result in lost data.

Using Automated Warnings

Some operating systems, such as Windows XP Professional, create an information log that lists important or unusual events that occur within the system. In Windows XP, this tool is called the Event Viewer. You can use the event viewer to see events relating to your system's applications, security, and hardware devices.

Windows' Event Viewer automatically generates information, error, and warning messages. You need to use the Event Viewer to see them (see Figure 5B.16). You also can use the Event Viewer to configure your own warnings, although that probably is not necessary. Still, it is a good idea to review the logs' contents occasionally, to see if any recurring events or warnings require attention. For this purpose, the Event Viewer can be very helpful to a technician if your computer needs repair.

updated drivers and utilities that can make your drive easier to use or more functional.

If you have purchased a new computer, operating system, application, or peripheral, and if the product is from a major manufacturer, there's a good chance the product offers online support of some kind. To learn what options are available for your specific products, check your online help systems and printed documentation. Look for Web addresses for software update, download, or support pages.

How often should you update? It depends on the software. If you use a new version of Windows, you should configure it to check for updates whenever you're online. That way, you won't miss a critical update, which could compromise your system's security. Check for updates to your antivirus software definitions at least once a week; if your antivirus program can receive updates automatically, set it to do so. Otherwise, it's a good idea to check for updated device drivers and support files occasionally, to keep your peripheral devices and other programs running as well as possible.

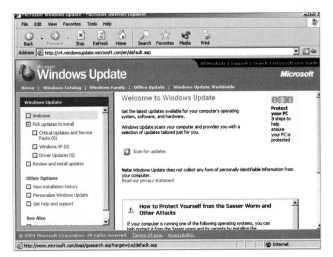

The Windows Update Web site, seen in the Microsoft Internet Explorer browser.

FIGURE 5B.16

Viewing a message about a system error, in the Windows XP Event Viewer.

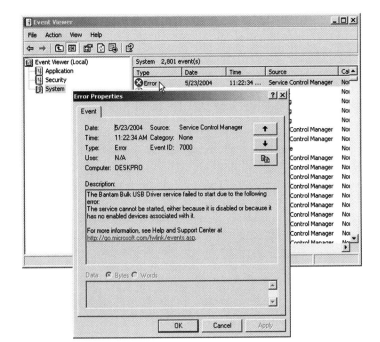

Computers In Your Career

As customer relationship management (CRM) supervisor for Jenny Craig Inc., in Carlsbad, California, Jon Kosoff starts his day when he clicks on his e-mail box in the morning to check his messages, and then prioritizes the day's projects. After that it's anything goes, and Kosoff wouldn't have it any other way.

"My job is very project-oriented, so no two days are ever the same," says Kosoff, who holds a degree in economics from the University of California Santa Barbara. He says the technical training he's learned along the way, combined with a solid financial foundation, has helped him to not only use technology, but also understand the return on investment that his employer gains from its use.

Kosoff oversees Jenny Craig's e-mail and Web site as well as the integration of customer data into the company's database and marketing efforts. That means using the Internet in conjunction with the firm's internal database to reach customers worldwide. "When I started here four years ago, we were sending out 4,000 text-based e-mails a month," says Kosoff. "Today we send out about 700,000 Flash and HTML messages a month."

Other key duties include updating Jenny Craig's Web site content to ensure that it represents the firm's current business objectives. That's not as easy as it sounds, says Kosoff, who explains that the firm has gone through a number of leadership changes over the last few years. Such changes lead to business objective changes and can have a profound effect on a firm's overall Web site and marketing strategy.

Perhaps the most satisfying aspect of working with the Internet, Kosoff adds, is the instant gratification that it provides. "You can see what you've done almost instantly, and share it not only with the company," he says, "but also with your friends and family 24/7."

Internet careers are among those expected to be the fastest growing occupations through 2010, according to the Bureau of Labor Statistics. Robert Half International reports

Handling Storage Media

You may think of your floppy disks and CDs as sturdy little objects. After all, they have your data encased in hard plastic. But storage media are a great deal more vulnerable than you might think. You should take precautions to protect your loose storage media (and the data they hold) from

>> **Magnetism.** Floppy disks should always be kept away from sources of magnetism. Remember, floppy disks (as well as storage tapes and other magnetic media) are magnetically sensitive. A floppy disk drive uses tiny electromagnets to store data on the disk's surface. If the disk is exposed to another magnet, degaussing can occur. Degaussing occurs when magnetic media is close enough to a magnetic source to erase its contents. Magnets are everywhere, and many electrical appliances generate magnetic fields. Loudspeakers, your computer's monitor, and fluorescent light fixtures are common examples.

>> **Heat and Cold.** Never store disks where they can be exposed to extreme heat or cold. If you leave a disk in front of a window on a sunny day (or, worse, in a car), it may warm up enough to melt a little. Extreme cold can cause media to shrink or crack. In either case, the data may be lost or the disk may not be able to spin properly when you insert it in a drive. Storage media survive best and last longer if you store them in a dry place, at room temperature, and away from direct light (see Figure 5B.17).

>> **Moisture.** Don't allow disks to get wet, especially floppy disks. You can dry a CD off with a clean towel, but that isn't possible with a floppy disk.

>> **Dust, Dirt, and Fingerprints.** Dust and dirt can make it impossible for a disk drive to read data on the disk's surface. Even a small smudge or fingerprint can interfere with a disk's operation. Keep disks as clean as possible, and always handle them by the edges.

FIGURE 5B.17

Keep your disks in a storage unit designed to hold them, away from sources of heat and light.

starting salaries in 2001 for Internet-related occupations ranged from $58,000 to $82,500 for Web masters, and $56,250 to $76,750 for Internet/intranet developers.

In the Internet age, there is a growing demand for network administrators, information system professionals, and data communications managers. Aside from careers that focus on architecture and administration of the Internet, many other professions require not only a working knowledge of the Internet but also a mastery of the tools used to create and distribute content across it. Here are a few such careers:

>> **Web Designers and Web Masters.** Corporate Web, intranet, and extranet sites are developed, designed, and maintained most often by teams of professionals. At the helm of such teams are experienced designers and Web masters.

>> **Multimedia Developers.** As more people connect to the Internet, companies face increasing competition to provide highly visual, interactive content that enables them to capture and retain visitors to their Web sites.

>> **Programmers.** Programmers are finding all sorts of opportunities in Internet development because Web sites are commonly used to support high-level functions such as interactivity, searches, data mining, and more.

Storing Computer Equipment

To reduce wear and tear on computer equipment and to protect it from possible theft and damage, it is important to store computer hardware properly:

>> Never store your equipment near large electrical equipment, such as refrigerators or generators.

>> Store your equipment in climate- and heat-controlled environments (see Figure 5B.18). Heat and humidity will deteriorate delicate boards and other delicate components. Like storage media, computers and other hardware components fare better in dry, room-temperature environments where dust and moisture are minimal.

>> Determine whether natural hazards such as fire and flood might affect the storage area, then take appropriate actions.

>> Ensure that the stored equipment is properly stacked. Don't store equipment in piles or stack computers on top of one another.

FIGURE 5B.18

If you need to store your computer equipment, it's best to put it back in the original boxes. Otherwise, be sure to cover it and store it off the floor to avoid water damage.

Keeping Your Computer Clean

Although it appears robust, the computer is a precision instrument and should be kept spotless. You should not place liquids on or near a computer or its media. In addition you should not eat or smoke while operating it. Even if you have not contaminated it with food or smoke, the computer requires regular cleaning using the commercial tools and products that are sold in most computer stores. Physical parts are subject to wear and tear; it is important to keep them clean and well maintained. A common cause of component failure is dust buildup, which affects everything from the mechanics of your drives to the integrity of your circuit boards and the reliability of the power supplies. Dust worsens heating problems by blanketing components and clogging vents. You should maintain the fans and filters that ventilate the inside of your CPU cabinet (see Figure 5B.19). If you do not feel capable of changing filters and "dusting" the internal components, you should schedule regular visits to commercial computer maintenance services.

FIGURE 5B.19

Special tools such as "canned air" and a small vacuum can keep your PC clean.

Summary ::

>> You can protect your privacy and avoid identity theft by handling important documents carefully—especially those that contain personal information such as your Social Security number or account numbers.

>> Another important step to protecting your privacy is to be careful about giving out personal information. It is never a good idea, for example, to give out account numbers or passwords via e-mail. Do so over the phone only if you are sure you are dealing with a legitimate business.

>> You should check your credit report once a year, to look for suspicious transactions and errors. The report can provide clues if someone else is making transactions in your name.

>> A variety of laws exist to protect your personal information from being misused. By learning more about these laws, you can better safeguard your privacy.

>> Your Web browser may provide tools for managing cookies, but a cookie-management utility will offer more options for identifying and removing unwanted cookies from your PC.

>> Similarly, you can use special anti-spyware software to find and delete spyware from your system. Some antivirus programs also target spyware.

>> To avoid receiving spam, avoid giving out your e-mail address. Otherwise, you can reduce spam by setting up a secondary e-mail account, using e-mail filters, and working with your ISP to block spam messages.

>> To secure your data, you must keep other people away from it. This means limiting physical access to your computer so other people cannot get to your data. It also means using a firewall to prevent hackers from accessing your system via the Internet.

>> Regular data backups are an effective countermeasure against threats to your data. Should any of your data become lost or damaged, you can restore it to your computer by using a backup copy.

>> By protecting your hardware, you are also protecting your data and avoiding the expense of replacing your PC. Make sure others cannot get to your PC and damage or steal it.

>> Take care when handling computer hardware and storage media, to avoid damaging them. If a disk becomes damaged, the data it stores may be lost.

>> Another way to protect your PC hardware and data is by keeping the system clean and avoiding exposure to magnetism or extreme temperatures. Dust can also cause system components to fail, so it is important to keep your PC clean.

Key Terms ::

adware, 229
always-on connection, 235
anti-adware utility, 231
anti-spyware utility, 231
cookie, 229
cookie-management utility, 230
credit report, 227
degaussing, 228
dumpster diving, 225
Electronic Communications
    Privacy Act, 228
Event Viewer, 236
Fair Credit Reporting Act, 228
filter, 233
Financial Modernization Act
    of 1999, 229

first-party cookie, 230
Freedom of Information Act, 228
identity (ID) theft, 225
opt-out option, 228
persistent cookie, 230
pop-up blocker, 231
pop-up window, 231
primary e-mail account, 232
Privacy Act of 1974, 228
restore, 235
Right to Financial Privacy Act
    of 1978, 229
rule, 233
screen saver, 234
secondary e-mail account, 232
session cookie, 230

shoulder surfing, 225
snagging, 225
social engineering, 225
spam, 231
spam blocker, 233
spyware, 229
stored cookie, 230
third-party cookie, 230
transient cookie, 230
unsolicited commercial e-mail
    (UCE), 231
USA PATRIOT Act, 229
Web bug, 229

Key Term Quiz ::

Complete each statement by writing one of the terms from the Key Terms list in each blank.

1. A(n) _____ is a document that lists all your financial accounts that can be a source of credit or that you can use to make purchases or other transactions.

2. If you select the _____ on a company's Web page or warranty form, the company promises either not to share your information or not to send you advertisements.

3. The _____ Act of 1970 mandates that personal information assembled by credit reporting agencies must be accurate, fair, and private.

4. A(n) _____ cookie is temporary; it is automatically deleted when you close your browser.

5. A(n) _____ cookie comes from a different Web site than the one you are viewing.

6. A(n) _____ window is a secondary browser window that may contain an advertisement and carry spyware.

7. Your _____ e-mail account is the one you set up with your ISP as part of your Internet access package.

8. By creating a(n) _____ in your e-mail program, you can tell the program to ignore messages from a specific sender.

9. A(n) _____ is a blank screen or a moving image that appears on the screen after the computer has gone unused for several minutes.

10. You can use a backup copy of your data to _____ lost files to your PC.

Multiple Choice ::

Circle the word or phrase that best completes each sentence.

1. From the moment they enter your mailbox until they reach the landfill, many of your most valuable documents are
   _____ .
   a. yours   b. vulnerable   c. missing   d. shredded

2. Before discarding them, you should _____ any document that contains sensitive information such as your Social Security number, account numbers, or passwords.
   a. read   b. hide   c. throw away   d. shred

3. A bank or legitimate business will never ask for your account number by _____ .
   a. law   b. itself   c. e-mail   d. any means

4. You should check your _____ at least once a year.
   a. credit report   b. e-mail filters   c. shredder   d. privacy laws

5. If a company asks you to complete a form on its Web site, you should first check the company's _____ .
   a. URL   b. privacy policy   c. security settings   d. warranty

6. Most Web browsers feature built-in settings that give you some control over _____ .
   a. Web bugs   b. cookies   c. ads   d. spyware

7. If the Web site you are viewing places a cookie on your system, the cookie is called a _____ cookie.
   a. session   b. third-party   c. first-party   d. expired

8. A key to avoiding _____ is to be careful about downloading files and programs from the Internet.
   a. spam   b. cookies   c. spyware   d. pop-ups

9. An e-mail program's filters also may be called _____ .
   a. spams   b. blockers   c. accounts   d. rules

10. _____ occurs when magnetic media is close enough to a magnetic source to erase its contents.
    a. Desensitizing   b. Demagnetizing   c. Defragmenting   d. Degaussing

Review Questions ::

In your own words, briefly answer the following questions.

1. Why should you tell your bank or credit card company about suspicious transactions or charges immediately?
2. List two methods you should not use to give out personal information such as an account number or a password.
3. How can you avoid spam by having two e-mail addresses?
4. Name two laws that require companies to give consumers notice of their privacy and information-sharing practices.
5. List four types of cookies that can be placed on your computer by a Web site.
6. What is the best way to deal with spyware and Web bugs?
7. What is a spam blocker?
8. How might your operating system help you protect the privacy of your files if you share your PC with other users?
9. When is it especially important to use a firewall?
10. Why is it important to protect storage media from dust, dirt, and fingerprints?

Lesson Labs ::

Complete the following exercise as directed by your instructor.

1. Check your cookie-management settings. To do this, launch your browser. If you use Internet Explorer, open the Tools menu, then click Internet Options. When the Internet Properties dialog box appears, click the Privacy tab, then click the ADVANCED button. When the Advanced Privacy Settings dialog box appears, check the cookie-management settings. Close both dialog boxes by clicking CANCEL.

   If you use Netscape Navigator, open the Edit menu, then click Preferences. When the Preferences dialog box appears, double-click the Privacy & Security category, then click Cookies. Check the settings that appear, then close the dialog box by clicking CANCEL.

   Do not change the settings unless your instructor directs you to do so.

Chapter Labs

Complete the following exercises using a computer in your classroom, lab, or home.

1. **Learn more about pop-up blockers.** Pop-up windows can make Web surfing a maddening experience. A good pop-up blocker can save you a lot of time and aggravation by preventing pop-up windows from appearing on your screen, while letting you decide if you want specific pop-ups to open.

   To learn more about pop-up blockers, visit your favorite search engine and conduct a search on the key words "pop-up blocker". Visit several sites and compare at least three programs. (Do not download or install any software without your instructor's consent.) Summarize the comparison in a one-page report, and be prepared to present your findings to the class.

2. **Back up a folder.** Use your operating system's Help system to find out if your OS has a built-in backup utility. If so, launch the utility and learn how it works. With your instructor's permission, use the program to back up at least one file or folder. You may be able to back up the data to a floppy disk, Zip disk, network drive, or recordable CD. Next, use the program's Help system to learn how to restore the backed-up data, in case it were accidentally deleted from the hard disk.

3. **Learn more about CAN-SPAM.** Go online and research the CAN-SPAM law, which took effect at the beginning of 2004. What measures does the law take to limit the amount of spam messages that consumers receive? What penalties does it assess spammers who violate the law? What recourse does the law give to consumers who continue to receive a lot of spam? Your instructor may ask you to focus on one aspect of the law, or to work with a group. Compile your findings into a one-page report, and be prepared to share it with the class.

Discussion Questions

As directed by your instructor, discuss the following questions in class or in groups.

1. Before you read this chapter, what steps (if any) were you taking to protect your personal information? How will you change your approach to guarding your privacy? Compare your thoughts and ideas with those of your classmates.

2. What makes society civilized are the norms by which it lives. Cellular phones have introduced a new challenge for the civilized world. Now that we can call anyone at any time, should we call or take a call while in restrooms, at meetings, eating dinner, or on a train? List 10 rules that we should apply to the use of cell phones.

Research and Report

Using your own choice of resources (such as the Internet, books, magazines, and newspaper articles), research and write a short paper discussing one of the following topics:

>> The various methods firewalls use to protect a computer or network.

>> The extent to which spyware is being used online, and the reasons for it.

>> The effects the environment can have on a computer.

When you are finished, proofread and print your paper, and give it to your instructor.

ETHICAL ISSUES

1. One of the primary reasons why it is easy to violate the rights of others is because of the relative anonymity that the Internet allows. Rather than having to go out and steal, or trespass, all you have to do is execute a programming routine in your own home. For instance, if you had to steal the software by going to the store and shoplifting a CD, you would get a sense that you were committing a crime. But if you download a file containing all of the same material, it is hard to get a sense that you are doing something wrong. Discuss the impact that the "virtuality" of the Internet has on our per-ception of ethical violations. In particular, what other areas of ethics might need a new set of definitions besides file sharing?

2. Many people who think about those sorts of things believe that the Internet will force us to define a new legal framework to embody the new powers it bestows. Specifically, where does the Internet blur the legal definitions? Consider issues of pornography, intellectual property, sabotage, government regulation, and taxation.

Appendix A

History of Microcomputers

1965

Honeywell corporation introduces the H316 "Kitchen Computer." This is the first home computer and is offered in the Neiman Marcus catalog for $10,600.

1970

Ken Thompson and Denis Ritchie create the UNIX operating system at Bell Labs. UNIX will become the dominant operating system for critical applications on servers, workstations, and high-end microcomputers.

1971

In 1971, Dr. Ted Hoff puts together all the elements of a computer processor on a single silicon chip slightly larger than one square inch. The result of his efforts is the Intel 4004, the world's first commercially available microprocessor. The chip is a four-bit computer containing 2,300 transistors (invented in 1948) that can perform 60,000 instructions per second. Designed for use in a calculator, it sells for $200. Intel sells more than 100,000 calculators based on the 4004 chip. Almost overnight, the chip finds thousands of applications, paving the way for today's computer-oriented world, and for the mass production of computer chips now containing millions of transistors.

Steve Wozniak and Bill Fernandez create a computer from chips rejected by local semiconductor companies. The computer is called the Cream Soda Computer because its creators drank Cragmont cream soda during its construction.

1972

Dennis Ritchie and Brian Kernighan create the C programming language at Bell Labs. The UNIX operating system is rewritten in C. C becomes one of the most popular programming languages for software development.

5.25-inch floppy diskettes are introduced, providing a portable way to store and move data from machine to machine.

1973

IBM introduces new mass storage devices: the eight-inch, two-sided floppy disk that can hold 400 KB of data and the Winchester eight-inch, four-platter hard drive that can hold an amazing 70 MB of data.

Bob Metcalfe, working at Xerox PARC, creates a methodology to connect computers called Ethernet.

1974

Intel announces the 8080 chip. This is a 2-MHz, eight-bit microprocessor that can access 64 KB of memory using a two-byte addressing structure. It has over 6000 transistors on one chip. It can perform 640,000 instructions per second.

Motorola introduces the 6800 microprocessor. It is also an eight-bit processor and is used primarily in industrial and automotive devices. It will become the chip of choice for Apple computers sparking a long-running battle between fans of Intel and Motorola chips.

1973

Model 8080 Microprocessor

1975

The first commercially available microcomputer, the Altair 880, is the first machine to be called a "personal computer." It has 64 KB of memory and an open 100-line bus structure. It sells for $397 in kit form or $439 assembled. The name "Altair" was suggested by the 12-year-old daughter of the publisher of *Popular Electronics* because Altair was the destination that evening for the *Enterprise*, the *Star Trek* space ship.

Two young college students, Paul Allen and Bill Gates, unveil the BASIC language interpreter for the Altair computer. During summer vacation, the pair formed a company called Microsoft, which eventually grows into one of the largest software companies in the world.

1976

Steve Wozniak and Steve Jobs build the Apple I computer. It is less powerful than the Altair, but also less expensive and less complicated. Users must connect their own keyboard and video display, and have the option of mounting the computer's motherboard in any container they

choose—whether a metal case, a wooden box, or a briefcase. Jobs and Wozniak form the Apple Computer Company together on April Fool's Day, naming the company after their favorite snack food.

1977

The Apple II computer is unveiled. It comes already assembled in a case, with a built-in keyboard. Users must plug in their own TVs for monitors. Fully assembled microcomputers hit the general market, with Radio Shack, Commodore, and Apple all selling models. Sales are slow because neither businesses nor the general public know exactly what to do with these new machines.

Datapoint Corporation announces Attached Resource Computing Network (ARCnet), the first commercial LAN technology intended for use with microcomputer applications.

1978

Intel releases the 8086 microprocessor, a 16-bit chip that sets a new standard for power, capacity, and speed in microprocessors.

Epson announces the MX-80 dot-matrix printer, coupling high performance with a relatively low price. (Epson from Japan set up operations in the United States in 1975 as Epson America, Inc., becoming one of the first of many foreign companies to contribute to the growth of the PC industry. Up until this point, it has been U.S. companies only. According to Epson, the company gained 60 percent of the dot-matrix printer market with the MX-80.)

1979

Intel introduces the 8088 microprocessor, featuring 16-bit internal architecture and an eight-bit external bus.

Motorola introduces the 68000 chip; it contains 68,000 transistors, hence the name. It will be used in early Macintosh computers.

Software Arts, Inc., releases VisiCalc, the first commercial spreadsheet program for personal computers. VisiCalc is generally credited as being the program that paved the way for the personal computer in the business world.

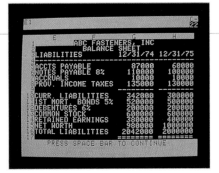

Bob Metcalf, the developer of Ethernet, forms 3Com Corp. to develop Ethernet-based networking products. Ethernet eventually evolves into the world's most widely used network system.

MicroPro International introduces WordStar, the first commercially successful word processing program for IBM-compatible microcomputers.

1980

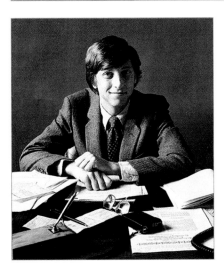

IBM chooses Microsoft (co-founded by Bill Gates and Paul Allen) to provide the operating system for its upcoming PC. Microsoft purchases a program developed by Seattle Computer Products called Q-DOS (for Quick and Dirty Operating System), and modifies it to run on IBM hardware.

Bell Laboratories invents the Bellmac-32, the first single-chip microprocessor with 32-bit internal architecture and a 32-bit data bus.

Lotus Development Corporation unveils the Lotus 1-2-3 integrated spreadsheet program, combining spreadsheet, graphics, and database features in one package.

1981

Adam Osborne creates the world's first "portable" computer, the Osborne 1. It weighs about 22 pounds, has two 5.25-inch floppy drives, 64 KB of RAM, and a five-inch monitor but no hard drive. It is based on the z80 processor, runs the CP/M operating system, and sells for $1,795. The Osborne 1 comes with WordStar (a word processing application) and Super-Calc (a spreadsheet application). It is a huge success.

IBM introduces the IBM-PC, with a 4.77 MHz Intel 8088 CPU, 16 KB of memory, a keyboard, a monitor, one or two 5.25-inch floppy drives, and a price tag of $2,495.

Hayes Microcomputer Products, Inc., introduces the SmartModem 300, which quickly becomes the industry standard.

Xerox unveils the Xerox Star computer. Its high price eventually dooms the computer to commercial failure, but its features inspire a whole new direction in computer design. Its little box on wheels (the first mouse) can execute commands on screen (the first graphical user interface).

1982

Intel releases the 80286, a 16-bit microprocessor.

Sun Microsystems is formed and the company begins shipping the Sun-1 workstation.

AutoCAD, a program for designing 2-D and 3-D objects, is released. AutoCAD will go on to revolutionize the architecture and engineering industries.

Work begins on the development of TCP/IP. The term *Internet* is used for the first time to describe the worldwide network of networks that is emerging from the ARPANET.

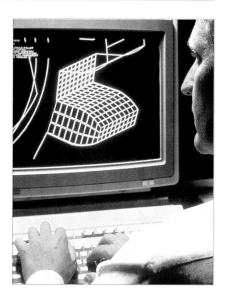

Time magazine features the computer as the 1982 "Machine of the Year," acknowledging the computer's new role in society.

Apple introduces the Lisa, a computer with a purely graphical operating system and a mouse. The industry is excited, but Lisa's $10,000 price tag discourages buyers.

IBM unveils the IBM-PC XT, essentially a PC with a hard disk and more memory. The XT can store programs and data on its built-in 10MB hard disk.

The first version of the C++ programming language is developed, allowing programs to be written in reusable independent pieces, called objects.

The Compaq Portable computer is released, the first successful 100 percent PC-compatible clone. (The term *clone* refers to any PC based on the same architecture as the one used in IBM's personal computers.) Despite its hefty 28 pounds, it becomes one of the first computers to be lugged through airports.

Adobe Systems releases its Post-Script system, allowing printers to produce crisp print in a number of typefaces, as well as elaborate graphic images.

Richard Stallman leaves MIT to start the GNU (GNU's not Unix) free software project. This project will grow adding thousands of programs to the library of free (open-source, available under a special license) software. This movement is supported by the Free Software Foundation, an alternative to expensive, closed-source software.

Apple introduces the "user-friendly" Macintosh microcomputer, which features a graphical interface.

IBM ships the IBM-PC AT, a 6 MHz computer using the Intel 80286 processor, which sets the standard for personal computers running DOS.

IBM introduces its Token Ring networking system. Reliable and redundant, it can send packets at 4 Mbps; several years later it speeds up to 16 Mbps.

Satellite Software International introduces the WordPerfect word processing program.

1985

Intel releases the 80386 processor (also called the 386), a 32-bit processor that can address more than four billion bytes of memory and performs 10 times faster than the 80286.

Aldus releases Page-Maker for the Macintosh, the first desktop publishing software for microcomputers. Coupled with Apple's LaserWriter printer and Adobe's PostScript system, PageMaker ushers in the era of desktop publishing.

Microsoft announces the Windows 1.0 operating environment, featuring the first graphical user interface for PCs mirroring the interface found the previous year on the Macintosh.

Hewlett-Packard introduces the LaserJet laser printer, featuring 300 dpi resolution.

1986

IBM delivers the PC convertible, IBM's first laptop computer and the first Intel-based computer with a 3.5-inch floppy disk drive.

Microsoft sells its first public stock for $21 per share, raising $61 million in the initial public offering.

The First International Conference on CD-ROM technology is held in Seattle, hosted by Microsoft. Compact discs are seen as the storage medium of the future for computer users.

1987

IBM unveils the new PS/2 line of computers, featuring a 20-MHz 80386 processor at its top end. This product line includes the MicroChannel bus, but is not a great success because consumers do not want to replace industry standard peripherals. To compete with IBM's MicroChannel architecture, a group of other computer makers introduces the EISA (Extended Industry Standard Architecture) bus.

IBM introduces its Video Graphics Array (VGA) monitor offering 256 colors at 320 × 200 resolution, and 16 colors at 640 × 480.

The Macintosh II computer, aimed at the desktop publishing market, is introduced by Apple Computer. It features an SVGA monitor. Apple Computer introduces HyperCard, a programming language for the Macintosh, which uses the metaphor of a stack of index cards to represent a program—a kind of visual programming language. HyperCard allows linking across different parts of a program or across different programs; this concept will lead to the development of HTML (hypertext markup language).

Motorola unveils its 68030 microprocessor.

Novell introduces its network operating system, called NetWare.

1988

IBM and Microsoft ship OS/2 1.0, the first multitasking desktop operating system. Its high price, a steep learning curve, and incompatibility with existing PCs contribute to its lack of market share.

Apple Computer files the single biggest lawsuit in the computer industry against Microsoft and Hewlett-Packard, claiming copyright infringement of its operating system and graphical user interface.

Hewlett-Packard introduces the first popular ink jet printer, the HP Deskjet.

Steve Jobs' new company, NeXT, Inc., unveils the NeXT computer, featuring a 25-MHz Motorola 68030 processor. The NeXT is the first computer to use object-oriented programming in its operating system and an optical drive rather than a floppy drive.

Apple introduces the Apple CD SC, a CD-ROM storage device allowing access to up to 650 MB of data.

A virus called the "Internet Worm" is released on the Internet, disabling about 10 percent of all Internet host computers.

1989

Intel releases the 80486 chip (also called the 486), the world's first one-million-transistor microprocessor. The 486 integrates a 386 CPU and math coprocessor onto the same chip.

Tim Berners-Lee develops software around the hypertext concept, enabling users to click on a word or phrase in a document and jump either to another location within the document or to another file. This software provides the foundation for the development of the World Wide Web, and is the basis for the first Web browsers.

The World Wide Web is created at CERN, the European Particle Physics Laboratory in Geneva, Switzerland, for use by scientific researchers.

Microsoft's Word for Windows introduction begins the Microsoft Office suite adoption by millions of users. Previously, Word for DOS had been the second-highest-selling word processing package behind WordPerfect.

1990

Microsoft releases Windows 3.0, shipping one million copies in four months.

A multimedia PC specification setting the minimum hardware requirements for sound and graphics components of a PC is announced at the Microsoft Multimedia Developers' Conference.

The National Science Foundation Network (NSFNET) replaces ARPANET as the backbone of the Internet.

Motorola announces its 32-bit microprocessor, the 68040, incorporating 1.2 million transistors.

1991

Linus Torvalds releases the source code for Linux 0.01 (a clone of UNIX for the 80386 personal computer) on the Internet. It quickly becomes the base operating system of the open-source movement. Linux will grow to become one of the most widely used open-source PC operating systems.

Apple Computer launches the PowerBook series of battery-powered portable computers.

Apple, IBM, and Motorola sign a cooperative agreement to design and produce RISC-based chips, integrate the Mac OS into IBM's enterprise systems, produce a new object-oriented operating system, and develop common multimedia standards. The result is the PowerPC microprocessor.

1992

With an estimated 25 million users, the Internet becomes the world's largest electronic mail network.

In Apple Computer's five-year copyright infringement lawsuit, Judge Vaughn Walker rules in favor of defendants Microsoft and Hewlett-Packard, finding that the graphical user interface in dispute is not covered under Apple's copyrights.

Microsoft ships the Windows 3.1 operating environment, including improved memory management and TrueType fonts.

IBM introduces its ThinkPad laptop computer.

1993

Mosaic, a point-and-click graphical Web browser, is developed at the National Center for Supercomputing Applications (NCSA), making the Internet accessible to those outside the scientific community.

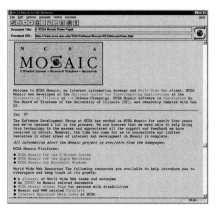

Intel, mixing elements of its 486 design with new processes, features, and technology, delivers the long-awaited Pentium processor. It offers a 64-bit data path and more than 3.1 million transistors.

Apple Computer expands its entire product line, adding the Macintosh Color Classic, Macintosh LC III, Macintosh Centris 610 and 650, Macintosh Quadra 800, and the Powerbooks 165c and 180c.

Apple introduces the Newton MessagePad at the Macworld convention, selling 50,000 units in the first 10 weeks.

Microsoft ships the Windows NT operating system.

IBM ships its first RISC-based RS/6000 workstation, featuring the PowerPC 601 chip developed jointly by Motorola, Apple, and IBM.

1994

Apple introduces the Power Macintosh line of microcomputers based on the PowerPC chip. This line introduces RISC to the desktop market. RISC was previously available only on high-end workstations.

Netscape Communications releases the Netscape Navigator program, a World Wide Web browser based on the Mosaic standard, but with more advanced features.

Online service providers CompuServe, America Online, and Prodigy add Internet access to their services.

After two million Pentium-based PCs have hit the market, a flaw in the chip's floating-point unit is found by Dr. Thomas Nicely. His report is made public on CompuServe.

Red Hat Linux is introduced and quickly becomes the most commonly used version of Linux.

1995

Intel releases the Pentium Pro microprocessor.

Motorola releases the PowerPC 604 chip, developed jointly with Apple and IBM.

Microsoft releases its Windows 95 operating system with a massive marketing campaign, including prime-time TV commercials. Seven million copies are sold the first month, with sales reaching 26 million by year's end.

Netscape Communications captures more than 80 percent of the World Wide Web browser market, going from a start-up company to a $2.9 billion company in one year.

A group of developers at Sun Microsystems create the Java development language. Because it enables programmers to develop applications that will run on any platform, Java is seen as the future language of operating systems, applications, and the World Wide Web.

Power Computing ships the first-ever Macintosh clones, the Power 100 series with a PowerPC 601 processor.

eBay, the premier online auction house, is formed.

1996

Intel announces the 200 MHz Pentium processor.

U.S. Robotics releases the PalmPilot, a personal digital assistant that quickly gains enormous popularity because of its rich features and ease of use.

Microsoft adds Internet connection capability to its Windows 95 operating system.

Several vendors introduce Virtual Reality Modeling Language (VRML) authoring tools that provide simple interfaces and drag-and-drop editing features to create three-dimensional worlds with color, texture, video, and sound on the Web.

The U.S. Congress enacts the Communications Decency Act as part of the Telecommunications Act of 1996. The act mandates fines of up to $100,000 and prison terms for transmission of any "comment, request, suggestion, proposal, image or other communication which is obscene, lewd, lascivious, filthy, or

indecent" over the Internet. The day the law is passed, millions of Web page backgrounds turn black in protest. The law is immediately challenged on constitutional grounds, ultimately deemed unconstitutional, and repealed.

Sun Microsystems introduces the Sun Ultra workstation that includes a 64-bit processor.

Intel announces MMX technology, which increases the multimedia capabilities of a microprocessor. Also, Intel announces the Pentium II microprocessor. It has speeds of up to 333 MHz and introduces a new design in packaging, the Single Edge Contact (SEC) cartridge. It has more than 7.5 million transistors.

AMD and Cyrix step up efforts to compete with Intel for the $1000-and-less PC market. Their competing processors are used by PC makers such as Dell, Compaq, Gateway, and even IBM.

The U.S. Justice Department files an antitrust lawsuit against Microsoft, charging the company with anticompetitive behavior for forcing PC makers to bundle its Internet Explorer Web browser with Windows 95.

Netscape Communications and Microsoft release new versions of their Web browser. Netscape's Communicator 4 and Microsoft's Internet Explorer 4 provide a full suite of Internet tools, including Web browser, newsreader, HTML editor, conferencing program, and e-mail application.

Digital Video/Versatile Disc (DVD) technology is introduced. Capable of storing computer, audio, and video data, a single DVD disc can hold an entire movie. DVD is seen as the storage technology for the future, ultimately replacing standard CD-ROM technology in PC and home entertainment systems.

Microsoft releases the Windows 98 operating system. Seen mainly as an upgrade to Windows 95, Windows 98 is more reliable and less susceptible to crashes. It also offers improved Internet-related features, including a built-in copy of the Internet Explorer Web browser.

Netscape announces that it will post the source code to the Navigator 5.0 Web browser on the Internet. This is a major step in the open-source software movement.

The Department of Justice expands its actions against Microsoft, attempting to block the release of Windows 98 unless Microsoft agrees to remove the Internet Explorer browser from the operating system. Microsoft fights back and a lengthy trial begins in federal court, as the government attempts to prove that Microsoft is trying to hold back competitors such as Netscape.

Intel releases two new versions of its popular Pentium II chip. The Pentium II Celeron offers slower performance than the standard PII, but is aimed at the $1,000-and-less PC market, which quickly embraces this chip. At the high end, the Pentium II Xeon is designed for use in high-performance workstations and server systems, and it is priced accordingly. Both chips boost Intel's market share, reaching deeper into more vertical markets.

Apple Computer releases the colorful iMac, an all-in-one system geared to a youthful market. The small, lightweight system features the new G3 processor, which outperforms Pentium II-based PCs in many respects. The iMac uses only USB connections, forcing many users to purchase adapters for system peripherals, and the computer does not include a floppy disk drive.

The new Internet Protocol, version 6 (IPv6), draft standard is released by the Internet Engineering Task Force.

Intel unveils the Pentium III processor, which features 9.5 million transistors. Although the Pentium III's performance is not vastly superior to the Pentium II, it features enhancements that take greater advantage of graphically rich applications and Web sites. A more powerful version of the chip (named Xeon) is also released, for use in higher-end workstations and network server systems.

With its Athlon microprocessor, Advanced Micro Devices finally releases a Pentium-class chip that outperforms the Pentium III processor. The advance is seen as a boon for the lower-price computer market, which relies heavily on chips from Intel's competitors.

Sun Microsystems acquires Star Division Corporation and begins free distribution of StarOffice, a fully featured alternative to Microsoft Office and other proprietary office productivity products.

Apple Computer introduces updated versions of its popular iMac computer, including a laptop version, as well as the new G4 system, with performance rated at one gigaflop, meaning the system can perform more than one billion floating point operations per second.

The world braces for January 1, 2000, as fears of the "Millennium Bug" come to a head. As airlines, government agencies, financial institutions, utilities, and PC owners scramble to make their systems "Y2K-compliant," some people panic, afraid that basic services will cease operation when the year changes from 1999 to 2000.

Peter Merholz coins the term *blog*, a contraction of Web-log. In early 1999, there are already 50 recognized blog sites on the Web. By 2005 the sites will number in the hundreds of thousands.

The Internet Assigned Number Agency begins assigning Internet Protocol addresses using the new IPv6 addressing structure.

Shortly after the new year, computer experts and government officials around the world announce that no major damage resulted from the "millennium date change," when computer clocks rolled over from 1999 to 2000. Immediately, a global debate begins to rage: had the entire "Y2K bug" been a hoax created by the computer industry, as a way to reap huge profits from people's fears? Industry leaders defend their approach to the Y2K issue, stating that years of planning and preventive measures had helped the world avoid a global computer-driven catastrophe that could have brought the planet's economy to a stand-still.

Microsoft introduces Windows 2000 on February 17. It is the biggest commercial software project ever attempted and one of the largest engineering projects of the century, involving 5,345 full-time participants, over half of them engineers. The final product includes almost 30 million lines of code.

On March 6, Advanced Micro Devices (AMD) announces the shipment of a 1GHz version of the Athlon processor, which will be used in PCs manufactured by Compaq and Gateway. It is the first 1GHz processor to be commercially available to the consumer PC market. Within days, Intel Corp. announces the release of a 1GHz version of the Pentium III processor.

In April, U.S. District Judge Thomas Penfield Jackson rules that Microsoft is guilty of taking advantage of its monopoly in operating systems to hurt competitors and leverage better deals with its business partners. Soon after the finding, the Department of Justice recommends that the judge break Microsoft into two separate companies: one focused solely on operating systems, the other focused solely on application development. Microsoft quickly counters by offering to change a number of its business practices. The judge rules to divide the software giant into two companies.

IBM (International Business Machines) announces that it will begin selling computers running the Linux operating system. As with other Linux vendors, the IBM version of Linux will be open source.

Microsoft releases the Windows XP operating system, with versions for home computers and business desktops. The XP version of Microsoft Office also is unveiled.

After blaming digital music pirates for lost revenue, the Recording Industry Association of America (RIAA) files lawsuits against purveyors of MP3 technology—most notably Napster, an online service that enables users to share MP3-format files freely across the Internet. The suits effectively shut down Napster, but do not stop individuals and other file-sharing services from exchanging music, text, and other files.

Apple introduces OS X, a new operating system for Macintosh computers that is based on BSD (Berkley Software Distribution) Unix with a beautiful graphical interface. It is an immediate success.

Several versions of recordable DVD discs and drives hit the market. Users instantly adopt the devices to store digitized home movies, data, and software; even though movie pirates soon begin copying and distributing movies on DVD, most users find the large capacity discs a wonderful storage and backup medium.

After several years of explosive growth, the "dot-com" revolution goes into sudden reverse. As thousands of Web-based companies go out of business (giving rise to the phrase "dot-bomb"), tens of thousands of workers lose their jobs, shareholders suffer billions of dollars in losses, and the world's financial markets learn a valuable lesson.

Apple introduces the iPod, the premier music player with a 5 GB internal hard disk that will store 1,000 CD-quality songs.

Technology takes an important new role in society after the United States is attacked by terrorists on September 11, 2001. Government agencies, the military, and airlines place a new emphasis on security, recruiting new high-tech methods to monitor travelers and inspect people and baggage for dangerous items. Almost immediately, billions of dollars are invested in the development of new bomb-detection technologies and the creation of a huge, multinational database that can allow airlines to track the movements of passengers through the flight system.

Europe and Asia adopt the new Internet Protocol standard IPv6; the United States has not yet moved to adopt the new standard.

Because of the high cost of flying and concerns about security, many American businesses drastically reduce business travel. Increasingly, companies rely on technologies such as videoconferencing, teleconferencing, and online document sharing to work with partners and customers.

After a year of devastating shakeouts, the dot-com world begins to pick itself up again. The new breed of online entrepreneur bases companies on sound business practices, rather than the glamour of simply being "new economy." Investments in new online ventures slow to a trickle, enabling only those companies with the best ideas and real promise of profits to flourish.

The wireless networking boom continues with an emphasis on enabling handheld computers and telephones to access the Internet via wireless connections. Products such as digital two-way pagers, wireless phones, and combination telephone/PDAs sell at unprecedented levels.

Michael Robertson releases Lindows, a Linux-based operating system that has a full graphical user interface and comes with Open Office software. Wal-Mart and Fry's, two large retail chains, market Lindows-based computer systems for as little as $199. Microsoft immediately sues Robertson to try to prevent the product from reaching the market but loses.

XML (eXtensible Markup Language) and Web-based applications take center stage in many businesses.

Microsoft releases Windows XP Server Edition and the .NET Framework.

OpenOffice.org announces the release of OpenOffice.org 1.0, a free, full-featured suite of productivity applications compatible with the file formats used by Microsoft Office and many other office suites. An open-source alternative to expensive application suites, OpenOffice.org runs under Windows, Solaris, Linux, the Mac OS, and other operating systems.

The National Center for Supercomputing Applications announces that Mike Showerman and Craig Steffen created a supercomputer based on 70 Sony PlayStation 2 gaming systems. The supercomputer cost about $50,000 to build, uses the Linux operating system and a Hewlett-Packard high-speed switch, and can perform 6.5 billion mathematical operations per second.

The Slammer worm does over $1 billion in damage and demonstrates that no network is truly secure.

Lindows explodes across the globe with several countries opting for this powerful and inexpensive alternative to high-priced proprietary software.

Microsoft releases Office 2003, the latest in the Office suite series.

Intel and AMD release 64-bit processors targeted for the home computer market.

Apple introduces the Power Macintosh G5, a 64-bit processor.

In a continuing attempt to control file sharing, the Recording Industry Association of America begins suing individuals who share files.

Apple opens an online music store, iTunes, offering more than 200,000 titles at $0.99 each.

Wi-Fi (Wireless Fidelity) or 802.11b/g comes to the consumer market with hot spots springing up both in home networking and in some commercial locations such as Starbucks. With this new technology comes the new technique called "war driving," where individuals drive around in automobiles with laptop computers looking for wireless networks that will allow them access.

2004

Spam (unsolicited e-mail) and malware (programs such as viruses, Trojan Horses, and worms) cause major problems across the Internet. Crackers use viruses to generate spam and attack companies. One example is Mydoom, which takes control of more than 250,000 personal computers and uses them to attack the SCO Group Inc. Web site. Some estimates made in mid-2004 show that nearly 85 percent of all e-mail messages can be classified as spam.

By March, Apple's Itunes store has sold 50 millions songs.

Centralized computing makes a resurgence in both home and business environments with mainframe-like servers feeding "stateless devices" formerly known as dumb terminals.

RFID (Radio Frequency Identification) tags, common on some products, are seen as an invasion of privacy when shoppers are scanned to see what brands they buy.

2005

The last of the old Internet Protocol addresses (IPv4) is assigned and now all Net devices worldwide must support the new standard, IPv6.

Microsoft releases the next version of Windows, code named Longhorn.

"Disposable computers" move into home computing. People no longer try to repair a broken personal computer; they simply throw away the old one and buy a new one that is quickly updated to contain everything on the old machine.

Bluetooth-enabled devices allow sharing of files, text, data, images, and music across a wide range of personal devices, allowing you to play tunes from your iPod on your cell phone or as background on your PDA.

Appendix B

Self-Check Answers

Chapter 1, Lesson A, page 8
1. C
2. A
3. B

Chapter 1, Lesson B, page 31
1. B
2. A
3. B

Chapter 2, Lesson A, page 57
1. B
2. A
3. C

Chapter 2, Lesson B, page 79
1. B
2. A
3. C

Chapter 3, Lesson A, page 117
1. A
2. B
3. C

Chapter 3, Lesson B, page 144
1. B
2. A
3. C

Chapter 4, Lesson A, page 167
1. B
2. A
3. B

Chapter 4, Lesson B, page 190
1. A
2. B
3. C

Chapter 5, Lesson A, page 216
1. C
2. A
3. B

Chapter 5, Lesson B, page 236
1. C
2. A
3. B

Glossary

Numerals

10Base-T   See *Ethernet*.

100Base-T   See *Fast Ethernet*.

A

activate   (1) To initiate a command or load a program into memory and begin using it. (2) To *choose*; for example, you can activate a resource by choosing its icon, toolbar button, or filename.

active matrix LCD   A liquid crystal display (LCD) technology that assigns a transistor to each pixel in a flat-panel monitor, improving display quality and eliminating the "submarining" effect produced by some types of flat-panel monitors. Also called a *thin-film transistor (TFT)* display.

adapter   See *expansion board*.

address book   A database that stores information about people, such as their names, addresses, phone numbers, e-mail addresses, and other details. Commonly part of a personal information management or e-mail program.

address bus   A set of wires connecting the computer's CPU and RAM, across which memory addresses are transmitted. The number of wires in the bus determines the amount of memory that can be addressed at any one time.

Advanced Micro Devices (AMD)   A chip manufacturer that makes processors for PC-compatible computers. AMD initially focused on chips for lower-price, lower-performance systems, but later became a major manufacturer of high-performance processors for the PC market.

adware   See *spyware*.

alphanumeric keys   On a computer keyboard, the keys that include the letters of the alphabet, numerals, and commonly used symbols.

ALU   See *arithmetic logic unit*.

always-on connection   An Internet connection that is always active, as long as the computer is running. Cable modem and DSL connections are examples of always-on connections.

AMD   See *Advanced Micro Devices*.

American Standard Code for Information Interchange (ASCII)   An eight-bit binary code developed by the American National Standards Institute (ANSI) to represent symbolic, numeric, and alphanumeric characters. The ASCII character set is the most commonly used character set in PCs.

anonymous FTP archive   An FTP site with files available to the general public. The user types the word "anonymous" as the account name in order to access the files.

anti-adware utility   See *anti-spyware utility*.

anti-spyware utility   A program that can locate and remove spyware programs from a user's computer. Some anti-spyware utilities can "immunize" a computer against known types of spyware, to prevent them from infecting the system.

antivirus utility   A program that scans a computer's disks and memory for viruses; when it detects viruses, it removes them. Some antivirus programs can help the user recover data and program files that have been damaged by a virus and can actively scan files as they are being copied from a disk or downloaded from the Internet.

application server   A network server that hosts shared application files, enabling multiple users to use a network version of a software program. Generally, an application server also performs some or all of the processing tasks required by users of the application.

application software   Any computer program used to create or process data, such as text documents, spreadsheets, graphics, and so on. Examples include database management software, desktop publishing programs, presentation programs, spreadsheet programs, and word processing programs.

architecture   The design of any part of a computer system, or of an entire system, including software and hardware. The design of a microprocessor's circuits, for example, is called its architecture.

arithmetic logic unit (ALU)   The component of the CPU that handles arithmetic and logical functions.

arithmetic operation   One of two types of operations a computer can perform, which are handled by the arithmetic logic unit (ALU). Arithmetic operations include addition, subtraction, multiplication, and division. See also *logical operation*.

ARPANET   Acronym for *Advanced Research Projects Agency Network*. An early network developed by the Department of Defense to connect computers at universities and defense contractors. This network eventually became part of the Internet.

article   A message posted to an Internet newsgroup. A series of related articles and responses is called a *thread*.

ASCII   See *American Standard Code for Information Interchange*.

audio port   A specialized computer port that accepts audio devices and transmits audio data.

B

B2B transaction   See *business-to-business transaction*.

B2C transaction   See *business-to-consumer transaction*.

backbone   The central structure of a network that connects other elements of the network and handles the major traffic.

bar code   A pattern of bars printed on a product or its packaging. A device called a *bar code reader* can scan a bar code and convert its pattern into numeric digits. After the bar code reader has converted a bar code image into a number, it transfers that number to a computer, just as though the number had been typed on a keyboard.

bar code reader   An input device that converts a pattern of printed bars (called a *bar code*) into a number that a computer can read. A beam of light reflected off the bar code into a light-sensitive detector identifies the bar code and converts the bar patterns into numeric digits that can be transferred to a computer. Bar code readers are commonly used in retail stores.

basic input output system (BIOS)   A set of instructions, stored in ROM, that help a computer start running when it is turned on.

binary number system   A system for representing the two possible states of electrical switches, which are on and off. (The binary number system is also known as *base 2*.) The binary number system gets its name from the fact that it includes only two numbers: 0 and 1. In computer storage and memory systems, the numeral 0 represents off and a 1 represents on.

BIOS   See *basic input-output system*.

bit   The smallest unit of data that can be used by a computer, represented by a 1 or a 0.

block   A contiguous series of characters, words, sentences, or paragraphs in a word processing document. This term is also sometimes used to describe a range of cells in a spreadsheet. Once a block of text or cells has been selected, the user can perform many different actions on it, such as moving, formatting, or deleting.

board   See *expansion board*.

Boolean operator   Special words—such as AND, OR, and NOT—that can be used to modify a keyword search in a Web-based search engine. These operators are commonly used in standard database queries.

boot   To start a computer. The term comes from the expression "pulling oneself up by one's own bootstraps."

boot sector   The portion of a disk that contains the master boot record—a program that runs when the computer is first started and determines whether the disk has the basic operating system components required to run successfully.

brick-and-mortar store   A business, such as a retail store, that has a physical location but does not have an online presence such as a Web site.

bridge   A device that connects two LANs and controls data flow between them.

browser   See *Web browser*.

buddy list   A list of people who can participate in chats, using instant messaging software.

bus   The path between components of a computer or nodes of a network. The bus's width determines the speed at which data is transmitted. When used alone, the term commonly refers to a computer's data bus.

bus topology   A network topology in which all network nodes and peripheral devices are attached to a single conduit.

business-to-business (B2B) transaction   A transaction (such as the placing of an order or the paying of an invoice) conducted by two businesses. A B2B transaction can be conducted in many ways, with or without the use of computers, but the term *B2B* is commonly used to describe transactions that occur online or through a private corporate network such as an extranet.

business-to-consumer (B2C) transaction   A transaction (such as the ordering of a product or the paying of a bill) conducted between an individual consumer and a business. A B2C transaction can be conducted in many ways, with or without the use of computers, but the term *B2C* is commonly used to describe transactions that occur via the Internet.

byte   The amount of memory required to store a single character. A byte is comprised of eight bits.

cache memory   High-speed memory that resides between the CPU and RAM in a computer. Cache memory stores data and instructions that the CPU is likely to need next. The CPU can retrieve data or instructions more quickly from cache than it can from RAM or a disk.

campus area network (CAN)   A larger version of a *local area network (LAN)*, usually used to connect adjacent buildings such as those found on college campuses.

CAN   See *campus area network*.

card   See *expansion board*.

cathode ray tube (CRT)   A type of monitor that uses a vacuum tube as a display screen. CRTs are most commonly used with desktop computers.

CD   See *compact disc*.

CD-R   See *CD-Recordable drive*.

CD-Recordable (CD-R) drive   An optical disc drive that enables the user to create customized CD-ROM discs. Data that has been written to a CD-R disc cannot be changed (overwritten). CD-R discs can be read by any CD-ROM drive. CD-R drives are commonly used to create backup copies of program or data files, or to create duplicates of existing compact discs.

CD-ReWritable (CD-RW) drive   An optical disc drive that enables the user to create customized CD-ROM discs. Unlike a CD-R disc, a CD-RW disc's data can be overwritten, meaning the data can be updated after it has been placed on the disc.

CD-ROM   See *compact disc read-only memory*.

CD-ROM drive   An optical disc drive that enables a computer to read data from a compact disc. Using a standard CD-ROM drive and compact disc, the computer can only read data from the disc and cannot write data to the disc.

CD-RW   See *CD-ReWritable drive*.

cell   In a spreadsheet or database table, the intersection of a row and a column, forming a box into which the user enters numbers, formulas, or text. The term also is used to refer to the individual blocks in a table created in a word processing program.

cell address   In a spreadsheet, an identifier that indicates the location of a cell in a worksheet. The address is composed of the cell's row and column locations. For example, if the cell is located at the intersection of column B and row 3, then its cell address is B3.

cell pointer   A square enclosing one cell of a spreadsheet, identifying that cell as the active cell. The user positions the cell pointer in a worksheet by clicking the cell or by using the cursor movement keys on the keyboard.

central processing unit (CPU)   The computer's primary processing device, which interprets and executes program instructions and manages the functions of input, output, and storage devices. In personal computers, the CPU is composed of a control unit, an arithmetic logic unit, built-in memory, and supporting circuitry such as a dedicated math processor. The CPU may reside on a single chip on the computer's motherboard or on a larger card inserted into a special slot on the motherboard. In larger computers, the CPU may reside on several circuit boards.

channel   Discussion group where chat users convene to discuss a topic.

character formatting   In a word processor, settings that control the attributes of individual text characters, such as font, type size, type style, and color.

characters per second (cps)   A measure of the speed of impact printers such as dot matrix printers.

chat   One of the services available to users of the Internet and some online services. Using special chat software or Web-based chatting tools, users can exchange messages with one another in real time.

choose   See *activate*.

circuit board   A rigid rectangular card—consisting of chips and electronic circuitry—that ties the processor to other hardware. In a personal computer, the primary circuit board (to which all components are attached) is called the *motherboard*.

click-and-mortar store   A business such as a retail store that has one or more physical locations as well as an online presence such as a Web site. Customers can conduct transactions with such a business by visiting a physical location or using its Web site.

client   An application program on a user's computer that requests information from another computer, such as a network server or Web host, over a network or the Internet. The term also may be used to refer to the computer itself, as it requests services via a network.

client/server network   A hierarchical network strategy in which the processing is shared by a server and numerous clients. In this type of network, clients provide the user interface, run applications, and request services from the server. The server contributes storage, printing, and some or all processing services.

Clipboard   A holding area maintained by the operating system in memory. The Clipboard is used for storing text, graphics, sound, video, or other data that has been copied or cut from a document. After data has been placed in the Clipboard, it can be inserted from the Clipboard into other documents, in the same application, or in a different application.

clock cycle   In a processor, the amount of time required to turn a transistor off and back on again. Also called a *tick*. A processor can execute an instruction in a given number of clock cycles, so as a computer's clock speed (the number of clock cycles it generates per second) increases, so does the number of instructions it can carry out each second.

clock speed   A measure of a processor's operating speed, currently measured in megahertz (MHz, or millions of cycles per second) or gigahertz (GHz, or billions of cycles per second). A computer's operating speed is based on the number of clock cycles, or ticks, it generates per second. For example, if a computer's clock speed is 800 MHz, it "ticks" 800 million times per second.

cluster   On a magnetic disk (such as a hard disk), a group of sectors that are treated as a single data-storage unit. The number of sectors per disk can vary, depending on the type of disk and the manner in which it is formatted.

coaxial cable (coax)   A cable composed of a single conductive wire wrapped in a conductive wire mesh shield with an insulator in between.

command   An instruction issued to the computer. The user can issue commands, usually by choosing from a menu, clicking an on-screen tool or icon, or pressing a combination of keys. Application programs and the operating system also issue commands to the computer.

command-line interface   A user interface that enables the user to interact with the software by typing strings of characters at a prompt.

compact disc (CD)   A type of optical storage medium, identical to audio CDs. The type of CD used in computers is called *compact disc read-only memory (CD-ROM)*. As the device's name implies, you cannot change the information on the disc, just as you cannot record over an audio CD. Standard compact discs can store either 650 MB or 700 MB of computer data, or 70 minutes or 80 minutes of audio data.

compact disc read-only memory (CD-ROM)   The most common type of optical storage medium. In CD-ROM, data is written in a series of lands and pits on the surface of a compact disc (CD), which can be read by a laser in a CD-ROM drive.

computer   An electronic device used to process data, converting the data into information that is useful to people.

computer system   A four-part system that consists of hardware, software, data, and a user.

configure   To adapt a computer to a specific need by selecting from a range of hardware or software options. Configuration may include installing new or replacement hardware or software or changing settings in existing hardware or software.

contact information   Data that can help communicate with individuals or businesses, such as names, mailing addresses, phone numbers, e-mail addresses, and other details. This kind of information is often stored and managed in special software, such as contact-management software, personal information managers, or e-mail programs.

contact-management software   See *personal information manager*.

contact manager   See *personal information manager*.

control unit   The component of the CPU that contains the instruction set. The control unit directs the flow of data throughout the computer system. See also *instruction set*.

cookie   A special text file that a Web server places on a visitor's computer. A cookie may store information about your visit at a Web site, or it may store personal information such as credit card data. Web sites create cookies and store them on the user's computer.

cookie-management utility   A program that allows the user to control the handling of cookies on the PC. Using a cookie-management program, you can determine what types of cookies to allow on your system and can selectively remove cookies at any time.

Copy command   An application command that makes a duplicate of data selected from a document and stores it in the Clipboard without removing the data from the original document. The data then can be used in other documents and other applications.

cps   See *characters per second*.

CPU   See *central processing unit*.

credit report   A document that lists all your financial accounts that can be a source of credit or that you can use for making purchases or for other transactions. These include bank accounts, mortgages, credit cards, and others.

CRT   See *cathode ray tube*.

cursor   A graphic symbol on the screen that indicates where the next keystroke or command will appear when entered. Also called the *insertion point*.

cursor-movement keys   On a computer keyboard, the keys that direct the movement of the on-screen cursor or insertion point, including the up, down, left, and right arrows and the HOME, END, PAGE UP, and PAGE DOWN keys.

Cut command   An application command that removes data selected from a document and stores it in the Clipboard. The data is no longer a part of the original document. While in the Clipboard, the data can be used in other documents or applications.

D

data   Raw facts, numbers, letters, or symbols that the computer processes into meaningful information.

data area   The part of the disk that remains free to store information after the logical formatting process has created the boot sector, file allocation table (FAT), and root folder.

data bus   An electrical path composed of parallel wires that connect the CPU, memory, and other hardware on the motherboard. The number of wires determines the amount of data that can be transferred across the bus at one time.

datagram   The term for data packets when traversing the Internet. A datagram (or packet) is a piece of a larger message that has been broken up for transmission over the Internet.

decimal number system   The system that uses 10 digits to represent numbers; also called *base 10*.

degaussing   The process of disrupting a magnetic field. If a floppy disk becomes degaussed, for example, the data stored on it can be corrupted or destroyed.

density   A measure of the quality of a magnetic disk's surface. The higher a disk's density, the more data the disk can store.

deselect   The opposite of *select*. In many applications, the user can select, or highlight, blocks of text or objects for editing. By clicking the mouse in a different location or pressing a cursor-movement key, the user removes the highlighting and the text or objects are no longer selected.

desktop   In a computer operating system, a graphical workspace in which all of the computer's available resources (such as files, programs, printers, Internet tools, and utilities) can be easily accessed by the user. In such systems, the desktop is a col-ored background on which the user sees small pictures, called *icons*. The user accesses various resources by choosing icons on the desktop.

desktop computer   A full-size personal computer whose system unit is designed to sit on top of a desk or table; such computers are not considered to be portable. One variation of the desktop model is the *tower model*, whose system unit can stand upright on the floor.

device   Any electronic component attached to or part of a computer; hardware.

dialog box   A special-purpose window that appears when the user issues certain commands in a program or graphical operating system. A dialog box gets its name from the "dialog" it conducts with the user as the program seeks the information it needs to perform a task.

digital   The use of the numerals 1 and 0 (digits) to express data in a computer. The computer recognizes the numeral 1 as an "on" state of a transistor, whereas a 0 represents an "off" state.

digital camera   A camera that converts light intensities into digital data. Digital cameras are used to record images that can be viewed and edited on a computer.

digital pen   See *pen*.

Digital Video Disc (DVD)   A high-density optical medium capable of storing a full-length movie on a single disc the size of a standard compact disc (CD). Unlike a standard CD, which stores data on only one side, a DVD-format disc stores data on both sides. Using compression technologies and very fine data areas on the disc's surface, newer-generation DVDs can store several gigabytes of data.

Digital Video Disc-RAM (DVD-RAM)   A type of optical device that allows users to record, erase, and re-record data on a special disc. Using video editing software, you can record your own digitized videos onto a DVD-RAM disc, and then play them back in any DVD player. (However, special encoding makes it impossible to copy movies from commercial DVD onto a DVD-RAM disc.) DVD-RAM drives can read DVDs, DVD-R discs, CD-R discs, CD-RW discs, and standard CDs.

digitize   To convert an image or a sound into a series of binary numbers (1s and 0s) that can be stored in a computer.

DIMM   See *dual in-line memory module*.

directory   See *folder*.

disk   A storage medium commonly used in computers. Two types of disks are used: magnetic disks, which store data as charged particles on the disk's surface; and optical discs, which use lasers to read data embossed on the disc in a series of lands and pits.

disk drive   A storage device that holds, spins, reads data from, and writes data to a disk.

diskette   A removable magnetic disk encased in a plastic sleeve. Also called *floppy disk* or *floppy*.

diskette drive   A device that holds a removable floppy disk when in use; read/write heads read and write data to the diskette.

display adapter   See *video card*.

distributed application   A program that is divided into parts, each of which executes on a different computer. In essence, the program's execution is distributed across multiple systems.

distributed computing   A system configuration in which two or more computers in a network share applications, storage, and processing power. Also called *distributed processing*.

document   A computer file consisting of a compilation of one or more kinds of data. There are many types, including text documents, spreadsheets, graphics files, and so on. A document, which a user can open and use, is different from a program file, which is required by a software program to operate.

document area   In many software applications, the portion of the program's interface in which the active document appears. In this part of the interface, the user can work directly with the document and its contents. Also called *document window*.

document format   In productivity applications, a setting that affects the appearance of the entire document, such as page size, page orientation, and the presence of headers or footers.

document window   See *document area*.

DOS   Stands for *Disk Operating System*. A popular operating system in early personal computers, DOS featured a command-line interface. Though limited in its power and ability to harness computing resources, DOS remained popular because of its stability and the abundance of applications that ran under it.

dot matrix printer   A type of impact printer that creates characters on a page by using small pins to strike an inked ribbon, pressing ink onto the paper. The arrangement of pins in the print head creates a matrix of dots—hence the device's name.

dot pitch   The distance between phosphor dots on a monitor. The highest-resolution monitors have the smallest dot pitch.

dots per inch (dpi)   A measure of resolution commonly applied to printers, scanners, and other devices that input or output text or images. The more dots per inch, the higher the resolution. For example, if a printer has a resolution of 600 dpi, it can print 600 dots across and 600 down in a one-inch square, for a total of 360,000 dots in one square inch.

dpi   See *dots per inch*.

driver   A small program that accepts requests for action from the operating system and causes a device, such as a printer, to execute the requests.

dual in-line memory module (DIMM)   One type of circuit board containing RAM chips.

dual-scan LCD   An improved passive-matrix technology for flat-panel monitors in which pixels are scanned twice as often, reducing the effects of blurry graphics and submarining (an effect that occurs when the mouse pointer blurs or disappears when it is moved).

dumpster diving   The act of searching through trash in hopes of finding valuable personal information such as account numbers, passwords, or Social Security numbers; commonly practiced by identity thieves.

DVD   See *Digital Video Disc*.

DVD-R   See *DVD-Recordable*.

DVD-RAM   See *Digital Video Disc-RAM*.

DVD-Recordable (DVD-R)   An optical disc drive that can record data onto the surface of a special, recordable DVD disc. Once data has been written to the disc, it cannot be overwritten.

E

EBCDIC   See *Extended Binary Coded Decimal Interchange Code*.

e-commerce   See *electronic commerce*.

edit   To make modifications to an existing document file.

electronic commerce   The practice of conducting business transactions online, such as selling products from a World Wide Web site. The process often involves the customer's providing personal or credit card information online, presenting special security concerns. Also called *e-commerce*.

Electronic Communications Privacy Act   A federal law (enacted in 1986) that prevents unlawful access to voice communications by wire. It originally regulated electronic wiretaps and provided the basis for laws defining illegal access to electronic communications, including computer information. It is the basis for protection against unreasonable governmental intrusion into Internet usage, stored electronic communications, and e-mail.

electronic mail   A system for exchanging written, voice, and video messages through a computer network. Also called *e-mail*.

e-mail   See *electronic mail*.

e-mail address   An address that identifies an individual user of an electronic mail system, enabling the person to send and receive e-mail messages. The e-mail address consists of a user name, the "at" symbol (@), and the DNS address.

e-mail client   See *e-mail program*.

e-mail program   Software that lets you create, send, and receive e-mail messages. Also called an *e-mail client*.

embedded operating system   A computer operating system that is built into the circuitry of an electronic device—unlike a PC's operating system, which resides on a magnetic disk. Embedded operating systems are typically found in devices such as PDAs.

encryption   The process of encoding and decoding data, making it useless to any system that cannot decode (decrypt) it.

enterprise directory   A collection of data about the users of a network and the computer resources of the network. This database typically is managed by the network operating system, which resides on a network server.

Ethernet   The most common network protocol. Also called *10Base-T*.

Event Viewer   In later versions of Windows, a program that records certain conditions, such as errors, and creates a log that is usable by the system's user or administrator.

execute   To load and carry out a program or a specific set of instructions. Executing is also called *running*.

expansion board   A device that enables the user to configure or customize a computer to perform specific tasks or to enhance performance. An expansion board—also called a *card*, *adapter*, or *board*—contains a special set of chips and circuitry that add functionality to the computer. An expansion board may be installed to add fax/modem capabilities to the computer, for example, or to provide sound or video-editing capabilities.

expansion slot   The area of the motherboard into which expansion boards are inserted, connecting them to the PC's bus.

Extended ASCII   An extension of the ASCII character set, which specifies the characters for values from 128 to 255. These characters include punctuation marks, pronunciation symbols, and graphical symbols.

Extended Binary Coded Decimal Interchange Code (EBCDIC) An eight-bit code that defines 256 symbols. It is still used in IBM mainframe and midrange systems, but it is rarely encountered in personal computers.

extranet   A network connection that enables external users to access a portion of an organization's internal network, usually via an Internet connection. External users have access to specific parts of the internal network but are forbidden to access other areas, which are protected by firewalls.

F

Fair Credit Reporting Act   A federal law (enacted in 1970) that mandates that personal information assembled by credit reporting agencies must be accurate, fair, and private. It allows individuals to review and update their credit record as well as dispute the entries.

FAQ   See *frequently asked questions*.

Fast Ethernet   A networking technology, also called *100Base-T*, that uses the same network cabling scheme as Ethernet but uses different network interface cards to achieve data transfer speeds of up to 100 Mbps.

FAT   See *file allocation table*.

fiber-optic cable   A thin strand of glass wrapped in a protective coating. Fiber-optic cable transfers data by means of pulsating beams of light.

file   A set of related computer data (used by a person) or program instructions (used by an application or operating system) that has been given a name.

file allocation table (FAT)   In a diskette or hard disk, a log created during the logical formatting process that records the location of each file and the status of each sector on the disk.

file server   The central computer of a network; used for shared storage. A server may store software applications, databases, and data files for the network's users. Depending on the way a server is used, it also may be called a *network server, application server*, or *server*.

file server network   A hierarchical network strategy in which the server is used to store and forward files to the nodes. Each node runs its own applications.

file system   In an operating system, a logical method for managing the storage of data on a disk's surface.

file transfer protocol (FTP)   A set of rules that dictate the format in which data is sent from one computer to another.

filter   In an e-mail program, a tool that allows the user to decide how messages are handled. For example, you can create a filter that automatically deletes messages from a certain sender or that stores certain messages in a specific folder. In e-mail programs, a filter also may be called a *rule*.

Financial Modernization Act of 1999   A federal law that requires companies to give consumers notice of their privacy and information-sharing practices.

firewall   A method for protecting private networks from unauthorized access via a public network, such as the Internet. Firewalls are available in both hardware and software form, and use a variety of techniques to block unauthorized users from accessing a network.

Fire Wire   See *IEEE 1394*.

first-party cookie   A cookie placed on a user's computer by the Web site he or she is currently viewing. First-party cookies are persistent and usually store preferences the user has set for viewing the site. Some first-party cookies store information that can personally identify the user.

flat-panel display   A thin, lightweight monitor used in laptop and notebook computers. Most flat-panel displays use LCD technology.

floppy   See *diskette*.

floppy disk   See *diskette*.

folder   A tool for organizing data stored on a disk. A folder contains a list of files and other folders stored on the disk. A disk can hold many folders, which can in turn store many files and other folders. Also called a *directory*.

font   A family of alphanumeric characters, symbols, and punctuation marks that share the same design. Modern applications provide many different fonts and enable users to use different fonts in the same document. Also called a *typeface*.

format   (1) As relating to magnetic storage devices, the layout of tracks and sectors in which data is stored. (2) In productivity applications, a setting that affects the appearance of a document or part of a document.

formatting   (1) The process of magnetically mapping a disk with a series of tracks and sectors where data will be stored. Also called *initializing*. (2) The process of applying formatting options (such as character or paragraph formats) to a document.

formula   A mathematical equation within a cell of a spreadsheet. To identify it and distinguish it from other spreadsheet entries, a formula begins with a special symbol, such as a plus sign or an equal sign.

formula bar   In spreadsheet programs, a special text box that displays the data or formula entered in the active cell. The user may be able to enter or edit data or formulas in this box.

frame   (1) In networking, a small block of data to be transmitted over a network. A frame includes an identifying header and the actual data to be sent. Also called a *packet*. (2) In animation, a single still image that, when viewed with many other images in rapid succession, creates the illusion of motion. (3) In many software applications, a special tool that enables the user to place an object—such as a text box or an image from a separate file—in a document. The frame surrounds the object in the document, enabling the user to position and resize the object as needed.

Freedom of Information Act   A federal law (enacted in 1966) that allows individuals to view and amend personal information kept about them by any governmental entity.

Freescale   A subsidiary of Motorola, Inc., that produces microprocessors used in many Apple computers, as well as in large-scale UNIX-based systems.

frequently asked questions (FAQ)   A document routinely developed by a newsgroup; it lists questions most commonly asked in the newsgroup, along with their answers. FAQs help a newsgroup's members avoid the repeated posting of the same information to the group.

FTP   See *file transfer protocol*.

FTP client software   Programs that enable users to download files from an FTP site.

FTP server   A computer used to store FTP sites, many containing thousands of individual programs and files.

FTP site   A collection of files stored on an FTP server; users can copy files from and to their own computer.

function keys   The part of the keyboard that can be used to quickly activate commands; designated F1, F2, and so on.

G

game controller   A specialized type of input device that enables the user to interact with computer games. Two popular types of game controllers are game pads and joysticks.

game pad   A type of game controller that usually provides two sets of controls—one for each hand. These devices are extremely flexible and are used to control a wide variety of game systems.

gateway   A computer system that can translate one network protocol into another so that data can be transmitted between two dissimilar networks.

GB   See *gigabyte*.

GHz   See *gigahertz*.

Gigabit Ethernet   The newest addition to Ethernet technology; capable of transferring 10 Gb of data per second. Gigabit Ethernet also can carry about 900 video signals at once, at about 1.5 MB per second of digital video.

gigabyte (GB)   Equivalent to approximately one billion bytes; a typical measurement of data storage.

gigahertz (GHz)   Equivalent to one billion cycles per second; a common measure of processor clock speed.

graphical user interface (GUI)   A user interface in which actions are initiated when the user selects an icon, a toolbar button, or an option from a pull-down menu with the mouse or other pointing device. GUIs also represent documents, programs, and devices on screen as graphical elements that the user can use by clicking or dragging.

GUI   See *graphical user interface*.

H

HAN   See *home area network*.

handheld personal computer   A personal computer that is small enough to be held in one hand.

hard disk   A nonremovable magnetic storage device included in most PCs that stores data on a stack of aluminum platters, each coated with iron oxide, enclosed in a case. The device includes the hard disk platters, a spindle on which the platters spin, a read/write head for each side of each platter, and a sealed chamber that encloses the disks and spindle. Many hard disks also include the drive controller, although the controller is a separate unit on some hard disks. Also called a *hard drive*.

hard drive   See *hard disk*.

hardware   The physical components of a computer, including processor and memory chips, input/output devices, modems, and cables.

header   The initial part of a data packet being transmitted across a network. The header contains information about the type of data in the payload, the source and destination of the data, and a sequence number so that data from multiple packets can be reassembled at the receiving computer in the proper order.

helper application   A program that must be added to your browser in order to play special content files—especially those with multimedia content—in real time. Also called *plug-in application*.

hertz (Hz)   The frequency of electrical vibrations, or cycles, per second.

high-capacity floppy disk   A small, removable disk that resembles a standard diskette, but provides much higher data storage capacity. Typically, high-capacity floppy disks have data densities of 100 MB or greater.

home area network (HAN)   A local area network that exists within a home, used to connect the computers and peripheral devices in the home. A HAN is commonly used to allow multiple users to share a single Internet connection.

host   A computer that provides services to other computers that connect to it. Host computers provide file transfer, communications services, and access to the Internet's high-speed data lines.

hot swapping   The process of removing a device (such as a disk drive) from a computer and replacing it without shutting down the system first and without disrupting the system's operations. Devices that can be changed in this manner are called *hot-swappable*.

hot-swappable hard disk   A magnetic storage device similar to a removable hard disk. A removable box encloses the disk, drive, and read/write heads in a sealed container. This type of hard disk can be added to or removed from a server without shutting down the server.

HTML   See *hypertext markup language*.

HTTP   See *hypertext transfer protocol*.

hub   In a network, a device that connects nodes and servers together at a central point.

hyperlink   See *hypertext link.*

hypertext   A software technology that provides fast and flexible access to information. The user can jump to a topic by selecting it on screen; used to create Web pages and help screens.

hypertext link   A word, icon, or other object that when clicked jumps to another location on the document or another Web page. Also called *hyperlink* or *link.*

hypertext markup language (HTML)   A page-description language used on the World Wide Web that defines the hypertext links between documents.

hypertext transfer protocol (HTTP)   A set of file transfer rules used on the World Wide Web; it controls the way information is shared.

Hz   See *hertz.*

I

I/O   See *input/output.*

IBM   Refers to the IBM Corporation, a leading maker of computer hardware, software, and technologies.

icon   A graphical screen element that executes one or more commands when clicked with a mouse or other pointing device.

identity (ID) theft   A type of crime in which a thief uses someone else's identity to obtain money or conduct business transactions. This crime usually involves the theft of the victim's personal information, such as a Social Security number, credit card number, or bank account information.

IEEE 1394   An expansion bus technology that supports data-transfer rates of up to 400 Mbps. Also called *FireWire.*

IM   See *instant messaging.*

image scanner   An input device that digitizes printed images. Sensors determine the intensity of light reflected from the page, and the light intensities are converted to digital data that can be viewed and manipulated by the computer. Sometimes called simply a *scanner.*

impact printer   A type of printer that creates images by striking an inked ribbon, pressing ink from the ribbon onto a piece of paper. Examples of impact printers are dot-matrix printers and line printers.

initializing   See *formatting.*

ink jet printer   A type of nonimpact printer that produces images by spraying ink onto the page.

input device   Computer hardware that accepts data and instructions from the user. Examples of input devices include the keyboard, mouse, joystick, pen, trackball, scanner, bar code reader, microphone, and touch screen.

input/output (I/O)   Communications between the user and the computer or between hardware components that result in the transfer of data.

input/output (I/O) device   A device that performs both input and output functions. Modems and network interface cards are examples of input/output devices.

insertion point   See *cursor.*

instant messaging (IM)   Chat software that enables users to set up buddy lists and open a window to "chat" when anyone on the list is online.

instruction set   Machine language instructions that define all the operations a CPU can perform.

integrated pointing device   A pointing device built into the computer's keyboard; consists of a small joystick positioned near the middle of the keyboard, typically between the G and H keys. The joystick is controlled with either forefinger. Two buttons that perform the same function as mouse buttons are just beneath the spacebar and are pressed with the thumb. One type of integrated pointing device, developed by IBM, is called *TrackPoint.*

Intel   A leading manufacturer of microprocessors. Intel invented the first microprocessor, which was used in electronic calculators. Intel's product line includes the Pentium, Celeron, and Itanium processor families.

Internet   Originally, a link between ARPANET, NSFnet, and other networks. Today, a worldwide network of networks.

Internet relay chat (IRC)   A multiuser system made up of channels that people join for exchanging messages either publicly or privately. Messages are exchanged in real time, meaning the messages are transmitted to other users on the channel as they are typed in.

Internet service provider (ISP)   An intermediary service between the Internet backbone and the user, providing easy and relatively inexpensive access to shell accounts, direct TCP/IP connections, and high-speed access through dedicated data circuits.

internetworking   The process of connecting separate networks together.

intranet   An internal network whose interface and accessibility are modeled after an Internet-based Web site. Only internal users are allowed to access information or resources on the intranet; if connected to an external network or the Internet, the intranet's resources are protected from outside access by firewalls.

IRC   See *Internet relay chat.*

ISP   See *Internet service provider.*

J

joystick   An input device used to control the movement of on-screen components; typically used in video games.

K

KB   See *kilobyte.*

keyboard   The most common input device, used to enter letters, numbers, symbols, punctuation, and commands into the computer. Computer keyboards typically include numeric, alphanumeric, cursor-movement, modifier, and function keys, as well as other special keys.

keyword   A term or phrase used as the basis for a search when looking for information on the World Wide Web.

kilobyte (KB)   Equivalent to 1,024 bytes; a common measure of data storage.

L

L1 cache   See *Level-1 cache*.

L2 cache   See *Level-2 cache*.

L3 cache   See *Level-3 cache*.

label   Descriptive text used in a spreadsheet cell to describe the data in a column or row.

LAN   See *local area network*.

land   A flat area on the metal surface of a CD-ROM that reflects the laser light into the sensor of an optical disc drive. See also *pit*.

laptop computer   See *notebook computer*.

laser printer   A quiet, fast printer that produces high-quality output. A laser beam focused on an electrostatic drum creates an image to which powdered toner adheres, and that image is transferred to paper.

LCD monitor   See *liquid crystal display monitor*.

Level-1 (L1) cache   A type of cache memory built directly into the microprocessor. Also called *on-board cache*.

Level-2 (L2) cache   A type of cache memory that is external to the microprocessor but is positioned between the CPU and RAM. Also called *external cache*.

Level-3 (L3) cache   A type of cache memory that is built into the computer's motherboard.

link   See *hypertext link*.

Linux   A freely available version of the UNIX operating system. Developed by a worldwide cooperative of programmers in the 1990s, Linux is a feature-rich, 32-bit, multiuser, multiprocessor operating system that runs on virtually any hardware platform.

liquid crystal display (LCD) monitor   A flat-panel monitor on which an image is created when the liquid crystal becomes charged; used primarily in notebook computers.

listserv   An e-mail server that contains a list of names and enables users to communicate with others on the list in an ongoing discussion.

local area network (LAN)   A system of PCs located relatively near to one another and connected by wire or a wireless link. A LAN permits simultaneous access to data and resources, enhances personal communication, and simplifies backup procedures.

logical formatting   An operating system function in which tracks and sectors are mapped on the surface of a disk. This mapping creates the master boot record, FAT, root folder (also called the *root directory*), and the data area. Also called *soft formatting* and *low-level formatting*.

logical operation   One of the two types of operations a computer can perform. Logical operations usually involve making a comparison, such as determining whether two values are equal. See also *arithmetic operation*.

M

Mac OS   See *Macintosh operating system*.

Macintosh operating system (Mac OS)   The operating system that runs on machines built by Apple Computer. The Mac OS was the first commercially available operating system to use a graphical user interface, to utilize Plug and Play hardware compatibility, to feature built-in networking, and to support common user access.

magnetic disk   A round, flat disk covered with a magnetic material (such as iron oxide), the most commonly used storage medium. Data is written magnetically on the disk and can be recorded over and over. The magnetic disk is the basic component of the diskette and hard disk.

magnetic storage   A storage technology in which data is recorded when iron particles are polarized on a magnetic storage medium.

mail server   In an e-mail system, the server on which messages received from the post office server are stored until the recipients access their mailboxes and retrieve the messages.

mainframe computer   A large, multiuser computer system designed to handle massive amounts of input, output, and storage. A mainframe is usually composed of one or more powerful CPUs connected to many input/output devices, called *terminals*, or to personal computers. Mainframe systems are typically used in businesses requiring the maintenance of huge databases or simultaneous processing of multiple complex tasks.

MAN   See *metropolitan area network*.

mb   See *megabit*.

mbps   See *megabits per second*.

MB   See *megabyte*.

MBps   See *megabytes per second*.

mechanical mouse   A mouse that tracks motion mechanically, using a ball, a set of rollers, and built-in sensors. As the mouse is moved across a flat surface, the ball's rolling motion is detected by the rollers and sensors, which send data about the mouse's direction and speed to the computer.

media   The plural form of the word *medium*. See *medium*.

medium   (1) In storage technology, a medium is material used to store data, such as the magnetic coating on a disk or tape, or the metallic platter in a compact disc. (2) In networking, a medium is a means of conveying a signal across the network, such as a cable.

megabit (mb)   Equivalent to approximately one million bits. A common measure of data transfer speeds.

megabits per second (mbps)   Equivalent to one million bits of data per second.

megabyte (MB)   Equivalent to approximately one million bytes. A common measure of data storage capacity.

megabytes per second (MBps)   Equivalent to one million bytes of data per second.

megahertz (MHz)   Equivalent to millions of cycles per second. A common measure of clock speed.

memory   A collection of chips on the motherboard, or on a circuit board attached to the motherboard, where all computer processing and program instructions are stored while in use. The computer's memory enables the CPU to retrieve data quickly for processing.

memory address   A number used by the CPU to locate each piece of data in memory.

menu   A list of commands or functions displayed on screen for selection by the user.

menu bar   A graphical screen element—located above the document area of an application window—that displays a list of the types of commands available to the user. When the user selects an option from the menu bar, a list appears displaying the commands related to that menu option.

mesh topology   An expensive, redundant cabling scheme for local area networks, in which each node is connected to every other node by a unique cable.

metasearch engine   A Web-based search engine that compiles the search results from several other engines, allowing for a wider range of results.

metropolitan area network (MAN)   A larger version of a local area network (LAN); it can be used to connect computer systems in buildings in the same town or city.

MHz   See *megahertz*.

microcode   Code that details the individual tasks the computer must perform to complete each instruction in the instruction set.

microcomputer   See *personal computer (PC)*.

microprocessor   Integrated circuits on one or more chips that make up the computer's CPU. Microprocessors are composed of silicon or other material etched with many tiny electronic circuits.

MIDI   See *Musical Instrument Digital Interface*.

midrange computer   See *minicomputer*.

minicomputer   A midsize, multiuser computer capable of handling more input and output than a PC but with less processing power and storage than a mainframe. Also called a *midrange computer*.

mobile computer   Any type of computer system that can the user can carry. Examples include notebook computers and PDAs.

modem   Abbreviation for *modulator/demodulator*. An input/output device that allows computers to communicate through telephone lines. A modem converts outgoing digital data into analog signals that can be transmitted over phone lines and converts incoming analog signals into digital data that can be processed by the computer.

modifier keys   Keyboard keys that are used in conjunction with other keys to execute a command. The IBM-PC keyboard includes SHIFT, CTRL, and ALT modifier keys.

monitor   A display screen used to provide computer output to the user. Examples include the cathode ray tube (CRT) monitor, flat-panel monitor, and liquid crystal display (LCD).

motherboard   The main circuit board of the computer; it contains the CPU, memory, expansion slots, bus, and video controller. Also called the *system board*.

mouse   An input device operated by rolling its ball across a flat surface. The mouse is used to control the on-screen pointer by pointing and clicking, double-clicking, or dragging objects on the screen.

multitasking   The capability of an operating system to load multiple programs into memory at one time and to perform two or more processes concurrently, such as printing a document while editing another.

multiuser/multitasking operating system   A powerful operating system that supports more than one user at a time, performing more than one task at a time. UNIX is an example of a multiuser/multitasking operating system.

Musical Instrument Digital Interface (MIDI)   A specialized category of input/output devices used in the creation, recording, editing, and performance of music.

N

.NET   A development environment that combines several programming languages, including Visual Basic, C++, C#, and J#. Using .NET, developers can write programs for Windows, the World Wide Web, and PocketPC.

.NET Framework   A set of technologies that support Web-based applications, large databases, e-commerce servers, and distributed applications.

network   (1) A system of interconnected computers that communicate with one another and share applications, data, and hardware components. (2) The act of connecting computers together in order to permit the transfer of data and programs between users.

network interface card (NIC)   A circuit board that controls the exchange of data over a network.

network news transfer protocol (NNTP)   A set of rules that enable news servers to exchange articles with other news servers.

network operating system (NOS)   A group of programs that manage the resources on a network.

network server   See *file server*.

network version   An application program especially designed to work within a network environment. Users access the software from a shared storage device.

news   A public bulletin board service on the Internet; organized into discussion groups representing specific topics of interest.

news server   A host computer that exchanges articles with other Internet servers.

newsgroup   An electronic storage space where users can post messages to other users, carry on extended conversations, and trade information.

newsreader   A software program that enables the user to post and read articles in an Internet newsgroup.

NIC   See *network interface card*.

NNTP   See *network news transfer protocol*.

NNTP server   Another name for news servers using the network news transfer protocol.

node   An individual computer or device that is connected to a network.

nonimpact printer   A type of printer that creates images on paper without striking the page in any way. Two common examples are ink jet printers, which spray tiny droplets of ink onto the page, and laser printers, which use heat to adhere particles of toner to specific points on the page.

nonvolatile   The tendency for memory to retain data even when the computer is turned off (as is the case with ROM).

NOS   See *network operating system*.

notebook computer   A small, portable computer with an attached flat screen; typically powered by battery or AC and weighing less than 10 pounds. Notebook computers commonly provide most of the same features found in full-size desktop computers, including a color monitor, a fast processor, a modem, and adequate RAM and storage for business-class software applications. Also called *laptop computer*.

NSFnet   Acronym for *National Science Foundation Network*. A network developed by the National Science Foundation (NSF) to accommodate the many users attempting to access the five academic research centers created by the NSF.

numeric keypad   The part of a keyboard that looks and works like a calculator keypad; it has 10 digits and mathematical operators.

O

object embedding   The process of integrating a copy of data from one application into another, as from a spreadsheet to a word processor. The data retains the formatting applied to it in the original application, but its relationship with the original file is destroyed.

object linking   The process of integrating a copy of data from one application into another so that the data retains a link to the original document. Thereafter, a change in the original document also appears in the linked data in the second application.

Object Linking and Embedding (OLE)   A Windows feature that combines object embedding and linking functions. OLE allows the user to construct a document containing data from a single point in time or one in which the data is constantly updated.

OCR   See *optical character recognition*.

OLE   See *Object Linking and Embedding*.

online   (1) The state of being connected to, served by, or available through a networked computer system or the Internet. For example, when a user is browsing the World Wide Web, that person's computer is said to be online. (2) Describes any computer-related device that is turned on and connected, such as a printer or modem that is in use or ready for use.

online banking   The use of Web-based services to conduct transactions with a bank, such as managing accounts or paying bills.

online finance   The use of Web-based services to conduct financial transactions such as investing or buying insurance.

online service   A telecommunications service that supplies e-mail and information search tools.

online shopping   The use of Web-based services to make purchases from online retailers, such as Web-based bookstores or clothing stores.

online store   A business that operates only online, such as through a Web site, and has no physical location.

operating system (OS)   The master control program that provides an interface for a user to communicate with the computer; it manages hardware devices, manages and maintains disk file systems, and supports application programs.

optical character recognition (OCR)   Technology that enables a computer to translate optically scanned text into character codes, which then can be edited.

optical drive   A storage device that writes data to and reads data from an optical storage medium such as a compact disc. Such devices typically use a focused beam of light, such as a laser, to read and write data.

optical mouse   A pointing device that tracks its location (and the pointer's location on the screen) by using a beam of light, such as a laser, bounced off a reflective surface.

optical storage   Refers to storage systems that use light beams to read data from the surface of an optical disc. Data is stored as a series of lands and pits on the disc's reflective surface. Generally speaking, optical storage systems provide higher storage capacities than typical magnetic storage systems, but they operate at slower speeds.

opt-out option   An option available on many Web sites and registration forms. By selecting this option, the user affirms that he or she does not want to be contacted by the company or its partners, and that he or she does not want the company to sell or share information about him or her.

OS   See *operating system*.

output device   A hardware component, such as a monitor or printer, that returns processed data to the user.

P

P2P   See *peer-to-peer network*.

packet   A small block of data transmitted over a network that includes an identifying header and the actual data to be sent. Also called a *frame*.

pages per minute (ppm)   A common measure for printer output speed. Consumer-grade laser printers, for example, typically can print from 6 to 10 pages per minute depending on whether text or graphics are being printed. See also *characters per second*.

paragraph   In a word processing program, any series of letters, words, or sentences followed by a hard return. (A hard return is created by pressing the ENTER key.)

paragraph format   A setting that affects the appearance of one or more entire paragraphs, such as line spacing, paragraph spacing, indents, alignment, tab stops, borders, and shading.

parallel interface   A channel through which eight or more data bits can flow simultaneously, such as a computer bus. A parallel interface is commonly used to connect printers to the computer; also called a *parallel port*.

passive matrix LCD   Liquid crystal display technology used for flat-panel monitors; it relies on a grid of transistors arranged by rows and columns. In a passive matrix LCD, the color displayed by each pixel is determined by the electricity coming from the transistors at the end of the row and the top of the column.

Paste command   An application command that copies data from the Clipboard and places it in the document at the position of the insertion point. Data in the Clipboard can be pasted into multiple places in one document, multiple documents, and documents in different applications.

payload   In a packet, the actual data being transmitted across a network or over telephone lines. Also refers to the executable portion of a computer virus or the output produced by a virus.

PC   See *personal computer*.

PC Card   A specialized expansion card the size of a credit card; it fits into a computer and is used to connect new components.

PC-to-TV converter   A hardware device that converts a computer's digital video signals into analog signals for display on a standard television screen.

PC video camera   A small video camera that connects to a special video card on a PC. When used with videoconferencing software, a PC video camera enables users to capture full-motion video images, save them to disk, edit them, and transmit them to other users across a network or the Internet.

PDA   See *personal digital assistant*.

peer-to-peer (P2P) network   A network environment in which all nodes on the network have equal access to at least some of the resources on all other nodes.

peer-to-peer (P2P) service   A special type of connection provided via the Internet that allows connected client computers to communicate and exchange data directly instead of using server computers.

pen   An input device that allows the user to write directly on or point at a special pad or the screen of a pen-based computer, such as a PDA. Also called a *stylus*.

persistent cookie   A cookie that remains on the user's hard disk after the current browsing session is ended. Persistent cookies are usually set to "expire" on a certain date; until then, they remain active.

personal computer (PC)   The most common type of computer found in an office, classroom, or home. The PC is designed to fit on a desk and be used by one person at a time; also called a *microcomputer*.

personal digital assistant (PDA)   A very small portable computer designed to be held in one hand; used to perform specific tasks, such as creating limited spreadsheets or storing phone numbers.

personal information manager (PIM)   A software program used for collecting and refining information about people, schedules, and tasks. PIMs are also called *contact-management software* or *contact managers*, because these programs are used primarily for managing information about people the user commonly contacts.

PhotoCD   A special optical disc technology, developed by Kodak, for digitizing and storing standard film-based photographs.

PIM   See *personal information manager*.

pit   A depressed area on the metal surface of a compact disc or digital video disc that scatters laser light. Also see *land*.

pixel   Contraction of *picture element*. One or more dots that express a portion of an image on a computer screen.

plug-in application   See *helper application*.

point   (1) A standard unit used in measuring fonts. One point equals $\frac{1}{72}$ inch in height. (2) To move the mouse pointer around the screen by manipulating the mouse or another type of pointing device.

pointer   An on-screen object used to select text; access menus; move files; and interact with programs, files, or data represented graphically on the screen.

pointing device   A device that enables the user to freely move an on-screen pointer and to select text, menu options, icons, and other on-screen objects. Two popular types of pointing devices are mice and trackballs.

POP   See *post office protocol*.

POP server   A server computer on an e-mail system that manages the flow of e-mail messages and attachments, using the post office protocol.

pop-up   See *pop-up window*.

pop-up blocker   A software program that prevents unwanted pop-up windows from appearing on the user's screen when browsing the Web.

pop-up window   A secondary browser window that unexpectedly appears when browsing the Web. Pop-up windows commonly contain advertisements and often host spyware.

post   To place a document online, such as on a Web server or a news server, so that it may be accessed via the Internet or a network. Also called *publishing*.

POST   See *power on self test*.

post office protocol (POP)   A networking protocol used by e-mail servers to manage the sending and receiving of e-mail messages and attachments.

power on self test (POST)   A routine stored in a computer's BIOS that runs whenever the computer is started. This routine conducts checks to determine whether various parts of the system are functioning properly.

ppm   See *pages per minute*.

presentation   A collection of slides that can be shown to an audience. Presentations are created using special software, called a *presentation program*.

presentation program   Software that enables the user to create professional-quality images, called *slides*, that can be shown as part of a presentation. Slides can be presented in any number of ways, but they are typically displayed on a large screen or video monitor while the presenter speaks to the audience.

primary e-mail account   An individual's main e-mail account, which is usually established as part of an account with an Internet service provider.

print head In impact printers, a device that strikes an inked ribbon, pressing ink onto the paper to create characters or graphics.

print server A special network server that is devoted to managing printing tasks for multiple users. A print server makes it easy for many users to share a single printer.

printer An output device that produces a hard copy on paper. Two types are impact and nonimpact.

Privacy Act of 1974 A federal law that restricts federal agencies from sharing information about individuals without their written consent.

processing A complex procedure by which a computer transforms raw data into useful information.

processor See *central processing unit (CPU)*.

program (1) A set of instructions or code to be executed by the CPU; designed to help users solve problems or perform tasks. Also called *software*. (2) To create a computer program. The process of computer programming is also called *software development*.

prompt In a command-line interface, the on-screen location where the user types commands. A prompt usually provides a blinking cursor to indicate where commands can be typed. Also called a *command prompt*.

protocol A set of rules and procedures that determine how a computer system receives and transmits data.

publish See *post*.

R

RAM See *random access memory*.

random access memory (RAM) A computer's volatile or temporary memory, which exists as chips on the motherboard near the CPU. RAM stores data and programs while they are being used and requires a power source to maintain its integrity.

random access storage device A storage device that can locate data at any point on the storage medium without going through all the data up to that point. Floppy disks, hard disks, and optical discs are examples of random access storage devices.

read-only memory (ROM) A permanent, or nonvolatile, memory chip used to store instructions and data, including the computer's startup instructions.

read/write head The magnetic device within the disk drive that reads, records, and erases data on the disk's surface. A read/write head contains an electromagnet that alters the polarity of magnetic particles on the storage medium. Most disk drives have one read/write head for each side of each disk in the drive.

real-time application An application that responds to certain inputs extremely quickly—thousandths or millionths of a second (milliseconds or microseconds, respectively). Real-time applications are needed to run medical diagnostics equipment, life-support systems, machinery, scientific instruments, and industrial systems.

real-time operating system An operating system designed to support real-time applications.

refresh rate The number of times per second that each pixel on the computer screen is scanned; measured in hertz (Hz).

register High-speed memory locations built directly into the ALU and used to hold instructions and data currently being processed.

resolution The degree of sharpness of an image, determined by the number of pixels on a screen; expressed as a matrix.

restore To replace a damaged or missing file on a hard disk with a copy from a backup.

Right to Financial Privacy Act of 1978 A federal law that requires companies to give consumers notice of their privacy and information-sharing practices.

ring topology A network topology in which network nodes are connected in a circular configuration. Each node examines the data sent through the ring and passes on data not addressed to it.

ROM See *read-only memory*.

root folder The top-level folder on a disk. This primary folder contains all other folders and subfolders stored on the disk. Also called the *root directory*, or sometimes just the *root*.

router A computer device that stores the addressing information of each computer on each LAN or WAN; it uses this information to transfer data along the most efficient path between nodes of a LAN or WAN.

rule See *filter*.

ruler An on-screen tool in a word processor's document window. The ruler shows the position of lines, tab stops, margins, and other parts of the document.

run See *execute*.

S

scanner See *image scanner*.

screen saver A utility program that displays moving images on the screen if no input is received for several minutes; originally developed to prevent an image from being burned into the screen.

scroll To move through an entire document in relation to the document window in order to see parts of the document not currently visible on screen.

scroll bar A vertical or horizontal bar displayed along the side or bottom of a document window that enables the user to scroll horizontally or vertically through a document by clicking an arrow or dragging a box within the scroll bar.

SCSI See *Small Computer System Interface*.

search engine A Web site that uses powerful data-searching techniques to help the user locate Web sites containing specific types of content or information.

secondary e-mail account A backup e-mail account that can be used as a collection place for spam and other unwanted e-mail messages.

sector A segment or division of a track on a disk.

secure sockets layer (SSL)   An Internet protocol that can be used to encrypt any amount of data sent over the Internet between a client computer and a host computer.

secure Web page   A Web page that uses one or more encryption technologies to encode data received from and sent to the user.

select   To highlight a block of text (in a word processor) or range (in a spreadsheet) so the user can perform one or more editing operations on it.

sequential access device   A storage device that must search a storage medium from beginning to end in order to find the data that is needed. Such devices cannot access data randomly. A tape drive is an example of a sequential access device.

serial interface   A channel through which data bits flow one at a time. Serial interfaces are used primarily to connect a mouse or a communications device to the computer. Also called a *serial port*.

server   See *file server*.

session cookie   A cookie that remains on the user's hard disk only during a Web-browsing session. The cookie is deleted when the session ends. Also called a *transient cookie*.

shell   Refers to a GUI environment that can run on top of a command-line operating system, such as Linux or UNIX.

shopping cart   At many e-commerce Web sites, a feature that lets the shopper store, review, and edit items to be purchased before checking out.

shortcut   Any means that enables the user to quickly execute an action or issue a command. On the Windows desktop, for example, icons serve as shortcuts by allowing you to quickly launch programs. Within programs, you may be able to click buttons or press specific keys to quickly perform tasks; these buttons and keystrokes are also shortcuts.

shoulder surfing   A method used by hackers and identity thieves to learn passwords and other personal information from their victims. In shoulder surfing, the thief watches as the victim enters a password or other information at a computer, ATM, phone, or other device.

SIMM   See *single in-line memory module*.

single in-line memory module (SIMM)   One type of circuit board containing memory chips.

single-user/multitasking operating system   An operating system that supports only one user at a time, but allows the user to perform multiple tasks simultaneously, such as running several programs at the same time. Examples include Windows and the Macintosh operating system.

single-user/single-tasking operating system   An operating system that supports only one user at a time and allows the user to perform only one task at a time. Examples include MS-DOS and some operating systems designed for use on handheld computers.

site license   An agreement in which an organization purchases the right to use a program on a limited number of machines. The total cost is less than would be required if individual copies of the software were purchased for all users.

slide   An individual graphic that is part of a presentation. Slides are created and edited in presentation programs.

Small Computer System Interface (SCSI)   A high-speed interface that extends the bus outside the computer, permitting the addition of more peripheral devices than normally could be connected using the available expansion slots.

small outline DIMM (SO-DIMM)   A small-format memory chip found in portable computers.

smart phone   A digital cellular phone that includes many of the features found in a personal digital assistant (PDA), such as schedule management, e-mail, Web access, and others.

snagging   A method used by identity thieves to gather passwords or other personal information from a victim. In snagging, the thief listens in on a telephone extension, through a wiretap, or over a cubicle wall while the victim gives credit card or other personal information to a legitimate agent.

snail mail   A term used to describe the U.S. Postal Service.

social engineering   Describes a variety of methods used by hackers and identity thieves to gather passwords or other personal information from victims. Social engineering usually involves tricking a victim into divulging personal information.

SO-DIMM   See *small outline DIMM*.

software   See *program*.

sound card   An expansion card that records and plays back sound by translating the analog signal from a microphone into a digitized form that the computer can store and process, and then translating the data back into analog signals or sound.

spam   (1) Another term for junk e-mail. (2) To distribute unrequested messages across the Internet or an online service. Spammers often flood newsgroups with messages and send e-mail messages to thousands of individuals. Spam messages often attempt to sell a product or service (like regular junk mail) but frequently carry negative, indecent, or obscene material.

spam blocker   A software program that is designed to prevent unwanted e-mail messages from reaching the user.

spammer   A person who distributes junk e-mail messages.

spawn   To launch a program from within another program. For example, to allow the user to view streaming multimedia content, a Web browser may spawn a second application, such as the QuickTime Player.

speech recognition   An input technology that can translate human speech into text. Some speech-recognition systems enable the user to navigate application programs and issue commands by voice control, as well as to create documents by dictating text; also called *voice recognition*.

sponsored link   In a page of results created by a search engine, a link that has been purchased by a merchant. Sponsored links usually appear before nonsponsored links in search results, or may appear separately from nonsponsored links.

spreadsheet   A grid of columns and rows used for recording and evaluating numbers. Spreadsheets are used primarily for financial analysis, record keeping, and management, as well as to create reports and presentations.

spyware   Software that tracks a computer user's activities and reports the activities back to someone else. Spyware can be used to monitor Internet use, e-mail, and keyboard or mouse actions.

SSL   See *secure sockets layer*.

star topology   A network topology in which network nodes connect to a central hub through which all data is routed.

START button   A Windows 95/98/2000/NT/XP screen element—found on the taskbar—that displays the Start menu when selected.

Start menu   A menu in the Windows 95/98/2000/NT/XP operating systems; the user can open the Start menu by clicking the START button; the Start menu provides tools to locate documents, find help, change system settings, and run programs.

start page   The page that opens automatically when a Web browser launches.

status bar   An on-screen element that appears at the bottom of an application window and displays the current status of various parts of the current document or application, such as the page number, text entry mode, and so on.

storage   The portion of the computer that holds data or programs while they are not being used. Storage media include magnetic disks, optical discs, tape, and cartridges.

storage device   The hardware components that write data to and read data from storage media. For example, a diskette is a type of storage medium, whereas a diskette drive is a storage device.

storage media   The physical components or materials on which data is stored. Diskettes and compact discs are examples of storage media.

stored cookie   See *persistent cookie*.

streaming audio/video   Multimedia content that is sent to the user's desktop in a continuous "stream" from a Web server. Because audio and video files are large, streaming content is sent to the user's disk in pieces; the first piece is temporarily buffered (stored on disk), then played as the next piece is stored and buffered.

stylus   See *pen*.

submarining   In older passive-matrix LCD displays, a problem caused by the monitor's inability to refresh itself fast enough. One characteristic of submarining is the disappearance of the mouse pointer when it moves across the screen.

subscribe   To select a newsgroup so the user can regularly participate in its discussions. After subscribing to a newsgroup in a newsreader program, the program automatically downloads an updated list of articles when it is launched.

Super VGA (SVGA)   An IBM video display standard capable of displaying resolutions up to 1024 x 768 pixels, with 16 million colors.

supercomputer   The largest, fastest, and most powerful type of computer. Supercomputers are often used for scientific and engineering applications and for processing complex models that use very large data sets.

SVGA   See *Super VGA*.

swap in   To load essential parts of a program into memory as required for use.

swap out   To unload, or remove, nonessential parts of a program from memory to make room for needed parts.

switch   A networking device that learns which machine is connected to its port by using the device's IP address.

system board   See *motherboard*.

system clock   The computer's internal clock, which is used to time processing operations. The clock's time intervals are based on the constant, unchanging vibrations of molecules in a quartz crystal; currently measured in megahertz (MHz) or gigahertz (GHz).

system operator (sysop)   In an online discussion group, the person who monitors the discussion.

system software   A computer program that controls the system hardware and interacts with application software. The designation includes the operating system and the network operating system.

system unit   In a personal computer, the case that contains the system's essential hardware components, including the processor, disk drives, and motherboard.

T

tablet PC   A newer type of portable PC, similar in size to a notebook PC; it allows the user to input data and commands with a pen rather than a standard keyboard or pointing device.

tape drive   A magnetic storage device that reads and writes data to the surface of a magnetic tape. Tape drives are generally used for backing up data or restoring the data of a hard disk.

taskbar   A Windows 95/98/2000/NT/XP screen element—displayed on the desktop—that includes the START button and lists the programs currently running on the computer.

TB   See *terabyte*.

telecommuter   A person who works at home or on the road and requires access to a work computer via telecommunications equipment, such as modems and fax machines.

teleconference   A live, real-time communications session involving two or more people in different locations, using computers and telecommunications equipment.

template   A preformatted document used to quickly create a standard document such as a memo or report.

terabyte (TB)   Equivalent to approximately one trillion bytes of data; a measure of storage capacity.

terminal   An input/output device connected to a multiuser computer such as a mainframe.

terminal client   Networking software that creates a user session when a user runs a program from a network server (the terminal server).

terminal server   In multiuser/multitasking networked environments, a server that gives multiple users access to shared programs and other resources.

terminator   In a bus topology network, a special device that is placed at the end of the network cable. The device prevents data signals from "bouncing back" after reaching the end of the cable, thus preventing data collisions.

text box   In word processing and presentation software, a special frame that enables the user to contain text in a rectangular area. The user can size and position the text box like a frame by dragging the box or one of its handles. Also see *frame*.

text code   A standard system in which numbers represent the letters of the alphabet, punctuation marks, and other symbols. A text code enables programmers to use combinations of numbers to represent individual pieces of data. EBCDIC, ASCII, and Unicode are examples of text code systems.

TFT   Acronym for *thin-film transistor*. See *active matrix LCD*.

thin-film transistor (TFT)   See *active matrix LCD*.

third-party cookie   A cookie that is placed on the user's computer by a Web server other than the one hosting the page being viewed.

thread   A series of related articles and responses about a specific subject, posted in a newsgroup.

tick   See *clock cycle*.

title bar   An on-screen element displayed at the top of every window that identifies the window contents. Dragging the title bar changes the position of the window on the screen.

token   In a network using ring topology, any piece of data that is being transferred across the network. Each node examines the data and passes it along until it reaches its destination.

Token Ring   IBM's network protocol, based on a ring topology in which linked computers pass an electronic token containing addressing information to facilitate data transfer.

toner   A substance composed of tiny particles of charged ink that is used in laser printers. The ink particles stick to charged areas of a drum and are transferred to paper with pressure and heat.

toolbar   In application software, an on-screen element appearing just below the menu bar. The toolbar contains multiple tools, which are graphic icons (called *buttons*) representing specific actions the user can perform. To initiate an action, the user clicks the appropriate button.

topology   The physical layout of wires that connect the computers in a network; includes bus, star, ring, and mesh.

touch screen   An input/output device that accepts input directly from the monitor. To activate commands, the user touches words, graphical icons, or symbols displayed on screen.

touchpad   See *trackpad*.

track   An area used for storing data on a formatted disk. During the disk-formatting process, the operating system creates a set of magnetic concentric circles on the disk; these are the tracks. These tracks are then divided into sectors, with each sector able to hold a given amount of data. By using this system to store data, the operating system can quickly determine where data is located on the disk. Different types of disks can hold different numbers of tracks.

trackball   An input device that functions like an upside-down mouse, consisting of a stationary casing containing a movable ball that is operated by hand. Trackballs are used frequently with laptop computers.

trackpad   A stationary pointing device that the user operates by moving a finger across a small, touch-sensitive surface. Trackpads are often built into portable computers. Also called a *touchpad*.

TrackPoint   See *integrated pointing device*.

transient cookie   See *session cookie*.

transistor   An electronic switch within the CPU that exists in two states: conductive (on) or nonconductive (off). The resulting combinations are used to create the binary code that is the basis for machine language.

twisted-pair cable   Cable used in network connections. Twisted-pair cable consists of copper strands, individually shrouded in plastic, twisted around each other in pairs and bound together in a layer of plastic insulation; also called *unshielded twisted-pair (UTP) wire*. Twisted-pair wire encased in a metal sheath is called *shielded twisted-pair (STP) wire*.

typeface   See *font*.

type style   An attribute applied to a text character, such as underlining, italic, and bold, among others. Most application programs provide a wide variety of type styles that the user can freely apply to text anywhere in a document.

U

UART   See *universal asynchronous receiver transmitter*.

UCE   See *unsolicited commercial e-mail*.

Unicode Worldwide Character Standard   A character set that provides 16 bits to represent each symbol, resulting in 65,536 different characters or symbols, enough for all the languages of the world. The Unicode character set includes all the characters from the ASCII character set.

uniform resource locator (URL)   An Internet address used with HTTP in the format *type://address/path*.

universal asynchronous receiver-transmitter (UART)   A chip that converts parallel data from the bus into serial data that can flow through a serial cable, and vice versa.

Universal Serial Bus (USB)   A new expansion bus technology that currently enables the user to connect 127 different devices into a single port.

UNIX   A 32-bit, fully multitasking, multithreading operating system developed by Bell Labs in the 1970s. A powerful, highly scalable operating system, UNIX (and variants of it) is used to operate supercomputers, mainframes, minicomputers, and powerful PCs and workstations. UNIX generally features a command-line interface, although some variants of UNIX feature a graphical operating environment as well.

unsolicited commercial e-mail (UCE)   The official term for *spam*. UCE is any e-mail message sent to multiple recipients that contains commercial content.

URL   See *uniform resource locator*.

USA PATRIOT Act   A federal law (enacted in 2001) that extends the authority of law enforcement and intelligence agencies in monitoring private communications and access to your personal information.

USB   See *Universal Serial Bus*.

user   The person who inputs and analyzes data using a computer; the computer's operator.

user ID   See *user name*.

user interface   The on-screen elements that enable the user to interact with the software.

user name   A code that identifies the user to the system; often the user's full name, a shortened version of the user's name, or the user's e-mail name. Also called a *user ID*.

user session   The period during which a user interacts with a terminal server, using a shared program on a network.

utility   A software program that may be used to enhance the functionality of an operating system. Examples of utility software are disk defragmenters and screen savers.

V

value   A numerical entry in a spreadsheet—representing currency, a percentage, a date, a time, a fraction, and so on—that can be used in formulas.

VGA   See *Video Graphics Array*.

video capture card   A specialized expansion board that enables the user to connect video devices—such as VCRs and camcorders—to the PC. This enables the user to transfer images from the video equipment to the PC, and vice versa. Many video cards enable the user to edit digitized video and to record the edited images on videotape.

video card   A circuit board attached to the motherboard that contains the memory and other circuitry necessary to send information to the monitor for display on screen. This controller determines the refresh rate, resolution, and number of colors that can be displayed. Also called the *display adapter*.

Video Graphics Array (VGA)   An IBM video display standard capable of displaying resolutions of 640 x 480, with 16 colors.

video RAM (VRAM)   Memory on the video controller (sometimes called *dual-ported memory*) that can send a screen of data to the monitor while receiving the next data set.

viewing angle   The widest angle from which a display monitor's image can be seen clearly. Generally speaking, cathode ray tube (CRT) monitors provide a wider viewing angle than liquid crystal display (LCD) monitors do.

viewing area   The actual portion of a computer monitor that displays an image.

virtual memory   Space on a computer's hard drive that acts as a backup to system RAM. Programs can store instructions or data in virtual memory that is not needed immediately; when an instruction or data is needed, it can quickly be moved into RAM, where the processor can access it.

virus   A parasitic program that infects another legitimate program, sometimes called the *host*. To infect the host program, the virus modifies the host so that it contains a copy of the virus.

virus definition   A database of information about specific viruses that enables an antivirus program to detect and eradicate viruses. Also called a *virus pattern*.

virus pattern   See *virus definition*.

Voice over Internet Protocol (VoIP)   A protocol that allows voice data to travel over the Internet.

voice recognition   See *speech recognition*.

VoIP   See *Voice over Internet Protocol*.

volatile   The tendency for memory to lose data when the computer is turned off, as is the case with RAM.

VRAM   See *video RAM*.

W

WAN   See *wide area network*.

Web browser   A program that enables the user to view Web pages, navigate Web sites, and move from one Web site to another. Also called a *browser*.

Web bug   A GIF-format graphic file, placed in a Web page or HTML-format e-mail message, that can be used to track a person's online activities. Web bugs are commonly considered to be a form of spyware.

Web page   A document developed using HTML and found on the World Wide Web. Web pages contain information about a particular subject with links to related Web pages and other resources.

Web server   An Internet host computer that may store thousands of Web sites.

Web site   A collection of related Web pages.

Webcam   An inexpensive video camera that connects directly to a PC and captures video images that can be broadcast over the Internet or through a network connection.

wide area network (WAN)   A computer network that spans a wide geographical area.

window   An area on the computer screen in which an application or document is viewed and accessed.

Windows   A family of operating system products developed and produced by Microsoft Corp. The vast majority of personal computers run Windows, with versions including Windows 3.*x*, 95, 98, Me, NT, 2000, and XP. Windows versions 3.*x* and earlier were actually operating environments—graphical interfaces that ran on top of the DOS operating system. In versions 95 and later, Windows is a full-fledged operating system.

wireless network   A network that transmits data without the use of wires or cables. Such networks typically transmit data via radio waves or infrared signals.

wireless NIC   A network interface card that connects a computer to a wireless network.

word processing program   Software used to create and edit text documents such as letters, memos, reports, and publications. Also called a *word processor*.

word processor   See *word processing program*.

word size   The size of the registers in the CPU, which determines the amount of data the computer can work with at any given time. Larger word sizes lead to faster processing; common word sizes include 16 bits, 32 bits, and 64 bits.

workbook   A data file created with spreadsheet software, containing multiple worksheets.

worksheet   The data file created with spreadsheet software.

workstation   A fast, powerful microcomputer used for scientific applications, graphics, CAD, CAE, and other complex applications. Workstations are usually based on RISC technology and operated by some version of UNIX, although an increasing number of Intel/Windows-based workstations are coming into popular use.

World Wide Web (the Web or WWW)   An Internet service developed to incorporate footnotes, figures, and cross-references into online hypertext documents.

WWW   See *World Wide Web*.

Photo Credits

Chapter 1

1A.1right CMCD/Getty Images; **1A.1 left** Ryan McVay/Getty Images; **1A.2** Courtesy Sun Microsystems, Inc.; **1A.3** Ariel Skelley/Corbis; **1A.4** Anthony P. Bolante/Getty Images; **1A.5** Courtesy palmOne, Inc.; **1A.6** Courtesy Nokia; **1A.7** Bob Stefko/The Image Bank/Getty Images; **1A.8** Bruce Ando/Index Stock; **1A.9** Yellow Dog Productions/Getty Images; **1A.10** Courtesy of Cray, Inc.; **p.9** David Pollack/Corbis; **1A.14** Aaron Haupt; **1A.15** Kingston Technology Company, Inc.; **1A.16 left** Courtesy Sony; **1A.16 top right** Courtesy IBM Corporation; **1A.16 bottom right** Mark Steinmetz; **1A.17** Teri Stratford; **1B.3** Courtesy Microsoft; **1B.7** Photo courtesy of Logitech.; **1B.9** Aaron Haupt; **1B.10** Siede Preis/Getty Images; **1B.11** Courtesy IBM Corporation; **1B.12** Pete Pacifica/The Image Bank/Getty Images; **1B.13** Bob Daemmrich/The Image Works; **1B.14** Matt Meadows; **1B.15** Courtesy IBM Corporation; **1B.17** Steve Cole/Getty Images; **1B.18** B. Busco/Getty Images; **1B.19** Photos of DC-CAM 3200Z and Sound Blaster Audigy 2 ZS provided courtesy of Creative Technology Ltd.; **p. 33** Roger Ball/Corbis Stock Market; **1B.20 left** Courtesy Silicon Graphics; **1B.20 center** Ryan McVay/Getty Images; **1B.20 right** Courtesy IBM Corporation; **1B.22** Courtesy palmOne, Inc.; **1B.23 both** Applied Optical Company; **1B.27** Courtesy Altec Lansing.

Chapter 2

2A.1 Bettmann/Corbis; **2A.2** Salus, CASTING THE NET: FROM ARPANET TO INTERNET AND BEYOND, p.64,© 1995 Addison-Wesley Publishing Company Inc. Reprinted by permission of Pearson Education, Inc. Publishing as Pearson Addison Wesley.; **p. 69 top** Dennis Degnan/Corbis; **2B.1** Courtesy Research in Motion.

Chapter 3

3A.6 Sandisk Corporation 2004; **3A.7 both** Kingston Technology Company, Inc.; **3A.14 left** Photo courtesy of Intel Corporation; **3A.14 top right** Courtesy Freescale Semiconductor, Inc.; **3A.14 bottom right** Photo courtesy of Intel Corporation; **3A.16 both** Photo Courtesy of AMD 2004.; **p. 117** Photo courtesy of Intel Corporation; **3A.17** Photo courtesy of Acer America; **3A.19** Mark Burnett; **3A.20** Courtesy 3Com; **3A.31** Courtesy IOMEGA Corporation; **3A.32** Photo courtesy Hewlett-Packard; **3A.34** Bigshots/Photodisc Red/Getty Images; **p. 129** Photo courtesy of Xybernaut Corporation; **3B.1** Christian Hoehn/Taxi/Getty Images; **p. 143** Epson America, Inc.; **3B.13** Aaron Haupt; **3B.14** Aaron Haupt; **3B.15** Aaron Haupt; **3B.17** Photo courtesy of Linksys; **3B.18** Courtesy TrippLite; **p. 151** Jim Craigmyle/Corbis.

Chapter 4

4A.21 Courtesy palmOne, Inc.; **4B.20** Mark Burnett; **p. 195 top** Photographers Choice/Getty Images; **p. 195 bottom** Jose Luis Pelaez/Corbis.

Chapter 5

5A.3 David Young Wolff/Photoedit; **p. 215 bottom** Michael Newman/Photoedit; **5A.12** Walter Hodges/Corbis; **5A.14** John Henley/Corbis; **p. 219** DiMaggio/Kalish/Corbis; **5B.1** Spencer Grant/Photoedit; **5B.13** Photo courtesy of Linksys; **5B.17** Property of Fellowes; **5B.18** David Young Wolff/Photoedit; **5B.19** David Young Wolff/Photoedit.

TIMELINE

p. 248-1965 Computer History Museum; **p. 248-1970** Lucent Technologies Inc./Bell Labs; **p. 248-1971** Photo courtesy of Intel Corporation; **p. 249-1972** W. Cody/Corbis; **p. 249-1973** Courtesy IBM; **p. 249-1974** Photo courtesy of Intel Corporation; **p. 250-1975, 1976** Computer History Museum; **p. 250-1977** Courtesy Apple Inc.; **p. 251-1978** Photo courtesy of Intel Corporation; **p. 251-1980 left** Courtesy Microsoft; **p. 251-1980 right** Box shot of Lotus 1-2-3 (copyright 1980) IBM Corporation. Used with permission of IBM Corporation. Lotus and 1-2-3 are trademarks of IBM Corporation.; **p. 252-1981 top** Computer History Museum; **p. 252-1981 bottom** Courtesy of IBM Corporate Archives; **p. 252-1982** Photo courtesy Hewlett-Packard; **p. 253-1983** Photo courtesy Hewlett-Packard; **p.253–1984** Paul Sakuma/AP Wide World; **p. 254 -1985 left** Courtesy Microsoft; **p. 254-1985 right** Photo courtesy Hewlett-Packard; **p. 254-1986, 1987 left** Courtesy of IBM Corporate Archives; **p. 255-1987 right** Courtesy Apple Inc.; **p. 255-1988** Shahn Kermani/Getty Images; **p. 256-1989 left** Photo courtesy of Intel Corporation; **p. 256-1989 right** Donna Coveny/MIT News; **p. 256-1990 left** Courtesy Microsoft; **p. 256-1990 right** Courtesy IBM; **p. 257-1991 left** Paul Sakuma/AP Wide World; **p. 257-1991 right** Courtesy of Apple Inc.; **p. 257-1992** Courtesy IBM; **p. 258-1993 left** Courtesy National Center for Supercomputing Applications and the Board of Trustees of the University of Illinois.; **p. 258-1993 right** Reproduced with Permission of Motorola, Inc.; **p. 258-1994 bottom** RED HAT is a registered trademark of Red Hat, Inc.; **p. 259-1995 left** Courtesy Microsoft; **p. 259-1995 right** eBay ™ is a trademark of eBay Inc.; **p. 259-1996 left** Amanita Pictures; **p. 259-1996 right** Paul Sakuma/AP Wide World; **p. 260-1997 left** Photo courtesy of Intel Corporation; **p. 260-1997 right, 1998 left** Amanita Pictures; **p. 261-1998 right,** 1999 Aaron Haupt; **p. 263-2000 left** Amanita Pictures; **p. 263-2000 center** Photo courtesy AMD 2004; **p. 263-2000 right** Photo courtesy of Intel Corporation; **p. 264-2001 left** Courtesy Microsoft; **p. 264-2001 center** Courtesy Apple, Inc; **p. 264-2001 right** AP Wide World; **p. 265-2002 top** Steve Chenn/Corbis; **p. 265-2002 bottom left** Courtesy palmOne, Inc.; **p. 265-2002 center** Denis Poroy/AP Wide World; **p.265-2002 bottom right** Open Office.org; **p.266-2003 left** © Robin Scholtz; **p. 266-2003 right** Courtesy Apple, Inc.; **p. 267-2004** Nathan Howard/AP Wide World; **p. 267-2005** Photo courtesy of Nokia.

Index

10Base-T, networks and, 148

A

Active matrix LCD technology, monitors, 34
address books, e-mail, 196
address bus, 112
Advanced Micro Devices (AMD)
    processors, 115, 263
Advanced Research Projects Agency
    (ARPA), 50
adware, 229–230
Allen, Paul, 250–251
alphanumeric keys, keyboards, 25
Altair 880, 250
always-on connections, 235
Amazon.com
    e-commerce, 210
    privacy notice at, 228
AMD processors, 115
American Micro Devices (AMD), 114
American Standard Code for Information
    Interchange, 105
AngelFire, web sites, 100
anonymous FTP archives, 83
anti-adware utilities, 231
anti-spyware utilities, 231
antivirus programs, 205
Apple I computer, 250
Apple II computer, 250
application servers, 138
application service providers, 189–190
application software, 14–15
architecture, chips and, 113
Arithmetic Logic Unit, operations performed
    by, 107
arithmetic operations, 107
articles, 82
artificial intelligence, ethical issues, 157
ASCII Codes, 105–106
At Issue
    Cyborgs among Us, 128–129
    On the Beat with Techno-Cops, 218–219
    Stomping Out Spam, 80–81
    Who Really Owns the Software on
        Your PC?, 176–177
Athlon processors, 116
audio ports, 118
AutoCAD, 3-D projects, 252
automatic vehicle location (AVL)
    software, 219

B

backbones, networks and, 51
Backup systems, 139–140
Bank of America, e-commerce, 214
Bar code readers, 29

bar codes, 29
Barry's Clipart Server, web sites, 96
basic input output system (BIOS), 108
Bellmac-32, 251
Berners-Lee, Tim, 256, 58
Best Buy, e-commerce, 213
Bimodal virus, 204
binary number systems, 104
Bipartite virus, 204
bits, definition of, 104
BlackBerry Wireless Handheld devices, 77
blocks, definition of, 184
blogs, 262
bombs, computer viruses, 204
Boolean operators, 66–68
Boot Sector viruses, 204
boot sectors, 124
booting, 124
brick-and-mortar stores, 211
bridges, 147
browsers, 54–55, 59–60
    closing and, 62–63
    getting Help with, 63
    launching and, 60
buddy lists, 85
Bureau of Labor Statistics
    computer support specialists, 195
    Internet careers and, 238–239
    technical writers, 87
bus
    address bus, 112
    components of a computer and, 111
bus topology, 145
business-to-business (B2B)
    transactions, 216–217
business-to-consumer (B2C) transactions, 210
Buy.com, e-commerce and, 211
bytes, definition of, 104

C

Cache memory, 112–113
cache speeds, 113
caches
    Level-1 (L1) caches, 113
    Level-2 (L2) caches, 113
    Level-3 (L3) caches, 113
cameras, PC video cameras, 30
campus area networks (CANs), 141
cathode ray tube (CRT), 31
CD-Recordable (CD-R) drive, 129, 13
CD-ReWritable (CD-RW) disc, 13
CD-ReWritable (CD-RW) drive, 130
CD-ROM drives, 13
    reading data and, 128
Cedant Web Hosting, web sites, 100
cell addresses, 186–187
cell pointers, 186–187

cells, 186
central processing unit (CPU), 11
CERT Coordination Center, viruses and, 206
Channels, chat rooms, 85
character formatting, 185
charts, creating a chart in PowerPoint, 192
chat, Web-based chat, 84–85
chat rooms, 85
chips, What Is a Computer Chip?, 116–117
circuit boards, 11
click-and-mortar stores, 211
client/server networks, 143
Clipboards, 165
    Object Linking and Embedding, 166
clock cycle, 111
clock speed, 111
Cluster viruses, 204
clusters, 124–125
coaxial cables, 146
command-line interfaces, 164
commands
    Copy command, 166
    Cut command, 166
    Paste command, 166
Communications Decency Act, 259
Compact Disc Read-Only Memory
    (CD-ROM), 13, 127
Compact discs (CDs), 13
CompactFlash card, 108
Compaq Portable computer, 253
Computer data, review questions
    and, 131–135
computer systems, parts of, 9–10
computerized disease management (DM)
    programs, 18
Computers
    application software, 14–15
    Career Opportunities and the
        Internet, 238–239
    common output devices, 31–32
    definition of, 4
    essential computer hardware, 10–11
    Handheld personal computers, 6
    history of microcomputers, 248–267
    Input and Output overview, 24
    Input devices, 25, 28–29
    keeping your computer clean, 240
    laptop computers, 5
    mainframe computers, 6
    microcomputer processors, 114–115
    microcomputers, 4
    midrange computers, 7
    minicomputers, 7
    mobile computers, 5
    Notebook Computers, 5
    operating systems, 14
    organizations and, 6–7, 6
    Outside of the IT Industry, 40–41

Computers—*cont.*
    overview of, 3
    personal digital assistant (PDA), 6
    processing data and, 107–108
    processors and, 10–11
    review questions and, 20–23, 42–47
    software and, 13–14
    storing computer equipment, 239–240
    Supercomputers, 8
    system units, 4
    tablet PCs, 5
    viruses and, 202
    Workstations, 5
Computing Keynotes
    adding pages and links to, 98
    choosing your design tools, 94–95
    finding a host for your web site, 99
    finding graphics online, 96
    free hosting services, 99
    modifying headings and, 98
    planning your Web page, 95
    selecting a template, 97
    Web Content and Intellectual
        Property, 101
    Web design tips, 99
contact information, tech support and, 194
contact-management software, 194
control unit, 107
cookie-management utility, 230–231
cookies, 212, 229–230
    first-party cookies, 230
    persistent cookies, 230
    session cookies, 230
    stored cookies, 230
    third-party cookies, 230
    transient cookies, 230
Copy command, 166
copyright, Intellectual Property Rights, 101
CPU
    Cache memory, 112–113
    definition of, 107
    memory and, 108–109
    performance specifications, 116
    processing speed, 109–110
    registers, 109–110
    system bus, 111
credit reports, 227
CRT monitors, 31, 33
cursor-movement keys, 26
cursors, insertion points, 26
customer service, 212–213
Customer Service Support, careers and, 150
Cut command, 166
Cyborgs among Us, 128

D

data, 16–17
    backing up, 235
    binary number systems, 104
    decimal number systems, 104

data—*cont.*
    definition of, 10
    entering data in worksheets, 186–187
    how computers represent data, 104
    keeping your data secure, 233–234
    overview of, 103
    text codes, 105
data area, 124
data backup, 139–140
data bus, 111
Data Communications Managers, careers
       and, 151
Data projectors, 193
databases, knowledge bases, 169
datagrams, 145
Dates, 187–188
decimal number systems, 104
Degaussing, disks and, 238
denial of service (DOS) attack, virus and, 203
density, disks and, 126
desktop computers, 4
devices, definition of, 10
Dialog boxes, 163–164
Digital cameras, 31
Digital Media Support, 172
Digital Pens, 5
    Pen-based systems, 28
Digital Video Disc (DVD), 13
Digital Video/Versatile Disc (DVD)
       technology, 260
directories, 124
    definition of, 63
    enterprise directory, 174
    using and, 65
disabilites, Ethical Issues and, 47
disk drives, 13
disc–read-only memory (DVD-ROM) drive, 129
diskettes (floppy disks), 125
disks
    floppy disks, 125
    handling storage media, 238–239
    hard disks, 126
    high-capacity floppy disk drives, 126
    hot-swappable hard disks, 127
    magnetic disks, 13
    removable high-capacity disks, 126
distributed applications, 174
distributed computing, networks and, 144
Do-It-Yourself Tech Support, 168–169
document area, 183
Document formatting, 185
documents, definition of, 17
Dogpile, metasearch engines and, 70
DOS (disk operating system), 166–167
DOS applications, 169
Dot matrix printers, 37–38
dot pitch, monitors and, 36
dots per inch (dpi), image quality and, 39
downloading files, Ethical Issues and, 246
Dreamweaver MX, 94
drivers, 166

dual in-line memory module (DIMM)
       chips, 108–109
dual-scan LCD technology, monitors, 34
dumpster diving, security and, 225
Duron processors, 116
DVD-RAM drives, 130
DVD-Recordable (DVD-R) device, 130

E

e-commerce
    business levels and, 216–217
    business-to-business (B2B)
       transactions, 216–217
    business-to-consumer (B2C)
       transactions, 210
    customer service and, 212–213
    Online banking, 213–214
    Online catalogs, 211–212
    Online finance, 215–216
    Online shopping, 210
    overview of, 209
    review questions and, 220–223
    security, 218–219
    shopping carts, 212
    telecommuters, 217–218
e-mail
    address books, 196
    buddy lists, 85
    definition of, 77
    file transfer protocol (FTP), 83
    instant messaging (IM), 85
    Internet relay chat (IRC), 84
    listserv Systems, 78
    Microsoft Messenger, 86
    online services, 85–86
    overview of, 76
    Peer-to-peer (P2P) services, 86–87
    primary e-mail account, 232
    receiving and reading messages, 79–80
    review questions, 88–93
    secondary e-mail account, 232
    spam and, 267
    unsolicited commercial e-mail (UCE), 231
    viruses and, 204
    web-based e-mail services, 81
E-mail addresses, 77–78
    user name, 77
e-mail client, 77
e-mail programs, creating a message, 77–79
eBay, e-commerce, 210
editing text, 184
EISA (Extended Industry Standard
       Architecture), 255
Electronic Communications Privacy Act, 228
Electronic Privacy Information Center,
       web sites, 229
embedded operating systems, 175–176
Enkeboll Designs, 40
Enriquez, Richard, 40
enterprise directory, 174

Epson, MX-80 dot-matrix printer, 251
Ethernets, 148
Ethical Issues
    artificial intelligence and, 157
    copying documents and, 201
    disabilites and, 47
    downloading files and, 246
    Internet and, 93
    unneeded printouts, 47
Event Viewers, 236
expansion boards, 120
expansion slots, 120
Extended ASCII, 105
Extended Binary Coded Decimal Interchange
        Code, 105
extranets, 217–218

F

Fair Credit Reporting Act, 228
Fast Ethernets, 148
faxing alternatives, 143
Federal Trade Commission (FTC), spam
        legislation, 81
Fernandez, Bill, 248
fiber-optic cables, 146
file server networks, 142
file servers, 137
file systems, 124
file transfer protocol (FTP), 83
File-Infecting Viruses, 204
files, definition of, 17
filters, 233
finance, online finance, 215–216
Financial Modernization Act of 1999, 229
firewalls, 234–235
Fireworks MX, 94
First-party cookies, 230
Flash memory, 108
flat-panel monitors, 31, 34–35
floppy disks, 13, 125
    handling storage media, 238–239
folders, definition of, 124
fonts, 185
formatting
    character formatting, 185
    disks and, 122
    Document formatting, 185
    logical formatting, 124
    Paragraph formatting, 185
formatting text, 185
formula bars, 186
formulas, definition of, 188
FortuneCity, web sites, 100
frames, 191
Free Servers, web sites, 100
Freedom of Information Act, 228
Freescale processors, 115–116
French, Michael, 150
frequently asked questions (FAQs), 82, 169
FTP client programs, 84

FTP client software, 83
FTP servers, 83
FTP sites, 83
function keys, 26

G

game controllers, 29
game pads, 29
Gates, Bill, 250, 251
gateways, nodes and, 147
Gigabit Ethernet, 148
gigabytes (GB), 12
Gigahertz (Hz), definition of, 111
The GIMP, 94
GoLive CS, 94
Google
    Help links and, 68
    web sites, 64
graphical user interfaces, 161–162
graphics
    adding to your Web page, 94–95
    finding graphics online, 96
The Gutenberg Project, 58

H

Handheld personal computers, 6
hard disks, 13, 126
hardware, 9–10
    essential computer hardware, 10–11
    managing hardware, 166–167
    safeguarding and, 235–236
headers, networks and, 145
headings, modifying headings and, 98
Help
    Digital Media Support, 172
    frequently asked questions
        (FAQs), 82, 169
    Help Desk and Technical Support
        Specialists, 194–195
    Online Help System Designer, 86–87, 168
Help window, browsers and, 63
helper applications, 56–57
Hertz (Hz)
    cycles per second, 36
    definition of, 111
high-capacity floppy disk drives, 126
Hoff, Ted, 248
home area networks (HANs), 141
Hosting.Com, web sites, 100
hosts, definition of, 50
hot-swappable hard disks, 127
Hotmail, 82
HTML tags, 54–55
hubs, 147
hybrid networks, 140–141
HyperCard, 255
hyperlinks, 53, 61–62
hypertext, 53
hypertext links, 53

hypertext markup language (HTML), 53
hypertext transfer protocol (HTTP), 53

I

IBM processors, 117
IBM-PC AT, 253
IBM-PC XT, 253
icons, 162
identity (ID) theft, cost of, 225
IEEE 1394 (FireWire), 120
iMac, release of, 261
Image scanners, 29–30
impact printers, 37
Industry Association of America (RIAA), 264
Information Systems (IS) Managers, careers
        and, 151
initializing, disks and, 122
ink jet printers, 39
input/output (I/O) devices, 7
insertion points, 26
instant messaging (IM), 85
instruction sets, 107
Integrated Pointing Devices, 28
Intel
    80386 processor and, 254
    80486 chip, 256
    8080 chip and, 249
    MMX technology, 260
    current Intel processors, 115
    Pentium III processor, 262
    Pentium Pro microprocessor, 259
Intellectual Property Rights, 101
Internet
    Boolean operators, 66–67
    closing the browser, 62–63
    Ethical Issues and, 93
    getting Help with your browser, 63
    growth of, 51, 257
    helper applications, 56–57
    history of, 50
    major services and, 52–53
    metasearch engines, 70
    navigating the Web, 60–61
    online help systems, 168
    overview of, 49
    plug-in applications, 56–57
    review questions and, 72–75
    search engines and, 63–64
    searching the Web, 63–64
    site-specific search tools, 71
    sponsored links, 70
    URLs, 60–61
    using advanced search options, 67–68
    using hyperlinks, 61–62
    using the browser's navigation tools, 62
Internet Archive, web sites, 59
Internet Explorer, 54–55, 60
    Help window and, 63
Internet Eye's Paint Shop Pro Resources
        page, 96

Internet relay chat (IRC), 84
    worms and, 205
Internet service providers (ISPs), 52, 140
internetworking, 51
intranets, 217–218
Iomega Zip system, 127
iPod, release of, 264
IPX/SPX protocols, 149

J

Jackson, Thomas Penfield, 263
Jensen, Mark, 86
Jobs, Steve, 250, 255
Joke programs, viruses and, 204
Joysticks, 29
Jupiterimages, 96

K

Kernighan, Brian, 249
keyboards, 25
    alphanumeric keys, 25
    modifier keys, 25
    numeric keypads, 25
keyword searches, 64
kilobytes (KB), 12
knowledge bases, 169
Kosoff, Jon, 238

L

L.L. Bean, e-commerce, 212
labels, 187
LAN technology, 250
lands, 127
laptop computers, 5
large-format monitors, 193
laser printers, 39
LaserJet laser printers, 254
Level-1 (L1) caches, 113
Level-2 (L2) caches, 113
Level-3 (L3) caches, 113
licenses, definition of, 176
LifeMasters Online, 18
links
    hyperlinks, 53
    non-sponsored links, 70
    sponsored links, 70
Linux
    networking services, 175
    operating systems, 173
    with an optional GUI desktop, 173
liquid crystal display (LCD) monitors, 34
listserv Systems, 78
local area networks (LANs), 140
logical formatting, 124
logical operations, 107
LookSmart home page, 64
Lotus Development Corporation, 251
LView Pro, 94

Lycos home page, 66

M

Mac OS System X, desktop of, 172
Macintosh operating system, 172–173
macro viruses, 204–205
magnetic disks, 13
magnetic storage devices, 121–122
mail servers, 78
Mail.com, e-mail accounts, 232
mainframe computers, 6
managing hardware, 166–167
marketers, keeping marketers at bay, 228
McAfee, web sites, 236
McGill University, FTP sites, 84
media
    network media, 146–147
    wire-based media, 146
megabytes (MB), 12
Megahertz (Hz), definition of, 111
memory
    basic input output system (BIOS), 108
    Cache memory, 112–113
    CPU and, 108–109
    dual in-line memory module (DIMM)
        chips, 108–109
    Flash memory, 108
    nonvolatile memory, 12, 108
    processing speed, 109–110
    random access memory (RAM), 11
    read-only memory (ROM), 12
    registers, 109–110
    Single in-line memory module
        (SIMM), 108
    small outline DIMM (SO-DIMM)
        chips, 109
    Units of Measure for, 12
    virtual memory, 110
memory address, 109
menu bars, 163
menus, definition of, 163
Merholz, Peter, 262
mesh topology, 146
metasearch engines, 70
Metcalfe, Bob, 249–251
metropolitan area networks (MANs), 141
microcodes, 107
microcomputer processors, 114–115
microcomputers, 4
    history of, 248–267
Microphones, 30
microprocessors, 11
Microsoft, releases Windows 3.0, 256
Microsoft Excel
    interface of, 187
    protecting a document in, 234
Microsoft Internet Explorer
    cookie-control settings in, 230
    Google toolbar and, 232
Microsoft Messenger, 86

Microsoft Outlook
    adding contact information for a
        person, 195
    contact lists, 194
    e-mail filter in, 233
Microsoft PowerPoint
    creating a chart in, 192
    interface of, 191
Microsoft Word
    interface of, 184
    Open dialog box, 165
midrange computers, 7
Millennium Bug, 262
minicomputers, 7
MMX technology, 260
mobile computers, 5
modifier keys, 25
monitors, 31
    Active matrix LCD technology, 34
    comparing and, 34–35
    CRT monitors, 31, 33
    dual-scan LCD technology, 34
    flat-panel monitors, 34–35
    large-format monitors, 193
    liquid crystal display (LCD) monitors, 34
    passive matrix LCD, 34
    plasma monitors, 193
    refresh rate of, 36
    resolution and, 35
    Super VGA (SVGA), 35
    thin-film transistor (TFT) technology, 34
    video cards, 36–37
    Video Graphics Array (VGA), 35
    video RAM (VRAM), 37
Mosaic, creation of, 258
motherboards, 11
mouse, 26–27
    mechanical mouse, 26
    mouse variants, 27–28
    optical mouse, 26
multi-user/multitasking operating
    system, 160
Multipartite viruses, 204
Musical Instrument Digital Interface
    (MIDI), 120
MX-80 dot-matrix printer, 251

N

Napster, 264
National Center for Supercomputing
    Applications (NCSA), 258
National Football League (NFL), web sites, 61
National Science Foundation (NSF), 50
National Science Foundation Network
    (NSFNET), 256
Navigator 5.0 Web browser, 261
.NET Framework, 174
NetBIOS/NetBEUI protocols, 149
NetObjects Fusion, 94
Netscape Communications, 258–259

Netscape Navigator, 54–55
network administrators, careers and, 151
Network Advertising Initiative (NAI), 233
network cards, 142
Network Interface Cards (NICs), 147
network linking devices, 147
network media, 146–147
network news transfer protocol (NNTP), 82
network operating system (NOS), 14,
    173–174
network servers, 6, 137
    application servers, 138
    print servers, 139
network versions, 138
networking
    Advanced Networking and
        Communications, 172
    campus area networks (CANs), 141
    careers in, 150–151
    client/server networks, 143
    data backup, 139–140
    file server networks, 142
    home area networks (HANs), 141
    hybrid networks, 140–141
    local area networks (LANs), 140
    metropolitan area networks (MANs), 141
    network media, 146–147
    overview of, 136
    peer-to-peer networks, 144
    review questions and, 152–157
    server-based networks, 141–142
    shared peripheral devices, 138–139
    site licenses, 138
    teleconferencing, 139
    Token Ring networks, 148
    uses of, 137–138
    Voice over Internet Protocol
        (VoIP), 139
    wide area networks (WANs), 140
    wireless networks, 146
networks
    beginning of, 50
    common types of, 140–141
    structure of, 141–142
    topology and, 145
news servers, 82
newsgroups, 81, 169
newsreaders, 82
Newton MessagePad, 258
Nicely, Thomas, 258
NNTP servers, 82
nodes
    definition of, 141
    gateways and, 147
non-impact printers, 37
non-sponsored links, 70
nonvolatile memory, 12
    basic input output system (BIOS), 108
Nordstrom, e-commerce and, 211
Northrop Grumman Mission Systems
    (NGMS), 219

Norton AntiVirus, 205
    setting options in, 206
Norton Notebook
    Business, the Internet, and
        Everything, 214–215
    Internet Time Travel, 58–59
    Speech Recognition, 32–33
    What Is a Computer Chip?, 116–117
    Why Own When You Can Rent?, 188–189
Notebook Computers, 5
Novell NetWare, 175
NSFnet, 51
numeric keypads, 25

O

Object Linking and Embedding, 166
Office 2003, release of, 266
Online banking, 213–214
Online catalogs, 211–212
online finance, 215–216
Online Help System Designer, 86–87
online help systems, 168
online services, 85–86
Online shopping, 210–212
Online Stores, versus Physical Locations, 211
Open dialog box, Microsoft Word and, 165
operating system (OS), overview of, 159
operating systems, 14
    command-line interfaces, 164
    communicating with the CPU and, 167
    DOS (disk operating system), 166–167
    embedded operating system, 175–176
    finding data on disks, 124
    graphical user interfaces, 161–162
    Linux, 173
    Macintosh operating system, 172–173
    managing hardware, 166–167
    multi-user/multitasking operating
        system, 160
    network operating system
        (NOS), 173–174
    PC Operating Systems, 166–167
    Pocket PC OS, 177
    real-time operating system, 160
    review questions and, 178–181
    running programs and, 164–165
    single-user/multitasking operating
        system, 160
    single-user/single-tasking operating
        system, 160
    Symbian, 177
    UNIX, 173
    Windows 9x, 170
    Windows 2000 Professional, 171
    Windows CE .NET, 176
    Windows NT Workstation, 168–169
    Windows XP, 171–172
    Windows XP Embedded, 175–176
opt-out options, 228

optical character recognition (OCR)
    software, 30
optical mouse, 26
optical storage, 121
optical technologies, recordable optical
    technologies, 129–130
OS X, release of, 264
Osborne, Adam, 252

P

packets, networks and, 145
PageMaker program, 254
pages per minute (ppm), 40
Paint Shop Pro, 94
Palm OS, PDAs, 176
PalmPilot, 259
Paragraph formatting, 185
passive matrix LCD, monitors, 34
Paste command, 166
payloads, 145
PC Cards, 120
PC convertible, laptop computers, 254
PC Operating Systems, 166–167
PC-to-TV converters, 193
PC video cameras, 30
Peer-to-peer (P2P) services, 86–87
peer-to-peer networks, 144
Pentium III processor, 262
Persistent cookies, 230
personal digital assistant (PDA), 6
personal information managers, 193–194
PhotoCD systems, 130
piracy, software piracy, 176
pits, 127
pixels, definition of, 31
plasma monitors, 193
plug-in applications, 56–57
Pocket PC OS, 177
pointing devices, 26
points, 185
Polymorphic viruses, 204
POP servers, 78
pop-up blockers, 231
pop-up windows, 231
ports
    audio ports, 118
    IEEE 1394 (FireWire), 120
    Musical Instrument Digital Interface
        (MIDI), 120
    parallel ports, 119
    serial ports, 119
    specialized expansion ports, 119–120
    standard computer ports, 118
post office protocol (POP), 78
PostScript systems, 253–254
Power Macintosh, 258
Power Macintosh G5, release of, 266
PowerBooks, 257
presentation programs, 190–191
Presentation software, 15

primary e-mail account, 232
print head, 37
print servers, 139
printers
    cost of, 41
    Dot matrix printers, 37–38
    impact printers, 37
    ink jet printers, 39
    laser printers, 39
    LaserJet laser printers, 254
    MX-80 dot-matrix printer, 251
    non-impact printers, 37
    pages per minute (ppm), 40
Privacy Act of 1974, 228
processing speed, 109–110
processors
    AMD processors, 115
    comparing and, 117
    current Intel processors, 115
    definition of, 10–11
    different architectures and, 114
    extending the power to other
        devices, 118–119
    Freescale processors, 115–116
    IBM processors, 117
    microcomputer processors, 114–115
    performance and, 113–114
Productivity Tips, 8
    Choosing the Right Tool for the Job, 8–9
    Do-It-Yourself Tech Support, 168–169
    Keeping Your PC Up to Date, 236–237
    Reliability of Search Results, 68–69
    The Telecommuter's Checklist, 142–143
programs
    adding graphics to your Web page, 94–95
    antivirus programs, 205
    application service providers, 189–190
    definition of, 10
    presentation programs, 190–191
    Red Hat Certified Engineer (RHCE)
        programs, 173
    running programs and, 164–165
    speech recognition, 30
    spreadsheet programs, 186–187
    voice recognition, 30
    Web design programs, 94
    word processing programs, 183
protocols
    LANs and, 149
    NetBIOS/NetBEUI protocols, 149
Prudential Financial, e-commerce, 216

Q

Q-DOS, 251
QuickTime, web sites, 57

R

RAM
    Cache memory, 112–113

RAM—cont.
    memory and computing power, 110
    system bus, 111
    virtual memory, 110
random access memory (RAM), 11
random access storage devices, 122
read-only memory (ROM), 12
Read/write heads, 13
real-time operating system, 160
recordable optical technologies, 129–130
Records Management System (RMS), 218
Red Hat Certified Engineer (RHCE)
        programs, 173
Red Hat Linux, 258
refresh rate, monitors, 36
registers, 107–110
removable high-capacity disks, 126
review questions
    Computer data and, 131–135
    computers and, 20–23
    e-commerce and, 220–223
    e-mail, 88–93
    networking and, 152–157
    operating systems and, 178–181
    security and, 241–246
    Word processing programs, 197–201
RFID (Radio Frequency Identification)
        tags, 267
Right to Financial Privacy Act of 1978, 229
ring topology, 145–146
Ritchie, Dennis, 248–249
Robertson, Michael, 265
root folders, 124
routers, 147
    firewalls and, 235
rulers, 184
rules, 233

S

scanners
    cleaning and, 96
    Image scanners, 29–30
screen savers, 234
scroll bars, 163, 184
search engines
    definition of, 63
    using and, 65–66
secondary e-mail account, 232
sectors, 123
secure sockets layer (SSL) technology, 219
secure Web pages, 219
security
    anti-adware utilities, 231
    anti-spyware utilities, 231
    credit reports and, 227
    firewalls and, 234–235
    guarding personal information, 226–227
    handling storage media, 238–239
    high-tech methods, 225
    identity (ID) theft, 225

security—cont.
    keeping marketers at bay, 228
    keeping your computer clean, 240
    keeping your data secure, 233–234
    knowing your legal rights, 228–229
    managing your papers, 226–227
    opt-out options, 228
    overview of, 224
    protecting your privacy, 227–228
    removing Web bugs, 231
    restricting access to your
        system, 234–235
    review questions and, 241–246
    storing computer equipment, 239–240
    using automated warnings, 236–237
Self-Encrypting viruses, 204
Self-Garbling viruses, 204
sequential access devices, tape drives, 127
serial ports, 119
server-based networks, 141–142
servers, 137
    application servers, 138
    file servers, 137
    FTP servers, 83
    mail servers, 78
    network servers, 6
    network versions, 138
    news servers, 82
    NNTP servers, 82
    POP servers, 78
    print servers, 139
    terminal servers, 160
    UNIX for Servers, 175
    Windows 2000 Servers, 174
    Windows NT Servers, 174
    Windows Server 2003, 174
service accounts, 143
Session cookies, 230
shared peripheral devices, 138–139
shells, definition of, 173
shopping carts, 212
shortcuts, 162
shoulder surfing, security and, 225
Showerman, Mike, 266
shredders, security and, 226
Single Edge Contact (SEC) cartridge, 260
Single in-line memory module (SIMM), 108
single-user/multitasking operating
        system, 160
single-user/single-tasking operating
        system, 160
site licenses, networking, 138
Slammer worm, 266
slides, 190
    adding text to, 192
    choosing layouts for a new slide, 192
    presenting slide shows, 192–193
Small Computer System Interface, 119
small outline DIMM (SO-DIMM) chips, 109
smart phones, 6
snagging, 225

snail mail, 193
social engineering, 225
software
    application software, 14–15
    automatic vehicle location (AVL)
      software, 219
    contact-management software, 194
    cookie-management utility, 230–231
    definition of, 10
    FTP client software, 83
    graphical user interfaces, 161–162
    managing hardware, 166–167
    network operating system, 14
    optical character recognition (OCR)
      software, 30
    overview of, 182
    overview of operating system (OS), 159
    personal information managers, 193–194
    presentation programs, 190–191
    Presentation software, 15
    spreadsheet programs, 186–187
    spyware, 229–230
    system software, 14
    word processing programs, 183
    Word processing software, 15
Software piracy, 176
sound cards, 30
sound systems, 37
spam, 231–232, 267
    stomping out spam, 80–81
    unsolicited commercial e-mail (UCE), 231
spam blockers, 233
spawning, 58
specialized expansion ports, 119–120
speech recognition, 30, 32–33
sponsored links, 70
spreadsheet formulas, 190
spreadsheet programs, 186–187
spreadsheets, interface of, 186
Spybot – Search & Destroy, 231
spyware, 229–230
    removing Web bugs and, 231
Stallman, Richard, 253
star topology, 145
Start menu, shortcuts and, 162
status bars, 184
Stealth Viruses, 204
Steffen, Craig, 266
storage, memory and, 12
storage devices, 121
    magnetic storage devices, 121–122
    random access storage devices, 122
storage media, 121
stored cookies, 230
streaming audio, 57
streaming video, 57
stylus, 5
submarining, definition of, 34
subscribe, news groups and, 82
Sun Ultra workstation, 259
Super VGA (SVGA), 35

Supercomputers, 8
swap in, 110
swap out, 110
switches, 147
Symantec, web sites, 236
Symbian, cell phones and, 177
system bus, 111
system clocks, 111
system operators, 86
system software, 14
system units, 4

T

tablet PCs, 5
Tape drives, 127
Target, Main Help page, 213
taskbars, 162
TCP/IP protocols, 149
technical support, Do-It-Yourself Tech
    Support, 168
technical support specialists, 194–195
technical writers, Bureau of Labor
    Statistics, 87
telecommuters, 217–218
    The Telecommuter's Checklist, 142–143
teleconferencing, 139
templates, 191
    selecting a template, 97
terabytes (TB), 12
terminal clients, 161
terminal servers, 160
terminals, 7
terminators, 145
text
    adding text to slides, 192
    entering and editing text, 184
    formatting text, 185
text boxes, 191
text codes, 105
thin-film transistor (TFT) technology,
    monitors, 34
Third-party cookies, 230
Thompson, Ken, 248
threads, 82
title bars, 163
Token Ring networking system, 253
Token Ring networks, 148
tokens, 146
toolbars, 163
tools
    choosing your design tools, 94–95
    Windows applications, 163
TopHosts.com, web sites, 100
topology, networks and, 145
Touch screens, 29
trackballs, 27
trackpads, 27
TrackPoint, 28
tracks, 123
transient cookies, 230

transistors, chips and, 117
Trojan Horses, 204
Twisted-pair cables, wire-based media, 146
type styles, 185

U

Unicode Worldwide Character Standard, 105
uniform resource locators (URLs), 55
universal asynchronous receiver-transmitter
    (UART), 119
Universal Serial Bus (USB), 119
UNIX, operating systems, 173, 248
UNIX for Servers, 175
unsolicited commercial e-mail (UCE), 231
URLs, 60–61
USA PATRIOT Act, 229
Usenet domains, common, 82
user interfaces, 161–162
user name, e-mail address, 77
user sessions, 161
utility, definition of, 14

V

values, 187
Versadex Computer Aided Dispatch (CAD), 218
video capture cards, 31
video cards, 36–37
Video Graphics Array (VGA) monitor, 35, 255
video RAM (VRAM), 37
Virtual Reality Modeling Language
    (VRML), 259
viruses, 202
    Boot Sector viruses, 204
    categories of, 204
    Cluster viruses, 204
    definition of, 202–203
    denial of service (DOS) attack, 203
    Millennium Bug, 262
    preventing infection and, 205–206
    web sites for, 206
    What Can a Virus Do?, 203
    worms, 204–205
    Y2K bug, 263
VISA, "zero liability" policy, 227
VisiCalc, spreadsheet programs, 251
Vista Development, 86
Voice over Internet Protocol (VoIP), 139
voice recognition, 30, 32–33
volatile memory
    dual in-line memory module (DIMM)
      chips, 108–109
    Single in-line memory module
      (SIMM), 108–109

W

wearable technology, 128–129
Weather Channel, web sites, 57
Web-based e-mail services, 81

Web browser, HTML tags and, 54–55
Web bugs, 229
   removing and, 231
Web design programs, 94
Web design resources, 101
Web pages
   adding graphics to your Web page, 94–95
   adding images to, 97–98
   adding pages and links to, 98
   free hosting services, 99
   publishing the page, 54
   using hyperlinked graphics on, 62
   Web Content and Intellectual
      Property, 101
Web sites
   AngelFire, 100
   Barry's Clipart Server, 96
   Cedant Web Hosting, 100
   Electronic Privacy Information
      Center, 229
   finding a host for your web site, 99
   FortuneCity, 100
   Free Servers, 100
   Google, 64
   Hosting.Com, 100
   Internet Archive, 59
   Internet Eye's Paint Shop Pro Resources
      page, 96
   Jupiterimages, 96
   McAfee, 236
   National Football League (NFL), 61
   QuickTime, 57

web sites—*cont.*
   Symantec, 236
   TopHosts.com, 100
   Weather Channel, 57
   ZDNet, 71
Webcams, 30
Wi-Fi (Wireless Fidelity), 266
wide area networks (WANs), 140
windows
   definition of, 162
   pop-up windows, 231
Windows 9x, 170
Windows 98 operating system, 261
Windows 2000, release of, 263
Windows 2000 Professional, 171
Windows 2000 Servers, 174
Windows applications, tools and, 163
Windows CE .NET, 176
Windows Me (Millennium Edition), 171
Windows NT Servers, 174
Windows NT Workstation, 168–169
Windows Server 2003, 174
Windows XP, 171–172
   folder listing in, 124
   release of, 264
Windows XP Command Prompt, 164
Windows XP Embedded, 175–176
Windows XP GUI, shortcuts and, 162
Windows XP Professional, firewalls and, 235
wire-based media, 146
wireless communications, 143
wireless network interface card (NIC), 143

wireless networks, 146
wireless NIC, 147
Word processing programs, 183
   review questions and, 197–201
Word processing software, 15
word processors, interface of, 183
word size, registers and, 110
workbooks, 186
worksheets, 186
   entering data in, 186–187
Workstations, 5
World Wide Web, creation of, 52, 256
worms, 204–205
   Slammer worm, 266
   viruses and, 255
Wozniak, Steve, 248, 250

X

Xerox Star computer, 252
XML (eXtensible Markup Language), 265

Y

Y2K bug, 263
Yahoo!, advanced search form at, 69

Z

ZDNet, web sites, 71
zero liability policy, security and, 227